# Only in NEW YORK

**Ferne Kadish**        **Shelley Clark**

*Printed on recyclable paper*

**PASSPORT BOOKS**
a division of *NTC Publishing Group*
Lincolnwood, Illinois USA

*Cover photo*: Courtesy of New York Convention & Visitors Bureau

Library of Congress Cataloging-in-Publication Data

Kadish, Ferne.
    Only in New York: the ultimate guide to the finest hotels,
shopping, dining & entertainment / Ferne Kadish, Shelley Clark.
        p.    cm.
    Includes index.
    ISBN  0-8442-9606-6: $14.95
    1. New York (N.Y.)—Guidebooks.    I. Clark, Shelley.  II. Title.
F128. 18.K333    1993
917.47' 10443—dc20                      93–39115
                                        CIP

Published by Passport Books, a division of NTC Publishing Group,
4255 West Touhy Avenue, Lincolnwood (Chicago), Illinois 60646-1975.
© 1994 by Ferne Kadish.

4 5 6 7 8 9 ML 9 8 7 6 5 4 3 2 1

# Dedication

*For my beloved husband, Stan — Yes! Yes! Yes!*

*Ferne*

# Contents

**Introduction**                                                    xiii

CHAPTER ONE
## Transportation                                                      1
*Up, down, and around the town*

Hoffman Travel Service    2

SCHEDULED    SERVICE
Amtrak   5   •   British Airways   6   •   New York
Helicopter   7   •   *Queen Elizabeth 2*   9   •   Virgin
Atlantic   12

CHARTERS
Jet Aviation Business Jets, Inc.   14

CAR/LIMO SERVICES
Dav-El   15

CHAPTER TWO
## Hotels                                                             17
*A home it is ... not!*

The Carlyle   18   •   The Doral Tuscany Hotel   21   •
Essex House   23   •   The Four Seasons Hotel   26   •
The Hotel Millenium   29   •   Hotel Westbury   32   •
The Lowell   34   •   The Mark   37   •   Mayfair
Hotel Baglioni   40   •   The New York Palace   43   •
The Peninsula   45   •   The Pierre   48   •   Plaza
Athénée   51   •   The Plaza Hotel   54   •   The
Regency Hotel   57   •   The Royalton   60   •

The St. Regis  63  •  The Stanhope  66  •  The
Waldorf-Astoria  69

CHAPTER THREE

# Restaurants 73
*On the count of three — open your napkins!*

Aquavit  74  •  Arizona 206  76  •  Aureole  79  •
Ballato  81  •  Bouley  82  •  Café des Artistes
86  •  Carnegie Delicatessen & Restaurant  89  •
Chanterelle  91  •  Docks  93  •  Ferrara  95  •
The Four Seasons  96  •  Fu's  99  •  Gallagher's
102  •  Gotham Bar and Grill  104  •  Grotto
Azzurra  106  •  Hudson River Club  108  •  J. G.
Melon  111  •  Jim McMullen  112  •  Joe Allen
114  •  La Caravelle  116  •  La Côte Basque  118
•  La Grenouille  120  •  Le Bernardin  122  •  Le
Cirque  125  •  Les Celebrites  127  •  Lespinasse
129  •  Lutèce  131  •  Mesa Grill  133  •
Montrachet  135  •  Natalino  137  •  One Fifth
Avenue  139  •  Orso  141  •  Parioli Romanissimo
143  •  Park Avenue Cafe  146  •  Patsy's  147  •
Petrossian  150  •  P. J. Clarke's  152  •
Primavera  154  •  Primola  156  •  The Rainbow
Room  158  •  Rosa Mexicano  161  •  The
Russian Tea Room  165  •  San Domenico  167  •
Sarabeth's Kitchen  170  •  Sfuzzi  172  •  Shun
Lee  174  •  Sidewalkers  176  •  Sign of the Dove
178  •  Snaps  180  •  Sparks  182  •  The "21"
Club  184  •  Zarela  188

CHAPTER FOUR

# A Sudden Yen for ... 190
*Something for every taste, every mood, every moment*

PURVEYORS OF FINE FOODS

Dean & DeLuca  191  •  Manhattan Fruitier  193
•  Murray's Sturgeon  194  •  Orwasher's  195  •
William Poll  196  •  Word of Mouth  198  •
Zabar's  200  •  Zito's Bread  202

CATERERS
Glorious Foods   203   •   Great Performances   205   •
Sylvia Weinstock Cakes   206

FLORISTS
Philip Baloun Designs   208   •   Renny   210   •
Robert Isabell, Inc.   212

CHAPTER FIVE

# Shopping                                                    214
*If it's not here, it doesn't exist*

FOR MEN
Arthur Gluck, Chemisiers   215   •   Beau Brummel
216   •   Brooks Brothers   218   •   Davide Cenci   220
•   Maurizio—Custom Tailors   222   •   Paul Stuart
223   •   Uma-Reddy, Ltd.   225   •   William
Fioravanti, Inc.—Custom Tailors for Men   226

FOR WOMEN
Chanel   228   •   Fendi   230   •   Givenchy   232   •
Helene Arpels   234   •   Henri Bendel   235   •   J. S.
Suárez   237   •   La Lingerie   238   •   Laura
Biagiotti   239   •   Maud Frizon   240   •   Rene
Mancini   241   •   Sylvia Pines—Uniquities   242   •
Ungaro   243   •   Vera Wang Bridal House, Ltd.   244
•   Walter Steiger   247

FOR MEN AND WOMEN
Barneys New York   248   •   Bergdorf Goodman   251
•   Billy Martin Western Classics   254   •
Bloomingdale's   255   •   Bottega Veneta   258   •
Burberry's   259   •   Cashmere Cashmere   262   •
Charivari   264   •   Emporio Armani   265   •   E.
Vogel—Custom Boots to Measure   267   •   Gianni
Versace Uomo   268   •   Giorgio Armani   269   •
Gucci   271   •   Hermès   272   •   Leggiadro   275   •
Macy's   276   •   Ralph Lauren at 72nd Street   280
•   Saks Fifth Avenue   282   •   Susan Bennis/Warren
Edwards   285   •   Tender Buttons   286   •   T. O.
Dey   288   •   Yves Saint Laurent Femme   290

FOR THE HOME
Asprey & Company, Ltd. 293 · Baccarat 295 ·
Bernardaud 297 · Christofle 300 · D.
Porthault & Co. 301 · Fortunoff 303 · Frette
304 · Lalique 306 · Pratesi 308 · Puiforcat
310 · Schweitzer Linens 311 · Steuben 312 ·
Tenzing & Pema 314

CHAPTER SIX

# Jewelry 316
*Baubles, bangles, and big bucks*

Buccellati 317 · Bulgari 318 · Cartier 320
· Ciner Fashion Jewelers 323 · The Gorevic
Collection 324 · Kenneth Jay Lane 326 ·
Marina B. 327 · Norman Landsberg 328 ·
Runsdorf, Inc. 329 · Tiffany & Co. 330 · Van
Cleef & Arpels 333

CHAPTER SEVEN

# Beauty and Health 336

SUPPLIES
Boyds of Madison Avenue 337 · Floris 339 ·
Kiehl's 341

LADIES' SERVICES
Elizabeth Arden 343 · García 344 · John
Sahag 345 · Leonardo 347 · Nathan 348 ·
The Wayne Webb Technique 348

UNISEX SERVICES
Georgette Klinger 350 · Il Makiage 352 · La
Coupe 354

GENTLEMEN'S SERVICES
Delta Men's Hair Stylists 357

EXERCISE
Lotte Berke 358 · Radu's Physical Culture Studio
359 · Vertical Club 360

CHAPTER EIGHT
# Miscellaneous Services 363
*"I can get it for you ...."*

Alice S. Mason, Ltd. 364 · Herman Agar Co. 365
· Jerry Kravat Entertainment Services 366 · Jill
Gill 367 · Michel Thomas Language Center 368
· Spencer Realty 369 · Tiecrafters 370

**Acknowledgments** 373

**Index** 375

# Introduction

$N$ew York is an easy city to enjoy. The easiest! The best! That's why it has been celebrated often in movies, musicals, and songs. It has *more* enjoyable places — restaurants, hotels, shops, and services — than anywhere else in the world. So go out and enjoy! You don't need help, *if* you have a lifetime of experience, to choose well from thousands of options.

But if you're coming to the city for a few days or a few weeks, or if you live here but are too busy to do the time-consuming research to discover the special places....

Well, that's why we wrote *Only in New York* — to help you make the most of your time and to help you enjoy New York in style, with no wasted effort. Within these pages are the inside stories on the city's special places and the people who run them. We hope you'll have the time, the energy, and the bankroll to visit them all. If not, we think you will be entertained reading about where the sophisticated, stylish New Yorker dines, drinks, and shops. This is a book about memories you will acquire and cherish and places you will want to visit again. While most memories exist only as mental images, we thought it would be fun to put a few on the tip of your tongue via succulent recipes from special restaurants. What better way to recall a wondrous meal than by eating it again?

You will, of course, make your own discoveries, so we've organized the book as a starting place, a series of beginnings. Did we cover everything? Of course not. We're talking about a city that, by some calculations, supports over 25,000 restaurants and even more shops. No doubt we missed some special places here and there — we leave it to you to fill in the blanks. And we *know* we skipped a few establishments that usually appear on the pages of guides to New York — some fell by the wayside because of time and space restrictions, other because, quite frankly, we don't feel they're worthy of our time or yours. Use this book as a resource of places and people you can count on — safe havens from which to launch a more hit-and-miss approach to the city.

In the process, you'll be struck by the vibrancy of this city we're proud to call home. It's constantly on the go, undulating with change. New York and New Yorkers are not inclined to leave well enough alone — renew, restore, replace are the three R's here. By the time this book is published, there will be any number of exciting, commendable new businesses and services that you can add to your list. By the same token, rates and prices quoted may have changed. But the good news is that where hotels and restaurants are concerned, they're not likely to increase by much. Hotel competition at the luxury end of the market is heating up, and restaurants are still trying to hold down prices, and some are even rolling them back in search of clientele.

So, whether you're in town for a weekend, a week, a lifetime or only thinking about your next jaunt to the Big Apple, help yourself to all the opportunities for indulgence, to all the possibilities of excitement that make New York one hell of a town!

Ferne Kadish
Shelley Clark

# CHAPTER ONE

# Transportation

*Up, down, and around the town*

*W*e wrote this book to get you to go to fabulous places. When you know where to go, the question for out-of-towners *and* native New Yorkers is: How do I get there?

Since that is the most-asked question by international diplomats, government officials, celebrities from the world of show business and sports, as well as the newlywed couple from the Midwest, New York has come up with a variety of answers. There's an army of entrepreneurs dedicated to Transportation with a capital *T* and that stands for "terrific" and not "trouble."

You will notice instantly that gridlock in New York is like everything else here — bigger and better (?) than anywhere else. And that is why, *mon cher*, the limousine was invented. It can be an understated town car or an overstated stretch limo, but it spells comfort and style while you spend forty-five minutes in crosstown traffic. There are a wet bar and television, a telephone and fax, and — best of all — a driver who knows which streets are one way (and which way the one way is), who speaks English and American, who knows that a spin through Central Park can be a visual restorative before plunging back into the muddle of midtown Manhattan.

For dramatic entrances, there's nothing like a limousine, the more stretched, the better. Color is key. Black is best, though increasingly difficult to come by. Navy blue will do. Gray is okay in a pinch, but white? Save it for weddings in Brooklyn.

Of course, one must always remember the most efficient mode of transportation that especially suits New Yorkers — walking. Indeed it's the one we tend to rely on as much as possible, but only in the interest of getting someplace on time, or what passes for on time in New York — there's an automatic fifteen-minute grace period built into any appointment.

To get here from wherever you are, there are, but of course, *mein liebchen*, chartered planes, chartered helicopters, luxury ocean liners, not to mention special first-class service on regularly scheduled flights. Arrive in style, then stay in style. Our motto is: First class or not at all.

Now that you know it's possible to get around New York and to enjoy it — get on your mark, get set, go!

## Hoffman Travel Service

| | |
|---|---|
| 155 East 55th Street | (212) 688-4444 |
| Suite 4H | Fax (212) 753-5974 |
| New York, NY 10022 | |

Although we've given you Hoffman's address, you really don't need it. The point of their service is just that — it's service that comes to you.

Hoffman offers the same kinds of things that any good travel agency does, but what makes them stand out is how they go beyond the basics. *USA Today* said it best: "Hoffman is probably the best travel agency in the country at pampering and coddling fist-class travelers."

What that means is that they'll see to everything, from the reservations on. They have seven people based at JFK, including Caren Hencken, their airport services manager. Caren or one of her staff will meet you at the airport and take care of you from the time you get out of the car to the time you get on the plane. You don't have to think about anything, including where you'll be seated. Before you get there, they've confirmed the flight (or booked you on another if there's been a cancellation) and reserved the best seat possible. After you arrive, they'll check your bags and escort you to a private waiting area, VIP lounge, or right onto the plane. You'll never have to stand in line. As you can imagine, this suits celebrities, corporate execs, and other VIPs to a *T.* And although Hoffman handles arrangements for fashion industry clients like Calvin Klein and Chanel, the entertainment industry accounts for most of its client base. Warner Brothers, MCA Universal, 20th-Century, A&M Records, and Electra are just a few of their regulars. New Line Cinema, Polygram Records, and Atlantic Records maintain a Hoffman outlet in their Manhattan offices for quick access.

Hoffman Travel Service has been owned since 1972 by Carol Dunn-Tompkins, who saw a need for an entertainment industry-oriented travel service. With her partner Tom Stout, they developed the meeting-and-greeting side of the business and it's been going gangbusters since then. Business travelers account for 80 percent of their $100 million-plus business, but they do have a leisure travel department that arranges for their business clients' hard-earned vacations.

The firm is based in Los Angeles (with branches in London and Paris), but with so much travel from the Big Orange to the Big Apple, the New York location (established in 1981) is as key a location for them as is L.A. And that's where Caren comes in. A self-described "airline brat" (her mother worked for the airlines and Caren grew up in airports), she knows every inch of JFK, La Guardia, and Newark and everyone she has to know to get you what you need, as does her staff. Although she's mostly at JFK, she visits La Guardia frequently to keep in touch with her contacts there. She and her staff are so ubiquitous at airports that they're often mistaken for airline employees.

If you're a high-profile celebrity who doesn't want to be seen, they know the ins and outs and the back corridors through which to take you. If you're an exec, on the other hand, being seen in the right places is critical. No self-respecting VIP dares to be spotted (or not spotted) seated in the Concorde's Siberia-like second cabin, so Hoffman will snare a coveted Cabin One, Row One seat where you're treated appropriately like the crème de la crème. Domestic flight equivalents are rows two or three in first class (of course) and Hoffman knows how to get you there, too.

Although Hoffman's people are good, even they must play by the rules when it comes to customs. If you're a VIP, or especially a highly visible celeb, however, they will alert the airlines and arrange for a representative to keep you out of the public eye.

Snowstorms and hurricanes? No problem. Hoffman's network of computers, beepers, and portable phones allows them to reach their people at a moment's notice. This was crucial during the recent snowstorm that shut down everything in three states; Hoffman was able to reach many clients en route to the airport to let them know that no planes were flying—anywhere. You can be sure, however, that when air service resumed, Hoffman clients were the first to know and the first to go.

On good-weather days, though, often their biggest challenge is getting their busy executive clients off the car phone. Somehow, they do. "I would never have made this flight without you" is one of the most common comments Caren gets.

Caren's office is her briefcase. With two and one-half miles to cover at JFK alone, she does a lot of running. It's a glamorous job, she told us, if you wear flats.

Celebrity regulars include Jack Nicholson, Bette Midler, Priscilla Presley, Danny DeVito, George Harrison, and Ringo Starr. Their ex-partner Paul McCartney is one of Caren's favorites. She's been escorting him and wife, Linda, for nearly all of the twelve years she's been with Hoffman, including the time that a security guard at the metal dectector exlaimed, "Oh, Ringo Starr, Ringo Starr! (Paul took it with good humor.) Dolly Parton is the biggest attention-getter Caren can recall, provoking spontaneous cheers from passers-by. The late Lucille Ball was another regular; the redhead wouldn't get out of the limo unless a Hoffman rep was there. She once challenged Caren to backgammon while they waited for a plane. After Caren beat her three times straight, Lucy wanted to buy her a plane ticket so they could play again during the flight. Needless to say, Caren had to decline, but she might have accepted if Lucy insisted; Hoffman people will do anything for their clients.

And believe it or not, you don't have to be a celebrity to be a Hoffman VIP. As long are you're going first class (in every sense of the word), all this TLC is provided free of charge to regulars.

# SCHEDULED SERVICE

## *Amtrak*

(800) 872-7245
(212) 582-6875

One thing about airports; they're never any place you want to be. Instead they tend to be at the end of the earth or at least a good forty-five minutes from anywhere that could be described as civilization. So even though we have some suggestions about the best way to fly and even the most convenient way to get to and from New York's airports, we still feel honor bound to tell you about an alternative — the train.

Not just any train. We have a specific class of service on a particular kind of train in mind — the club car on Amtrak's Metroliner between Washington, D.C., New York, and such points as Baltimore and Philadelphia. The D.C.–Manhattan trip takes what Amtrak calls two hours and fifty-five civilized minutes. When you consider the crucial downtown-to-downtown element of the trip, it's about the same time you'd be likely to spend getting to National (which in all fairness is one of the few major airports within shouting distance of the city it serves), grabbing the shuttle to La Guardia, and schlepping to midtown Manhattan.

And the train is really more comfortable than the plane. For one thing, you don't feel so confined to your seat. You can take a stroll and belly up to the bar. Although since there is a waiter in the club car (read *First Class*), you really don't need one.

In fact, in the club car, you don't need to do much of anything except sit back and relax in your oversized seat and wait to be served your complimentary meal, beverage, and a newspaper. Now a word about the food — it isn't bad. And it's nicely presented, topped off with a hot towel that does refresh and invigorate. If you must, you can conduct business on the telephone, more reliable and infinitely more satisfying in its private booth than those available on planes.

The current one-way fare is $90, but since fares tend to have short life spans, call to check and make the required reservation.

Although we ride Amtrak for the comfort and convenience, there's another very appealing factor—the social possibilities. We don't know exactly what it is, but there's a feeling about the train that brings out a sense of camaraderie. Instead of studiously avoiding any human contact by burying our heads in a magazine or pretending to be asleep, as we do on planes, we find ourselves chatting away with neighbors. We've actually met people on the train—people we like and have made our friends. When was the last time you had that experience on a plane?

# British Airways

530 Fifth Avenue                                    (800) 247-9297
Between 44th and 45th Streets
New York, NY 10036

British Airways claims to be "the world's favourite airline." We have no way of verifying that typically bold British assertion, but there's no question that as far as we're concerned British Airways' supersonic Concorde is the only way to fly—at least between London and New York. Yes, it's glamorous. Yes, having one of the Concorde's leather identification tags on your briefcase is a status symbol. But our reason for flying the Concorde (indeed the only reason for anyone in his or her right mind to do this) is that it's fast—very fast.

The transatlantic flight, Concorde-style, averages only three hours and twenty-five minutes (or as little as three hours westbound). There are four crossings daily, two originating from Heathrow, two from JFK. A 10:30 A.M. departure from London means an early morning arrival in New York in the nick of time for a power breakfast at the Regency, Carlyle, or 21, with a whole business day ahead. The 7:00 P.M. departure from New York allows a full day in London, but arrival back in New York in time for dinner. By the same token, leaving New York in the morning gets you to London in time for dinner, while the lunchtime departure allows plenty of time for a morning meeting stateside with an evening arrival in London. Best of all, when you get there, you can look forward to a full night's sleep.

Flights also depart from D.C. if you happen to find yourself there on a Tuesday, Friday, or Sunday. Or, if you need to return to D.C. from London, you can do so on a Monday, Thursday, or Saturday.

Time, as they say, is money, and all this time-saving doesn't come cheap. A New York-to-London round-trip ticket is $8,334; half that for a one-way fare. But that includes VIP treatment from check-in to baggage claim and some first-class food. At both airports there are ticket counters reserved for the exclusive use of Concorde passengers. After check-in, travelers relax in a special lounge, where complimentary libations and snacks, appropriate to the time of day, are served. Once on board, the gracious flight crew tempts you with delicate canapés, accompanied by vintage champagne. Brunch, lunch, or dinner follows, the creation of British Airways' master chefs and served on damask table linens and fine Royal Doulton china accented with fresh orchids flown in daily. For dinner, the meal might consist of smoked Scottish salmon and grilled filet of Angus beef. Caviar is always on the menu. Any dietary restrictions will be catered to, if you call in advance. It's bound to be the best in-flight meal you've ever had.

Now, you should know that despite all of British Airways' admirable efforts, there is a slight discomfort factor associated with supersonic travel. The Concorde is on the narrow side, the cushy leather seats lined up very closely in pairs on either side of the aisle. The headroom reminds you of a forty-foot yacht — adequate, but barely. It's not for the claustrophobic. (You will find seats far forward — in front of the wings — less noisy.)

Still, the close quarters are a small price to pay for such a quick, convenient flight and an end to the miseries of jet lag — another sensible reason for flying the Concorde. As we settled into our seats one recent morning, we recalled the seventeenth-century English poet Andrew Marvell: "But at my back I always hear Time's wingèd chariot hurrying near." He must have had a vision of the Concorde, rapidly becoming one of life's more delectable necessities.

## *New York Helicopter*

Heliport: 34th Street
and East River Drive

Scheduled Service
(800) 645-3494
Charters (516) 228-8300
(National Helicopter
Corporation)

Schlepping out to JFK is a drag under any circumstances and when time is, shall we say it, on the wing, the trip can turn into pure torture. Sitting on the Van Wyck Expressway in bumper-to-bumper traffic while the minutes to flight time tick away can be very nerve-racking. But wait! There's a quick, comfortable, reliable alternative provided by New York Helicopter. Ride in style in one of their four 14-passenger Sikorsky choppers. With 13 flights on weekdays and 10 on weekends, there's bound to be one to suit your agenda.

It's only $65 one way—unless you're traveling business or first class on most major airlines, in which case it's "free." Likewise, if you're flying a foreign carrier in from Europe, the service is generally included. Even full economy fares on many airlines allow substantial discounts or free rides on New York Helicopter.

Book the chopper flight at the same time you book your airline reservations—they're connected to all major airline computer systems—whether you're coming or going. When going, you check in at the heliport located at 34th Street and the East River Drive. Luggage is checked through to your final destination. If, on the other hand, you're arriving, a New York Helicopter representative will meet you at the gate, help you retrieve your luggage, and escort you to the American Airlines terminal, which serves as their JFK facility.

It's just a ten-minute flight into Manhattan: fast, easy, and fun. In fact, there's only one way to make the trek any easier—charter a helicopter of your very own. The Manhattan–JFK route, either way, can be exclusively yours at rates ranging from $595 to about $1,200. For $595 ($395 from January through March) you get a tidy little four-passenger BellJet Ranger; $1,200 rents a Sikorsky. The folks at New York Helicopter liken the former to picking you up in a Ford station wagon, while the latter is more akin to riding in a Rolls-Royce. For security reasons, they're reluctant to cite high-profile types who use their service, let alone who opts for the Ford and who goes for the Rolls, but they do allow that private charter tends to be the way most celebrities choose to make the JFK–Manhattan jaunt.

Bear in mind, however, that New York Helicopter charter services are by no means restricted to runs back and forth from the airport. They are regularly called on to take private parties to the Hamptons or to fly a group to any of the tristate area's elite country clubs for a friendly game of golf. Atlantic City is also a big destination.

Call the operations department for any such special requests. Charter rates are by the hour—$750 each for the little Bell helicopter and $1,950 for the big Sikorsky, with several sizes and prices in between. With eight aircraft, they're down from their high of 30 helicopters but still the largest fleet in the East.

## Queen Elizabeth 2

Cunard                                           (800) 221-4770
555 Fifth Avenue
New York, NY 10017

We firmly believe (with apologies to that old Western Airlines ad) that a voyage via Cunard's *Queen Elizabeth 2* is truly the *only* way to travel. From New York to Southampton or vice versa — or round-trip for that matter — you will never spend five more glorious days.

*QE2* is the only passenger ship to operate regularly scheduled transatlantic service (about twenty-six crossings a year between April and December), and when winter weather makes that voyage unpleasant, her versatility allows conversion to a cruise liner with forty-five ports of call, from Asia to South America. She's the largest passenger ship able to pass through the Panama Canal, and it's a close call with barely twelve inches to spare on each side! *QE2* sails from New York to just about everywhere she goes: Hawaii, Bermuda, Canada, Nassau, the Caribbean, the Canary Islands, Iberia, the Mediterranean, and Norway, besides the Canal.

With a length that equals three football fields, *QE2* certainly lives up to her billing as a "city at sea." She boasts 13 decks with 4,500 square yards of space, 900 passenger cabins, 4 restaurants, a 20,000-bottle wine cellar, 4 swimming pools, a 40-car garage, an executive boardroom, a full-service hospital (whose staff includes a dentist), a 6,000-volume library, and the only shipboard tuxedo rental service in the world.

*QE2* is not a mere cruise ship. She combines the grandeur of an oceanliner with state-of-the-art onboard facilities, evoking an elegant era when sea travel was the way to see the world. And despite competition from airplanes and newer vessels, *QE2* continues to appeal. Any particular crossing might bring you face to face with the likes of Elizabeth Taylor, Meryl Streep, Walter Cronkite, Calvin Trillin, or Rod Stewart. While you're sailing on the fastest passenger ship still in service (her cruising speed is a brisk 32.5 knots), you'll find no shortage of things to do. Cunard claims that it would take one person four months to participate in all the activities offered on board, and they may be right. Start your morning with breakfast in bed while you peruse the newspaper that's published daily on board. When you're in the mood to shop, boutiques by Gucci, Christian Dior, Burberry's, Louis Vuitton, Harrods and others await, duty free. For entertainment, the Art Deco-style theater has been completely remodeled and its bar area is adorned with a photo gallery of stars snapped by renowned photographer Jane Hunter-Cox. Culture? Try the new art gallery, complete with lectures and guided tours. Keep in touch with the world, if you must, via the computer center or the 20-channel television sets. You can pamper yourself at the brand-new two-level *QE2* spa, one of the most complete health and fitness facilities at sea, or on land, for that matter. Whatever you want, they have: rowing machines, StairMasters, Lifecycles, treadmills, free weights, a ten-station Keiser body workout and cross-training system, exercise classes, one-on-one training, steam rooms, saunas, whirlpools, hydrotherapy baths, beauty treatments, and even computerized nutritional and life-style evaluation. if you're the outdoorsy type, there's everything from shuffleboard and swimming to volleyball, golf putting, and laser skeet. More? Try financial lectures, dancing, movies, concerts, gaming—we could go on and on.

With a passenger capacity of 1,850, there are nearly as many crew members and employees as there are guests, including 239 waiters, 16 bakers, 18 wine stewards, 5 exercise specialists, 4 printers, 2 nannies, and 1 disk jockey.

For accommodations, we highly recommend either the Queen Mary or Queen Elizabeth suite. Located on *QE2*'s top deck, each has its own sun deck, private enough to permit sunbathing au naturel. Both are bi-level, with lots of blond wood and brass fittings. Perhaps best of all are their big bathrooms with separate stall showers and tubs. These suites will set you back anywhere from $26,145 to $57,520 for the transatlantic trip, depending upon the time of year. But it is perhaps some small consolation that the fare is per suite, not per person, and does include return airfare.

You can, of course, travel for lots less. As they say, there's "a level of luxury for every taste." About $6,000 per person buys an outside cabin with a veranda for the transatlantic trip. "Penthouse Service" amenities are provided for all the luxury suites and staterooms. These include the services of a butler or attendant and chefs from the Queen's Grill, a bon voyage bottle of French champagne, fresh fruit daily, personalized stationery, and in-cabin videocassette players.

Where you stay, though, does determine where you eat. The Queen's Grill, with its 240 seats and custom-designed Wedgewood china, is for guests in the suites and top-price cabins. Several of the five nights require black-tie attire, so come prepared; people really do dress. But no matter what day it is, you'll always find caviar on the menu. In fact, it's served daily for breakfast, with shirred eggs and cream. If you have special needs or desires, just ask. We're told that if they have it, they'll make it. And if they don't have it, they'll do their best to get it for your next voyage. We read about a lady who had been disappointed not to find her favorite brand of bottled water; the next time she sailed, the management ordered several cases and stocked her cabin.

You'll be assigned one of the other restaurants depending on where you stay. In descending order of cabin price, they are: the Princess Grill—there are two actually, one port, one starboard, each with about 100 seats; the Columbia, which has outstanding views; or the more informal 420-seat Mauretania restaurant. But no matter where you stay, you'll find each restaurant to be top quality, befitting *QE2*, of course.

And whatever your choice, be assured that you'll experience that wonderful tradition begun by Cunard when its first ship, *Britannia*, was launched in 1840, kicking off regular transatlantic service. Over a century later, in 1965, *QE2*'s keel was laid; she was launched in 1967 by her namesake, the queen of England, and her maiden voyage took place in 1969. Since then, *QE2* has operated not only as a transatlantic liner and a cruise ship, but has also done service as a troop ship in 1982 during the Falklands conflict. In fact, two weeks were all that were necessary to get the old girl shipshape for that mission! *QE2* has undergone several refurbishments since then (including conversion from steam engines to diesel power), the most recent being an $8 million refit in 1992.

Well, we've done our best, but our *QE2* discussion doesn't begin to cover the range of services, activities, and amenities you'll find on board or the grandeur of this experience. The only option you have is to check it all out for yourself!

# Virgin Atlantic

96 Morton Street                                    (800) 862-8621
New York, NY 10014

Richard Branson is a man with the Midas touch. A self-made millionaire at the tender age of 17 (courtesy of a discount record mail-order business), he is now a billionaire who, against all odds, has made a hit out of Virgin Atlantic Airways. Indeed the brash Branson has succeeded where so many others have failed with economy-oriented start-up airlines. And while aviation pioneers like Pan-Am and TWA were floundering in bankruptcy courts, Virgin Atlantic moved into the black in 1983, its third year of operation.

Today, for its size, Virgin Atlantic is one of the most profitable carriers in the world, with routes from Great Britain to six U.S. destinations and to Tokyo. Apparently Richard understood what others did not: it isn't enough to be just cheaper than the competition; you've got to be different. And different is what Virgin Atlantic is all about.

Richard drew on his roots in the music business to minimize the boredom of flying. He instituted an ambitious entertainment policy on Virgin, from live events such as musical acts, wine tastings, and book signings to personal video screens at every seat. No wonder *Executive Travel Magazine* honored Virgin Atlantic with its Best In-Flight Entertainment Award for 1993.

Besides being fun, Virgin Atlantic is a bona fide good deal, in each of its three classes of service. Its Upper Class is equal and indeed superior to many a competitor's first class, while its prices are comparable to their business class service. Upper Class passengers are treated to dedicated check-in desks and lounges equipped with phones, faxes, and other business facilities. On board, they have roomy sleeper seats and the freedom to explore exclusive lounges and stand-up bars. In fact, it's our experience that flying Virgin's Upper Class can be a very social experience, never more so than the transatlantic flight we spent autographing our *London on 1,000 Pounds a Day (Before Tea)*.

However, with conspicuous consumption being frowned upon these days, we're just as likely to fly Virgin's Economy Class, which remains remarkable on the entertainment and amenity fronts. There are those screens (Virgin was the first line to install them throughout all of their planes) offering six video channels and ten audio channels — and you get to keep the complimentary headphones! Moreover, drinks are on the house throughout the flight and the food is better than you might expect. You get a choice of four different meals, including a vegetarian selection, which are as close to gourmet as it's possible to get on an airline — award-winning, even. *Executive Travel* gave Virgin its 1993 Best Food and Wine award.

But Richard and Virgin are not content to rest upon their culinary laurels. They've engaged the consulting services of one of Britain's premier chefs, Raymond Blanc of the legendary Le Manoir aux Quatre Saisons, with a view toward transforming "the whole nature of on-board catering," according to Richard. Upper Class passengers already have the choice of an entrée created especially for Virgin by Raymond, who suggests companion wines for each and supplies a souvenir recipe.

There are two flights daily from London's Heathrow to the New York area, either to Newark International or to JFK. The Newark-bound flight leaves at 4:00 P.M. and arrives at 6:40 P.M., while the JFK flight leaves at 12:40 P.M. and arrives at 3:20 P.M. We generally opt for the former, because Newark's customs and immigration procedures tend to run much faster and smoother than JFK's. The fare for Upper Class runs $3,293 round trip; depending upon the season, Economy Class ranges from $412 to $646.45 round trip with a 21-day advance purchase.

If you were paying attention, you noticed we mentioned *three* classes of service. The third is called Mid. Its principal claim to fame is having its own cabin, as well as more seat and leg room than Economy. At least, that's what they tell us. We've never bothered with it — for us it's either blow budget caution to the wind with Upper or tighten our belts with Economy!

# CHARTERS

## *Jet Aviation Business Jets, Inc.*

(212) 868-1122
(800) RENT-JET

It can be *so* tiresome worrying about getting to the airport in time to make a scheduled flight. You break your neck getting there, only to discover it's been delayed or canceled. Even if it does take off on time, there's that dreary food to contend with. Jet Aviation to the rescue! Theirs is really the only way to go. They've been in the business of supplying private planes and jets for charter for nearly twenty-five years.

With more than 120 aircraft, over 200 flight personnel, and facilities in the United States, Europe, Singapore, and the Middle East, Jet Aviation operates one of the world's largest executive fleets. If it flies, they have it — from a five-passenger twin-engine King Air turboprop for those quick jaunts to Washington or Boston at $725 a flight hour to a 16-passenger Gulf Stream jet with a range of 4,800 miles and a fee of $5,000 an hour.

They even have 727s for charter, in several different configurations seating up to a hundred. The pride of the pack is an Executive B727, complete with full working galley stowing Baccarat crystal, Puiforcat silver, and Limoges china, two bedrooms with king-size beds, and an elegant salon area outfitted with couches, club chairs, telephones, fax machine, and VCR. It can take about twenty-five of your very closest friends anywhere in the world for about $7,000 an hour.

Jet Aviation's very professional staff (no tipping, ever) employs considerable resources to make flying as painless as possible. All major newspapers and periodicals are routinely supplied, and the food alone is worth the price of admission — cold lobster salad and champagne for lunch or perhaps a little beluga washed down with chilled vodka just before landing tend to soothe even the most white-knuckled flyers.

While most of Jet Aviation's charters use the Teterboro, New Jersey, airport, only twenty minutes from midtown Manhattan through the Lincoln Tunnel and just beyond Giants Stadium, arrangements can be made to fly into or out of any of the area's facilities. If you've set your sights on one of the 727s, it's easiest to pick it up at Newark as many CEOs do. Wish we could tell you who, but confidentiality is of paramount importance to Jet Aviation, for security and business reasons. Use your imagination. We're sure you'll think of one or two people who rely on their 24-hour dispatch service — and on their discretion.

# CAR/LIMO SERVICES

## *Dav-El*

---

(212) 645-4242
National Reservations (800) 922-0343
New York Reservations (800) 543-5719
Corporate Fax (212) 463-8620

Nearly fifteen years ago, Scott Solombrino blew his $600 savings on a limousine rather than his year's college tuition. Both he and the car were nineteen years old. His gamble allowed him to work his way through school. His books stayed under the front seat, so he studied whenever he had a break. In the process, he managed to build a tidy little business. By 1987, his Boston-based Fifth Avenue Limousine had a thirty-two-car fleet and annual revenues of $3 million. In 1988, he blew his savings again, but there was considerably less risk involved. Scott, along with a partner, purchased the already well-established Dav-El Limousine Service. Founded by the late David Klein, it is one of the world's largest with an international network of over 5,000 cars.

Today, Dav-El is piloted alone by Scott, still practically a youngster at thirty-three years old. He divides his time between New York and Boston while also managing to visit Los Angeles on a regular basis. It is to his credit that Dav-El, which boasts 300 cars in New York alone, has long had an enviable reputation for polite, efficient service and beautifully maintained cars. One of the first services to have phones and writing desks in every car, it is especially popular with busy corporate types who, Scott says, now spend 90 percent of their time in his cars on the phone. Big-time celebrities like chatting on the phone, too, but it's Dav-El's discretion and respect for their privacy that's of even greater importance to them. Limo drivers are traditionally a great source for gossip columnists — but not Dav-El's limo drivers.

Scott insists that, in addition to keeping their mouths shut, his drivers be well-groomed and well-versed in the goings-on of the cities they serve. In fact, a Dav-El driver is generally as helpful as some of Manhattan's best concierges when it comes to suggesting places to dine and dance. Most know all about the in spots of the moment and are happy to share the knowledge.

And speaking of concierges, Dav-El has its own fleet, who service area airports. Upon request, they will meet you at the airport to assist with all your travel arrangements and anything else you might need. There's no charge for their services, but Dav-El does tend to be the most expensive act in town when it comes to cars. Sedans (Lincoln town cars) are $42 an hour or $1.45 per mile, whichever is greater, while the deluxe variety (stretch limos) are $55 or $1.75 a mile. There's a two-hour minimum and a gratuity is automatically added to the bill — 15 percent for the sedans, 20 percent for the deluxe cars.

Interestingly enough, Dav-El, in keeping with our assertion that, limowise, bigger is better, has eliminated formal limousines altogether. They only offer stretches and only in approved colors: black, navy, and silver. Each comes equipped with oriental carpets, phone, moon roof, bar, television, VCR, and radio/tape player. CD players are standard, but it's the VCRs that hold the greatest appeal and are giving Dav-El an edge in this highly competitive market. Scott sees corporate execs as "video-conscious," now demanding VCR-equipped cars as insistently as they once demanded those with phones. He says they now forego reading the paper in favor of reviewing tapes of meetings or seminars.

All major credit cards are accepted, but house accounts are so much more convenient and you can charge it in any of the 350 cities worldwide that it services.

There's no doubt about the quality of Dav-El's service. And Scott, who has come a long way since that $600 investment, still delivers on his promise of "clean cars on time."

# CHAPTER TWO

# Hotels

*A home it is ... not!*

You think a hotel should be "a home away from home"?
Wrong! Unless your home has maid service twice a day, room
service around the clock — for everything from a diet drink to
caviar to a mushroom omelette — a valet service to press the suits
and iron the dresses, a concierge to help get theater tickets and
make all travel arrangements. You say your home has all that?
Good, we'll come to visit *you*.

Seriously, the choice of the hotel is the most important travel
decision you will make. If you're not comfortable and happy in your
space, it won't matter how bright the sun, how tuneful the show,
how inexpensive the shopping. Hotel time is escape time, fantasy
time, romance time. It should be free of the alarm clock, the constant interruptions of the normal day at home, a chance to smell
the flowers, taste the wine, to be pampered and pleasured.

"You'll find me at the Pierre" (or The Carlyle or The Mark, or
the whatever) may be as much a social (or a business) statement
as a way of reaching you when you're "in town." Each has a different look, a different feel, a different statement of who you are,
where you're from, what you'll be doing, and what you're all about.
You are, after all, where you visit. So, of course, you are where you
stay.

We know all about that even though we New Yorkers don't stay in the local hotels; we just visit them. We visit them to eat, to socialize, to show off our latest gowns and jewels, our latest coiffures and beaus. But that's why they've become so important. When we're "seen" in public, we want the background to be just right. Like everything else in New York, the choice is boggling. Hotels seem to be exempt from the harsh economic law that says, "This too shall pass." Unlike restaurants, boutiques, and many other commercial endeavors, hotels are rarely victims of trendiness, going from red-hot to stone cold dead in the market. The hotels remodel, their prices escalate, and sometimes they offer weekend bargains. And in recent years, a number of new hotels have joined the fray.

To help you along, we've narrowed the field to our favorites. We're sure that your selection, whatever it may be, will make you very happy that a hotel is not a home.

# The Carlyle

| Madison Avenue at 76th Street | (212) 744-1600 |
| New York, NY 10021 | Fax (212) 717-4682 |

Often referred to as the "grande dame" of New York hotels, even by managers of rival properties, The Carlyle's 190 rooms make it neither the largest nor the smallest, nor do its sixty-two years make it the oldest. It may simply be the best—the only hotel in the city to rate Mobil's prestigious Five-Star Award, an honor it has held for a quarter of a century thanks to its quiet luxury underscored by a large, friendly staff.

Tucked away in a peaceful residential neighborhood on upper Madison Avenue, The Carlyle caters to a faithful clientele, who've been staying here for decades and wouldn't dream of staying elsewhere. The absence of glitz in favor of an extraordinarily comfortable and very tasteful atmosphere appeals to their old-money sensibilities. There's the ring of truth about the oft-told tale of a wealthy frequent guest who called The Carlyle's front desk to announce, "I'm at the _____ (another famous New York hotel)." And then she pleaded, "Please get me out." In search of greener grass, she'd ventured outside the private preserve that The Carlyle is to its devoted clientele only to be bitterly disappointed by a more commercial establishment—one of those places that actually spends money on promoting its charms. The Carlyle eschews such self-serving practices in favor of expenditures on guest comforts (upwards of $100,000 a room) in the constant upgrading and renovation program orchestrated by internationally renowned decorator Mark Hampton. Then there are the salaries of some five hundred employees—The Carlyle has the highest guest-to-staff ratio in the city.

Individually and as a whole, The Carlyle's staff has traditionally been its best asset—unfailingly discreet, sincerely accommodating, and perpetually polite. It's no coincidence that well-heeled New Yorkers seeking sanctuary from scandals of a matrimonial kind head for The Carlyle, where they know their privacy will be insured by the protective staff. But it goes both ways: the guests are equally protective and solicitous of the staff. Consequently, a position at The Carlyle is not just a job; it's a career. A number of employees have been here for more than thirty years, and there's a five-year waiting list to become a bellman!

Managing Director Dan Camp enjoys telling the story of the young man who applied to The Carlyle for a position as a bellman. He was told, "Your mother had to have put you on the list at birth, and someone has to die." The poor chap wasn't destined to join the ranks of a staff dedicated to making the hotel worthy of the likes of Prince Philip.

When he's in town, the prince opts for Suite 2701 with its sweeping views across Central Park to the West Side. We don't know if he plays, but a grand piano is at His Highness's disposal in the huge living room. The suite goes for $1,250 a night if just one bedroom is required; $1,500 includes a second bedroom.

For less princely sums, there are the single or double rooms from $260 to $385 a night, each unique in its decor. But you can count on rich colors—Chinese red, burnt orange and green— world-class artwork, porcelain vases and lamps, chintz coverlets and antique satin boudoir chairs. All this old-world sophistication is complemented by contemporay high-tech amenities, such as VCRs, CD players, fax machines, mini-bars, and marble bathrooms decked out with hairdriers, makeup mirrors, and Jacuzzi tubs. Some even boast bidets. We are especially enamored of one of The Carlyle's little extras—the breakfast tray tucked away in the closet of every room. What a treat to cope with New York's

Sunday morning ritual of poring through *The Times* while enjoying breakfast in bed. Room 305 is a particularly pleasant place to play the person of leisure. A warm and cheerful double overlooking Madison Avenue, it takes on a residential air with its nice-sized foyer and outlandish closet space. Yours for $335 a night.

The Carlyle is very much an integral part of its tony environs. Indeed, the hotel is considered by many New Yorkers to be a civilized retreat from their manic city. A sense of serenity surrounds you upon entering the spacious marble lobby, glorious in its Aubusson carpets and Gobelin tapestries. Beyond, the Gallery has long been a neighborhood haunt for tea or late-night snacks. Once its muted grandeur was enlivened only by a high people-watching quotient. No longer. The Gallery has taken on a new, bold life in the form of a Turkish palace, thanks to a recent re-do by designer Renzo Mongiardino. Granted, the kaleidoscopic effect of the Italian handpainted wallpaper, colorful screens, couches covered in burgundy velvet appliquéd with antique kilims, and a paisley carpet seems incongruous in the midst of The Carlyle's English country-house elegance. But management, as well as your knowledge of decorative trends, is quick to point out that the great European rural residences of the 18th and 19th centuries often included a fantasy space designated as the Turkish room.

The more familiar elements of English hunt prints, brass-studded leather armchairs, and banquettes sprinkled with pillows, in combination with excellent food, makes the Carlyle Restaurant so inviting that many area residents consider it an annex of their dining rooms. The bar (called Bemelman's after Ludwig Bemelman, the creator of the endearing *Madeline* books), whose delightful murals of New York vignettes adorn the walls, serves as a local pub. The drinks are generous, the service is attentive, and the lighting is just dim enough to lend a sense of intimacy; it's just bright enough to observe regulars like Senator Pat Moynihan holding court.

The Cafe Carlyle offers some of the best entertainment in town with Karen Akers, Barbara Cook, Dixie Carter and, of course, Bobby Short who has called it home for nearly 26 years. The pied piper of café society never fails to charm with his witty renditions of popular songs, old and new. Bobby and his fellow performers do two shows a night, at 8:45 and 10:45. There's a $40 cover charge.

Reservations are hard to come by (the room only seats 90), so plan ahead.

Of course, if you're a guest at the hotel, the resourceful head concierge John Neary (a rookie by Carlyle standards with only 15 years in service here) will make sure you get a table at the Cafe or any other difficult-to-get-reservations spot in town. He knows all the tricks of his resourceful trade. In fact, John's the national president of Les Clefs d'Or, the international association of career concierges. Note the emphasis on "career." These men and women are the real pros because only 170 out of an estimated 500 concierges nationally meet the elite organization's stringent requirements. "Our raw material is information, our technology is service, and our product is a satisfied guest," explains John. And satisfy he does, no matter how outlandish the request. And you can bet with a clientele that includes Jack Nicholson, Goldie Hawn, Kurt Russell, Sylvester Stallone, and Johnny Carson, he's had some doozies!

Debonair Executive Manager James Sherwin, who joined the staff several years ago from the Savoy Group in London, does a terrific job. It's always such a pleasure to catch sight of that twinkle in his eye.

While committed to maintaining The Carlyle's unique brand of classic sophistication, James Sherwin has bowed to current trends in order to improve the hotel's services. A fitness center has recently been installed on the third floor. James calls the 1,500-square-foot facility complete with beautifully appointed locker rooms, sauna, steam room, gym, and massage room "a gem"—one that sparkles in its strikingly contemporary design. Predictably, it is small, understatedly elegant, hospitable, well equipped, and efficient—in a word, a microcosm of the hotel it serves.

# *The Doral Tuscany Hotel*

| 120 East 39th Street | (212) 686-1600 |
|---|---|
| New York, NY 10016 | Fax (212) 779-7822 |

Clive Perrygore, Resident Manager of the Doral Tuscany, loves to remind people that his is a hotel at which, "neither the past nor the present is forgotten." He is referring to the fact that the dual themes of then and now are intertwined throughout this delightful property hidden away in a residential neighborhood, yet conveniently midtown. It flaunts all the modern amenities expected of a fine hotel, as well as the old-fashioned personalized service, so often forgotten by other luxury properties.

The Doral Tuscany is located in the historic Murray Hill section of the East Side, nestled between brownstones, courtyards, and mews. It's small (136 rooms and 16 suites), but elegant and caters to an upscale corporate crowd, attracted by its proximity to the centers of New York's business, entertainment, and fashion worlds, which are all within just a few short blocks.

The rooms tend to be large and sunny, with some having push-button drapes, exceptionally good lighting, and walk-in closets. They have refrigerators stocked with beverages. All have marble bathrooms with immense tubs suitable for good, long, relaxing soaks—just the ticket at the end of a pressure-filled day of high-powered negotiations. The bathrooms are also thoughtfully equipped with phones, scales, hairdriers, and magnifying mirrors.

Exercise bikes are just a phone call away. And newspapers arrive at the doorstep every morning as a matter of course.

Our favorite suite is 1501 with its welcoming foyer and large living room. A pleasing combination of overstuffed sofas and good reproductions makes it cozy and comfy, and the large desk makes it practical. It rents for $400 a night.

Regular room rates run from $195 to $220 a night. The rates for one-bedroom suites range from $350 to $700, and there is a two-bedroom suite at $650.

If you're a regular, your preferences in such things as flowers and room service will be solicited and duly noted, ready thereafter for your arrival. Should you become a special favorite of Clive's he might have some of his beloved chocolate popcorn delivered. That and a good book have kept us company through many an evening— delicious, but addictive.

Clive's remark about things past and present comes to mind when you enter the Doral Tuscany's restaurant, Time & Again. Designed to evoke turn-of-the-century New York, it is extremely attractive. The antiques, chandeliers, etched glass, and beveled mirrors truly recapture the style and grace of a bygone era. However, while Time & Again may favor the decor of yesterday, the food is definitely that of today. As conceived and executed by Chef Christophe Barbier, the food has earned the *Zagat* guide's respect as one of the best hotel restaurants in the city.

The sweet potato soup with bacon, scallions, and sour cream followed by pheasant breast stuffed with foie gras, truffles, and vegetables julienne wrapped in a cabbage leaf is representative of the kitchen's flair. Open for breakfast, lunch, and dinner, Time & Again can accurately be described as moderately expensive or just about what you would expect at a good hotel restaurant. Breakfast, including complimentary newspaper, pads with pens, and the use of tape recorders or portable telephones, starts at $7.50. Dinner is at least $90 for two, if you include a reasonably priced bottle of wine from the rather impressive list.

For private parties, Time & Again sets up the hotel's uniquely spectacular two-level Renaissance Room on the second floor. The upper level is encased in glass, allowing the sun, moon, and stars to join the fun. And the view is terrific.

Finally, you should know that the Doral Tuscany owns a fitness center right around the corner at 90 Park Avenue. The facility is available free to hotel guests and opens at 6:00 A.M. for early-rising fitness buffs.

Whether you're more comfortable with the past or with the present, this sophisticated little enclave of civilized living enchants everyone.

# *Essex House*

| Hotel Nikko New York | (212) 247-0300 |
|---|---|
| 160 Central Park South | Fax (212) 315-1839 |

between Sixth and Seventh Avenues
New York, NY 10019

When it opened in 1931 as New York's tallest hotel, much was made of all the Seville Towers' (as it was then known) rooms being equipped with radios. Today, after an $80 million renovation which went so far as to address the hotel's infrastructure, the Essex House's rooms still have radios. But they also boast all the amenities that befit a modern deluxe hotel: VCR players, with a 500-video-tape library; remote-control TVs; safes; mini-bars; individual controls for heat and the newly installed central air conditioning; and dual-line telephones with an emphasis on "phones." Each room has three: one on the desk, one at bedside (each of these has a data port for a PC or fax), and one in the bathroom. Further-

more, the rooms have been enlarged by reducing the hotel's 690
guest quarters to 593. Thoughtfully, while the hotel was gutted to bring it up to
modern standards of luxury, none of its Art Deco splendor was
diminished. The building's ornamented exterior once again
glitters with gold leaf and the black marble colonnaded lobby is
such a paradigm that Warren Beatty and Annette Bening declared
it a perfect location for their remake of the classic *An Affair To Remember*. We wonder, however, if they also noticed the one jarring
note in this bastion of good taste—two truly dreadful portraits of a
Gatsby type and his significant other flank the corridor leading to
elevators. Any distress caused by those unfortunate paintings is
dispelled once you get to the elevators. Your sensibilities have
been soothed by the fascinating black-and-white photographs of a
prewar New York, and the elevators themselves are an unexpected
dose of Deco luster. In fact, the intricately carved brass doors are
the only remnant from the old Essex House. And once inside, you
can't help but be captivated by the old-world touch of a single red
rose perched in a corner-mounted bud vase.

We also doubt that you can resist the charms of Journeys Bar
just to the left of the elevators. It gets our vote as the city's best
wintertime lounge with its blazing fireplace casting a warm glow
over the dark wood paneling, Oriental carpets, decoratively plas-
tered ceiling, and gilt-framed oil paintings.

The paintings, by a collection of high-profile names not pro-
fessionally associated with the art world, serve a similiar purpose
at the hotel's showcase restaurant, Les Celebrites (detailed in the
restaurant section of this book). One of the city's premiere dining
venues, it can be difficult to get into even as an Essex House guest.
Never mind. The decidedly more casual, but only slightly less ambitious Cafe Botanica is a more than acceptable alternative, benefiting as it does from Executive Chef Christian Delouvrier's
kitchen. A large, airy space fronted by huge picture windows facing
Central Park, and well-spaced tables surrounded by enveloping
wicker armchairs make Cafe Botanica an exceedingly comfortable
restaurant. Soothing too, thanks to the gurgling of a fountain in
the plant-strewn *faux* solarium at the rear of the room.

Open for breakfast, lunch, and dinner, it is a special treat at
lunch when the restaurant's surprisingly pleasing California health
bar with Palladian decor is flooded with light streaming through

its windows. The menu is eclectic, including superlative Maryland crabcakes for $12, grilled breast of chicken on toasted brioche sandwich at $14.50, and a $27 grilled porterhouse steak served with mashed potatoes. You can also take advantage of New York's new love affair with value-loaded fixed-price lunches—$19.94 for three courses, such as Louisiana crabmeat and house-smoked salmon on a bed of frisé, sauteed jumbo shrimp, radicchio risotto, and a choice of goodies from the dessert trolley; remember in 1995 the price adjusts accordingly.

Upstairs, Cafe Botanica's handsome casualness gives way to the propriety of English and French antique reproductions. Even the elevator lobbies possess a stately demeanor, the result of specially commissioned hand-screened wall coverings depicting the monuments of Paris. The refined, "more Park Avenue co-op than hotel look" continues, with the recessed doorways dressed up in attractive wood detailing. Furthermore, each room is equipped with a doorbell and a marble threshold.

For suites, we like The Delacorte (401), which can be either a one-bedroomer for $850, or a two-bedroomer at $1,050 a night. Either way, you get the treetop view over Central Park from the gracious living room with is decorous fireplace. The formality of the Louis XVI-style furniture is softened by the tranquilizing blend of gold, beige, and green. Lovely as it is, we could live in the breathtakingly pretty bedroom, so homey in the inspired mixing and matching of floral and striped wallpapers and fabrics. A black lacquered Chinese armoire lends drama to the bouquet of yellows and greens, while the huge mirrored closets make it possible to hole up for a very long stay indeed. Then there's the magnificent bathroom that's the size of many a New York efficiency apartment. The glass-enclosed shower stall and large tub make it practical; the dark green marble floor and vanity make it regal.

Considerably more modest, but no less charming, are any of the Park Queen rooms like 514. Among the Essex House's smaller rooms (and cheaper at $275) they benefit from park views flattered by a cozy Chippendale-like blue-and-gray-hued decor. Other room prices range from $255 to $345, and suites start at $450 a night.

All have access to the hotel's new spa, exclusively the redwood preserve of hotel guests. The respectably sized gym is outfitted with Cybex equipment and augmented by a number of special treatment rooms, including one designed for European footbaths. The very glamorous locker rooms sport steam and sauna rooms. And if you forgot your workout togs, the energetic staff will happily supply you with the basics.

Once the home-away-from-home of Eleanor Roosevelt, the Essex House in its most recent incarnation is just beginning to develop a following. No doubt its members will be just as colorful as the irrepressible Lily Pons who shared her suite here with a pet jaguar or the legendary recluse who never set foot outside his room during his thirty-year residency. Even his meals, always delivered by room service, were left outside the door. Only when he was sure the waiter had departed, would he open the door wide enough to roll the cart inside.

There are some who maintain he was crazy. We're not so sure.

## The Four Seasons Hotel

57 East 57th Street                      (212)758-5700
between Park and Madison Avenues   Fax (212)758-5711
New York, NY 10022

Common wisdom would dictate that the last thing Manhattan needed was another luxury hotel. The crippling 19.25 percent hotel tax on top of some of the nation's highest room rates in this era of general belt-tightening have been sending occupancies into a tailspin — especially at the top end of the market. These days, bosses are inclined to treat expense accounts with bills from Holiday Inn more benevolently than those with receipts from the Plazas, Pierres, and, yes, The Four Seasons of this world.

So what, then, would possess the well-respected Four Seasons Hotels and Resort, by all accounts one of the most successful, well-run hospitality organizations in the world, to enter into the fray? Granted, they already had a pretty strong toehold in New York as the operators of The Pierre since 1981. Consequently, they had a more-than-fair idea of what they were getting into at the high end of the market. In all fairness, we should also point out that the Four Seasons didn't set out to build the most expensive New York hotel ever built (in current or any other dollars). The total cost is close to $400 million, well over $1 million for each of its 367 rooms. (To put this in perspective, consider the fact that the

Holiday Inn Crowne Plaza Manhattan opened its 770 rooms in 1991 for about $300 million.)

It was the Regent organization that set out to build an I. M. Pei-designed flagship hotel on the most powerful retail street in the world. When the Four Seasons bought the Regent—amid rumors that the cost overruns on the New York property were threatening to bankrupt its parent—the fifty-two-story building was part of the deal.

So it fell to the Four Seasons to finish Mr. Pei's vision of a late 1900's grand hotel. As such, it is nothing short of monumental. Clad in the same honey-colored French limestone that Pei used for the interior of his expansion of the Louvre, it is the city's tallest hotel, and its guest rooms, at an average of 600 square feet, are the largest.

If the lobby is not the largest, it certainly seems the highest, with its thirty-three-foot-high back-lighted onyx ceiling supported by massive limestone columns. Make no mistake; it's big enough to remind you of a train station, with its central elevated rotunda circled by pillars and terraced conversation areas. Pei wanted to create a "sense of theater and arrival." He certainly succeeded, although you may not be exactly sure *where* you've arrived. There's not a hotel trapping in sight: no registration desk, concierge station, bell-captain's-stand, or even an elevator. They're tucked away in all their Danish beech-paneled splendor in the core of the building, up the stairs at the rear of the front lobby.

Beyond is the rest of the lobby, facing 58th Street with a sweeping staircase leading to the 5757 Restaurant and The Bar. While the restaurant is attractively done up in polished cherry floors and bronze chandeliers, it doesn't compete with some other luxury hotel dining rooms (notably those at The Mark, The Carlyle, and the Essex House) for culinary kudos. Nor was it meant to, because the Four Seasons folks made a deliberate decision not to enter the top-toque competition with a signature restaurant. That would have required a lot of time, energy, and money, which they thought were best spent elsewhere. So they put in what is best described as a contemporary American grill that does a perfectly pleasant job of serving breakfast, lunch, and dinner in order to concentrate on making the guest quarters worth every penny of their $295 minimum.

We've mentioned their size, but if you're like us, you haven't the foggiest idea of what six hundred square feet means. Let's put it this way: we know comfortable one-bedroom apartments that size. We were stunned when we walked into room 511. The foyer (distinguished by a handsome inset bar stocked with a complete set of glasses) would have done most houses proud. It empties into a chamber that, with its 10'3" coffered ceilings and huge wood-trimmed windows, dwarfs the king-size bed and the full-size sofa. Serene in caramel tones accented by peaches and creams, it features stunning limited edition artwork circa 1950; modernist custom-designed English sycamore furniture, including an oval partners desk; fax caddy with your own line; compact disc player; two softly upholstered leather chairs; and two two-line phones. (All rooms have these features.)

What really overwhelmed us was the separate dressing room that was *not* a glorified closet. Paneled in the same richly textured English sycamore that is used to such great advantage throughout the hotel, it has a full-length mirrored walk-in closet, a leather-surfaced luggage bench, more built-in drawers than you can possibly use, and a safe. Then there's the bathroom in all its floor-to-wall-to-ceiling marble glory, complete with separate shower stall; a deep tub suitable for long, relaxing soaks; TV; telephone; and— most appreciated of all—a scale.

After stepping on that scale, we were even more grateful for the regularly scheduled aerobics classes in the fitness center. In addition to all the usual workout equipment, it also has saunas, steam rooms, and whirlpools. A take-no-prisoners massage put an end to our plans for a night on the town. However, we appreciated the fact that a simple call to the desk secures a complimentary VCR and the opportunity to take advantage of the hotel's extensive video library.

Just when we thought it couldn't get much better than that, we found out that twenty-three of The Four Seasons' rooms have terraces like the one off room 504, which goes for $390. A wall of sliding glass doors leads to a private balcony, the size of many a hotel room we have known. The view of the city is terrific and, typical of all the rooms, are push-button-controlled window treatments.

Of course there are suites here, fifty-eight to be exact. They range in price from $525 to $3,000 (for the two-bedroom Presidential, which occupies the entire top floor of the hotel). However, when you can have a room with a view (and a terrace!) for considerably less, why bother?

# The Hotel Millenium

| 55 Church Street | (212) 693-2001 |
|---|---|
| New York, NY 10007 | Fax (212) 571-2316 |

Before we get into a discussion of this new addition to the Lower Manhattan skyline, right across the street from the World Trade Center, we want to make one thing very clear — Millenium is not a typo. The name is deliberately misspelled for aesthetic reasons. The two "n's" following the two "l's" just didn't make it for a logo. So owner Peter Kalikow, who knows something about artistic license as the former owner/publisher of the *New York Post*, decided to forsake the *Webster's* spelling in favor of one with a better look.

And look is what the Millenium is all about. It's a stunner — with its shiny black lines, resembling nothing so much as a domino minus spots — as the world's tallest, narrowest hotel. That's not to say that at fifty-eight stories and just short of six hundred feet high the Millenium is the world's tallest hotel. We're talking ratios here. It's the tallest in relation to its fifty-foot depth and 125-foot width. What that means to you is that there is a maximum of only twelve rooms on a floor, each blessed with sweeping river, harbor, and/or city views from oversized windows. There's even a picture-postcard-perfect view from each of the corridors. Windows are strategically placed just where you step out of the elevators, which in and of themselves are very much a part of the Millenium look.

Their stripes of lustrous rosewood and rough pinkish granite, set off by chrome accents, appear to mirror the lofty lobby. In fact, it's the other way around — the elevator cabs were designed first. Both are visually successful, exuding a subtle warmth for all their polished functionality. The same goes for the guest quarters.

Peter Kalikow asked his designers to come up with rooms that would appeal to hard-working executives because the hotel's financial district location dictated that they would be its client base. The result is that each of the Millenium's 561 rooms has a sleekly tranquil quality. Soft hues of taupe, peach, and platinum blend soothingly against the backdrop of contoured custom-made teak and curly maple furnishings. Thoughtful little touches lend a residential air to their almost too-masculine look: extra pillows in the ample closets; a built-in cabinet in which to stow the bedspread; an umbrella; slippers; and a bar setup that includes a full complement of glasses, ice bucket, bottle opener, and corkscrew. Naturally the target audience's business interests are also addressed by two-line fax and computer-ready telephones with speaker and conference capabilities (including one in the marble-trimmed bathroom). Voice mail message service (which can be activated prior to arrival), large work areas, and an expanded concept of room service are other features. Not only does a single call access the full 24-hour menu, but it can order up daily necessities such as newspapers and client gifts. No telling how many transactions have been celebrated with the $60 Deal Maker, which features a book detailing the lively history of Wall Street; a crystal ice bucket; a choice of Absolut vodka, Tanqueray gin, or Johnnie Walker Black Label scotch; and a Tiffany perpetual calendar.

In fact, novel services for the business traveler are a Millenium specialty. The hotel stocks changes of Brooks Brothers clothes, underwear, and toiletries for those whose unexpected overnight or extended stays catch them without the "wearwithal" to appear corporately crisp the next day. These "All-Nighter" items, available twenty-four hours a day, are also sold at prices comparable to retail.

Naturally, in such an executive-friendly hotel, there's a well-appointed business center offering a wide array of services. You can also rent equipment for use in the privacy of your room, including personal computers, fax machines, VCRs, and mobile telephones.

But it's not all business at the Millenium. A fitness center features that rarest of New York hotel amenities: a pool — and a very glamorous one at that. Located on the fifth floor, it's glass-enclosed to take advantage of a beautiful view of historic St. Paul's Chapel. Across the hall, a gym is loaded with all the expected state-of-the-art workout machines. If you prefer your exercise outdoors, a jogging map of lower Manhattan is provided in each of the rooms.

Having worked up a healthy appetite, you have several options: Taliesin and The Grille restaurants, the Connoisseur Bar, or room service. If you take our advice and book a corner Millenium room like 4702 for $325, you'll probably order by phone. Why bother going anywhere, when you can pull back the curtains and get lost in the staggering vista of New York Harbor? And the separate living space affords the luxury of in-suite dining without getting crumbs in your bedroom.

Should you prefer to live or entertain quite literally higher on the hog, try the top-floor Governor's Suite at $2,000 per night. It benefits from a private reception area and exclusive concierge service, but the big news in this two-bedroom aerie is the bathrooms. The master is immense, the Taj Mahal of bathrooms in its marble magnificence, complete with Jacuzzi and a window framing another of the Millenium's hallmark views. Even more intriguing is the half-bath off the living/dining area, which appeals to voyeuristic urges with a telescope at its window.

Fogged in? Turn to the built-in entertainment center that occupies one wall of the living room, or consider puttering in the kitchenette. Less commodious and entertaining accommodations start at $225. On the lower floors, the Millenium Rooms are $305 and the one-bedroom suites go for $395.

For our dining dollars, when claustrophobia *finally* sets in, we head for Taliesin on the third floor. Named after a Welsh god who signified warm hospitality, the showcase restaurant delivers on the attributes of its namesake. Burnished wood and brass accents distinguish the gracious room, which in its Frank Lloyd Wright-inspired decor reminds us of a great ocean liner's dining room. It's impressive without being overwhelming, a description that is equally apt for the food. The diverse menu focuses on fresh local and regional ingredients prepared and presented in a simple yet artful manner by chef Albert De Angelis.

While we've concentrated on the Millenium's appeal to the business traveler, we should tell you that the hotel doesn't discriminate against the leisure-oriented. It offers fascinating programs for those who want to experience the history, culture, shopping, and dining attractions of lower Manhattan.

The Millenium is rapidly fulfilling its promise of becoming the preeminent hotel of the downtown community, a goal set by its managing director Susan Ricci. Herein the Millenium boasts an amenity even rarer than the pool — a woman at the helm!

# Hotel Westbury

| | |
|---|---|
| 69th Street at Madison Avenue | (212) 535-2000 |
| New York, NY 10021 | Fax (212) 535-5058 |

If you have been wondering where celebrities, who are as skittish about the spotlight as Yves St. Laurent, hole up, wonder no longer. As often as not, it is at the Hotel Westbury, a small hostelry nestled in the midst of one of Manhattan's tonier neighborhoods, which offers a cocoonlike sense of privacy to its guests.

The Westbury's cosseting tranquility is apparent the moment you step into the small lobby. No hustle and bustle here. Rather, it's a quiet, dignified place for conducting business with the staff, schooled in what General Manager Stefan Simkovics calls, "active hospitality. We specialize in fulfilling guests' wishes before they have to ask." It's a neat trick and to a great extent his multilingual crew delivers on anticipating guests' requests. But, if something pops into your mind that they haven't thought of, talk to Anthony Pike, the Westbury's resourceful concierge. In fact, as a matter of course it's a good idea to check in with Anthony at his lobby station because he always knows what's going on in town and how to organize your participation in it.

Otherwise, this lobby is meant for passing through, which is not to say that it's not impressive. Quite the contrary. We liken it to the two-story-high great hall of a modestly sized castle, aglow in polished travertine and swathed in 18th-century Flemish tapestries. Massive columns support the domed ceiling and exquisite, hand-woven rugs crafted exclusively for the Westbury cover the floors.

Just as imposing is the wood-paneled elevator. It's large enough to move into, but why bother when the Westbury's rooms and suites await? Walking into any of them is more like entering one of the neighborhood's historic brownstones than a hotel room. Here you actually turn a doorknob, a vintage brass one at that, neatly inscribed with the hotel's address: 15E69. They are holdovers from the Westbury's 1920s roots as a residential hotel built by the family of a polo player. Hence the name, in honor of Westbury, Long Island's polo grounds.

The residential ambience grows as you cross the threshold because there's no cookie-cutter commercial decor here. Each of the Westbury's 235 rooms retains its individuality in shape and design. No two are alike; each has its distinctive cachet. Yet the theme is that of an English country manor as interpreted by wallcoverings and fabrics by Ralph Lauren or Laura Ashley.

English chintz, comfy sofas, and a bright, cheery look make Suite 715 a favorite choice at $850 a night. No doubt its extra half bath and practical kitchenette are also part of its appeal, but we think the high four-poster bed accounts for most of its popularity.

Despite the threat from the outside world posed by the two telephone lines that service each room, there is a charming serenity here. Maybe it's the traditional English prints and drawings that decorate every room or the coziness of the sitting areas defined by Oriental rugs. Then again, perhaps it's due to the vases of cut flowers that perfume the rooms. Whatever, it costs $245 to $295 a night for standard and deluxe rooms. Junior suites are available at $325, and one bedrooms start at $400. For $1,500 a night, you can get an entire one-bedroom apartment replete with fireplace (albeit cosmetic); formal dining room; kitchen; two bathrooms (one with Jacuzzi); and the ultimate in hotel gadgets, a fax/phone. Two-bedroom suites go for $850 to $1,500 for one with a sauna.

Admittedly even we, who have always considered the Westbury close to perfection, had noticed that it had begun to take on the patina of a faded heirloom. So did the ownership, Forte, which operates a whole crown of similarly jewel-like properties throughout the world. They spent three years and untold millions polishing and even adding to the Westbury's many facets. As the result of this "stately facelift," the Westbury now sports a health club. Like the lobby, it's small but impressive, equipped with Cybex exercise machines, treadmills, StairMasters, free weights, and locker rooms.

Fortunately, Forte demurred when it came to tampering with that outpost of civilized dining in the often too trendy Upper East Side, The Polo. Long a favorite spot for breakfast, lunch, and dinner for everyone from visiting Russian dignitaries to Natalie Cole, the Westbury's restaurant has always been just as chic and smart as it can be. Of course, the life-size portrait of Prince Charles in full polo regalia now borders on the politically incorrect, but the rest of the cushy men's club decor holds up well—prints of thoroughbreds and their jockeys, leather chairs, deep red carpeting, dark paisley-printed banquettes, mahogany paneling, and brass sconces.

What the folks at Forte did do with The Polo is make it a contender in the hotel dining sweepstakes by installing Kerry Hefferman in the kitchen. A veteran of the wildly popular One Fifth Avenue, Kerry has developed his own following further uptown. Ted Danson enjoys his multicultural cooking, and Al Pacino dines at The Polo so often that he's gotten very chummy with manager Michel Pimienta. He's gotten so chummy that Michel has a new hobby—appearing in his buddy's movies. He played a waiter, which he admits wasn't much of a stretch, in *The Scent of a Woman* and has been recruited for Al's next picture.

The possibility of being "discovered" aside, the Westbury's location in the heart of upper Madison's best stores and just south of "Museum Mile" makes The Polo an ideal respite from shopping or sightseeing. You can have a fast and light lunch with velvety potato and leek soup complemented by a salad of mixed field greens in a red wine vinaigrette, both $8, or with the $15 grilled club sandwich dressed up with artichoke crisps and a confiture of shallots. There's also a vegetable platter representing the market's freshest legumes at $16. For a more leisurely repast, you can't go wrong with the strudel-wrapped shrimp served on a bed of shaved fennel and mesclun greens for $12 followed by the $22 sirloin steak garnished with a tasty fricassee of wild mushrooms and Roquefort-stuffed ravioli.

After one such meal, we enviously observed the departure of a very famous director who keeps a suite at the Westbury. We suspected he was going upstairs to take a nap—would that we could have done the same.

## The Lowell

28 East 63rd Street          (212) 838-1400
New York, NY 10021       Fax (212) 319-4230

The Lowell has been characterized as the sort of place that would "scream class, if class did that sort of thing." So what is Madonna doing hanging out here, especially given the fact she owns not one, but two, apartments just across town on Central Park West? It seems that before becoming a real estate mogul, she, like many other shining stars—David Bowie, Jeremy Irons, Debra Winger, and Danny DeVito are examples—appreciated the pampered privacy of this most discreet of hostelries. So, with her in mind, General Manager Martin A. Hale (who knows about coddling royalty of both the Hollywood and constitutional variety, thanks to his years at Claridge's) spent $150,000 to install a mirrored state-of-the-art gym in one bedroom of a two-bedroom suite.

Madonna was the Gym Suite's first guest and, typical of most things the Material Girl touches, it turned to gold. And why not? For $680 a night, where else can you get an elegantly appointed one-gbedroom flat with fireplace, kitchen, terrace, *and* gym equipped with StairMaster, treadmill, exercise bench, stationary bicycle, ballet bar, and free weights, not to mention CD player, stereo cassette deck, and remote control television? It has become so popular, Martin considered installing another one. But then he decided to build a complete fitness center on the second floor to suit other clients' needs. And suit them it does daily from 6:30 A.M. to 10:00 P.M.

Other than such high-tech touches, including fax and computer-ready two-line phones and VCRs in every room, former occupants of this gracious building (circa 1928), such as Scott and Zelda Fitzgerald, Dorothy Parker, and Noël Coward would feel right at home today. The hotel, one of the smallest in New York with only 61 rooms and suites, maintains a residential air. And the boutique-sized lobby, where there is never any check-in or check-out line, echoes The Lowell's original Art Deco splendor, with a rare console signed by Edgar Brandt and the ornate doors connecting it to the Post House restaurant next door.

The Fitzgeralds, among others, would be less familiar with the Empire style that now dominates the boutique-sized room. But we doubt they would object. Who can quibble with pale gray silk walls, *faux* marble wainscoting accented by gold-plated bronze moldings and a carpet inspired by one made for Empress Josephine's bedroom?

Taking a cue from that carpet's origins, the staff makes you feel like royalty. A liveried doorman ushers you into the hotel with pomp and circumstance. The charming reception staff, outfitted in formal morning attire, greets you by name and escorts you to your quarters. You will quickly come to think of it as your very own pied-à-terre as does our pal British couturier Victor Edelstein.

While each room and suite is unique, you can count on comfortable sophistication courtesy of a selective blend of period French and Oriental pieces, fine artworks, and rich fabrics in muted tones.

Thirty-three of the forty-eight suites have wood-burning fireplaces, and ten of those glory in private terraces with stunning cityscape views. All have Italian marble baths, down comforters, sound-proof double-casement windows that you can actually open, and kitchens that lend new meaning to "fully equipped." Truly complete and meant to be used, they feature refrigerators stocked with food fit for entertaining; dishwashers; ovens; and, most impressively, high-quality cooking equipment; china; crystal; and silverware.

Our buddy Victor is especially fond of The Lowell's suites, the hotel's two largest one-bedroom numbers. They are stacked one on top of the other on the 12th and 13th floors; he has a slight preference for 12B at $680 because of its cunning little balcony. We like it because of the entertaining possibilities in the formal dining area; Victor likes it because sans dining table and chairs it becomes an ideal showcase for breathtaking haute couture creations.

For us though, we adore the Fleur Cowles Garden Suite. Indeed it is a very special one-bedroom suite on the 14th floor. You'll be delighted with the living room and its antique bird cage, along with a private library filled with books on garden topics as well as Fleur Cowles's latest book *The life and Times of a Rose*. The bedroom is glorious with its hand-painted, stenciled ceiling, lace pillows, and vanity table. This glorious Garden Suite was inspired by the two terraces, one a sitting area with a fountain; the other, a cozy dining area. Each terrace has manicured flower beds. What a special way to live in New York for a day, a week, or a season at a time.

For such a small hotel, the rate schedule is convoluted. There are singles and doubles from $280 to $340 a night. A junior suite is $440, while full-blown one-bedroomers go for $540. Then there are the Lowells, as well as the Garden Suite sporting two terraces. One is decked out as an English garden complete with fountain at $680. And you can get a two-bedroom suite for $840. The marvelous three-bedroom penthouse rents for $1,500 a night.

Until recently, the Post House, one of New York's most celebrated chop houses, served as a convenient appendage next door, but it was the smart Pembroke Room on the second floor that was the hotel's culinary gem. The Lowell's purchase of the Post House changed all that, relegating the Pembroke Room to what always best categorized its decor: a traditional English tea salon. Tucked away on the second floor, this exquisite little room of needlepoint carpets, yellow chintzes, crystal wall sconces, and chairs upholstered in a "nice English stripe" only seats thirty-two for breakfast and tea. But tea's only served as the season warrants—in other words don't look for it in August—and at private parties, of course, as are cocktails and hors d'oeuvres.

That leaves the Post House as the real culinary story here, one that began in September 1980 when it opened as an independent operation, part of Alan Stillman's New York Restaurant Company empire (Cite, Manhattan Ocean Club, Park Avenue Cafe, and Smith & Wollensky). Stillman and company still run the Post House; it remains what *The New York Times* described as a "paragon of a New York steakhouse." As such, it's better looking than most of its brethren because the tan and burnt sienna tiles topping the polished wooden wainscoting are particularly attractive. And the strategically placed massive floral arrangements are a dramatic, unexpected touch in a place heavily populated by conservative looking "suits" comfortably ensconced in leather arm chairs and chowing down on gargantuan portions of steak and seafood.

True to New York steakhouse tradition, the Post House is pricey; for example, classics like the prime rib and sirloin steak are $29.75 at dinner, $26.50 at lunch. Other than the prices, there's no difference in the menu. So if you're counting pennies, go for lunch and split an appetizer *or* an à la carte vegetable. You won't go away hungry, and you might feel better about taking advantage of the Post House's excellent cellar, winner of *The Wine Spectator*'s Best Award for Excellence. Extensive and hardly budget conscious, it's drawing some of the city's most sophisticated wine drinkers, many of whom are especially intrigued by The California Cache—a group of California wines from small vineyards that are sold exclusively in New York at the Post House.

The restaurant is a most agreeable all-American counterpoint to the very European hotel, but don't expect any Madonna sightings, even if she stops by to visit "her" suite. She's a vegetarian.

# The Mark

Madison Avenue at 77th Street       (212) 744-4300
New York, NY 10021       Fax (212) 744-2749

The first time we romped through The Mark, a newcomer invading the Upper East Side territory long dominated by The Carlyle and The Stanhope, we predicted it would give them a run for their money and we were right. Five years after a much heralded $35 million renovation of the old Madison Hotel, The Mark is firmly ensconced as one of New Yorkers' favorite small hotels.

The entrance, on a lovely tree-lined street between Madison and Fifth, is distinguished by the building's landmark tower and four brass flagpoles, all of which are lit at night to emit a welcoming beacon. A striking retro entry, accented with brass and elegant black vitroglass, hangs over the doorway, opening onto the neoclassical lobby. The decor was inspired by the rich style favored by the 18th-century English architect Sir John Soane, comprising Italian marble and 18th-century Piranesi prints and floral motifs, all of which lend a delicate refinement to the English-Italian elegance.

Beyond the marble entrance and reception area with its cozy and wildly popular Mark's Bar (we don't know of another watering hole where reservations are suggested) is the three-tiered Mark's Restaurant. Reminiscent of London's chic dining clubs, Mark's is graced with gentle hues of burgundy, rose, and teal enhanced by brass-topped, wrought-iron balustrades, marble columns, ebony and gold-leafed moldings. The look is unabashedly romantic and the food lives up to the setting. Executive Chef Philippe Boulot, an alumnus of such Parisian landmarks as Jamin and Maxim's, is a rising culinary star. His self-described "cuisine Bourgeoise—with an international perspective" reflects Philippe's Normandy roots and his classical training. Unpretentious, yet refined and light-hearted, just like their creator, signature dishes include kitchen-smoked salmon with crisp potato layers, barbequed striped bass with creamed savoy cabbage, and roasted breast of pheasant complemented by a celery root puree. All serve as perfect foils to a delightful dessert finale, courtesy of Pastry Chef Susan Boulot — Philippe's wife.

Like her husband, whom she met when they both worked at L'Archestrate in Paris, Susan doesn't believe in ostentatious food. She notes there's a temptation among pastry chefs to overdo with elaborate presentations. "I keep my desserts fairly uncomplicated, and I concentrate on the flavor and freshness." Her efforts are uniformly delicious.

Susan's philosophy of simple things presenting the greatest satisfaction in practicing one's profession is amplified by Head

Concierge Giorgio Finocchario. "Too many people think the secret of being a good concierge is the ability to accomplish the impossible for a guest. But that is not really true.... The secret of a good concierge is to anticipate and provide for a guest's small needs; to ensure the simple requests a guest makes are handled with speed, discretion, and good taste." Which is not to say that Giorgio doesn't relish the challenge of performing miracles. His war stories rank with the best of those offered by his fellow members of Les Clefs d'Or, the worldwide organization of concierges. He was once called upon to organize for the transport of perishable medicine from the Mayo Clinic to South America where it was needed for a delicate operation. Then there was the time when a couple, frequenters of The Mark, were stranded in Europe, unable to escort their child home from summer camp. Alerted to the situation, Giorgio came up with the perfect solution. He arranged for the child to stay with him and his family until the parents could return.

No wonder General Manager Raymond Bickson stole Giorgio away from The Pierre. It's been his goal since the hotel opened to achieve a level of personalized service that allows guests to feel genuinely at home. "I want to ensure that The Mark establishes a reputation as the kind of hotel one keeps returning to." That The Mark has become a haunt of a crowd normally partial to splashier digs, like the Hollywood contingent led by Michael Eisner, Harrison Ford, and Bette Midler, along with Alexander Haig and General Norman Schwarzkopf, is testimony to the fulfillment of Raymond's ambitions for the hotel.

As good as the food and the service are here, though, we suspect the real draw, particularly for the show biz set, is the bathrooms. They're large and luxurious; gorgeous in gleaming black and white tile or earth-tone marble; practical in separate glass-enclosed showers and tubs, heated towel racks, scales, hairdriers, thick terry robes, and an abundance of toiletries from Molton Brown in London. Running a close second to the appeal of the bathrooms is that of the sleek black kitchens attached to most of The Mark's rooms, complete with microwaves, refrigerators, dishwashers, and cooking equipment. Granted, they seldom get more of a workout than producing a cup of coffee, but the kitchens are a nice homey touch, as are the bowls of potpourri that scent every room.

And speaking of home, we've been tempted to move into the Presidential Suite, which is nothing short of spectacular, with its marble circular foyer dominated by graceful columns. The corner living room overlooking both Madison Avenue and East 77th Street is sumptuously decorated in beige and blue. It boasts a wet bar, antique prints, and access to a terrific terrace. The library is perfect for curling up with a good book (preferably this one), while the master bedroom and bath are larger than many a Manhattan studio apartment. Three televisions, in the living room, bedroom, and den, keep you in touch with the outside world. A VCR and CD player, stocked by the hotel's extensive video and CD library, assure endless entertainment. Call it home for $2,200 a night.

If you arrive in the winter and think you can forego the terrace, the layouts of the Tower Suites 1510 and 1610 are otherwise identical to that of the Presidential. With one bedroom and one and a half baths (the library has a powder room), they rent for $1,900. A second bedroom can be added for $325.

Number 1405 is called the Terrace Suite. Its large living room in shades of doe and forest green flows out to a glorious terrace outfitted with pretty patio furniture and flower boxes. The bedroom on the other side of the graceful double set of French doors features a king-size bed and window seats. The enormous bathroom is divided into three sections: one for the double-sinked vanity, one for the tub, and one for the shower. Tough to beat even at $1,600 a night.

Actually, any of The Mark's 180 accommodations are on the special side. A warm, residential feeling prevails throughout. The oversized "regular" rooms, ranging from $275 to $525 a night, feature a table and chairs placed by the window for in-room dining, as well as a writing desk and a comfy, richly upholstered sofa.

No doubt about it, The Mark has hit its mark at the high end of New York's hotel hierarchy.

# *Mayfair Hotel Baglioni*

610 Park Avenue                                    (212) 288-0800
at 65th Street                               Fax (212) 737-0538
New York, NY 10021

A number of New York's current crop of deluxe hotels can lay claim to long histories, but only the Mayfair Hotel Baglioni's Dario ◄ Mariotti contends his is a "hotel with soul." As general manager and resident since 1978, he should know. In fact, we maintain he is the very embodiment of that soul. As proof, we offer the fact that he engineered a remarkable feat: keeping his job in the face of new ownership.

Of course, any buyer would have been foolish to turn Dario loose. To many, he and his wife, Gabriella, *are* the Mayfair. Certainly, they have imbued it with their effervescent personalities and exquisite taste. Who else would have thought of operating a pillow bank? Just exactly what the name suggests, it is a repository for all manner of pillows filled with down, foam, or water, ranging from "snore stopper" to "reading wedge." Each is described and pictured in a brochure placed in every room. To secure the pillow of your dreams, just call housekeeping and order it by name or number.

Such novel albeit endearing touches notwithstanding, Dario has imbued the Mayfair Hotel Baglioni with the elegantly intimate aura of a posh European hotel—the sort of place that used to be the seat of a noble family before inheritance taxes. There is something about the exquisite lobby that is reminiscent of an Italian palazzo. Perhaps it's the lush tones of sienna, ochre, and terra cotta that manage to harmonize what might otherwise be considered a compilation of fifty years worth of decorating trends, including Tudor beamed ceilings and a baronial fireplace alongside Moorish arches. It's very grand, yet warm and inviting. It begs to be sat in and, in fact, is one of the few hotel lobbies truly conducive to meeting and greeting.

Like any palazzo worth its salt, the Mayfair plays host to several varieties of royalty. There's the regular garden variety like the King of Spain. Then there's the Hollywood strain as embodied by Sophia Loren and Barbra Streisand. The Mayfair's special brand of luxury is also appealing to representatives of fashion royalty, Gianni Versace and members of the Missoni family, although rumor has it there have been some defections to the St. Regis among the designing contingent.

If we know Dario, he'll get them back, even if it means installing an atelier for them. After all, he created the only golf course on Park Avenue. There's a full-fledged putting green fashioned after those of Casa de Campo's world-famous courses in the hotel's fitness center. Located on the 12th floor, the center has a terrific view, so you can practice sinking those long putts while getting a taste of the great outdoors. Need more evidence of Dario's dash?

Take the gray umbrella tucked away in every one of the 201 rooms and suites. Feel free to take it — Dario expects it — and delights in telling tales of Mayfair regulars saluting each other with their umbrellas on rainy streets all over the world.

The level of service that Dario affords his guests is another element of the palacelike quality of the hotel. It's as if you have been assigned your own personal staff during your stay, which is standard operating procedure in any palace. You have *your* affable doormen capable of cab-hailing miracles in even the foulest weather. Likewise, the gloved elevator attendants seem exclusively at your service. Surely that puller of strings par excellence, Concierge Tito Fornari, must be part of your personal entourage. And then there's Mel, for whom everyone clamors. Mel oversees the hotel's laundry. He has such a way with shirts that many guests make it a regular practice to send them to the Mayfair for Mel's tender loving care from wherever they happen to be, even from their homes!

With so much to offer, it's little wonder the hotel is often full. Particularly in September, October, April, and May, you should be sure to book well in advance.

When you call, you might want to reserve Suite 1015, if you're in the market for one bedroom at $410 per night. Tones of green abound. The living room has a plush yet homey feel to it, with its mirrored bar all ready for entertaining. Another favorite in the one-bedroom category is 206, complete with wood-burning fireplace and dining area for $800 a night.

If you prefer a two-bedroom suite, try 803, which runs $1,700 a night. It, too, has a fireplace, not to mention Jacuzzi, enormous closets (a Mayfair trademark), and delightful views of Park Avenue. Less spectacular, but equally elegant single and double rooms can be had from $275 to $295.

No discussion of the Mayfair Hotel Baglioni would be complete without mention of the legendary Le Cirque, which serves as the hotel's restaurant, but that is all we're going to do here. Still the city's most chic eatery after all these years, the house that Sirio Marcionni built rates a separate account in our restaurant overview.

We would be equally remiss if we failed to note the hotel's afternoon tea, a New York institution. Admittedly, almost every luxury hotel in the city now engages in the custom. But, when

Dario started it as one of the European traditions he brought to the Mayfair, afternoon tea was considered novel. It remains the best one in town, attracting a glamorous crowd of natives. They happily nibble away at the delicate finger sandwiches and sinful pastries, while comparing notes on the day's news as reported by society chroniclers Liz Smith, Billy Norwich, Richard Johnson, Cindy Adams, Jeanette Walls, and Deborah Mitchell. Dario relishes their presence. He knows a little gossip is good for the soul and particularly good for his cherished Mayfair Hotel Baglioni.

## The New York Palace

| | |
|---|---|
| 455 Madison Avenue | (212) 888-7000 |
| between 50th and 51st Streets | (800) 697-2522 |
| New York, NY 10022 | Fax (212) 888-7000 |

The queen is gone! Long live The Palace! Those exclamations sum up sophisticated New Yorkers' feelings about the present invisibility of Mrs. L. Helmsley and the delightful ongoing presence of what is now called the New York Palace. Long a favorite of the well-traveled set, it has not lost a step by putting the managerial reins in the hands of efficient Alfred Heim.

Alfred is the benevolent regent for the Pittsburgh-based Interstate Hotels Corporation, the firm that was brought in to manage the hotel. Thanks to Alfred's regime, there's a new vitality in what has always been one of New York's prettiest properties (thanks to mansions designed by Stanford White that form the nucleus of its public rooms). Indeed, the palace portion of the name does not refer to its palatial (some 1,180 rooms) size but to the origins of those mansions. Built in 1882, the former Villard Houses were inspired by the grandeur of Rome's Palazzo della Cancelleria. This cluster of townhouses, once the home of the Archdiocese of New York, were later acquired by Harry Helmsley. He restored many of the rooms to their original splendor and added a dark bronze fifty-one-story tower to create the Helmsley Palace in 1979.

Today, you can marvel at the ornate gold-leafed carved wall panels, the vaulted two-story-high gilt ceiling, the stained-glass windows, and the John La Farge murals of the aptly named Gold Room, where princes of the church once strolled. True to its roots as a music room, a harpist or string quartet is usually on duty in this exquisite sanctuary, now dedicated to breakfast and afternoon tea. Actually the $24 tea, served daily from 2:00 to 5:00 P.M., is one of the city's great pleasures (not to mention bargains, if you consider the plentiful selection of sandwiches and pastries at lunch or dinner) — it's just so tranquilly civilized. And thanks to Alfred, if you want a cup of tea sans accoutrements, you can have it. Formerly, you had a choice of the full tea, or nothing.

A former dining room offers similarly serene surroundings for cocktails. The Hunt Room and Bar, with its carved walnut paneling and mammoth dark red marble fireplace, has a comforting clubby atmosphere. The unusual sliding doors embellished with tiny nailheads add to the reassuring masculinity of the room — you want to take the room home with you. But it's more fun to relax here and partake of what may be the most munificent spread of complimentary hors d'oeuvres in the city.

Beyond the Madison Room, overlooking its namesake avenue, is another beautifully restored chamber. Designed as a triple drawing room, it is preserved as a sophisticated setting for socializing. The walls bear the original framed panels depicting royalty at play, painted by French artist P. V. Galland.

The historic part of the Palace also boasts a reconditioned library as conference room, the Le Trianon restaurant (a belle epoque gem right down to the nineteenth-century china and silver service) and the city's only oval-shaped ballroom. All the sleeping quarters are found in the adjoining tower despite the fact that only 200 are specifically designated as tower rooms or suites. Located on the higher floors, they tend to be larger than the non-Tower rooms, and benefit from "private" (read faster) registration desk and elevators.

Naturally, you pay a bit more for such privileges, but it's worth it. Take Suite 4109, with its truly spectacular view across Rockefeller Center all the way to the Hudson River. You can gaze to your heart's content from almost anywhere in this beauty. There's even a window in the full-scale kitchen, a feature coveted by most New Yorkers. Done in the same dusty-rose-colored tones as the glorious sunsets it so often witnesses, this suite rents for $695 for one bedroom, $950 for two.

Single rooms in the main part of the hotel run $225 and doubles are $250, while the rates in the Tower are $285 for singles and $310 for doubles. But rest assured the Palace's service in all rooms under Alfred Heim's direction is superb.

But if you really want to live, quite literally, high on the hog, reserve one of the triplexes that occupy significant portions of the hotel's top three stories. Nestled in the tower's four corners, they were the first triplex apartments in New York to be offered for transient occupancy. As such, they are immense and booked 3 to 4 weeks in advance, even at $3,000 a night. Michael Jackson always stays in one, although his chimp (presumably chaperoned) usually stays across town.

The triplexes are the closest we've seen to the Hollywood take on sumptuous suites, the kind in which Fred Astaire and/or Ginger Rogers were always dancing around in elegant dressing gowns. They are nothing short of drop-dead glamorous. In 5301, the marble foyer opens into a two-story glass-walled living room, suitable for entertaining seventy-five of your closer friends. The formal dining room seats twelve with room to spare, and the spacious kitchen is equipped to deal with virtually any food-related activity.

A curved staircase, perfect for very noticeable entrances, sweeps up to the two bedrooms on the mezzanine level overlooking the living room scene (there is a third bedroom on the first floor). For more furtive comings and goings, there is a lilliputian elevator.

The third floor is a solarium made special by a wood-burning fireplace, full bar, powder room, and private rooftop terrace. In fact, standing on that terrace with all Manhattan spread out below, beckoning with the exhilarating combination of sights and sound that is the city's siren song, you can't help but feel regal.

## The Peninsula

| | |
|---|---|
| 700 Fifth Avenue | (212) 247-2200 |
| New York, NY 10019 | (800) 262-9467 |
| | Fax (212) 903-3949 |

For seven years, the once proud Gotham Hotel (a beaux arts landmark built in 1902) stood forlornly boarded-up despite its prime location at the corner of 55th and Fifth. Then in 1988, after extensive renovation, it reopened ever so briefly and with a spectacular lack of success as Maxim's de Paris. Just as people began to wonder if the site was jinxed, the fabled Peninsula Group stepped in to dispel that notion.

With The Peninsula New York, their first foray into the American market, the company that gifted the world with The Peninsula Hong Kong has a winner. The hotel's 250 rooms and suites and three restaurants and bars are predictably posh in their art nouveau finery, but it's the two *s*'s — service and spa — that really make The Peninsula stand out.

Of course, you expect the first. The Peninsula Hong Kong practically invented the word "service," and then refined it to its highest art form for over 60 years. Mindful of that, the New York hotel recruited an enthusiastic staff thoroughly schooled in the traditions of the Hong Kong property. In fact, a number have been sent to that international flagship to to be trained in The Peninsula style of gracious attention to detail. They learned how to anticipate guest needs and how to enjoy providing attentive assistance.

Consequently, they routinely pack and unpack guests' clothes, as well as park their cars and do their laundry seven days a week. Room service is offered twenty-four hours a day, with only a fifteen-minute wait for breakfast if you order in the morning. They'll even serve breakfast on a tray, so you won't have to stumble into a large bulky cart. Most impressively, fresh buckets of ice are placed in each room twice a day, so refreshments from the mini-bar can actually be acceptable substitutes for a drink in any of the hotel's bars.

As for the second *s*, the tri-level 35,000-square-foot spa, well, there's just nothing else like it in the city. The largest, most luxurious fitness center of any New York hotel, its rooftop, glass-enclosed site affords fabulous views along with a swimming pool, whirlpool, sauna and massage rooms, a gym, an aerobics studio, and facilities for complete body and skin treatment.

Naturally, such a complex is not supported by hotel guests alone. The Peninsula Spa is available to guests on a complimentary basis but relies on memberships for survival. As the only facility in Manhattan truly worthy of the name spa, it is very popular. But since membership has been limited to 700 lucky souls it is not plagued with the overcrowding that affects the quality of fitness life in other New York, less luxe, clubs.

As for the rooms we so cavalierly dismissed as being predictably posh, they are. They're generously proportioned and munificent in their art nouveau splendor, right down to the hardwood headboards designed to replicate an original French design. The oversized marble bathrooms with six-foot tubs and padded silk hangers are also noteworthy. And the rooms are wired. It seems

General Manager Niklaus Leuenberger brings not only his decade-long experience with the Peninsula Group to the premises, but also his electronic expertise. He's an electronics nut and is putting his avocation to good use at the hotel. Thanks to Niklaus, there are now fax machines and electronic safes in every room, along with what he proudly describes as a "bedside comfort management system." That's hotel talk for a bedside console housing a multifunctional digital clock, an AM/FM radio, a two-line telephone, and a panel from which you can control the room's lighting, temperature, and television. It's even guest-friendly, using touch-sensitive screens capable of displaying easy-to-follow directions in English, French, German, Italian, Japanese, and Spanish.

Not content to leave well enough alone with this innovation, Niklaus has also installed stereo systems in all of the hotel's 35 suites, including our favorite, 1601. Its more than 1,000 square feet overlooking Fifth Avenue landmarks to the north like Tiffany, Trump Tower, and Central Park go for $950 a night. The living room is done in soothing tones of rose and celadon and benefits from a large powder room and a wet bar. There's a small dining area that doubles as a respectable work space. The bedroom is spacious enough, and the bathroom is large with one of those big tubs you can stretch out in when you activate the Jacuzzi, and there's a separate shower stall.

Room 1805 is another winner, a junior suite with an extra-large foyer and cozy sitting area from which you get a spectacular view of Fifth Avenue's southern route, from St. Patrick's all the way downtown, which makes it great for parade watching. There's even a window in the bathroom, so you won't miss a step, all for $495. Other rooms, described as superior to deluxe, range from $295 to $395 a night. Executive suites start at $595 and one bedrooms, at $950. Two bedrooms go for $1,250, and the price of the 2,500 square feet of luxurious space that is the Presidential Suite costs $3,000.

Granted it's tough to venture out of any of these sumptuous sanctuaries, but do rouse yourself to check out the stately Gotham Lounge. You get a bird's-eye view of the gracious postage-stamp-sized lobby, distinguished by an imposing double staircase sporting a magnificent Art Nouveau armoire by J. Cherbonnier that was featured at the 1904 Exposition des Beaux Arts in Paris. You also get a gander at a group of remarkably good-looking and well-dressed people who find this lovely, rather regal room ideal for conversational cocktail rendezvous. Evocative of another more formal era, it serves as a perfect contrast to the breezier Pen-Top Bar and Terrace.

We mean that in the literal sense as well—during the warmer months you can imbibe on one of the city's few rooftop terraces open to the public. It's a thoroughly engaging experience, made all the more so by a menu of light snacks. On a summer afternoon, get there by 5:15 P.M. to snare a table.

The Adrienne Restaurant and Le Bistro Adrienne offer a similar contrast. While both evoke a sense of joie de vivre with their belle epoque decor, the former is for really memorable dining; the latter, for more unceremonious meals. In either case, Chef Nicholas Rabalais's kitchen is highly rated.

So in retrospect it's the two s's, the t and the r that set The Peninsula apart—service, spa, terrace, and restaurant.

# The Pierre

| Fifth Avenue at 61st Street | (212) 838-8000 |
| New York, NY 10021 | Fax (212) 940-8109 |

In real estate, they say "location, location, location" is everything. In the hospitality business, it's "service, service, service." The Pierre offers the best of both worlds: an unbeatable site at the corner of 61st and Fifth within walking distance of New York's finest museums, restaurants, galleries, and shops. And the service is impeccable, thanks to the careful management of Four Seasons Ltd., which has operated it since 1981. No wonder The Pierre acts as pièd-a-terre to many a globe-trotter, including the indefatigable Lady Fairfax, who has created one of the city's most spectacular apartments out of what once was a ballroom. Indeed most of The Pierre is devoted to private residences. Only 203 rooms and suites are available for transients.

It was Charles Pierre's goal to create a hotel "with the atmosphere of a private club or residence." Five years in the making (with a little help from some notable friends like E. F. Hutton and Walter P. Chrysler), his dream was realized with the October 1, 1930, opening of The Pierre. The New York Times described the hotel as "exclusive" and "characterized by its simplicity and refinement" designed to appeal to an elite clientele.

Sixty-odd years later, "elite" remains the best way to describe the clientele, be they guests or locals, who use The Pierre's extraordinary catering facilities for some of the city's most talked-about parties. The ballroom is a gleaming jewel; the food, perfection. The landmark ballroom aside, The Pierre had begun to look a little dated, and we'd always hated the uninviting, institutional look of the lobby cum corridor serving the Fifth Avenue entrance. It, like much of the rest of the hotel, has recently enjoyed a facelift, overseen by Managing Director Herbert Pliessnig, that will ensure it keeps winning awards like being named by *Institutional Investor* as one of "The World's 50 Best Hotels."

Both the Fifth Avenue faux lobby and the real McCoy off 61st have benefited tremendously. The former has been warmed up by trompe l'oeil tapestries, while the latter's once monochromatic decor has been glitzed up with splashes of vibrant blues and reds. Yet while the gilt gleams golder, it continues to reflect that *Times*'s description of simplicity and refinement. It doesn't bowl you over with noveau luxury. Rather it is a hospitable, comfortable place somewhat reminiscent of living rooms we have known, right down to the coffee table-centered furniture arrangements, book-lined secretaries, and respectable oil paintings. What a delightful place to camp out while doing a little people-watching.

There's plenty to watch. The Pierre is a favorite with Hollywood's old guard *A* list: Jimmy Stewart, Kirk Douglas, and Charles Bronson. The hotel also attracts an international clientele. Indeed, Herbert, who presides over The Pierre with such thoughtful, meticulous care, maintains that only 40 percent of his guests are American. The remainder include the likes of Princess Michael of Kent.

No doubt she appreciates the new élan of another beneficiary of the hotel's refurbishment: the elevators. Not so long ago, the only thing that saved them from being unbearably pedestrian was their attendants. They maintain that distinction, but they have been lined with gilt-trimmed wood panels, and little leather-tufted benches have also been installed.

And it's likely that her royal highness is just as appreciative that Herbert did not tamper with The Rotunda, already one of the prettiest public rooms in New York. Appropriately round, this enchanting room envelops you in whimsy — floor-to-ceiling murals soar two stories to meet the domed ceiling. Cherubim frolic with pagan gods. Toga-clad men converse with women in Renaissance garb. Speculating about the story line of the murals and spotting all their historical contradictions can amuse for hours. We recommend doing it over tea, a particular treat here, and at $18 a good buy. During the summer, should you prefer your tea cold, rest assured it will be dutifully brewed and arrive with its own little ice bucket.

Just beyond The Rotunda is the Café Pierre, a dignified urban retreat in soothing tones of gray, enlivened by gold accents, lovely crystal chandeliers, and etched Italian mirrors. It is an intimate, seductive room which caresses rather than assaults you with its luxurious elegance. The food lives up to the setting, and the little bar is the perfect place to cap off any evening. Actually, it's a popular place to repair to after a lot of activities, such as work. The daily 5:00–7:30 P.M. happy hour is made happier by complimentary hors d'oeuvres. The Café Pierre also attracts the posttheater crowd who relax in the comfortable armchairs and loveseats while they review the show.

As for our review of The Pierre's guest rooms, it is predictably enthusiastic. Commodious with white-tiled bathrooms (each further brightened by a single red rose) and ample closet space, they range in price from $280 to $490 a night. Suites, which constitute almost 25 percent of the hotel's guest quarters, run the bedroom gamut from one to three, starting at $630 and ending at $2,500. Their number has just been augmented by the addition of 15 grand suites, making The Pierre one of the city's leading purveyors of the suite life. Formerly private apartments, they have the genuinely residential atmosphere to which so many other hotel suites aspire. As freshly appointed as they are, they feel lived in. Just place a silver-framed picture or two on the mantel and you're "home," particularly in the Getty Suite, 1025. Configured to offer one to three bedrooms ($1,400 to $1,725), it is truly grand. A wall of French doors opens the living room onto a vast terrace. Tennis anyone? Each of the bedrooms is equally impressive in size, but we are fondest of the one to the left as you enter. What it lacks in the way of a view is more than made up for by a fabulous Chinese deco mirror. Other amenities include a pantry, full bath off the living room, Frette linens, and Lancôme toiletries.

For something cozier, there are several boudoir suites — 3801 for instance at $630 a night. The view from the blue-hued bedroom, stretching across the park to the Wollman ice-skating rink and beyond to imposing buildings lining Central Park West, is marvelous. Elaborate chintz window treatments and dark Chippendale-style furniture dress up the interior, while a large dressing area, decked out with a lounge chair and desk set, makes it a real suite.

Yes, life at The Pierre is indeed sweet, made all the more so by Herbert's edict that guests' needs should be anticipated and satisfied before they have a chance to voice them. With a staggering three-to-one staff-to-guest ratio, his philosophy is not just lip service; it is a reality.

Service and location; location and service. Either way you rank them, they are the hallmarks of which The Pierre is justifiably proud.

# *Plaza Athénée*

| 37 East 64th Street | (212) 734-9100 |
|---|---|
| New York, NY 10021 | Fax (212) 772-0958 |

Given the frenzy produced by a public sighting of the Princess of Wales, the Duchess of York, and the "last movie star" Elizabeth Taylor, we forgive the rather forbidding presence of the three security guards permanently installed in the small lobby of the Plaza Athénée. They keep a watchful eye on the hotel's single entrance, making the Plaza Athénée one of the most secure hotels in New York. Everyone has to pass the guards' scrutiny, which is not terribly friendly, though always polite, for the privilege of comparing this sister hotel to Paris's renowned Plaza Athénée.

Rest assured, it's worth the effort. After all, this intimate property (only 200 rooms) had a formidable reputation to live up to. Every effort was made to insure that the New York hotel captures the ambience and spirit for which its Paris counterpart is so beloved. This was not an easy or inexpensive task. The vintage 1927 former Hotel Alrae had been declared a landmark. Since no exterior changes could be made, creative solutions had to be devised to deal with basics, like the installation of central air conditioning. Furthermore, the internal structural beams typical of 1920s construction made transforming the interior an equal challenge.

The bi-level lobby is the first clue to the extraordinary success of the project. While relatively small, its division into two levels by a *faux* marble balustrade and a set of shallow steps lends a sense of grandeur. The decor is magnificent with its Italian marble floor, French antiques, large gilt mirrors, and Oriental rugs. The classic and pastoral scenes of the specially commissioned Gobelin-style tapestry wall coverings are reminiscent of the priceless originals hanging in the long gallery of the hotel's Parisian counterpart. After registering at the eighteenth-century ormolu desk, management escorts guests to their rooms. The ride in one of the lovely leather-lined elevators is the harbinger of the delights of the Plaza Athénée's guest quarters. Paisley fabrics coordinate the richly elegant look of directoire-style furnishings designed exclusively for the hotel and complemented by specially commissioned Navarian carpets imported from Ireland. Most rooms have practical little pantries with a refrigerator and two-burner Corning stove. The rose-colored Portuguese marble bathrooms sport the usual luxury amenities like hairdriers, make-up mirrors, scales, and designer toiletries (Crabtree & Evelyn, in this case), but Hollywood-handsome General Manager Bernard Lackner also insists on another very special touch: fresh flowers.

Room prices start at $275 a night, going up to $390 for a luxury double. One-bedroom suites cost $590. If you want one with a dining room and solarium, you're talking $975. For $895 you can get a two-bedroom suite. The rate for either of the two duplex penthouse suites with solariums and rooftop terraces is $1,950 a night for one bedroom; $2,300, for two.

And it's worth every penny; they are truly majestic. The sumptuous living rooms with their marble floors, fireplaces, and silk moiré walls are certainly fit for a princess or a duchess, and have lodged both. Let's talk about eclectic clientele — Richard Pryor loves the Plaza Athénée so much he once stayed three months. Julio Iglesias is also a fan. To a great extent, their loyalty is inspired by Bernard's singular treatment of them. Dedicated to the niceties that distinguish the European approach to hospitality, he routinely treats his guests to tasty surprises — a sampling of smoked salmon, caviar, or perhaps a bottle of Dom Perignon. Bernard also delights in sending up a tray of canapés and a half bottle of wine for what he describes as a little respite before dinner. Then there are the slippers that guests find next to their turned-down beds every night, which is another old-world touch from Bernard.

You should make no mistake, though. Bernard is very much attuned to what modern travelers increasingly consider necessities; for instance, he recently installed a health club, as well as a fax- and modem-ready phone system.

And Bernard is just as concerned about his guests' dining experience as he is about their exercise and communications needs. In keeping with his theory that Plaza Athénée guests deserve only the best, Bernard forged an association with Michel Rostang, one of the world's greatest chefs. He hired Michel and his two sons as consultants to the hotel's lavish Le Regence restaurant. Under their guidance, it became one of the city's premier hotel dining rooms, a position it still retains while no longer benefiting from the Rostangs' expertise. Under chef Marcel Agnez, Le Regence continues to offer an original menu of imaginative cuisine with classical French origins. It also offers one of the most opulent atmospheres in town, a rococo-inspired fantasy of magnificent mirrored panels set against turquoise walls that cast endless reflections under glittering chandeliers hanging from the sweeping cloudscape ceiling.

Le Regence is a popular luncheon spot with those seeking a quiet meal in what seems more like a private dining salon than a public restaurant. Barbara Walters is among the regulars who make a choice between the à la carte and $25.50 prix-fixe menus. The latter represents a new element at Le Regence: lowered prices. Indeed it is a very tempting value, given the surprisingly generous number of choices for each of the three courses. Among them, we like the classic escargots and the absolutely sublime calf's liver (which has always been our measure of a truly great French restaurant).

Dinner here is often enjoyed by Dudley Moore, Mel Gibson, and Ryan O'Neal and Farrah Fawcett. Again, the prix fixe at $49.50 is a deal, but we prefer greater freedom of the à la carte. How could anyone resist the warm lobster salad garnished with baby carrots and basil for $18.25 or the $15.50 smoked salmon on a warm potato pancake topped by crème fraiche and onions? For the main course, we like the grilled sea scallops with candied tomatoes and a coulis of fennel at $26.25, although the grilled veal chop in mustard and rosemary is a close second at $32.50.

We've all had the experience of agreeing with Charles Dickens's assertion that, "To travel with high expectations is better than to arrive." The Plaza Athénée may be the exception that proves the rule. To arrive here is to satisfy, indeed exceed, even the most grandiose of expectations.

## The Plaza Hotel

Fifth Avenue at Central Park South      (212) 759-3000
New York, NY 10019      Fax (212) 546-5234

Sometimes you have to run twice as fast just to stay in place. I believe a character in *Alice In Wonderland* first noted that interesting fact of life. Certainly, it is well known to hoteliers the world around. Opening a quality hotel is difficult; maintaining the quality is even more difficult.

Of all the New York hostelries, none knows this better than The Plaza. For many years the jewel in the crown, the hotel saw many management companies come in and dull the luster, tarnish the dreams, and turn a once-elegant emporium into a merely mediocre one.

The Plaza began its rise back to the heights in the guise of a white knight named Donald Trump, whose sympathetic refurbishment of the hotel is almost enough to make us forgive him for Trump Tower and the Taj Mahal. With considerable assistance from then-spouse Ivana, who actually supervised the work, the hotel was restored to its former grandeur. The physical restoration was breathtaking: Elaborate ornamental plaster ceilings long hidden by acoustical tile were revealed; the Tiffany ceiling of the celebrated Palm Court, destroyed during the Hilton regime, was reconstructed; long-concealed mosaics reappeared in the Oak Room; and the charming cast-iron canopies at the entrances were stripped of modern trimmings, as were the lamps and flagpoles that adorn them. The Trumps even raised $3,000,000 from the community to restore the city-owned landmark fountain that separates the hotel from Fifth Avenue.

In keeping with early advertisements that described it as the world's "most luxurious hotel," every bathroom in the "new" Plaza's 815 guest rooms has been redone in marble and equipped with two-line telephones, hairdriers, and makeup mirrors. Dazzling turn-of-the-century crystal chandeliers and elaborate plaster moldings decorate every VCR- and safe-equipped room, 450 of which are further embellished with the original marble fireplaces.

The bed and bath linens are custom-made Frette. Kitchenettes on each floor ensure prompt delivery of a Continental breakfast.

But a hotel is more than amenities and appointments. Our recent stays have shown that the hotel is well maintained, but there are signs of a slide in management's care and concern for travelers and their problems. Personally, we have encountered one highly cavalier handling of a serious overcharge, plus a certain — shall we say — lack of interest in making an apology. One hopes corrections have been made.

True to its origins as a residential hotel for very wealthy New Yorkers, the Plaza glories in some of the most remarkable suites in town. The 7,802-square-foot Presidential Suite is quite literally over-the-top, located as it is on the nineteenth floor with a spectacular view of Central Park from its *two* living rooms and terrace (not to mention dining room, kitchen, four bedrooms, four bathrooms, and powder room). There's also a sauna and a 2,000-bottle wine cellar, all for $15,000 a night.

A little too rich for your blood? What about the Vanderbilt Suite for only $4,000? Named in honor of Mr. and Mrs. Alfred Gwynne Vanderbilt (the first guests to sign The Plaza's register when they moved into a $10,000-a-year apartment eighty-seven years ago), the suite's 2,400 square feet offers one the opportunity to roam or to do some very lavish entertaining. The living/dining room is beautifully done in rose and celadon, accented by striking moldings and made most comfortable by remarkable Empire reproductions resting on a 300-year-old rug. The topiary trees flanking the fireplace are a nice touch. Indeed, an abundance of lush flowers and plants in all rooms are a trademark. Each of the suite's bedrooms exults in a different color scheme, but the master bathroom is the real eye-catcher. More like a boudoir, its white leather chaise lounge, hand-painted screen, and huge marble Jacuzzi tub make it very glamorous indeed.

Somewhat smaller at "only" 1,500 square feet, the Frank Lloyd Wright Suite is so-named because he actually lived in the space while he was designing the Guggenheim Museum. No doubt he enjoyed the three fireplaces and the wonderful Fifth Avenue views. Today, its occupants also savor fine reproduction Wright furniture and accessories, complemented by a few originals like the high-backed chairs in the corridor leading to the two bedrooms. The marble floor in the entry is also worthy of note. It is a pattern created by Wright but never actually used in the Guggenheim, or anywhere else for that matter. The Trumps found it while researching the Wright archives and had it specially commissioned and installed. With both bedrooms, the suite rents for $2,500 a night. Should you require the use of only the master bedroom, you can save $500.

Alternatively, if you want to experience the unique Wright ambience on a budget, you can rent the second bedroom on its own for only $500. That's a bargain when you consider its extra large proportions, two queen-size beds, fireplace, and grand desk that doubles as an elegant dining table.

Other guest quarters, all decorated in traditional French or English country manor-style, carry more modest price tags. Standard rooms start at $205 and go to $275 a night for a "deluxe park view." Suites can be had for as little as $650. Whatever the cost, make sure you secure accommodations on floors 2 through 11, so that you can relish the spaciousness accorded by the 14-foot ceilings on those levels.

While Ivana (now a member of the rarefied set identified simply by first name) is no longer The Plaza's grown-up Eloise, her personal stamp remains on a number of fronts. Some ascribe the tad-too-brilliant colors of the specially woven carpets and the eye-popping-gilding in the public rooms to her nouveau riche taste. *You* should know, however, that Ivana took great pains to make sure the renovation exemplified the spirit and intent of architect Henry Janeway Hardenbergh, who also designed another New York landmark, The Dakota. The colors are true to the periods, and all that glittering gilt was part of the original decor, although it was considered a bit much even by opulent Edwardian standards. (Just before opening, The Plaza's first manager ordered that a coat of dulling varnish be applied to tone it down.)

One has only to visit any of the hotel's six dining establishments to experience feeling important, Plaza-style. The Palm Court has for decades been a favorite gathering spot for New Yorkers, particularly for tea, when guests are serenaded by violins. A new kitchen solely dedicated to this sumptuous palm-garnished oasis has dramatically improved the quality of the service and the food.

Similarly, the clubby Oak Room, the English publike Oyster Bar, and the romantic Edwardian Room are profiting from a renaissance. They have reclaimed their standing as destinations of choice for natives as well as tourists (the Edwardian Room is even credited with instituting the current craze for kitchen dining), while the Oak Bar overlooking Central Park never lost its luster as one of New York's most popular watering holes. Even Trader Vic's, long a fixture (if a somewhat anachronistic one) in the Plaza's basement, is enjoying a new lease on life.

Once again fit for royalty—the King of Morocco is a frequent guest and that prince of Hollywood, Eddie Murphy, chose it as the site of his extravaganza of a wedding—The Plaza now fulfills everyone's fantasy of the quintessential New York hotel. Does it? Sometimes yes, sometimes no—you be the judge.

# The Regency Hotel

| | |
|---|---|
| 540 Park Avenue | (212) 759-4100 |
| New York, NY 10021 | (800) 233-2356 |
| | Fax (212) 826-5674 |

The Regency stands proudly on Park Avenue as the flagship of the Tisch-family-controlled Loews Hotels. You know the Tisches. They emerged from wealthy obscurity to powerful celebrity when they engineered a stranglehold on communications in America; Preston Tisch became postmaster general not long after brother Larry bought CBS. Their offspring are also making power waves. Jonathan Tisch is one of the hotel industry's brightest stars as president and chief executive. He pulled off one of the dynastic mergers of the century by marrying Laura Steinberg, daughter of corporate raider Saul. Then there's Steve Tisch, who has earned his own Hollywood-style star status as the producer of a number of hit movies.

The site of many a Tisch family breakfast, it's only fitting that The Regency is credited as the birthplace of that hallmark of the 1980s: the *power breakfast*. In the post-barbarians-at-the-gates 90s (the term may be politically incorrect and the trappings down-sized), town cars now idle curbside where limousines once roamed. But "power" aptly describes the reality of breakfast here. Marie Hallas, who knows everyone with a capital E, continues to oversee the frenetic scene that is The Regency dining room every weekday from 7:00 to 9:00 A.M. Whether by her design, or happy circumstance, things have settled down a bit into a pattern. The finance crowd led by Felix Rohatyn stakes out its territory at 7; the real estate and media moguls as personified by Mort Zuckerman check in at 8, while the entertainment honchos show up at 9. Whoopi Goldberg stakes out a favorite corner table as Disney's Jeffrey Katzenberg demonstrates table-hopping par excellence by conducting two, three, and even four meetings simultaneously (starting at 7 A.M.)!

However powerful and even healthy (there are now egg substitutes on the menu) it may be, breakfast is only one of the Regency's attractions. As the name suggests, there is a Regency-period flavor to the decor throughout. But it isn't stuffy or institutional. Rather, The Regency's unpretentious elegance imitates a tastefully decorated, albeit very grand home. Suffice it to say, the Grimaldi family finds it an adequate substitute for Monaco's palace.

In fact, we would gladly trade our respective abodes for the comfort of Suite 1831. One of the hotel's four suites designated as "presidential," it is available in either one- or two-bedroom configurations. The living room with its good-looking original artwork is so expansive that the grand piano is almost lost in one corner. That goes for the oversized television, too. Equally large, the terrace overlooking Park Avenue readily accommodates 75 people for cocktails on a warm evening. With both bedrooms, it's yours for $1,200 a night.

In deference to The Regency's popularity with the bicoastal set, such as Sharon Stone, Steve Guttenberg, Goldie Hawn, Jane Fonda, and Jimmy Smits, another of the hotel's more lavish suites has been dubbed the California. Also priced at $1,200 with two big bedrooms, its bleached wood floors complement dramatic but comfortable overstuffed furniture. George Hurell's portraits of Tinsel Town greats add a glamorous touch. And the sauna explains why The Regency has assumed the nickname "Hollywood East"!

Other one- and-two bedroom suites range from $600 to $850. Single-and double-occupancy room rates range from $245 to $395, with junior suites at $350.

Regardless of size or price, all the Regency's 450 guest quarters offer several nifty features, including loads of closet space, refrigerators, two telephone lines, and well-appointed rose-colored marble bathrooms equipped with mini-TVs, telephones, and enough counter space to provide a home for all your toiletries. Many also boast kitchens and canopied beds.

Lest you think breakfast is the only food story at The Regency, you should know that amid the much ballyhooed explosion of fine (read "elaborate" and "expensive") restaurants in New York hostelries, Jonathan Tisch has set another course for 540 Park (yes, the address is the hotel's restaurant's name). He charged Chef Philippe Feret with simplifying the menus to that of a neighborhood haunt in scale and price. And he set David Rockwell, the current king of restaurant design, about deplushing the interior to make it more contemporary and casual. The result is a refreshingly unassuming dining enclave on Park Avenue, despite the decor which remains decidedly formal even after David's softening touches. Actually the contrast between the look and the food is one of 540's charms. Where else in New York can you sit on a tapestried banquette under a crystal chandelier and dine on a $12.50 hamburger at lunch or a $16 pan-roasted chicken at dinner? Andrew's kitchen produces cuisine that reflects today's dining trends toward simplicity and value.

It will be interesting to see how many other hotels follow Jonathan's lead on the dining front. They certainly fell into line with regard to the installation of fitness centers. At Jonathan's direction, the Regency was one of the first to add such a facility. It proved so popular with hotel guests, as well as with some of his high-profile New York-based friends, that he doubled its size in 1988. What its ensemble of exercise equipment, free weights, whirlpool spa, sauna, and professional staff doesn't offer, you don't need.

For those who consider exercise bending an elbow at a bar, there are few better places to do it than in the Regency Lounge. The fiefdom of bartender John Mahon, who has been there since the hotel's 1963 opening, it is a popular gathering spot for the chic set. Not surprisingly, John has seen and heard it all. Fortunately, or not, he is very discreet. Still, John does engage his considerable wit to regale his subjects with amusing anecdotes while pouring his generous drinks.

John's yarns aside, you will probably leave the Regency with a tale or two of your own. Unless you are so enamored of your room that you live the life of a recluse, it's impossible to spend any time here without observing (or participating in) a celebrity slice of life. Once, while just waiting in the lobby for our pal Susan Anton, we watched Terry Bradshaw descend on the Regency full of venom about the guy who lifted his wallet at the airport. And when Susan strode out of the elevator, she literally bumped into Prince Albert of Monaco, who engaged her in conversation. Over his shoulder, she kept looking at us quizzically as we made frantic hand signals which didn't quite get across the fact that her dazzling smile was marred by bits of her beloved John's pizza. C'est la vie — at the Regency, that is.

# The Royalton

| | |
|---|---|
| 44 West 44th Street | (212) 869-4400 |
| between Fifth and | Reservations (800) 635-9013 |
| Sixth Avenues | Fax (212) 869-8965 |
| New York, NY 10036 | |

In 1898, Manhattan sat up and took notice when The Royalton was built as an exclusive residential hotel. Now, almost a hundred years later, this small hostelry is once again commanding attention as a hotel frequented by a rarefied breed of New Yorkers. The lobby and restaurant known as "44" have become the nexus for the editors of high-profile magazines such as *Vogue, Vanity Fair, GQ, Harper's Bazaar*, and *The New Yorker*. The designers, photographers, models, and celebrities of the moment that are their inevitable entourage also come here. It is a scene that would have warmed the cockles of the late Steve Rubell's heart. He was one half of the team that immortalized Studio 54. Before he died, Steve and surviving partner Ian Schrager had successfully ventured into the hotel business with the Morgans hotel and were embarking on the renovation of The Royalton with the goal of creating "the hotel of the 90s," one that would become "a new kind of gathering place." They predicted that hotel lobbies would become the social hubs of the 1990s, just as restaurants were in the 1980s and nightclubs/discos were in the 1970s.

So far, we think restaurants are holding their own, but The Royalton is certainly leading whatever vanguard there may be in terms of what Rubell and Schrager termed as "lobby socializing." Superstar interior designer Philippe Starck produced a fantastic stage set for a constantly changing cast of characters who really socialize with a vengeance. At lunch, the 110-seat restaurant spills out into the lobby to accommodate another 50 diners, some of whom have to eat bending over cocktail tables normally used for drinks or tea. Later, the participants in the cocktail party that is the nightly scene here are so comfortably familiar with their surroundings that they avail themselves of any space for seats. This includes arms of chairs, the aforementioned cocktail tables, the stairs that define the gathering areas, and even the floor.

Despite its block-long ten thousand square feet of space, the room has a sophisticated, inviting warmth due to its clever multi-level division into distinct spaces. There is the study, with a twenty-foot library table and an extensive selection of reading materials. Beyond the study, and deliberately hidden, lurks the descriptively named Round Bar. Resembling a very blue padded cell, it was ostensibly inspired by Ernest Hemingway's favorite bar at The Ritz in Paris. However, we suspect it is also a takeoff on the legendary Round Table of the venerable Algonquin, just across the street.

In any event, The Royalton clearly subscribes to the theory that if you can't find the bar or if you don't know where it is, you don't belong there. Don't worry; there are other areas to explore. Take the living room boasting Starck's specially designed visions of futuristic overstuffed furniture. Sink into a settee or armchair to survey the often frenetic scene, but be wary of the three-legged chairs — they have been known to tip over, with great fanfare.

Then there's the "sushi-bar-without-sushi." It's another graphically named space, so avant garde a version of a sushi bar that it doesn't serve sushi. But it does offer light fare on a twenty-four-hour basis. For more serious eating, the dining room, as Restaurant "44," serves breakfast, lunch, and dinner. As a hotel guest, your best bets are at either end of the meal spectrum. It's not that the food is any better; it is always ingeniously sophisticated and good. It's just that at lunch "44" is less hospitable to mere mortals, populated as it is with the powerful of periodicals' publishing. The queens — Tina Brown and Anna Wintour — hold court almost every day. The restaurant also serves as commissary to Susan Kamil, Editorial Director of Dial Press; Art Cooper of *Gentlemen's Quarterly*; and the men's style editor of *The New York Times*, Hal Rubenstein, along with Paul Goldberger, cultural editor of the *Times*.

The bottom line is that if your editorial experience is limited to proofing term papers, you'll be seated in the worse-than-Siberia front section of "44," where the waiters seem embarrassed to be seen serving you. (That is, *if* you can get a table at all.)

Otherwise, The Royalton succeeds admirably at its goal of being more like a home than a hotel—albeit a somewhat futuristic residence. The Royalton represents Rubell's and Schrager's notion of a "mansion hotel" with living and entertaining areas on the first floor and sleeping quarters upstairs. Speaking of which, they are every bit as captivating as the lobby—all 170 of them. Forty have fireplaces and all are equipped with VCRs, stereo cassette decks, two-line telephones with speaker and conference capabilities, refrigerators stocked with Japanese lacquer-boxed goodies from Dean & DeLuca, and candles. Yes, candles, which may be the homiest touch of all.

Our fancy was particularly struck by room 516, described as a "loft suite." Starck's sleek modern decor is executed in tones of gray, warmed by the glow from the fireplace and punctuated by a single piece of art: a postcard that's changed three times a day. In addition, like all of The Royalton's sleeping rooms, it sports a cushioned window seat, writing desk, and a glamorous bathroom.

At $380 per night, 516 is at the high end of The Royalton's tariff card. Minus the fireplace and the extra square footage, you can experience Starck's unique environments in standard and deluxe doubles for $255 to $320.

Regardless of your economic participation in the hotel's runaway success, you can be sure you'll be treated royally by the staff. Your every wish will be considered a command. If your evening is planned around a movie that is not part of The Royalton's large video library, just call the front desk. Someone will scurry out into the night to find it. And now that The Royalton has installed a fitness facility, open 24 hours a day, it's no wonder the hotel has become "home" to the young, restless, and glamorous set—Jodie Foster, Johnny Depp, Jason Priestley, John Stamos, and John Cusack.

Extraordinary decor, exemplary service, and the opportunity to refine your lobby social skills—what more could one possibly want in a hotel? We might be interested in slightly larger closets, but we're awfully picky!

# The St. Regis

| 2 East 55th Street | (212) 753-4500 |
|---|---|
| at Fifth Avenue | Fax (212) 541-4736 |
| New York, NY 10022 | |

For three years, an integral thread of the city's social fabric was missing. The St. Regis, first opened as Colonel John Jacob Astor's palatial pride and joy in 1904, was closed for renovation. New Yorkers mourned the loss of one of their favorite watering holes — the King Cole Grill, home of a beloved Maxfield Parrish mural of the jolly old king and his court, and the famed St. Regis Roof, the city's only rooftop ballroom.

Now, after an extraordinary $100 million plus renovation by ITT Sheraton, the St. Regis is back in all its Art Nouveau glory right down to the Waterford chandeliers and the gilt letterbox in the lobby. In fact, with nary a computer or telephone in sight, the lobby is virtually a museum. It is the epitome of turn-of-the-century hotel luxury: soaring ceilings, ornate plaster moldings, and loads of gilt. (In fact, the restoration of the St. Regis to its original splendor represented the second largest gold leafing operation ever undertaken in the United States.)

By modern tastes, the lobby, its monochromatic marble unrelieved by carpets or much in the way of furniture (the notable exception being a set of red thronelike chairs) is cold. So, too, is the colonnaded meant-for-tea Astor Court beyond, despite its fanciful trompe l'oeil ceiling. Thank goodness for the beguiling salon with its impressive carved marble fireplace and fabulous chandelier of dancing cherubim and for the seductive King Cole Bar. Granted, its cherry-oak paneled walls need a little smoke in them to dull their shine, but the bar is a fitting showcase for its namesake mural and has become one of midtown's favorite after-work haunts, despite the hefty $7.50 for a glass of house wine.

Indeed, the St. Regis has, since its fall 1991 reopening, been plagued by a reputation for being New York's most expensive hotel. With rooms starting at $350, it's true. But you get a lot for your money, including unlimited local telephone calls, unmonitored enjoyment of a private bar, and the privilege of pressed clothing. Just add up your telephone, mini-bar, and valet charges on your last hotel bill to see what a value that $350 represents. All of a sudden, it's not such a staggering amount. And you haven't yet taken into consideration the worth of your "maître d'etage," the butler assigned to each floor whose raison d'être is to serve as your point of reference throughout the hotel. Out of toothpaste? Call the butler. Have a hankering for a midnight snack? Call the butler. Plumbing problems? Call the.... You get the idea. No more poring over the guest services directory trying to decide who to call for what. Don't worry about getting too dependent on your butler (or more accurately your staff of butlers, as there is 24-hour coverage) because you will be assigned to his floor on your next visit.

And return you will, at least if Managing Director Rick Segal has anything to do with it. He knows that the "success of the St. Regis depends largely on the return guest factor, which is insured by the highest level of personal service." That means your butler welcomes you to his floor at the elevator, escorts you to your room, and unpacks your belongings, while ascertaining what else can be done to assure your comfort. His hospitable efforts are enhanced by fresh flowers and a digital greeting from your bedside telephone cum computer, which serves as command central. It controls the room's lighting, temperature, radio, and television and can tell you the time anywhere in the world in six languages!

If it and its twenty-four-page instruction book are enough to make you feel uncommunicative, don't worry. There are two other less-sophisticated phones in every room, one on the desk and one in the bath. Speaking of which, the St. Regis's bathrooms are rated best in show. Not only are they cavernous in their Italian marble, double sink and separate shower stall grandeur, but they profit from the unexpectedly homey touch of decorative gilt-framed prints and mirrors.

Actually, space and reassuring residential elements are St. Regis trademarks. The rooms with their twelve-foot ceilings are, on average, the second largest of any of the city's hostelries, thanks to a reduction in their number from 557 to 317. Intricately patterned crown moldings set off soft-hued silk wall coverings; sparkling crystal chandeliers cast a warm glow over exceptionally fine mahogany Louis XV reproductions. Any hint of institutional decor is further diminished by the occasional comforter tossed over a sofa or an Oriental rug laid over the carpeting to anchor a sitting area. Even the corridors are relieved of monotony by strategically placed consoles displaying delicately colorful dried flower arrangements or bowls of potpourri.

Typical of a *basic* (though we hesitate to use that word to characterize anything about the St. Regis) room is 311, a symphony of blues and creams, the color scheme of choice throughout most of the hotel's guest chambers. There's enough room to set up your computer and fax machine on the desk facing the heavily swagged window. And there's plenty of space to store them in the closet, which is also notable for its high-tech lighting—open the door and the light goes on. Step away from the closet and the light switches off, only to shine again when next you approach. Cute, even entertaining. But our favorite thing about the room is the bench at the foot of the bed, another of those homey St. Regis touches.

For longer stays, ask about the St. Regis's inventory of suites, which come in an astounding number of configurations and range in price from $550 for an Astor to $3,000 for the Presidential. If one is available and you're prepared to ante up the $1,750 tab, take one of the designer numbers. We adore The Tiffany, decorated by that venerable company's design director, John Loring, for its drop-dead glamour. Here the St. Regis's tendency toward subtlety is thrown to the winds in favor of the drama of bold colors executed in a riot of florals and stripes. The living room, dominated by a large green marble-mantled fireplace, is a stunner, but it's the dining room that is everyone's favorite. Dark red walls are animated by paisley print silk insets framed by green molding. An antique secretary displays exquisite Tiffany china; the lustrous table seats twelve and often does, as the suite is a hit with hostesses.

No wonder! Not only is the room beautiful, but the St. Regis also serves up sumptuous cuisine, courtesy of Executive Chef Gray Kunz. In fact the hotel's signature French restaurant, Lespinasse, has been catapulted into multistar status and is addressed as a separate entity in this book's restaurant section. For the purposes of this discussion, suffice it to say that after a meal at Lespinasse, you'll be very grateful for the hotel's grottolike health club. It rates as the city's prettiest with its murals of classical gardens. And while it may be small, the facility is well equipped and underutilized.

We're usually on our own when we take advantage of it, which is the good *and* the bad news. Certainly, it's a luxury to work out without an audience, but at the St. Regis any fellow exercise hounds are likely to be very recognizable characters from the fashion and show biz worlds. We wish we could tell you who, but Rick made us promise not to. Protecting the privacy of his (very) high-profile clients is yet another way to insure they will return.

# The Stanhope

995 Fifth Avenue                           (212) 288-5800
at 81st Street                         Fax (212) 517-0088
New York, NY 10028

To some, The Stanhope might seem like a money pit, a silk-lined bottomless one that keeps swallowing millions of dollars with no end in sight. But according to general manager Neil Trubowitch, if that's "what it takes to leave a favorable and lasting impression on every guest... to convince them there is no better place to stay in New York," then so be it. As operations manager a few years back, Neil lovingly oversaw the $25 million renovation that launched the former and very faded American Stanhope into the luxury market. For a small hotel (only 148 rooms and suites), that is an astonishing sum—and it shows. The quality of the 18th-century French antiques in the lobby is self-evident, as is that of the custom-designed Baccarat crystal chandeliers, the Oriental rugs, the museum-quality Gobelin tapestries, and the 24-carat gold leaf on the moldings. In fact, the decor of the hotel's public rooms and corridors is best described as "mini Versailles."

Fortunately the rather too precious, formal magnificence is more restrained in the sleeping rooms. The style is still Louis XVI, but first-class reproductions replace the real McCoy here, and only the occasional touch of Chinoiserie is welcome. These are generously proportioned guest quarters (more than half are suites, many of which are equipped with kitchenettes), easily settled into for extended stays. This helps explain The Stanhope's not-surprising appeal to international CEO types. After all, the hotel is nowhere near anyplace where one normally conducts business, although the upper Fifth Avenue location in the heart of "Museum Mile" is dandy for those in search of cultural enrichment. But the hotel's weekday complimentary limousine service solves any geographical undesirability.

Actually, the slightly-off-the-beaten track location ensures a great degree of privacy, which is why The Stanhope is also popular with high-profile personalities like Paul McCartney, Liza Minelli, Quincy Jones, and Oliver Stone.

Rooms start at $275; suites start at $375, with a cap of $750 for a two-bedroom. The only exception is the phenomenal Penthouse Suite, which goes for $2,500. It's only a one-bedroomer, but this former abode of Edward G. Robinson also has a wraparound terrace with sensational views of Central Park and the city beyond, as well as a dining room which, according to the press materials, can seat the rather odd number of 55.

In the less pricey, two-bedroom category, our favorite is large and airy suite 1110. Done in warm tones of beige, it counts two full bathrooms and three telephones among its amenities. Sinfully soft Italian leather binds all the desk appointments. Even the hangers are special: ladies' are padded silk, and the gentlemen's are heavy wood. All of them are removable, for which we are eternally grateful.

For half the $650 charge for 1110, you can settle into 1008. It is smaller, but still very charming and quite peaceful in its sea-green decor. Should it prove a little too quiet, you can always crank up the CD and stereo cassette player, provided in every room. For further amusement, you can check out The Stanhope's new fitness club or use the complimentary pocket-sized map of jogging trails in Central Park. Alternatively you can test the mettle of the hotel's 24-hour room service by requesting supper for six at 2:00 A.M., or take advantage of its personal shopping service at Galeries Lafayette.

Leave it to The Stanhope to hook up with a Paris-based department store. A French influence is pervasive throughout the hotel, except in Gerard's, the bar off the lobby. Gerard's looks like the inner sanctum of a very gentlemanly English men's club, with its mahogany-paneled walls, hunter-green velvet Chesterfield sofas, leatherbound books, and hunt paintings. Gerard's is a warmly inviting spot for cocktails and it stands in dramatic contrast to the rather intimidating formal French Dining Room.

There you're surrounded by Louis XVI antiques, Baccarat crystal chandeliers, and eighteenth-century-style pastoral wall murals done in the neoclassical manner by Robert Jackson. The Limoges china and Baccarat crystal place settings are well suited to their rich surroundings, as are the luxurious pigskin-swathed armchairs. There's no doubt about the room's beauty, but its stateliness tends to stilt our conversation. We always feel compelled to whisper!

Card-carrying chatterers that we are, we prefer the cozier ambience of Le Salon (a contemporary rendition of a manor house conservatory), where continental breakfast, light lunch, and a very respectable tea are served. We highly recommend taking tea here to rejuvenate the senses after exploring the wonders of The Metropolitan Museum across Fifth Avenue. For $23.00, you can indulge in an intriguing assortment of delicate finger sandwiches, followed by hot scones with Devonshire cream and an array of tempting pastries. Of course, there is a selection of teas — Fortnum and Mason, House of Twining, Jackson's of Piccadilly, even Grace Rare Teas. In case you haven't tried it, a glass of sherry or one of The Stanhope's vintage ports makes a fine substitute for tea at tea!

And when it's open (spring, summer, and fall, weather permitting), The Terrace — the city's only Parisian-style outdoor cafe on Fifth Avenue — is a must.

While The Stanhope excels at providing luxurious accommodations well-serviced by an efficient staff, we do have a bone to pick. In an admirable effort to insure security and privacy, the automatic elevators are key-activated and will only take you to the floor on which you are staying. Therefore, if you're inclined to visit friends or business associates on other floors, you have to go down to the desk and enlist the aid of a "guest service representative" (we used to call them clerks). He or she, in turn, has to call the object of your intended visit, announce your impending arrival, then escort you to the elevator and access the appropriate floor with a master key.

It's more than a bit of a nuisance. Certainly, Neil Trubowitch is to be commended for his remarkably successful program of instilling a "sense of responsibility and authority in each of our staff members that encourages them to anticipate our guests' every need." But, in our experience, even he has not been able to figure out a way to train his staff to know when and where we want to go before we do!

# The Waldorf-Astoria

301 Park Avenue                    (212) 355-3000
New York, NY 10022          Fax (212) 872-6380

Ever since it opened as the world's largest and New York's first skyscraper hotel in 1931, The Waldorf-Astoria has been the traditional site of some of New York's grandest occasions. But the Waldorf legacy predates that auspicious opening by almost 40 years. In 1893, William Waldorf Astor launched the original Waldorf Hotel on the corner of Fifth Avenue, the site of his former mansion and currently home to the Empire State Building. This opening was a truly historic affair, inaugurating the now de rigeur institution of holding charity balls in hotels. Furthermore, the evening proved significant on the culinary front because the Waldorf salad made its debut.

Several years later, John Jacob Astor IV followed cousin William's example and razed his mansion on the corner of Fifth and 34th to build the Astoria Hotel. The two hotels were linked by an enclosed walkway; hence, the Waldorf-Astoria tie. The walkway became a promenade for those interested in showing off the late 19th-century's feathered fashions, prompting one journalist to note, "They are like peacocks on parade." Whether he was referring to the plumage or their hauteur remains uncertain. In any case, the walkway was dubbed Peacock Alley and lives on today as an elegant lounge and restaurant off the main lobby of the present Waldorf-Astoria.

As the most prized possession of the Hilton Hotel Corporation, the Waldorf remains worthy of its illustrious history. For years Conrad Hilton kept a picture of the Waldorf on his desk and across the picture was written "the greatest of them all." In 1949 he secured the management rights and finally bought the property outright in 1977. Subsequently the hotel was treated to a five-year, $150 million renovation that uncovered and restored the building's original Art Deco treasures, like the extraordinary 148,000-piece mosaic that had been hiding under a carpet in the Park Avenue lobby. In fact, no less an authority than the Smithsonian Institution has designated the Waldorf as one of the three major Art Deco buildings in the country.

Actually, the Waldorf was the first hotel in the United States to give prominence to the Art Deco style. But that's only one of the

Waldorf's many firsts. It was the first hotel to abolish the "ladies' entrance," the first to introduce room service, and the first to establish "a hotel within a hotel," the Waldorf Towers.

Occupying the 28th through 42nd floors, with accommodations designed to suggest the grandeur typical of Park Avenue apartments, the Towers offers complete privacy and highly personalized service. It maintains a separate entrance on 50th Street, serviced by a private lobby, elevators, and exclusive concierge staff. Here the rich and often famous have been holing up ever since the Waldorf originated the notion of people living in hotel suites on a long-term basis. Since first instituting that practice, the Towers has been home to an elite corps including General and Mrs. Douglas MacArthur, Cary Grant, the Duke and Duchess of Windsor, President and Mrs. Herbert Hoover, Lowell Thomas, Ambassador and Mrs. Walter Annenberg, and Cole Porter, whose piano now has a place of honor in Peacock Alley. But you don't have to take up residence to enjoy the Towers' 191 elaborate suites and rooms; you just have to have the wherewithal. Rooms range from $350 to $375 a night, depending on location and decor. But you can rest assured there's not a bad one, on either count, among them. One-bedroom suites start at $550 and end at $3,300 a night, two and three bedrooms range from $1,150 to $3,500. It also helps to have the presence to deal with the butler who appears at your doorstep, ready, willing, and able to do just about anything your heart desires from running errands to performing valet services. When Boris Yeltsin arrived for his first New York visit, the Towers butlers washed, ironed, and returned the shirts of his entire delegation in less than an hour!

The Presidential Suite in the Towers is one of the few such establishments truly worthy of the appellation. Every U.S. president since Herbert Hoover has stayed there, and a case could be made that only Buckingham Palace has lodged more heads of state. The suite's 3,100 square feet rent for $5,000 a night, for which you get four bedrooms. Each has enormous closets and dressing rooms, full kitchen, large living room, and palatial formal dining room with a table that can seat 22. Like all the suites (and rooms) in the Towers, there is a decidedly residential but opulent ambience, given the abundance of antiques, intricately carved moldings, custom-designed carpets, ornate window treatments, and crystal chandeliers.

If the Towers stretches the limits of your pocketbook or social conscience, there is nothing shabby or shameful about the rest of the Waldorf's 1,410 rooms and suites which start at $185 and $400 respectively. No two are alike and all display the whimsical touch of original Art Deco features. And no matter where you stay, you will have access to the Waldorf-Astoria's four restaurants and two cocktail lounges, all of which are serviced by the amazing Waldorf kitchen. Covering an entire city block, it is divided into fourteen separate operations, including dedicated space for room service, the restaurants, and the hotel's twenty-five banquet or meeting rooms. It has the capacity to feed nearly 10,000 guests on any given day and often does.

The Grand Ballroom alone, the only four-story ballroom in the world, can accommodate up to 2,000 and is the site of innumerable contemporary incarnations of the first Waldorf hotel's earliest invention — the charity ball, and not an inconsiderable number of bar mitzvahs and weddings. All of them lavish, but none more so than the wedding that EMI Record Group Chairman Charles Koppelman recently threw for daughter Stacy. For only the second time in the Waldorf's history, the Park Avenue entrance was closed to hotel guests (the first time was for Frank Sinatra's 75th birthday party) so it could be transformed into a sprawling garden. Chandeliers dripped with gardenias, walls were lined with ivy and boxwood, and the traditional wedding huppah was made of 20,000 pink roses. Five hundred guests ate in the ballroom and were entertained by Barry Manilow and a fifty-nine-piece orchestra. Pundits quipped that EMI really stands for Extraordinary Marriage Investment, claiming an expenditure of close to $3 million!

Another record to add to the amazing list of Waldorf statistics may be that the wine cellar houses some 200,000 bottles, the majority of which are sold and restocked monthly. More than seventy languages are spoken by the employees, making it the United Nations of the city's hotel staffs. Appropriately enough, the UN has been known to borrow one of the hotel's 115 national flags.

However, the gold china service for 1,600 — the only one of its size in the world — never leaves the premises. Stored in a computerized safe, it is used daily for VIP room service. We couldn't get a count on the cutlery and glassware, but it must be enough to service a small town.

While we haven't seen a statistic on this either, we imagine a lot of guests check in and never leave the hotel during their stay. Why bother? You can conduct business in the 48,000 square feet of function space, work out in the fully equipped fitness center on the nineteenth floor, and enjoy a number of different culinary experiences. There's contemporary French provincial in elegant Peacock Allcy, all-American steaks and seafood from the clublike Bull and Bear, sandwiches and salads at the casual Oscar's, and some of the city's better Japanese fare at the exotic Inagiku.

The Waldorf-Astoria is virtually a self-contained world dedicated to guests' comfort and enjoyment. Maybe you should take a tip from Ginger Rogers and spend a *Weekend at the Waldorf.* In that delightful movie, she didn't get any of the great package deals currently available, but Ginger did give the Waldorf another of its firsts—it was the first hotel to be featured in a major film.

# CHAPTER THREE

# Restaurants

*On the count of three —
open your napkins!*

*B*istro, tavern, café, brasserie, trattoria, diner, pizzeria, cafeteria, taverna, deli, restaurant — your tastebuds can go on an around-the-world pleasure trip without ever leaving New York. Eating — high-, medium-, and low-priced; plain or fancy; haute cuisine or hot dogs — is what the Big Apple (there's food again) is all about. Everyone in New York, a friend of mine says, has two jobs: his own and restaurant critic. It's to be expected. With literally thousands of places to dine — or, at least, to eat — one wants to find that handful that consistently deliver the best.

The best is made up of many parts: the chef, the maître d', the owner, the ambience, the culinary distinction that makes one restaurant's fettucini Alfredo far tastier than the same-named dish in a dozen other places.

As a visitor to New York, you need to know more than restaurant names, but we'll get to them in a moment. First, it is only fair to warn you that a meal in this city will cost more than eating at home or even eating out in your home city. But there are three things to keep in mind that will slice the price problem: (1) it tastes delicious; (2) compared to theater, concert, or opera tickets, one of these meals will cost about the same, will deliver several hours of real enjoyment, and will leave you with a warm glow and physical satisfaction unmatched anywhere else; and (3) with celebrity chefs in the kitchen, you are getting a custom-tailored, handmade item, not prêt-à-porter. Second, you cannot expect to just pop in and sit down. Apart from wanting to eat well, these are the dining spots chosen by New Yorkers for that special birthday or anniversary celebration, to share the happiness when your name goes on the door as partner, or when you close that multi-million-dollar deal. So reservations are a must. The longer in advance your request, the better your chance. Making your reservation early in the week rather than on a Friday or Saturday will also affect the odds dramatically.

We've given you some hints about whom to call, but use whatever it takes: the name of a friend who is a regular, or the concierge at the hotel, may work wonders. Sometimes simple persistence pays: a restaurant that was fully booked three days ago may be facing some last-minute cancellations.

Still, it is better than it was in the go-go 1980s, when the diners heading for these watering holes were a veritable stampede. Nowadays, it's crowded but not crazy. Just as there is a bit more elbow room, there is also a slight, but discernible, downward slide in the right-hand columns.

Now go! Enjoy! Who knows how long this trend will last?

# *Aquavit*

13 West 54th Street                              (212) 307-7311
between Fifth and Sixth
New York, NY 10019

Nestled in a landmark townhouse, formerly a Rockefeller residence, Aquavit used to be the only Scandinavian restaurant in town worth mentioning. Make that restaurants. Aquavit has a split personality, encompassing two eateries—a casual à la carte café upstairs and a gracious dining room on the lower level. Both are captivating in their very distinct ways and have been so successful that they've sprouted another noteworthy restaurant, Snaps on Park Avenue.

The café at Aquavit is publike in its congenial atmosphere, encouraged by the long polished blond wood stand-up bar displaying various flavors of the restaurant's namesake beverage. Unpretentious as it may be, the prices are a notch or two above modest. Downstairs, Aquavit evokes a well-bred formality that is seductive enough to steer clear of stuffy. Predictably, the food and the prices are fancier.

Mâitre d' Darren Siegfried will guide you to the Aquavit of your choice. Either way, you're in for a treat because Aquavit is as much a superior seafood restaurant as it is Scandinavian, offering a lot more than raw herring and gravlax, salmon, or halibut. Menus change daily, but you can count on other denizens of cold Northern waters like turbot, sea scallops, and Arctic char (reminiscent of salmon trout) or venison for landlubbers.

Regulars like to trade off between Aquavit's personalities, especially at lunch. The café is for slightly sloppy Danish open-faced sandwiches piled high with ingredients like chicken curry salad or steak tartare ($14 for any two), the dining room for a more decorous meal. Some split the difference by dining downstairs, then stopping by the cafe for takeout — hors d'oeuvres for a pretheater gathering or the makings of a late-night supper. The smoked Swedish salmon at $7 per quarter pound is a popular choice, as is the gravlax at $6.50. Don't forget the sauce, horseradish cream, or lemon mayonnaise for $.75 per ounce.

Opting for luncheon in the serenity of the art-filled atrium usually means serious business in what is arguably the most civilized eating space in town. Well-spaced tables, coupled with the sound absorbency quotient of black leather chairs and carpeted floors, assure private conversation. And the curiously silent waterfall gliding down a massive blue-gray tile wall coupled with colorful, gently swaying mobiles lend visual interest if your attention starts to wander. Given the height and breadth (125 seats) of this lofty chamber, it could be overwhelming. However, there is something almost snug about it. Maybe the stands of birch trees bring it into scale.

For lunch, the dining room is an à la carte affair; dinner is prix fixe. The large, dense Swedish potato pancake called "raggmunk" is a nice foil for the tasty smoked Arctic venison that accompanies it as a filling $9 appetizer. The "one-side sautèed" salmon served with nettle sauce, mushrooms, and beets for $24 has long been a signature dish here. But we lean toward the poached North Atlantic cod in a red pepper sauce with artichoke and olives. The cod holds up to the pungent sauce and is the least expensive entrée at $19.

That's also the price of the café's pretheater dinner, which for a menu like matjes herring, complemented by the expected condiments and followed by grilled salmon steak with cucumber salad and dill mayonnaise, is a steal. À la carte means $25 to $30 for two courses. And the dining room's pretheater rendition is $39, the reason most Aquavit aficionados like Bill Murray, Jackie Onassis, Bryant Gumble, and Kathie Lee Gifford don't bother. For the extra $21, they know they can savor the best Aquavit has to offer— in terms of food and atmosphere.

At night, basking in the glow of candles, the atrium takes on romantic dimensions and the food becomes more intriguing. Witness the cakelike buckwheat blini iced with bleak and trout roes, crème fraiche, and red onion. Then there's the fried pickled herring. You can't go wrong with any of the salmon dishes as a main course, especially the succulent seared version with mesclun salad, sherry vinaigrette, and roasted peppers. But if you like turbot (or have never tried it), spring for the $6 supplement it entails. Here, the flavor of this light white fish is enhanced by a heavenly brown butter sauce made gutsy by horseradish.

All the desserts rank in the good but not memorable category. Actually the whole concept seems an unnecessary afterthought to such rich fare since Chef Johan Ahlstedt remains committed to cream- and butter-based sauces. As far as we're concerned, they should make dessert optional and lob a few bucks off the dinner price. It would help with digesting the dollar figures attached to the wine list.

These are minor quibbles with an otherwise thoroughly enjoyable dining experience, one of the few that is truly unique in a city of so many options.

HOURS:      Noon to 3:00 P.M., Monday through
            Friday; 5:30 P.M. to 10:30 P.M., through
            Saturday.

CREDIT CARDS:      All major.

## Arizona 206

206 East 60th Street                    (212) 838-0440
between 2nd and 3rd Streets
New York, NY 10022

What do you do with a space designed to be an Austrian restaurant, complete with specially commissioned tables, chairs, and benches, that isn't setting the world on fire? If you're the Santos family—Dr. Joseph, his brother Berge, and sister-in-law Henny— you turn Tyrolean into Sante Fe. Stucco walls become adobe, European furniture becomes rustic American, après-ski fireplace becomes Indian hearth, possibly starting the trend for and setting the standards of Southwestern eateries in New York City.

Along the way, Arizona 206 garnered a coveted three stars from *The New York Times*'s Bryan Miller, making the Santoses the only two-time three-star family in town as owners of the equally highly rated Sign of the Dove.

Admittedly our sense of geography mirrors the famous *New Yorker* cover depicting everything west of the Hudson as sort of a vague vastness. And despite its popularity, we're not exactly sure what Southwest fare is. But then maybe Arizona 206 isn't either, which is the ultimate irony of this restaurant. The Santoses' charge to their first chef, Brendan Walsh, was to create a cuisine using ingredients indigenous to the region but not necessarily to duplicate Southwestern dishes. His successor, Marilyn Frobuccino, steered the kitchen to new heights, but in the process flirted with Mediterranean influences.

Now under the youthful guidance (almost thirty) of David Walzog, Arizona 206 has returned to its roots. David keeps both his lunch and dinner menus limited, but they're full of innovative combinations that make sense of Southwestern ingredients. Yet his unfamiliar mergers are provocative; David's menus truly whet the appetite for the zestful food they promise. For lunch, the roast chicken breast in an artichoke sauce, served with a spinach and eggplant salad, is a tasty and representative choice. The same goes for the even more intriguing braised rabbit tortilla laced with asparagus tomato in a wild turkey sauce. Both cost $14.

A three-course sampling of David's creativity, which might include barbequed pork tamales, sautéed rainbow trout garnished with a serrano pepper/yellow tomato salsa, and toasted coconut flan is a bargain at $19.93.

At dinner, often a crowded free-for-all that includes being corralled at the bar for a while, we love the assertive black bean terrine with goat cheese and pear-tomato salad ($8) for a starter. And we can't resist the pan-seared scallops in a translucent garlic broth with oven-dried tomatoes and pumpkin seed pesto (also $8). Then we usually succumb to roasted red snapper in a frothy broth of pickled shallot and serrano, accompanied by grilled Vidalia onion and orzo salad for $23. Grilled Muscovy duck with roast corn flan and an ancho oil-laced cranberry relish is just as seductive for $1 more. Personally, we don't think desserts are the strong suit here. It's not so much that they're not good; it's just that our tastebuds, all revved up a by chilied and peppered meal, don't cotton all that well to sweets afterward.

Any reservations? We don't have many about Arizona 206, despite a high noise level and a seating arrangement that's too close for comfort and that we would find objectionable elsewhere. Here it seems part of the self-consciously informal (though not necessarily unpretentious) scene, right down to the casually attired waiters, who are nonetheless very professional. Of course, we always *do* make reservations for dinner, giving General Manager and Mâitre D'hotel Larry Lazzarro the obligatory week's notice. Still, it is possible to enjoy Arizona 206 on a more spontaneous basis. Just pop into the very casual Arizona Cafe next door, which is just as loud and colorful as its parent. It serves essentially the same food in smaller portions at smaller prices: $8 to $16. The Cafe has a tasting menu, with dishes like the rich $9 fois gras stuffed tortillas that encourage sharing. It's a congenial practice, but one guaranteed to promote the rapid escalation of the tab. Your response to a check here can be akin to the shock which often attends the presentation of the bill for a meal of sushi.

Speaking of sharing, you may notice on the way to the facilities (at least the ladies will) that the Cafe, entered via Arizona 206, also shares space with two other restaurants, Yellowfingers and Contrapunta. These are two more members of the Santos family's restaurants, both delightful venues for a quick sandwich or pasta fix, respectively. Neither is competition in the culinary sweepstakes for its three-star siblings, but given the Santoses' penchant for reincarnations, you never know.

HOURS:      Noon to 3:00 P.M. and 5:30 to 11:00 P.M.,
            Monday through Saturday. 6:00 to 10:30
            P.M. on Sunday.
            The Cafe is open noon to midnight
            Monday through Saturday, till 11:00 P.M.
            on Sunday.

CREDIT CARDS:      All major.

# *Aureole*

34 East 61st Street                    (212) 319-1660
between Park and Madison
New York, NY 10021

Charlie Palmer wins the award for best career move because he traded in his aspirations of playing professional football for becoming a chef. Charlie scored early in the game at The River Cafe and made the all-star team as chef/owner of Aureole. Instantly popular with New York foodies, Aureole gained national recognition in 1992 when DiRONA named it one of the top 25 restaurants in America. As far as we're concerned, that award, along with the three stars from *The New York Times* and the first-place ranking from a New York City restaurant poll, is the classic good news/bad news scenario. The good news is for Charlie, who is getting the credit he deserves; the bad news is for the rest of us, who now find it even more difficult to get a reservation.

Since Aureole's 1988 kickoff, it's taken at least two weeks to get a reservation for the fixed-price dinner; these days, you can count on three. (Reservations for the à la carte lunch remain relatively easy; only a week's notice is generally required!) Of course, the dinner price tag has risen from those first heady days when it was a $45 bargain. Now you're looking at $59, which hovers near the top of the city's fixed-price firmament. Still, fans keep coming. It's a stylish crowd that appreciates the unpretentious yet comfortable atmosphere and Charlie's playful culinary inventions. Charlie was one of the first to explore the now-common practice of combining fish and potatoes into a single dish. His sea scallop "sandwiches," with crisp sautéed potatoes acting as the "bread" and citrus juices filling the role of mayonnaise, are an appetizer staple on the dinner menu and should not be missed. But we're getting ahead of ourselves. We haven't told you that when the evening of your long-awaited dinner reservation arrives, you may be asked to wait a little longer (one of our pet peeves) at the tiny bar. You'll wait even longer if you insist on sitting downstairs. This is the preferred of the two rooms, done in soft, soothing beiges brightened by glorious eruptions of flowers.

Granted, there are diversions. The two-story glass wall fronting the converted townhouse provides a dramatic window of opportunity for watching passersby who go to amusing lengths to camouflage their efforts to look at you! And a review of the wildlife motif of the plaster frieze adorning the cream-colored walls serves as a preview of the daily specials that make good use of the bounty of the American continent.

If you're here at lunch, you should be forewarned. The portions are so large that you may not want both an appetizer and a main course. Two appetizers easily suffice. Try the sugar snap pea soup with poached lobster, laced with Riesling and topped with fresh chervil, followed by the tartare of tuna and salmon dressed with fennel-chive oil and served on brioche toasts with crème fraiche ($12 and $13). Main courses like the pan-seared grouper with a vegetable couscous, given texture by crispy shrimp beignets and flavor by a rich "soup de poisson" sauce, range from $18 to $24. When ordering fish here, take heed of the menu's statement that it is "prepared slightly underdone" — Charlie means it.

For dinner, should the sea scallop sandwiches not appeal, opt for the terrine of natural foie gras with pressed duck confit, accompanied by a new potato salad and confiture of plums as a first course. Despite Charlie's winning way with seafood, we're usually drawn to other entrées, such as seared veal medallions in a roasted garlic sauce with a robust ragout of morels and a cunning little herb potato tart, for instance. And then there is the quail, a bird we generally find pretty useless on the dinner table, but worth ordering for the sensational corn and sweetbread pudding garnish.

The dessert list is a little overwhelming with 13 choices *and* a little plate of handmade chocolates, fancy fruits, and cookies that Charlie treats you to. With that in mind, we like the unusual ricotta cheese tart with caramelized banana. Just as silken as the menu promises, it's a particularly agreeable companion to the chocolates, which also play the role of souvenir. Aureole sells them by the pound — $28 for a half, $14 for a quarter.

HOURS:      Noon to 2:00 P.M., 5:30 to 11:00 P.M.
            Monday through Friday; 5:30 to 11:00 P.M.
            Saturday. Closed Sunday.

CREDIT CARDS:      All major.

# *Ballato*

55 East Houston Street                           (212) 274-8881
between Mulberry and Mott Streets
New York, NY 10022

If you've had it with the city's temples of contemporary Italian chic
and/or their contrived trattoria counterparts, or if you seek Italian
food instantly recognizable as the exotic tomato-laden cuisine you
grew up with, try Ballato.

Founded by John Ballato in 1957, the restaurant operated successfully on a frontier bordering Little Italy and "nowhere," a location which kept Ballato a treasured secret among geographically
adventurous diners. Later, when neighboring Soho was invaded by
the city's art world and long before its axis of the intersection of
West Broadway and Grand became restaurant central, Ballato
served as commissary to the likes of Andy Warhol. And the coming
of the galleries lent a sort of roguish class to the area that induced
such establishment stalwarts as S. I. and Victoria Newhouse to
sample Ballato's well-bred cannelloni.

John's passing did nothing to dim Ballato's siren's song. His
widow Lucia carried on with warm efficiency until retirement
beckoned in 1990. Rumors spread among alarmed patrons that
this signaled the end of an era; there were even prematurely
published reports of Ballato's demise. But Anthony Macagnone,
owner of Grammercy Park's popular Sal Anthony's, had other
ideas. It occurred to him that the tiny (only fifteen tables) Ballato
would be an ideal arena for his sons Anthony, Jr., and William to
earn their restaurant stripes.

In making Ballato their own, the Macagnone boys have made
some changes. The cannelloni has been banished from the menu
(a nod to the 1990s preference for lighter examples of classic
southern Italian fare), and Ballato now takes credit cards. Visual
drama has been replaced by cozy clichés with Lucia's removal of
part of her inheritance from John, the signed Warhols that had
been Andy's gifts over the years. Now the narrow dining room is
sheathed in a dark exotic jungle print wallpaper, brightened by the
gold leaf of ornate frames encasing classic still life and landscapes.
And there has been an expansion of sorts. The backyard, hand-

somely defined by a white picket fence and green-and-white striped awning, serves as a dining annex during the warmer months.

Mercifully, what hasn't changed is the high quality of the food and the astonishingly low prices (two-course fixed-price lunches at $7.50, the three-course dinner version that runs $14.50 until 6:30 P.M.). We're especially taken with the "seafood abbondanza," a sea of calamari, shrimp, and clams covering rice moistened by a sweetly pungent tomato sauce for only $10.50. And we delight in dishes that seldom darken the menus of more au courant establishments, such as chicken breast sautéed in a light cream sauce redolent with fennel and anise for $9.50.

You can count on any of the four pastas at $9 to please. The cold mixed antipasto is a special favorite, a bountiful classic which easily serves two for $5.50. However we construct our meal here, we top it off with the extravagantly delicious ricotta cheesecake. Another holdover from the Ballato family regime, it gets our vote as the galaxy's best. As does this enchanting little restaurant in the best family-run Italian category.

HOURS:   Weekdays 12:00 noon to 3:00 P.M. and 4:00 to 11:00 P.M.; 4:00 P.M. to midnight on Saturday. 1:00 P.M. to 11:00 P.M. on Sunday.

CREDIT CARDS:   All major.

# Bouley

165 Duane Street                     (212) 608-3852
Hudson and Greenwich
New York, NY 10013

Few among the city's growing list of celebrity chef/owners have traveled so illustrious a route to their current status. Born into a French-American family, David Bouley studied with Roger Verge and Paul Bocuse. He's a veteran of Le Cirque, and his talents launched Montrachet, which lured even those who claimed ignorance of territory south to TriBeCa.

With Bouley, David has put this increasingly trendy neighborhood on the world's culinary map. It has been a hit since opening day in August of 1987. Now David and Bouley have outdistanced legends such as Andre Soltner and the venerable Lutèce to top most lists of the city's best eateries. (Of course, frequent gossip column items about sightings of David tête-à-têting with Bernadette Peters haven't hurt his star status either!)

Like Lutèce, Bouley is homey rather than grand despite the outstanding and very formal dining it offers. The result of a labor of love on the part of David, his brother, and a makeshift crew of helpers who hammered every nail and painted every wall, the restaurant has a pleasant rather than spectacular ambience. As Provençal as the pastel scenes of that French region that adorn them, the walls are whitewashed and the ceilings vaulted. Both glow from discreet overhead lighting and the charming little lamps on each table with their pleated shades. An 18-foot flower box runs the length of the front windows and is always bursting with seasonal blooms.

It's all very low key, very understated, just like the waiters who nonetheless serve each morsel as if it were a precious jewel. And well they should. The food emanating from David's kitchen is sublime, made all the more so by his eschewing the use of heavy cream or copious amounts of butter in any of his dishes.

Lunch, peopled primarily by men of the Wall Street and City Hall species, is served either as a five-course menu degustation for $32, or à la carte. If you opt for the latter, it'll probably run you a little more. We suggest the menu, but not because it's less expensive. We like the fact that it represents David's best efforts and eliminates agonizing decisions, allowing concentration on the serious business of eavesdropping about the power politicos' plans for the city's future. You'll be treated to a feast that might start with a vibrant mixture of fresh asparagus and Maine crabmeat in a chive and leek dressing.

Next, choose between delicacies like Maine monkfish in a tomato coriander sauce, accented with sweet roasted garlic and savory cabbage or roast Pennsylvania chicken with French flageolot beans. A salad course comes after the entrée — warm goat cheese, last time we checked — succeeded by a refreshing fresh fruit sorbet and dessert. Try the chocolate soufflé!

For dinner, we advise skipping the $70 seven-course menu in favor of the à la carte suggestions. It's not any less tempting than the luncheon version, nor are eavesdropping opportunities any less compelling. Bill Cosby, Warren Beatty, Richard Gere and Cindy Crawford, Steven Spielberg, and, *of course*, Dustin Hoffman often enjoy dinner here. (David says it's such a pleasure watching Dustin in a restaurant because "he's so much at home and he *loves* to eat!") But since you're here for the evening, you should make the most of it — foodwise. Part of the fun is discussing all the selections, each more mouthwatering than the last, and enjoying bites of your companion's choices, as well as relishing your own.

Just when you and yours have settled on appetizers of creamless asparagus soup garnished with sweet roasted beets for $8 and the panache of three salads — hot goose foie gras, grilled shrimp, and wild mushrooms — for $15, you spot the extensive list of daily specials. All of a sudden you have to think long and hard about the $10 eggplant terrine topped by a parsley sauce or a lobster salad which showcases David's uncanny intuition for textures and flavors. Poached lobster rests on glazed endives and watercress, moistened by a yellow pepper and orange dressing for $16.

Having delighted in a debate on the merits of each, you move on to the entrées. Here again, David always slides in seasonal specials, but we have developed a passion for the honey-glazed duckling with roasted shallots, turnips, and sweet peas. At $24, it's a robust dish and such a relief from the ubiquitous, often tasteless duck breast found at less exciting restaurants. We're equally enamored of the roast loin of veal, accompanied by Bermuda onions braised in red wine and a rich puree made from the vegetable of the moment, the Yukon gold potato, for $32.

Dessert provides another quandary. The selection of imported and domestic cheeses (always the mark of a *real* French restaurant) usually gets our vote at $12, although similarly priced chocolate soufflé crowned with hot chocolate sauce and garnished with maple ice cream melting over a banana tart is awfully tempting. And where else would we even dream of ordering rice pudding? Here this humble dessert is made regal by a fresh fruit compote and apricot coulis for $9. The best solution is to ask the waiter for a sampling of each. Don't be shy about asking; they're used to it.

Indeed, requests — rather exceptional ones at that — are a house specialty. We know a gentleman who wanted to give his gourmet cook lady love a very special birthday present. So he took her to dinner at Bouley armed with a brand-spanking-new sauté pan, which he asked David to season. David graciously complied.

Always the innovator, in and out of the kitchen, David employs a computer to keep track of his patrons, their reservations, and meals.

On the downside, if you're one of that breed most despised by restaurateurs, a "no-show," manager Melissa Gossnel will know it next time you call. Expect a chilly reception. On the upside, each of your Bouley meals will be kept on file so you can always track down the source of that unforgettable taste sensation and request it.

As for reservations, they are an absolute must. And you wouldn't be overly cautious by giving them four weeks' notice of your desired date, at least for dinner. But if you breeze into town with Bouley on the brain, don't hesitate to call about last-minute cancellations. Afraid of David's and Melissa's censure, most people really do notify Bouley of a change in plans—you might just get lucky!

HOURS: Noon to 2:30 P.M., Monday through Friday. 5:30 to 11:00 P.M., Monday through Saturday. Closed on Sunday.

CREDIT CARDS: All major.

## Grandmother Bouley's Rice Pudding

**Ingredients**

**Rice**

1 cup rice (Carolina)
3 cups milk
1 vanilla bean
1/2 zest of one orange
1/2 cup sugar

**Anglaise**

1 cup milk
4 egg yolks
2 ounces sugar
1 ounce gelatin
1 pint whipped cream (soft)
2 ounces sugar

**Plum or Apricot Compote**

1 pound sugar cooked to 250°F
2 pounds 2 ounces pitted plums or apricots
1 vanilla bean

## Preparation
### Rice Pudding

1. Blanch rice in water 3-4 minutes. Strain and rinse.
2. Pour the boiling milk with the vanilla, the zest, and the sugar over rice and bake covered in the oven at 350 °F, about 35 minutes or until rice has absorbed all the liquid. Stir occasionally.
3. Cook the anglaise with the milk, yolks, and sugar until thickened. Be careful not to curdle the eggs.
4. When thickened, remove from heat and add softened gelatin while anglaise is still hot.
5. When rice has cooked, spread out on a pan to cool. And when both rice and anglaise are cool, mix with whisk in bowl and fold in whipped cream over rice.
6. Place rice in molds and chill.

### Compote

1. Add 1/2 cup of water to sugar and cook to 250 °F.
2. Pour over halved fruit in wide-bottomed stainless steel pot.
3. Stir gently when necessary and cook over medium flame till sugar reaches 220 °F.
4. Some compote can be placed in the bottom of the mold filled with rice pudding or served on the side.

# Café des Artistes

One West 67th Street          (212) 877-3500
between Central Park West and
Columbus
New York, NY 10023

Café des Artistes, New York's archetypal neighborhood restaurant, may also be its best loved. According to the *Zagat New York City Restaurant Survey*, it is the restaurant most often visited by the publication's five-thousand-plus contributors. One survey respondent went so far as to describe Café des Artistes as a rendezvous where "you could fall in love with your IRS agent during an audit."

Certainly only the most cynical could fail to fall under the Café's spell from the moment they first cross the threshold to be greeted by Howard Chandler Christy's effervescent murals. Some thirty-six perky nymphs called the "Christy Girls" (more flirtatious than their chaste Gibson contemporaries) frolic across the walls in a verdant fantasy forest, unashamed of their seductive but never naughty nudity. Indeed, for decades the Café des Artistes was justifiably more celebrated for the romance of its decor than for its food.

A call from media maven Dave Garth to internationally renowned restaurant consultant George Lang in 1975 marked the beginning of a new, more gustatorily glamorous era for the venerable establishment. Representing the board of directors of the Café's parent building, the Hotel des Artistes, Garth asked George if he would be interested in taking over the restaurant. He wasn't until a couple of nights later when, in the midst of a downpour, he and his wife, who live just down the street from the Café, were unable to get a cab. Then it occurred to George: "If I had a successful restaurant on this block, we could always get a cab."

The rest, as they say, is history, one to add to the Café's already considerable heritage. It debuted in 1917 as the commissary for the Hotel des Artistes, the apartments of which were purposely built without kitchens. Residents sent ingredients to the Café via dumbwaiter with instructions as to how they should be fashioned into a meal. However, the system soon broke down and the Café was opened to a devoted public that soon included Rudolph Valentino, Isadora Duncan, and Noel Coward. Today their ghosts mingle with the likes of Paul Newman, Peter Jennings, Barbara Walters, and James Levine, who consider Café des Artistes home. Their proprietary feelings don't bother George; he wanted to "re-create the warmth of a middle European coffeehouse restaurant that is occasionally left by the habitués for such necessities as brief and dutiful visits to their homes before returning to their *stammtisch* or regular table."

The fact that reservations are a must and not easy to come by is testimony to George's success. Weekends are crowded, especially at pretheater and Sunday brunch time, both requiring a good two weeks' advance notice. Three days to a week usually does it Monday through Thursday for dinner. Week day lunches are the best spur-of-the-moment bet — you can often get a table with a call by mid-morning.

Once you secure that coveted reservation, expect to be cosseted, not only by the captivating atmosphere, but by solicitously professional service and most importantly by what George describes as "Sunday supper comfort food—good solid middle-class food, cuisine bourgeois—cooked with the best ingredients and without any shortcuts." We buy his analysis of the actual cooking, but we don't remember too many homecooked meals featuring smoked sea scallops or sweetbreads in a crust of Japanese bread crumbs served with smoked tenderloin of pork!

Still, despite not growing up in Europe, the very thought of pot-au-feu, lentil cassoulet, and ragout of wild boar warms our hearts, while roast beef hash or chicken casserole does sound like Sunday supper at Grandma's (although we doubt she ever even heard of jalapeño peppers, let alone used them in this dish).

Whatever your definition of comfort food, you may find the prices here a tad discomforting. Except for a single pasta dish at $17, dinner main courses range from $20 to $29, making the $32.50 prix fixe a steal. If you are operating on a budget, the same goes for lunch. The $19.50 three-course lunch is a bargain on a menu where the appetizers go for $5 to $14 and the entrées start at $14.

Of course, we never let anything so crass as money interfere with our enjoyment of Café des Artistes. We go for dinner, when candlelight makes the restaurant downright bewitching, and indulge. We start with salmon four ways—smoked, poached, dill-marinated, and tartare—at $30 for two, and then go on to the ultimate extravagance of a second appetizer. We just can't resist the $6 sweetbread headcheese with its piquant vinaigrette. For the main event, the Provençal specialty called bourride, which is essentially a seafood casserole laced with aioli, never fails to beckon for $23. The steak tartare is made unforgettable with a hint of curry at $20.

Then it's back to sharing the to-die-for $19.50 chocolatissimo, a platter of chocolate-based cakes and tortes flavored with raspberries, hazelnuts, walnuts, and other sinfully rich ingredients.

As for wine, the list is refreshingly short and fairly priced. Look for George's selections, respectable and usually under $20 a bottle, or for the assortment of $22 wines which are presented by the waiter in a basket—yet another nice homey touch in this warmest of restaurants.

HOURS:      Noon to 3:00 P.M., Monday to Saturday.
            10:00 A.M. to 3:00 P.M. on Sunday. 5:30 P.M.
            to 12:15 A.M., Monday through Saturday.
            Sunday from 5:00 to 11:00 P.M.

CREDIT CARDS:    All major.

# Carnegie Delicatessen & Restaurant

854 Seventh Avenue      (212) 757-2245, 2246, or 2247
at 55th Street                     (212) 757-9889
New York, NY 10019

Carnegie Deli has long been synonymous with mountains disguised as sandwiches, peaks of savory meats capped with tasty condiments, and long lines of people waiting to take a crack at them. The sandwiches remain awesome, but waiting in line has improved somewhat since feisty owner Milton Parker recently added a new dining room, doubling the seating capacity.

That was a welcome improvement for this ever-popular New York institution. It doesn't matter that the chairs are decidedly uncomfortable and the tables so close together that you need to be a contortionist to unfold the giant menu without socking your neighbor. So why do so many people bother to come here so often?

Simple — the good food and long hours. Where else can you find a whopping $15.95 reuben to give you that much-needed second wind at 3:00 A.M.? And the crowded hustle and bustle is all part of the fun. Somehow you don't mind having your plate whipped off the table as you consume that last morsel of food. Apparently Jackie Mason (smitten with the borscht with chopped vegetables), Sharon Stone, Alec Baldwin, Meryl Streep, Danny Aiello, Joe DiMaggio, and Joan Rivers don't, either. They all come in — and yes, they have to stand in line like anybody else.

It's Milton's law, one of many that make this sixty-year-old landmark unique. Other laws are not accepting credit cards, slapping you with a $3 fine if you choose to share, not accepting substitutions in any of the gargantuan sandwiches, and keeping food standards high. The last is so important to Milton that he built a commissary to do Carnegie's baking and food processing, making it the only deli in town to smoke and pickle its own meats.

Another of Milton's laws is that no one take advantage of Carnegie's good name and reputation: "Even Mickey Mouse is trying to get into the act. They illegally opened a Carnegie in Euro-Disney. I'm suing." And as far as the Beverly Hills Carnegie goes... well, Milton admits that movie mogul Marvin Davis has the right to use the name. But he wants you to know that Marvin's place doesn't carry any of the real Carnegie products and, in his not so humble opinion, Marvin's people don't have the foggiest idea how to run a Carnegie satellite. He even said, "I totally disown it!"

Don't get us wrong. Milton's no curmudgeon and he does have a sense of humor. During the 1992 presidential campaign, he offered topical sandwiches, such as the Al Gore—lettuce, tomato, cucumber, and sliced green peppers on toasted wheat with mayonnaise, which he described as "a nice clean sandwich for an environmentalist." Then there was the President Bush—chopped egg and tuna on white, "no meat and soft like the economy."

But sandwiches are only part of the story here. The scope of the menu is staggering, from omelettes to sardine salad. The fabulous $10.95 blintzes are made to order with your choice of cheese, strawberries, blueberries, or cherries. The prime brisket of beef drenched in gravy and served with potato pancake, vegetable, and coleslaw is an icon at $16.95. The corned beef or pastrami hash is made with Milton's home-processed meats and made only when you order it, for $11.95.

As you might imagine, the staff consists of a true cast of characters. One of our favorites is Jack Sirota, who's been here for at least thirty-five years. He claims he doesn't look any different today than he did the day he first set foot on the premises. But then Jack has a reputation as quite a storyteller!

If you're shy about being a *fresser* (Yiddish for big eater) in public, you don't have to do without the Carnegie. They deliver, any time between 6:30 A.M. and 4:00 A.M. It's free in the area bounded by 50th and 60th streets; a nominal fee is charged for points farther north or south.

HOURS:       6:30 A.M. to 4:00 A.M. Seven days a week.

CREDIT CARDS:       None.

# *Chanterelle*

2 Harrison Street                                    (212) 966-6960
New York, NY 10013

Karen and David Waltuck's first Chanterelle paved the way for destination restaurants in Soho. Its much-anticipated second coming at the corner of Harrison and Hudson streets is another bright star to TriBeCa's growing restaurant firmament, which includes Bouley and Montrachet. Indeed, Chanterelle's chic has been given the imprimatur of no less an expert than *Vogue* editor-in-chief Anna Wintour, who hosted a gala there for legendary fashion photographer Irving Penn. A parade of the city's premier party-goers crossed Chanterelle's threshold to pay homage to Penn and to treat their jaded palates to David's clever but never cutesy combinations of flavors and textures, enhanced by his classic sauces. Calvin and Kelly Klein, Oscar de la Renta, Bruce Weber, Henry Kravis and Carolyne Roehm, Grace Mirabella, and Patrick de Marchelia were among the guests who serenaded both masters with praise.

Of course Penn and David have heard it all before, and from equally stellar sources. Since the days of the first Chanterelle, David's cooking has attracted a sophisticated clientele. Robert de Niro along with Naomi Campbell (or Toukie Smith), Frank and Barbara Sinatra, Issac Mizrahi, Sandra Bernhard, Robert Redford, and Sonia Braga are devotees. But you don't have to be a "name" to be sure that you won't be left languishing at the bar because there isn't one. Your reservation will be honored in a timely fashion, despite Chanterelle's extraordinary success and the fact that it only seats sixty.

In no time at all, you'll be escorted through the small entrance foyer into the simple majesty that is the dining room. Towering windows facing both streets rise to meet the ornate, pressed-tin ceiling and its three brass chandeliers, which are the room's focal point. No art adorns the peach walls; no flowers clutter the tables because Karen continues to do the room in sumptuous flowers. Chanterelle's is a studied, pure environment that forces concentration on the food. It is a place meant for serious dining, especially at dinner. There's a three-course $68 menu with a number of choices in each category, and the six-course tasting menu at $87. There's no à la carte and you should plan on a leisurely meal. You might even want to choose the $40 market menu (chef's choice). The menus are revamped monthly and their covers are revamped twice a year. Saluting Chanterelle's first incarnation as a popular spot with Soho's artsy crowd, each cover features the work of a different master, such as Elsworth Kelly, Roy Lichtenstein, Robert Maplethorpe, John Cage, Francesco Clemente, or Robert Indiana. Even Bill Cosby's work has been showcased, adding him to the growing list of show business people who have found restaurants appropriate venues for the display of their artistic avocation.

Inside the colorful covers, the menus are outlined in a sprawling handwritten black script. When we last visited, the $70 dinner featured a selection of five appetizers, eight entrées, and six desserts. We dove into David's signature dish, which appears on almost every menu: sublime grilled seafood sausage and sautéed foie gras with the unusual accent of gingered carrots for a first course. The poached salmon in basil butter and red snapper in a lime vinaigrette are testimony to David's daily forays to the Fulton Fish Market. The blood orange soup with winter fruits is a terrific seasonal choice for dessert, as is a strawberry and rhubarb shortcake. And anytime of year, you can count on a delicious assortment of homemade ice creams and sherbets.

Needless to say, the tasting menu is always tempting. Just be sure you've gone into training for a week before you attempt it. Last time we took the plunge, it began with a rich terrine of foie gras punctuated by blond raisins. A truffled chicken consommé with truffled quenelles lightened things up a bit and was followed by succulent Maine sea scallops dotted with sesame seeds, ginger, and tomato sauce. Rack of lamb distinguished by a cumin and salt crust rounded off the meal, which was topped by a selection of cheese and a passion fruit crepe in raspberry sauce. When you consider the quality of the requisite three hours of gustatory entertainment, the $87 price tag becomes pretty palatable.

If you want to sample Chanterelle on the (relatively) cheap—go for lunch when the $68 menu is abbreviated in terms of choice and priced to $30. À la carte selections, ranging from $7.50 to $13.00

for appetizers and $18.50 to $24.00 for entrées, are also available. *And* it's a lot easier to get a reservation!

HOURS:          Noon to 2:30 P.M. and 6:00 P.M. to 10:30
                Tuesday through Saturday.

CREDIT CARDS:   All major.

# Docks

Oyster Bar and Seafood Grill          (212) 724-5588
2427 Broadway
New York, NY 10024

633 Third Avenue                      (212) 986-8080
New York, NY 10017

In search of a restaurant concept, pals Howie Levine, Barry Corwin, and Arthur Cutler stumbled on the fact that Manhattan lacked a good, reasonably priced seafood restaurant. They filled the void with Docks on the Upper West Side at 89th and Broadway, an instant smash hit. Barely three years after the 1985 Broadway opening, a second Docks debuted, on Third Avenue. It seems that East Siders had been clamoring for the same fresh fish, mollusks, and crustaceans that had been the draw on the West Side. Indeed, the menus are identical at both locations, but the atmosphere is somewhat different.

For starters, the Third Avenue restaurant is considerably larger than its predecessor. And though Howard, Barry, and Arthur claim it was unintentional, it has a slightly more upscale look and feel to it. There are better prints on the walls and fancier lighting fixtures. Still, both restaurants benefit from a handsome decor featuring lots of tile, brass, and wood. They are the visual version of onomatopoeia. They look exactly like what they are —comfortable, old-fashioned, basic seafood houses where fish and their shelled brethren are cooked to pure perfection.

As such, they attract a cross-cultural crowd. Docks on Broadway tends to draw from the neighborhood, an eclectic lot, while Third Avenue gets more than its share of legal, publishing, and garment industry people who find its just slightly east-of-midtown location handy for lunch and dinner. In fact, we must admit that while we hold a sentimental place in our hearts for the first Docks, the people-watching at its East Side offspring is better.

At 5:00 in the afternoon, you see little old blue-haired ladies in search of their manhattans and broiled sole. Later on, the power ties and suspenders group comes in for their belon oysters, 3-lb. lobsters, and bottles of Chardonnay. It's about this time that the Third Avenue Docks becomes a bit of a meat market (despite what it serves) — a single woman threading her way to her seat through the packed bar does so at her own risk. Still, the regulars' ranks are enlivened by the frequent presence of William F. Buckley, Kathleen Turner, Robert Duvall, Paul Simon, Jerry Orbach, Jackie Mason, and Harrison J. Goldin.

We generally start our Docks seafood binge with a selection of the four varieties of oysters offered nightly. Priced per piece and according to market value, we've been known to mix them with some littleneck or cherrystone clams—they're all just so succulently moist and fresh. The fried calamari, just as light and scrumptious as can be at $6, is another favorite starter. For the most part, fish is either simply grilled, broiled, or fried, with an occasional sauced rendition among the specials. You can't go wrong with any of the grilled "steaks"—salmon, swordfish, tuna, snapper, or halibut, all in the $17 to $18 range. And the fried oysters served with a sublime tartar sauce are terrific at $16. All entrees are served with Docks's sensational coleslaw (tartly sweet and mercifully not drowned in mayonnaise) along with a choice of potato (baked or fried) or rice. Be sure to order the french fried yams on the side for $2.75—you won't regret it.

Reservations for dinner, at either location, are a good idea even on Sunday and Monday. Clever restaurateurs that they are, Howie, Barry, and Arthur have made those traditionally slow nights hot with a bargain-priced New England clambake—only $27 for a two-pound lobster crowning a wave of mussels, clams, new potatoes, and corn on the cob. If you care, it also includes key lime pie or ice cream!

As for "land-locked" items, there are some on the menu like a $21 grilled New York shell steak and an $8.75 burger, but why bother? If you think fish belongs in the water and not on a plate, go elsewhere.

HOURS:         11:30 A.M. to 11:00 P.M., Sunday through
                      Thursday; till midnight on Friday and
                      Saturday.
CREDIT CARDS:      All major.

# Ferrara

195 Grand Street                                    (212) 226-6150
New York, NY 10013                          Fax (212) 226-0667

New York in the Gay Nineties had everything, except for a place
where an Italian opera singer (or anyone else, for that matter)
could sit, relax, and sip a few cups of espresso, chased by a sweet or
two. Enter opera impresario Antonio Ferrara and his pal Enrico
Scoppa. In 1892, they opened Caffe A. Ferrara in the heart of what
is now known as Little Italy.

Even though no less an authority than Enrico Caruso loved the
place, the neighborhood café didn't come into its own as a world-
famous destination until the arrival of Antonio's nephew Peter
shortly after World War I. The enterprising youth, who made his
way to America as a stowaway on a New York-bound ship, united
the founding partners by marrying Enrico's daughter. This created
the family dynasty that still owns what has become simply Ferrara.

Famous and commercial though it is with its mail-order catalogue, Ferrara retains an old-world charm. The little rectangular
marble tables are squeezed close together and the atmosphere
depends on the crowd that comes from all over the city. It remains
the sort of place you drop by on the spur of the moment, at almost
anytime of day or night. Ferrara opens every morning at 7:30 and
doesn't close until midnight. It's busiest after 6 P.M. By nine o'clock
there's a line outside because seating is on a first-come, first-
served basis. If you show up late in the evening as many do, expect
a fifteen- to twenty-minute wait.

Ferrara is so popular because it's the perfect "after" place —
after lunch or after dinner. Lee Iacocca, Frank Sinatra, and the
last three U.S. Presidents have come here to sample the decadent
pastries, not to mention the best espresso and cappuccino in town.
During the summer, they set up an ice cream stand, so you can
stop for a cone and then continue your stroll through Little Italy
on to Chinatown.

Light breakfasts and lunches are also served, but the allure of Ferrara is the desserts, all made on the premises. The cannoli, those most traditional of Italian pastries, are superb. At $2.25 you can have as many as you wish. Even the tiramisu (a concoction we usually dread) is nothing short of addictive. Here the Italian pick-me-up really does so with lady fingers doused in espresso laced with coffee liqueur and smothered in blended cream. It packs a wallop for only $4.50!

The cookies can be packaged for takeout at $12 per assorted pound. They make great gifts and can be shipped anywhere in the world—as can all the Ferrara products, as outlined in the aforementioned catalogue.

As it enters its second century, Ferrara has carved a unique niche in the heart and appetite of New York.

HOURS:        7:30 A.M. to midnight, daily.

CREDIT CARDS:    All major.

# The Four Seasons

99 East 52nd Street                    (212) PL4-9494
between Park and Lexington
New York, NY 10022

A culinary landmark since 1959, The Four Seasons became an architectural one as well in 1990 when it was granted landmark status by the New York City Board of Estimates. The Philip Johnson-designed restaurant is the first interior to be so honored in Manhattan, a source of great pride to the owners even though the designation means they no longer control its aesthetics. They feel very strongly about the space, originally planned as an automobile showroom. "We treated it as a landmark, even when it wasn't," explains Vice President and General Manager Alex von Bidder. "We're just caretakers" of a space that Richard Lippold, whose dramatic sculpture of hanging brass rods defines the bar, describes as "One of the great rooms of the world."

Actually, The Four Seasons is two rooms and, increasingly, two restaurants. Both the Grill and Pool rooms are large, square, twenty feet tall, and framed on two sides by walls of windows swathed in chain metal which plays hypnotic rhythms with the light. There the similarities end. The Grill is monumental, as befits a room which *Forbes* described as having "more power personalities per meal than any other place on earth including the White House." Widely spaced tables, along with the sound absorption capacity of leather banquettes and French walnut walls ($1 million worth in 1959) assure privacy for their power-punched parleys. The somehow more frivolous Pool Room, connected to The Grill by a travertine-lined corridor hung with a huge Picasso tapestry, is arranged around a gurgling white-marble pool, illuminated trees planted around its four corners.

At lunch, the unflappable Alex holds the key to the prized tables in The Grill. The Pool Room is open, but only the uninitiated happily walk down that corridor to "Siberia." The regulars, people like Henry Kissinger, Jackie Onassis, Bill Blass, Si Newhouse, Michael Korda, Philip Johnson, and Grace Mirabella vie for the restful Mies van der Rohe-designed chairs in the Grill. Once settled, they dive into meals that by Four Seasons' standards are unassuming and uncomplicated, created by tag-team chefs Christian Albin and Stefano Battistini *not* to compete for attention with important conversations. As such the food is perfection. The menus are in a constant state of flux, both seasonally and daily, so there's always something new to try—no doubt in deference to those very regular regulars.

During the spring look for appetizers like a velvety sweetbread and corn terrine for $14.50, Parma prosciutto with fresh figs at $13.50, and a $17.50 shrimp cocktail. As for the entrées, the roasted swordfish with asparagus and porcini, and a skewer of grilled sea scallops, both at $34, are good choices. Ditto sautéed calf's liver sweetened by Vidalia onions at $31.50. Lunch for two in The Grill with wine can and will probably edge into the $160 neighborhood.

You should consider ordering a bit of the grape here. The wine list, renowned for its breadth of selections and prices, has long served as a guide to other restaurants. Because of The Four Seasons' buying power, the owners are often able to get good deals on some exceptional wines, which are added to the list with a relatively low markup.

There was a time when we would have instructed you to sit only in the elegantly relaxed Pool Room for dinner; at night the Grill was moribund. No longer. In the interests of making The Four Seasons more accessible to an increasingly price-conscious public,

Alex and manager Julian Niccolini banished the $85-per-person à la carte menu in favor of three-course fixed-price offerings at $29.50 to $37.50 (determined by the main course) and instituted The Grill at Night—essentially a second restaurant. "People were afraid of The Four Seasons," says Alex. "We wanted to attract new, younger diners so in our advertisements we even made the logo playful and virtually buried The Four Seasons name in small type." The ploy worked and the Grill Room at Night is now booked in advance every night.

On our last outing, the list of six appetizers included delightful "scallopops" (sesame-coated scallops on a stick), shrimp fried in rice paper with a mustardy apricot marmalade, and an eruption of spring greens from a volcano of tomatoes in a maple mustard and lime vinaigrette. Among the entrées, we liked the grilled mahi mahi with roasted onions, pineapple, and green peppercorns, as well as luscious lamb filet and mushroom mixture encased in a thin baked pastry ($35 and $34). For dessert, don't miss the bittersweet chocolate cake or the strawberry rhubarb shortcake.

To complete the wallet-friendly premise, The Grill at Night features an all-American wine list, which started out as "30 Under $30." Now it's up to forty wines, but $30 remains the top tag.

Miraculously, Alex and Julian have made a success of the "new" restaurant without losing their Pool Room dinner business. Its sophisticated, innovative à la carte menu and gracious luxury continue to attract a nightly full house. Diners savor dishes such as braised frogs' legs arranged over savoy cabbage at $14.50 and a sublime sorrel and crayfish chowder for $11.50 as starters. Filet of red snapper caressed by a merlot sauce and barbecued whole sweetbreads served with a pepper tart ($37 and $35) are representative entrées, as is the classic chateaubriand for two, carved tableside, at $45 per person. Dinner can easily run up to $225 a couple with a salad or vegetable ($6.50 to $9.50), wine, and dessert.

For those watching their diets, the Pool Room tenders low-sodium, low-cholesterol, and low-fat spa cuisine selections. Developed in accord with recommendations from the Columbia University School of Nutrition, the spa dishes might include mussels in green chili sauce for $13 and roast loin of rabbit with asparagus and bulgar at $32.

There's also a popular three-course $41.50 pre-and post-theater menu, augmented by spa cuisine items. And no matter where you dine, which Four Seasons you experience, or what menu you order from, you will be treated to service that can only be described as seamless.

Clearly The Four Seasons is a restaurant that not only celebrates all seasons but covers all bases. There's something here for everyone, depending upon mood and budget. For dinner, either in The Pool Room or The Grill on the weekend, reserve a week in advance. Three days should do it during the week. As for lunch in The Grill, call Alex and beg for mercy!

HOURS:   Lunch: Noon to 1:45 P.M. (till 2:30 P.M. in the Pool Room), Monday through Friday. Dinner: 5:00 to 9:00 P.M. Monday through Friday; Grill Room 5:30 P.M. to 10:30 P.M., Park Room 5:30 to 11:15 P.M. Saturday.

CREDIT CARDS:   All major.

# *Fu's*

972 Second Avenue                    (212) 517-9670
between 51st and 52nd
New York, NY 10021

You could almost hear the neighborhood's sigh of relief when it was announced that Fu's was finished. Everyone's favorite Chinese restaurant would lose its lease, but at least it would stay put on Second Avenue just below 52nd Street. All hell broke loose when it became known that Fu's was losing something even more valuable than its lease — the indomitable Hostess/Manager Gloria Chu.

To many people, Gloria *was* Fu's. Gloria was the magnet for a high-powered clientele, such an integral part of Fu's appeal that there was a common misperception that she owned the place. It's one she used to encourage. No longer — not since the latest Fu's flap, when the restaurant ran afoul of the IRS.

In actual fact, Gloria is a noted restaurant consultant, a dynamite cook, and an old friend of owner Michael Leung. He asked her to help out with Fu's when it first opened, and somewhat to her surprise, she remained until all the fuss with the feds made it "impossible for me to stay."

So now the restaurant she still describes as "my baby" is Gloria-less. For the time being, the reasonable prices, better-than-good food, and surprisingly sophisticated contemporay decor are holding their own. But habitués miss Gloria's whirling dervish imitation as she darted among tables telling who's who and what's what. She'd whisper conspiratorially that Paul Newman actually sat in "your" burgundy arm chair the other night or that it was such a thrill to see John Kennedy, Jr.'s too-handsome-for-words face reflected in Fu's strategically placed mirrors. In rapid-fire, only slightly accented English she would reel off names of Fu's fashion-crowd regulars — Missoni, Laura Biagiotti, and Saks's Mel Jacobs — as well as the media people like Mike Wallace, Barbara Walters, and Cindy Adams.

Fortunately for Fu's, what the regulars do not miss is the coddling that made it unnecessary to even glance at a menu. Gloria's protégé Michael To carries on her tradition of custom designing memorable meals. All you have to do is answer a couple of questions about your taste in Chinese food and inform him about any dietary restrictions you may have. The rest is up to him. And like his predecessor, Michael never fails to please.

Unless you're a vegetarian, he usually includes Peking duck. It's a house specialty and quite a show. The whole duck, all crispy golden brown, arrives tableside, where it is flamboyantly carved and served. At $32.95, one duck serves at least four.

If you leave it all to Michael, you'll experience a rich variety of textures and flavors, generally four or five courses not counting dessert, which he tends to ignore other than passing out the ritual fortune cookie. In addition to the duck, we always look forward to the delicately sweet Grand Marnier® shrimp, another house specialty although it's not on the menu. But if you take our advice and let Michael do the ordering, it usually appears — four jumbo shrimp breaded with water chestnut flour, deep fried, and then sauced with Grand Marnier® as an appetizer for two at $9.95. It's a complementary precursor to that old reliable that is made special at Fu's — crispy orange beef for $15.95 — and another Chinese standard which is particularly well turned out here, the hot and spicy sesame chicken for $11.95. All of the dishes are beautifully presented and impeccably served, according to exacting standards set during Gloria's reign and continued by Michael.

Dinner for two, Michael-style, usually runs about $70 for food. He makes no decisions about libations, so in that area, at least, you're on your own and in control of costs.

HOURS:         Noon to 11:30 P.M, daily.

CREDIT CARDS:         All major.

## Crispy Orange Beef from Fu's

**Ingredients**

    1 pound flank steak
    1 green pepper
    1 red pepper

    1/2 teaspoon salt
    2 teaspoons baking soda
    1 egg
    3 ounces cornstarch

    soy bean oil

**A Ingredients**

    5 pieces dried orange peel, crushed
    1 teaspoon minced garlic
    1 teaspoon minced ginger
    1 teaspoon diced scallion (white portion)
    5 pieces dried red pepper (varies according to degree of spice)

**B Ingredients**

    1/2 cup chicken stock
    5 teaspoons sugar
    2 teaspoons white vinegar
    2 teaspoons Gold Medal soy sauce
    1 teaspoon Maggi seasoning sauce
    1 teaspoon oyster sauce
    1 dash pepper powder
    1 teaspoon cooking sherry

**C Ingredients**

    1 teaspoon cornstarch mixed with 2 teaspoons water
    1 teaspoon sesame oil

    parsley and turnips for garnish

**Preparation**

1. Cut flank steak into 14 to 16 pieces, 2" × 1", 1/2" thick. Flush thoroughly with water and drain. Pat dry and set aside.
2. Dice green and red peppers; set aside.
3. Combine salt, egg, baking soda, cornstarch, and 1 teaspoon soy bean oil, then coat beef with the mixture.
4. Heat more soy bean oil (enough to cover the beef) in a wok until it's very hot.
5. Cook the beef on medium heat for about five minutes or until it's crispy.
6. Remove from heat and drain.
7. Drain most of the oil from the wok, then add peppers and all *A* ingredients. Stir fry for about 30 seconds.
8. Re-add beef and all *B* ingredients. Stir fry for another 30 seconds.
9. Add all *C* ingredients. Stir fry for another 30 seconds.
10. Garnish with parsley and turnips.

Serves four.

# Gallagher's

228 West 52nd Street                    (212) 245-5336
between Broadway and 8th Avenue
New York, NY 10019

Big, bold, brassy, and oh, so Broadway, Gallagher's has remained a stalwart on the steak house circuit for 66 years and countless musicals since opening a few nights before the debut of the immortal *Funny Face* next door in 1927. In fact, Gallagher's claims to have been the nation's first steak house, the brain child of former Ziegfeld girl Helen Gallagher and her flamboyant Jack Solomon.

Like "21," Gallagher's was first operated as a speakeasy, but when Prohibition became an unpleasant memory, Helen and Jack decided to broaden its horizons into a full-fledged restaurant. Their concept added a new dimension to American cuisine. They retreated from the formal, plush elegance and fancy food then de rigueur for restaurants. They went back to basics: plain plank floors, wood-paneled walls, red-checkered tablecloths, and steaks. As the genesis of a new breed, Gallagher's pleasing blend of speakeasy and country inn decor dressed up by row upon row of celebrity photographs and its à la carte meat and potatoes menu have been widely copied. Walk into any steak house in the U. S. and you'll get a sense of Gallagher's.

What you won't get is its barely West of Broadway location that makes Gallagher's a show-biz biggies' haunt. We've seen Raul Julia sing for his supper (literally), and when George C. Scott is on (or off) Broadway, he practically lives here. Nor are you likely to find too many other massive horseshoe-shaped bars dominating the center of the restaurant, the nightly site of much merrymaking. And we don't know of any other such establishment that so proudly displays its prime product in a giant glass-enclosed meat locker.

As the ever-so-Irish General Manager, Bryan Reidy, says, "It takes a pretty confident restaurant to showcase its main ingredient that way." But it's not just for show. All those dark red, bordering on black, heavily veined slabs of meat are experiencing the flavor-enhancing and tenderizing process of dry aging that lasts for at least twenty-one days at thirty-six degrees. The result is very tasty and shouldn't be missed. In other words, don't even think about menu items like fried shrimp in beer batter or Dover sole. Stick with the steaks and you'll be very happy. If you must digress, go for the giant $25.75 lamb chops or the fresh-from-the-tank Maine lobsters, $44 for 3- to 3-1/2-pounders.

Never one to stray from a sure thing, we stick to our Gallagher's guns and always order either the $29.75 sirloin (the New York strip cut invented here) or the filet for a dollar less. In fact, theirs is one of the few filets flavorful enough to stand on its own, thank to broiling over hickory logs. Consequently, Gallagher's is the only place our pal Ken Hall, a Texas steak stickler from way back, orders this usually overrated cut. When they're in town, it's where you'll find Richard Chamberlain and George C. Scott.

Like us, Ken whets his appetite with the $7.95 marinated herring, whole melt-in-your-mouth filets immersed in sour cream and onions. When complimented on his best-in-town herring, Bryan allows as how it is "homemade by a little old Jewish man, who also makes our pickles. He's been selling to Gallagher's forever and he still follows me around, making my life miserable, every time he makes a delivery until I give him money!" Keep him happy, Bryan. We're not the only ones addicted to the herring — or to Gallagher's top-notch onion rings, at $5.25 a generous serving.

They're another element of the cholesterol and fat fix we never miss here. Ditto for the crispy hash browns for $4.75. So it may surprise you to know that we skip the creamed spinach in favor of the plain boiled $5.25 rendition. It has been known to surprise the waiters, too, especially the delightful Benny Stevens who shakes his curly, salt-and-pepper head in disbelief at our otherwise uncharacteristic restraint. Like all the waiters here, Benny's a real pro, having made a career at Gallagher's. (What a relief not to be served by youngsters rather grudgingly waiting tables until that big break comes along!) And like most of his associates, Benny is a real character who relishes the frontierlike, you-never-know-what-might-happen atmosphere.

He got as much a kick as we did out of the night a large group of Italian businessmen who, upon learning one of us was celebrating our birthday (information most likely imparted by Benny), held us hostage with heartfelt serenades. Every time we made a move to leave, they burst into song again and sent over another round of drinks. Then there was the time several very big-time professional baseball players decided baked potatoes could be wielded to show us their pitching prowess. It was just another night at Gallagher's — the longest running show on Broadway.

HOURS:        Noon to midnight daily.

CREDIT CARDS:        All major.

# Gotham Bar and Grill

12 East 12th Street                                (212) 620-4020
between Fifth and University Place
New York, NY 10003

The term "Bar and Grill" may conjure up notions of informality (an impression enhanced by the vast postmodern former warehouse space and the sneaker-shod waiters), but this is a very serious restaurant. Gotham's initial heat may also have been somewhat frivolously generated by its location across the street from Fairchild Communications since it was commissary to the fashion world's arbiters of taste along with the designers, photographers, and models, and the PR people trying to impress them. However, its staying power is testimony to the talents of Executive Chef Alfred Portale.

In fact, Fairchild's move uptown didn't affect Gotham's popularity one iota, and Alfred's reputation continues to grow as disciples of his architectural approach to food presentation fan out across the city. John Schenck at West Broadway and One Fifth's Kerry Hefferman are graduates of Alfred's kitchen. It's particularly fertile training ground, not only because it produces more than 350 meals a day, but because Alfred insists that his cooks learn how to excel in each of the kitchen's stations because "unfinished work is everyone's responsibility."

The result is invigoratingly good food, made spectacular by its towering dimensions. Dishes are arranged to stand up to six inches high, invariably rousing even the most frequent of diners to "Ooh!" and "Ah!" Consequently, while Alfred has begun to tire of the vertical style, he's stuck with it; his audience expects it.

Furthermore, the surroundings almost demand the high design. Less dramatic presentations would be lost in this larger-than-life multilevel room brought into some semblance of perspective by neoclassical columns and parapets. A Statue of Liberty governs the room (although she fails miserably at controlling the noise level) as what appear to be parachutes billow overheard.

A little far afield for lunch, we think of Gotham as a dinner destination. In fact, we count on the drama of the food and decor, coupled with the sure-footed but leisurely pace of the service, to provide the evening's entertainment. We start the show with the monumental goat cheese salad, which is a tower of cheese and grilled bread built on a floor of beets, grilled leeks, and marinated peppers with an antenna of greens for $12. Then we order the tender $13 roast squab hovering over a cloud of couscous with a surprisingly harmonious curry and apple-cherry chutney.

Then it's a tough call between the yellowfin tuna steak on a beach of canary beans and grilled fennel with a stimulating burgundy sauce for $28, the mustard-bathed $29.50 rack of lamb with its smooth-as-silk garlic flan, or the red-currant-sauced duck breast perched on a nest of roasted vegetables lined with onion marmalade at $28. Here, even the ubiquitous roasted free-range chicken appeals, with its roost of sautéed rosemary-infused vegetables and shoestring potatoes for $26.50.

When it comes to dessert, the chocolate cake wins hands down. Now, that may seem a rather down-to-earth ending for such a high-flying meal, but consider its flourless state and the fact that it is served warm with a generous scoop of toasted almond ice cream. As if that weren't enough of a pedigree, at $8.50 it has become a menu staple, surviving a parade of pastry chefs who have gone on to preach the dessert gospel according to Alfred Portale at other establishments.

HOURS:    Noon to 2:00 P.M., Monday through Friday; 5:30 to 10:00 P.M. Monday through Thursday; till 11:00 P.M. on Friday and Saturday; 5:30 to 9:45 P.M. on Sunday.

CREDIT CARDS:    All major.

## Grotta Azzurra

387 Broome Street                                    (212) 925-8775
at the corner of Broome and Mulberry
New York, NY 10013

Lately, the agonized groans uttered by Grotta Azzurra fans arriving at their favorite Little Italy restaurant have been reduced to a dull roar. Not that "the Grotta," as it's known to the cognoscenti, is any less popular. Rather, the D'Avinos, the Grotta's founding family, have finally broken with a 95-year tradition and have started taking reservations — albeit grudgingly. It's more like they *can* take reservations than they *do* take them.

Either way, it's an improvement at this vintage establishment, which has always stood out, in a neighborhood full of alternatives, as the one place people would resign themselves to an often long wait instead of going elsewhere. Why? The two *F*s — food and fun. Grotta Azzurra has plenty of both, all of it good. It's a crowded, good-naturedly noisy place, often enlivened by a roving guitar player who whips everybody into a sing-along frenzy. When not singing or downing the generous portions of first-class Neopolitan specialties, patrons often busy themselves making new acquaintances. The tables are so closely packed together that individual party boundaries are blurred. It's virtually impossible to get through a meal without engaging your neighbors in conversation.

As the walls attest with autographed pictures of decades worth of celebrities, the crowd tends to be interesting. On any given night you might run into Bill Cosby, Neil Diamond, Dolly Parton, Barbra Streisand, Van Halen, or Lanie Kazan. One night Frank Sinatra called owner John D'Avino to announce he was coming down with a party of twenty-five. John checked with wife/hostess/

cashier Cathy about the feasibility of taking proper care of Ol' Blue Eyes. Since a number of regulars were already seated (and no one under any circumstance is ever rushed at the Grotta) and people were lined up on the steep stairway leading down to the dining room, they regretfully suggested he go elsewhere. Now, rumor has it that Frank doesn't deal well with "No," but in this instance he graciously accepted the decision. He knew the D'Avinos treat everyone equally.

Moreover, he probably figured they know what they're doing. The D'Avino family has been running the Grotta for four generations, since its 1908 opening. John's been here for the last forty-one years, thirty of them as chef. These days, son Vincent mans the kitchen at lunch, and daughter Connie is on hand at night. So there's always a member of the family on the premises. And most of the staff is part of an extended family; for instance, waiters Giovanni and Frankie have been around for twenty-eight and thirty years respectively. And current head chef Joe Amato has logged forty years with the D'Avinos.

Joe is responsible for what may be the best lobster Fra Diablo in town. Priced according to the size of the lobster (about $48 for a three-pounder), it's a lusty, well-sauced treat and the restaurant is justifiably proud of it. But it's not the only star on a menu that sets the standard for all the new and very popular family-style Italian uptown eateries, such as Carmine's. The outstanding chicken, steak, and sausage contadino easily serves four to five for $41.95. Try a side order of spaghetti with white or red clam sauce for $11.95, but plan on divvying that up, too. You'll get a mountain of pasta, and no half portions are offered.

Among the appetizers, the spedini alla Romana — breaded and fried mozzarella dressed with an anchovy sauce — is a big dish, literally and figuratively. The D'Avinos sell a lot of it and at $8.50 it serves four admirably. Likewise the cold, assorted antipasti for $7.50. And if you're a minestrone maven, don't miss Grotta's $6.50 rendition. You just have to add a salad and you can call it lunch or dinner.

Indeed, a very satisfying meal can be had at Grotta Azzurra for as little as $18 a person or for as much as the traffic, not to mention appetite, will bear. But rest assured that the bill will not be inflated by the bar tab because there is none. The D'Avino family has always believed that good food and liquor don't mix. Only wine and beer are available, with a $33 Bartolo at the high end of the small list of imported wines or try their own house wine at $17 a bottle. In the sparkling category, you can indulge in a $120 bottle of Dom Perignon, but bring plenty of cash. The D'Avinos believe credit cards and good business don't mix either.

HOURS:    Sunday and Tuesday through Thursday, noon to 11:00 P.M., till 12:30 A.M. on Friday and Saturday.

CREDIT CARDS:    None.

## Hudson River Club

4 World Financial Center          (212) 786-1500
Lobby Level
New York, NY 10281

There's a *new* New York rising majestically above the Hudson at the southern tip of the island. Once a no-man's land of decaying piers and rubble-strewn lots, Battery Park City (just west of the World Trade Center) is a gleaming testimony to the promise of responsible urban planning and development. People live, work, and play here amidst shimmering skyscrapers humanized by lots of open space. You'll find landscaped parks for picnics, fountained squares for concerts and promenading, an esplanade for strolling along the river, and marinas for dreaming.

The focal point of this bucolic city-within-the-city is the World Financial Center, which, in keeping with the curiously suburban feel of the area, boasts an indoor mall of shops and restaurants. Both run the gamut in terms of price and quality, the Hudson River Club topping both.

Poised on the second floor of one extension of the Center, the restaurant offers unobstructed views of its namesake river, straight down to Ellis Island, the Statue of Liberty, and beyond. But the Hudson River and the valley it dominates are more than the source of a name; they provide a theme for chef Waldy Malouf's inspired cooking. His kitchen truly celebrates the seasonal bounty of the Hudson River Valley. Waldy's menus reflect the historic area's unique heritage by utilizing its game, dairy products, produce, and wines.

The theme embraces the ambience as well—terraced levels facing a glass wall allow panoramic river views for every table. And the swank, clubby decor of muted colors, tapestried banquettes, and polished brass, in combination with the long, narrow proportions of the space, creates an illusion of a shipboard dining room. As captain of this daily voyage up the Hudson, general manager Chris Carey is as affable and as knowledgeable as they come. He may have gleaned some of his charm from dad, former New York Governor Hugh Carey, but the right-on restaurant intuition is all his. It's the result of having spent most of his professional life in the hospitality industry.

Consequently, Chris has no compunction about going against an overwhelming tide of policy elsewhere by allowing the smoking of cigars in designated areas. He recognizes that this is Wall Street turf; at lunch the Hudson River Club is a canteen for the Merrill Lynch, American Express, and Dow Jones execs who work in the World Financial Center's office buildings. Smart—he knows his Irish blarney can sweet-talk anyone who objects.

We don't. But we still recommend dinner over lunch here. Except for Saturday night, when it's packed with suburbanites, it's less crowded, making for the leisurely dining that the setting and food command. Moreover, you don't feel as if you've landed in the middle of a club to which you don't belong and to which you weren't invited.

If you are at least two like-minded souls with very hearty appetites, we recommend the $65 six-course tasting menu. A beautifully orchestrated gustatory tour of the Hudson Valley, it changes nightly according to Waldy's whim but can be counted on to be a heady and very filling experience.

For us it was a once-in-a-lifetime one. We now stick to the à la carte menu where we're less likely to run aground, appetite-wise in midstream. We usually get into the swim of things with one of Waldy's wonderful soups. Few other establishments in town present so many (at least five) with such variety. Depending on the season, there's wild leek and asparagus puree liquefied by red pepper cream for $7.50, scallop and crab bisque given bite by sherry and fennel at $8.25, or chilled mussel and shrimp chowder. And when Waldy's menu offers his wildly popular pumpkin-apple soup with cinnamon croutons in autumn, people ask for it. Of course, they ask for it in the dead of summer, too!

All of which is not to suggest that the range of hot and cold appetizers is not worthy of consideration. Take particular note of those dishes with smoked ingredients—Waldy does all his own on the premises. The Napoleon of smoked salmon and tuna layered with caviar cream is a marvel to behold and taste for $16.50.

The entrées are also divided into categories: fish and seafood, seasonal game, and meat and poultry. We tend to concentrate on the first two. Trout, sautéed and served with a tasty coulis of lovage and parsley, has a surprisingly lush flavor at $26.50, while a mustard seed crust gives juicy swordfish steak a new dimension for $28.50. Okay, so you can't eat trout from the Hudson these days (Waldy relies on a Catskill hatchery) and swordfish are oceangoing vessels, but their preparation reflects the restaurant's theme.

As for the venison, its origins are pure Hudson Valley, as are those of game birds like squab. Grilled venison chops are exquisitely complemented by one of Waldy's unique garnishes, a red wine and black pepper marmalade ($32.50), while the moistly tender squab is enriched with potato puree and foie gras at $28.50.

There are a number of boisterous desserts, including the aptly named "Tower of Chocolate" as in chocolate brownie, chocolate mousse, and chocolate meringue for $10.50, but we suggest the selection of New York cheeses. It's rare for a restaurant in the city to serve cheese as dessert (no matter how many other European customs they adhere to), even rarer to serve such tasty local varieties.

And speaking of rare, the wine list is, too. Well-priced and diverse, it focuses on domestic regionals, reaching far beyond the Hudson Valley to places like Texas. Indeed the restaurant is so justifiably proud of its wines that one room is devoted to their display and functions as the site of the monthly Wine Room Dinners. The first Monday of every month, a fortunate thirty folks who had the foresight to make reservations well in advance are treated to a six-course, six-wine feast made even more palatable by the presence of "illustrious guest speakers"—usually the purveyors of the food or wine, who deliver entertaining discourses on their origins. At $85 per person (including tip), it's an unforgettable evening. But then, any meal at the Hudson River Club is memorable.

HOURS:        11:30 A.M. to 2:30 P.M. and 5:00 to 9:30
              P.M. Monday through Friday; 5:00 P.M. to
              10:00 P.M. on Saturday; 11:30 A.M. to 3:30
              P.M. for Sunday brunch.

CREDIT CARDS:     All major.

# *J. G. Melon*

1291 Third Avenue                          (212) 650-1310
at 74th Street
New York, NY 10021

When Jack O'Neil and George Mourges opened their Upper East
Side bar/restaurant in 1972, they had a decorating budget of a
whopping $100. In need of bargains, they wandered around the
corner to an antique store about to go out of business and
happened upon four affordable prints, each depicting melons.
Voilà! Jack and George (J. G.) and melons. They found a name and
motif for their place in one outing! Friends and patrons (invariably
one and the same) have been donating melon items to the
decorating cause ever since. Indeed, when melons threatened to
overrun the first site, Jack and George opened a second West Side
location (almost directly across town) to house the collection. Alas,
the second restaurant recently fell victim to rising rents after a
fifteen-year run.

Rents are even higher in the original Melon's neighborhood, but
their business keeps pace. It's daily from late morning to the wee
hours, from 11:30 A.M. to the kitchen's close at 2:20 A.M. And then
the front barroom keeps hopping until 4(!) A.M. closing time.

Egalitarianism is the rule. No matter who you are, if there is
a line, you wait. There are no reservations for anyone — not
even Warren Beatty, Julia Roberts, Sigourney Weaver, or John F.
Kennedy, Jr. Affable manager Sean Young claims that even President Ford waited!

Once seated, you *can* consult the strategically placed black-
boards that serve as menus, but that serves to call attention to
yourself as one of the uninitiated. Afficionados don't even bother
to look; they already know what they want: the $4.95 hamburger,
the club sandwich at $7.50, and/or chili for $3.95. Our buddy,
banking guru Darla Moore, never fails to order the $8.75 salade

Niçoise, claiming it's the best in the city. Whether or not you bother with the menu, expect informal, friendly service which mirrors the cozy atmosphere.

In fact, the formula of good, solid food at modest prices in an inviting, old-fashioned tavern setting appeals to just about everyone in every mood. It's not unusual to see a couple in jeans seated next to a party in black tie. And neither bats an eye.

However you're dressed, if you're dining alone, sit at the bar, where you're sure to strike up a conversation with someone; if you're lucky, it could be Sam Shepard. But the amiable John Roney, a bartender who barely looks old enough to drink, will do nicely too. Ask him about the secret ingredients in his unforgettable Bloody Marys.

But be careful not to get carried away with the conviviality of the place and lose track of your cash reserves. Melon's does not take credit cards.

HOURS:      11:30 A.M. till 2:30 A.M., daily. The bar is
            open until 4:00 A.M.

CREDIT CARDS:      None.


# Jim McMullen

1341 Third Avenue                        (212) 861-4700
between 76th and 77th Streets
New York, NY 10021

Jim McMullen thought "there's no reason why you couldn't have a small town attitude toward your neighbors in New York. Being honest, friendly, and straightforward is all that it takes." So he created a friendly place where trendy types can devour straightforward food at honest prices. Jim's is a restaurant whose Upper East Side celebrity-studded clientele can call their own. Here they can see and be seen but still feel at home. Not as preciously chic as Mortimer's used to be or as power-charged as Elio's, Jim McMullen (the restaurant) nonetheless has a certain élan that elevates it well above the conventional neighborhood joint.

Of course, the restaurant's size distinguishes it too. At 170 seats, it's the largest on the East Side while remaining surprisingly warm because of the comforting brick walls, bentwood chairs, planked wood floors, and Art Nouveau sconces. A succession of rooms also helps.

The long, narrow bar is a popular gathering place for a young, stylish crowd. It's fun watching them pretending not to admire themselves and each other in the large mirrors that line the wall. Three dining rooms forming a *U*-shape flow behind the bar. Each of them is usually filled, producing a noisy, informal conviviality. Jim McMullen is a club to which everyone automatically belongs simply by virtue of having the good sense of being there. Devotees like Blaine Trump and Robert Trump, Joanna Carson, Reggie Jackson, Kim Basinger, Alec Baldwin, John McEnroe, and ex-Mayor Ed Koch casually acknowledge each other with a nod of the head or a glass raised in salute.

Social considerations aside, there's a lot to be said for the food. It's pretty good and increasingly innovative, especially the daily specials. Frankly, we miss the "nursery" food, those soothingly familiar dishes that used to be the mainstays of the menu. Mercifully, the warm corn bread and homemade biscuits remain, as do the *real* mashed potatoes, complete with lumps. And we're still reminded of Mom's admonitions about starving children in China when we try to cope with the generous portions! Just try to get through the mountain of an appetizer that is the fried calamari ($4.75 at lunch, $5.50 at dinner) or the Caesar salad ($5.00 and $5.50) for that matter. Then there's the chicken pot pie, an exemplary rendition at $10.50 for lunch, $14.50 at dinner.

Generally speaking, you can get away with lunch for two for $30 or less, if you steer clear of seafood, except for the superior shrimp salad at $10.75 or the salmon salade Niçoise at $9.75. The $6.75 hamburgers, predictably served with a mound of french fries, are good, and the chicken club sandwich for $7.25 should not be overlooked.

Dinner runs closer to $50 with decidedly non-nursery items such as duck roll with scallions and sashimi tuna ($6 and $6.75) as starters. More bowing to culinary trends is evidenced by the daily risottos at $14.50 and the $16.50 fettucine with lobster. But you can still get a great and unadulterated pork, veal, or lamb chop ranging from $14.75 to $19.75.

Though the restaurant is now being managed by Ark Restaurant Corporation, Jim is still keeping a watchful eye, so the next time you want to do some first-class mingling, while dining on reliably good food, without having to dress or extend the limit on your credit card, check out Jim McMullen.

HOURS:        11:30 A.M. to midnight, 365 days a year.

CREDIT CARDS:        All major.

# Joe Allen

326 West 46th Street                (212) 581-6464
between 8th and 9th Streets
New York, NY 10036

The last time out, we described this warm-to-cozy restaurant as "what Sardi's used to be — an integral part of the theatrical community serving up good food and better company." Joe Allen remains a favorite Broadway stomping ground. But in all fairness to Vincent Sardi, who has since repurchased his namesake restaurant, we should interject that, in true show-biz fashion, Sardi's has made a comeback.

Meanwhile, the more informal Joe Allen, both man and restaurant, just keeps rolling along the rocky restaurant road. In Joe's own estimation, the original Joe Allen has become somewhat of "a gray eminence" by virtue of its nearly thirty-year run and the spawning of international counterparts in Paris and London. Both of them have on more than one occasion served us admirably as welcome reminders of home. But how much homage can you pay a restaurant that relies on posters from Broadway's most disastrous flops for color, in both the literal and figurative senses? They line the brick walls, reminding the star wannabes, who staff the place, and the stars of the moment, who frequent it, of the precarious nature of their chosen careers.

Moreover, the restaurant cannot be accused of running a successful formula of basic food, casual ambience, and reasonable prices into the ground. Evolution is at work here, guided by Joe's daughter Julie who really runs the show these days. The prices have inched up, though not alarmingly so, and gone are the checkered tablecloths and chalkboard menus. They've been replaced by white cloths and handheld numbers, made all the more unfamiliar by what is and is not printed therein. Where's the old reliable, downright sublime meatloaf? And what's grilled porcini and veal sausage and warm wild rice salad or a hot focaccia sandwich dressed by grilled eggplant, spinach, black olives, and tomato doing on them? Granted, the $13 and $9 price tags are reassuring, but when did Joe Allen go fancy on the food front?

Joe demurs at the notion. It's not so much going fancy, he says, "as going with the trends. But we sure can tell when there are a lot of people here from out of town; we sell a lot of red meat." Like the noteworthy burgers—regular, cheese, and bacon cheese—at $6.50, $7.00, and $7.50, or the $19 grilled sirloin steak with french fries. Our guess is that when Joe Allen is overrun by tourists, a lot of the $5.50 buffalo chicken is sold, while the superb sweet potato vichysoisse at $3.75 goes begging. In any case, we're just so grateful that our favorite La Scala salad is still on the menu. A very large dose of diced salami, provolone, and iceberg lettuce laced with chick peas—it's a great combination of flavors and textures for $13.

While you can still get away with less than $30 for a very respectable meal for two, you should consider the reservation lead time here to be comparable to that of pricier, multistarred venues, especially for a pretheater meal. Call a week ahead; they start accepting reservations at 11:00 A.M. seven days in advance. The same goes for lunch on Wednesday, matinee day. But don't bother. Even Joe warns against it, as the restaurant is crowded with folks "who split everything and are so shrill...usually about everything being so wrong." So why, we wonder, do they keep coming back?

There's the location, of course; it's right in the middle of Restaurant Row in the very heart of the theater district, with the probability of getting a glimpse of whoever happens to be headlining on Broadway at the moment. We doubt it's the excellent selection of beers, although that is certainly a big draw for a younger, less critical crowd who keep the large, old-fashioned bar hopping.

Maybe the fact that they can count on one section of the menu being devoted to eggs appeals. Either the spinach and cheddar omelette served with a mixed green salad or the frittata with potato, scallion, roasted pepper, and three cheeses, $9.50 each, makes a great matinee brunch, as well as a gratifying late-night supper.

Undoubtedly, like us, they consider Joe Allen one of the better acts in town—its agreeable combination of satisfying food, convivial atmosphere, comfortable prices, and ample opportunity for star-gazing make it a perennial hit.

HOURS:          Noon to midnight daily. Matinee days (Wednesday and Saturday) from 11:30 A.M.

CREDIT CARDS:          MasterCard and Visa.

## La Caravelle

33 West 55th Street                              (212) 586-4252
between Fifth and Sixth Avenues
New York, NY 10019

When it opened in 1960, La Caravelle was the quintessential Camelot restaurant. It was formal and glamorous and served classic French fare. Indeed, almost since day one it was embraced by the Kennedys. Their regular patronage and the superb food assured its success for a decade or two.

But by the early 80s, La Caravelle was a restaurant whose time had passed. Its stately glamor was considered stuffy and fussy; its classic food, too heavy and old fashioned by a new generation of diners. They trekked to every corner of Manhattan to pay homage to French chefs of the nouvelle variety, but were conspicuously absent from this centrally located establishment.

La Caravelle disappeared from lists of the city's great restaurants. A lot of people thought it had closed. It was rapidly becoming a distant memory, except for Andre and Rita Jammet, who were determined that La Caravelle would not fall entirely by the wayside. Indeed, since the effervescent couple took over in October 1988, things have been looking up — way up.

Under the Jammet regime, La Caravelle has been rejuvenated. The kitchen has taken a softer, gentler approach to haute cuisine; the decor has been refreshed (including the famous Jean Pages' murals that line the walls); and the always well-mannered service has taken on a proper inconspicuousness. La Caravelle has regained its status as a restaurant in which to see and be seen. In fact, it's set up better than most for a meal-long survey of the scene — an aisle of banquettes, now peach shantung, opens into a large, square room lined with more banquettes. From almost any seat you can keep an eye on any other, including the bar which (oddly) is situated in the far corner. To rendezvous there is to march across the entire room as the subject of scrutiny by a good-looking crowd—the likes of Jackie Onassis, Anne Bass, John and Susan Gutfreund, David Frost, Joan Collins, Tony Randall, and Blaine Trump—who are clearly enjoying the still-serious food.

The prices are appropriately serious, too. Fixed-price dinner is $59 with the occasional supplement ranging from $5 to $25, making the pre-theater menu—featuring a generous range of dishes from the main menu—a bargain at $38. For lunch, you can order the fixed-price three-course meal for $35 or order à la carte with a $25 minimum.

Chef Tadashi Ono has added new luster to La Caravelle's classic cuisine with inspired Asian touches. Sweetbreads are coated with sesame, and snails are fortified with curry. Yet pike quenelles in truffled lobster sauce and crispy roast duck (carved and sauced tableside) remain menu mainstays.

At dinner, we can't resist what the menu calls "hors d'oeuvres": the featherlight fluke marinated in lemon and chive oil or the sea scallops and asparagus in a sweet chile sauce. But the real appetite teasers are those presented compliments of Andre shortly after you're seated. They're dear little surprises like a marinated mussel or two, a refreshingly light shrimp-topped canape, and perhaps a mushroom stuffed with a tasty concoction.

Among the entrées, other than the duck, which continues the Caravelle tradition of being one of the best in town, we like Chef Ono's lamb—a textbook example of his cross-cultural cooking. Sautéed medallions of lamb are crisped by a spicy breading and flavored with a black bean sauce. Less adventuresome palates will enjoy rediscovering time-honored dishes like roast chicken in a wicked Champagne sauce or black angus filet mignon made luscious with a rich wine sauce. Then there is the enchanting grilled smoked salmon, served with its roe fertilized by a basil sauce and tomato fondue.

In truly French fashion, an array of cheeses served with a full complement of breads, crackers, and biscuits is available for dessert, as is a selection of soufflés (at a $5 supplementary charge). Either seems a fitting finale to a meal here, until you find out that pastry chef Laurent Richard's signature dessert is a luscious lemon tart shaped like a caravelle propelled by white and dark chocolate sails!

As for the aristocratic wine list, allow Andre to act as your captain for smooth sailing. He will steer a clear course to bottles suited to both your budget and culinary voyage, just as he has plotted La Caravelle's course to renewed success.

HOURS:  Noon to 3:00 P.M., Monday through Friday; 5:30 to 10:15 P.M., Monday through Saturday.

CREDIT CARDS:  All major.

# La Côte Basque

5 East 55th Street                                    (212) 688-6525
between Fifth and Madison
New York, NY 10022

La Côte Basque has weathered a number of storms since opening in 1959, not the least of which was the furor created by its being the setting of Truman Capote's wicked exposé of the antics of New York society, *Answered Prayers*. The publication of excerpts in *Esquire* created a sensation that resulted in Capote's brutal ousting from the company of those whom he had only thinly disguised.

More recently, owner Jean-Jacques Rachou raised a ruckus by removing himself from the kitchen to play host. He was well meaning. Maître d' Pascal was always at his wits' end trying to accommodate the hordes of high-profile regulars insisting on the sixteen "good" tables in the bar and front gallery. There may be plenty of room in the back, but the likes of Roger Moore, Brooke Astor, Georgette Mosbacher, the King of Morocco, Diana Ross, and Donald Trump (especially Trump) do not take kindly to being asked to sit there. Maybe Monsieur Rachou thought he could cajole them into it.

Instead, he alienated many of the faithful as the food suffered in his absence from the kitchen. "Sacrilege!" they cried. After all, Jean-Jacques had a culinary pedigree to uphold. His restaurant was the original site of the almost mythical Le Pavillon, the dominant French restaurant in America in the 1940s and 1950s. After moving Le Pavillon to 57th Street, its legendary owner Henry Soule returned to open a second restaurant, La Côte Basque. Jean-Jacques has been on the scene since 1979 and was doing a spectacular job carrying on the legacy until he traded in his chef's whites for a suit. Realizing his mistake, Jean-Jacques is back where he belongs, and all is forgiven. The pretty people are back to their daily basks in this glamorous setting — exposed beams, sheltering red leather banquettes and velvet chairs, a profusion of flowers, silk-shaded lamps on the table, and Bernard LaMotte's charming murals of the French coast and countryside. All of this is just as beguiling in the back as it is in the front, so don't be too disappointed if you are seated there.

And *Chef* Rachou is back to serving his classical cuisine on over-sized plates in Brobdignagian portions. However, he has changed the fixed prices of his lunch and dinner. Perhaps as a measure of penance, he has lowered lunch to $31 and gotten rid of the $3.50 supplement formerly attached to the popular cold asparagus vinaigrette. To make up for it, he's rounded off dinner to $58.

At lunch, we tend not to experiment and instead stick to a couple of eagerly anticipated favorites: the aforementioned asparagus, so beautifully arranged, followed by the Cassoulet du Chef Toulousin, archetypal in all its sausage, duck confit, and pork and beans glory. Hearty and flavorful, it's the best and one of the few genuine cassoulets in the city.

For dinner, we go a more sophisticated route. The scintillating salade gourmande — duck breast, lobster, artichoke hearts, and foie gras — is about as cosmopolitan an hors d'oeuvre as you can get. Witness the $8.50 surcharge. While not taxed with a supplement, the seafood stuffed cannelloni sauced by a tomato and fresh basil coulis is hardly pedestrian as a hot starter. It is, however, a throwback. When was the last time you saw cannelloni on a gourmet menu, even an Italian one? Same goes for duck à l'orange, touted right up there with the cassoulet as a house specialty no less! If you've forgotten how much you *used* to like this dish, try it here at its very best — the skin crispy brown, the meat juicy, and the sauce not too sweet. Another old French familiar given a new lease on life is braised sweetbreads in a Madeira sauce.

After such filling fare, you probably won't have much appetite for dessert. That's just as well since it's not included. But if you must, spring the $4 for the Grand Marnier ® soufflé with raspberry sauce. With a supplement here and there, dinner for two can easily hit $170, depending upon how far you dip into the wine cellar. For lunch, figure on at least $100 if you want to leave a generous enough tip to make sure you're noticed by the experienced staff.

It may mean your rescue from the Siberia of the back room on your next visit. But it will not relieve you of the necessity of making a reservation several days in advance, especially for lunch now that Jean-Jacques has got his toque on straight again.

HOURS:    Noon to 2:30 P.M., Monday through Saturday; 6:00 to 10:30 P.M., Monday through Friday; 5:30 to 11:00 P.M. on Saturday. Closed Sunday.

CREDIT CARDS:    All major.

# La Grenouille

3 East 52nd Street           (212) 752-1495
between Fifth and Madison
New York, NY 10022

Any number of New York restaurants have national, even international, reputations for excellence. For many, image and reality are miles apart. Not so at La Grenouille, which is everything you've ever heard about it and then some. From the glorious symphony of color in the spectacular flower arrangements to the excellent, formal (but never haughty) service, from the scrumptious food to the extraordinarily high celebrity quotient, La Grenouille never disappoints.

Indeed, it is considered by many to be one of the city's great gastronomical treasures. And for most such icons, the notion of anything of import changing at La Grenouille was unthinkable. The operative word here is *was*.

Whether it was a case of sibling rivalry or, as was announced to the press, simply "time for a change" has been a matter of much conjecture among La Grenouille's glitterati. What is clear is that, after 18 years, the elegant Charles Masson is out and his younger, motorcycle-riding brother Phillippe is in (albeit under the watchful eye of his lovely mother Giselle, who "is in charge, as always"). Phillippe's persona may be somewhat racier than his brother's, but it is clear that charm runs in the family. His cordial greeting, long a La Grenouille trademark, is every bit as warm as Charles's. And if Phillippe is not at the door, you'll be welcomed like a long-lost friend (even if they have never set eyes upon you before) by either Giselle or mâitre d' Armel Gren. Their hospitality effectively softens the blow of being seated in the room which prompted the coining of the term "Siberia" by the press. Regulars and that large daily dollop of celebs sit in the front.

Make that *only* in the front, preferably on the banquettes so *intime* that they can all natter away at each other without raising the noise level unduly. Indeed, Phillippe is just as careful as Charles was about the seating of fashiondom's favorite eatery. He places his guests as if he were seating them for a private dinner party, always sensitive to who knows whom, who *should* know whom, and who's feuding with whom. God knows it's a delicate business, when he's dealing with the likes of John Fairchild, Brooke Astor, Bill Blass, Pauline Trigere, Annette and Oscar de la Renta, Diane von Furstenberg, and Hanae Mori.

The first bite of the three-course $39.50 "Prix du Dejeuner" or $70 "Prix du Diner" explains their attraction to the place. Despite its classic French origins, there is a lightness, a delicacy about La Grenouille's food. The varied but not overwhelmingly extensive menu is augmented by daily specials, which may include fresh sole or turbot flown in from France. At lunch, we often put ourselves in the capable hands of our waiter, allowing him to select a plate of assorted hors d'oeuvres from the always-tempting buffet in the bar. When we're not in the mood for appetizer surprises, we order the sublime Le Saint-Germain—cream of split pea soup—or the sinful La Crêpe de Mais et Foie blond de volaille—small corn blinis with chicken livers sautéed in sherry. Generally, we ask for the fish of the day as the main course and follow it with the deliciously comforting warm apple tart served with homemade vanilla ice cream.

At night, La Grenouille takes on a romantic blush from the sweet silk-shaded lamps. The flowers soften into a riotous blur complemented by impressionist-style paintings. The seductive atmosphere encourages you to throw calories and cholesterol concerns to the wind and linger luxuriously over a long, leisurely meal. Accordingly, we suggest the ravioli stuffed with lobster in a beurre blanc sauce laced with vermouth (Les Raviolis de Homard) or the so-rich-it's-wealthy lobster bisque to start. Then it's a toss-up between filet of beef glazed with a black truffle and Madeira sauce snuggled up to a fricassee of artichokes and the frogs' legs sautéed in garlic butter and tomatoes (for a $5.50 supplement). But there's no contest in the dessert department as far as we're concerned. The warm, bittersweet chocolate torte is a must.

As much as we enjoy La Grenouille for lunch or dinner, we also like to visit when nothing is being served at all. Every morning at about 10 A.M., even on Sundays and Mondays when the restaurant is closed, Phillippe can be found working magic with the restaurant's fabulous floral displays. It would seem that more than charm and seating sensibility runs in the Masson family. Here, too, Phillippe takes after his brother. When last we wrote about La Grenouille, we suggested that should it ever flounder, Charles could have a future as a florist or perhaps as an artist. It is his paintings, along with those of his and Phillippe's late father, that decorate the walls. They really are quite wonderful, having benefited from the inspiration of painter Bernard LaMotte, whose studio once occupied the upstairs room.

The Massons have wisely refrained from remodeling the studio, leaving LaMotte's wine racks and paintings lining the walls. Even his easel is in its place. The high ceilings, leaded windows, and woodburning fireplace make it one of the most charming private dining rooms in the city. If you're considering a dinner party for up to thirty, by all means book it.

So here's to the new regime at La Grenouille, living proof that, as much as things change, they also stay the same.

HOURS:      Noon to 2:30 P.M., 6:00 to 11:30 P.M.,
            Tuesday through Saturday.

CREDIT CARDS:      All major.

# Le Bernardin

155 West 51st Street                    (212) 489-1515
between 6th and 7th Avenues
New York, NY 10019

When the charismatic brother/sister team of Gilbert and Maguy Le Coze first tried to duplicate the success of their Paris-based two-star Le Bernardin in New York, they did so without the preopening fanfare that accompanied other transatlantic transplants. Nonetheless, the day after they opened, the phone started ringing off the hook. Fed by an ongoing series of rave reviews, it has never stopped.

The reason is a four-letter word—fish—fresh, extraordinarily prepared, and beautifully presented. Okay, so the Le Cozes have bowed to the pressure of American tastes and added a couple of nonseafood entrées to the menu. But clichés that they are (filet of beef and that ever-free-roaming chicken), it is almost as if the Le Cozes are pointing out what sacrilege it is to order anything but fish here. After all, Gilbert and/or his right hand Eric Ripert are at the Fulton Fish Market in the wee hours of every morning to hook the best of the catch of the day. They stalk the stalls in search of succulent sea scallops, perfect pompano, tender tuna, and heavenly halibut. If a particular variety is not up to Gilbert's demanding standards born of a childhood on the Brittany coast and refined by a lifetime in the restaurant business, they don't buy, even if the menu promises it. A little star is simply placed by the entry indicating that it is temporarily unavailable.

Gilbert's fanaticism extends beyond the selection of his precious fish. Eric's talented presence was supposed to relieve him from some of his duties in the kitchen, to give him some time for a little beauty sleep—though the city's best-looking chef hardly needs it! But he's almost always there at Eric's side. Clearly Gilbert's hands-on approach pays off with food that has critics frantically exploring their thesauruses, looking for new superlatives.

Both lunch and dinner are prix fixe, $42 and $68 respectively, with some supplements in the $6 to $15 range. For lunch, it's a straightforward presentation of first course, main course, and dessert. We find the luxurious mussel and saffron soup smoothes the way for sweet and flaky monkfish on a bed of leeks garnished with an intense rouille sauce. And while for some it may be too liquid a lunch, we like the melodious exotic fruit soup as the finale.

Later, the menu gets a little convoluted. You're still presented with three courses, but the first is subdivided into four groupings. First you have several mollusk selections. Then there's the heading "Simply Raw"—as opposed to the oysters and clams on the half shell listed above? With choices like a tangy black bass ceviche and tender tuna pounded with chive-flavored olive oil, this category could be more aptly described as "cured." Next come "lightly cooked" items—don't miss the ethereal paper-thin sliced sea scallops, quickly poached in a rich fish stock and served in light chive sauce. Finally there are the soups. Our favorite is mussel and saffron, along with a bountiful seafood chowder. As for the main courses, we've never landed one we didn't like. Dive into the roast salmon with wild mushrooms (chanterelle, oyster, or black trumpet, depending on the season). The poached halibut served with sliced asparagus in warm herb-laden vinaigrette is another great catch. For dessert, the plate of artfully arranged caramel goodies is tasty; the homemade bitter chocolate ice cream is even better.

It used to be that while Gilbert was toiling in the kitchen, his coquettish sister was running a tight ship out front. But Maguy has decamped to the Miami branch of Le Bernardin, turning the bridge over to maître'd Jacques Le Magueresse. And what a lovely ship his is—spacious, gracious, posh, and plush, the dining room is strikingly elegant. The sea-blue velvet upholstered walls soar up to a dramatic teak ceiling and are hung with what, next to the Four Seasons, is the city's best art collection—large gilt-framed 19th-century oils depicting fish and fishermen. Vaguely Oriental lamps cast a muted glow on patrons reposed in roomy armchairs—patrons like Warren Beatty and Annette Bening, Mick Jaggar and Jerry Hall, and the Dustin Hoffmans.

Yes, at night it's a couples kind of place. While not flagrantly romantic, it is certainly one of the city's most comfortable restaurants—a sea of tranquility with fewer seats per square foot, and thus less noise, than any comparable establishment. It invites long, languorous dining, but does not demand it. Neither the kitchen nor the waitstaff have any problem accommodating the more time-conscious luncheon clientele, heavily laden with people from publishing and fashion of the female persuasion who find that only their expense accounts are fattened by dining here.

Of course, these days expense accounts are a little on the lean side too, which explains the reduction of the lead time on reservations from a month to a week or less. Actually, you shouldn't be shy about same-day calls; they can often be accommodated. This is not to imply that you should be concerned about Gilbert and Maguy. They have cast their net quite successfully stateside. Le Bernardin of New York continues to thrive, and the Miami location is just as hot as that rejuvenated resort. Only the Paris operation has fallen by the wayside, sold so the Le Cozes could keep things shipshape in the United States.

HOURS:        Noon to 2:30 P.M., Monday through Friday; 6 to 10:30 P.M., Monday through Thursday; 5:30 to 11 P.M. on Friday and Saturday. Closed Sunday.

CREDIT CARDS:      All major.

## *Le Cirque*

58 East 65th Street                (212) 794-9292
between Madsion and Park Avenues
New York, NY 10021

What can we possibly say about this most celebrated of New York restaurants that hasn't already been said? That the John Wayne look-alike ringmaster Sirio Maccioni is a driven perfectionist, albeit a hand-kissing, charming one? That it's a hotbed of rich and famous activity? That your social standing can be measured by your ability to get a luncheon reservation on short notice? That the importance of the food finally rivals that of the scene? That the pertly pretty room is saved from being pretentious by strategically placed monkeys? That it's almost impossible to get through a day's reading of Cindy, Billy, Charlotte, Liz, or Suzy without one of them mentioning who was dining here with whom? No, it's all been said, ad nauseam. Since March 1974, when this French restaurant opened just off the lobby of the Mayfair Regent, it has taken center stage with no sign of relinquishing that position.

There's something about being at Le Cirque that makes you feel socially secure, although your day can be ruined if you're not seated on the banquettes alongside Larry Tisch, Walter Annenberg, Brooke Astor, Henry Kravis, Regis and Joy Philbin, Ivana Trump, Alice Mason, Barry Kieselstein-Cord, or Judy Price. It really is a game, one that enthusiastic contestants play two to three times a week.

To join the fun, you have to make a reservation. No hard and fast rules here. On some days or evenings, five minutes' notice might be enough; at other times, five weeks may not do it. When you show up to claim your prize, you're sure to be effusively greeted by Benito. Should Sirio scurry over to offer his welcome, you get two points. Now comes the dreaded table assignment. If you're worried that you won't rate a banquette placement, bring a party. There are no demerits for groups of four or more seated at a table in the center of the room, but the closer to the front the better.

Once seated cheek by jowl (there are twenty-eight tables jammed into this former doctor's office), you pretend to study the menu when in reality you're straining to eavesdrop on your high-profile neighbors. Fortunes have been made (or saved) by information gleaned here. But you don't lose any ground if you're seated next to a boring conversation; you're just better off genuinely devoting yourself to the menu, which is certainly worthy of your attention. Executive chef Sylvan Portay has brought a new, deftly light touch to the food, concentrating on reinterpreting classic French cuisine by steering clear of butter and cream in favor of vegetable reductions for sauces. Before taking over Le Cirque's kitchen, he earned three Michelin stars in France, despite criticism for his audacity at redefining Gallic tastes.

*You* get three stars if Sirio drops by your table to give advice on the menu or to suggest his favorite among the daily specials. He's most persuasive, so you get bonus points if you stick to your guns by ordering what first captured your fancy rather than bowing to Sirio's counsel.

The prix fixe of $29 is a bargain, even with the $2 cover. Start with a brightly flavorful fresh pea, onion, potato, and asparagus casserole or the pasta of the day. Sirio delights in reminding you that he had five pastas on his menu back in 1975, long "before any other French restaurant discovered it." Entrées might include a tasty but unadulterated grilled filet of rabbit or roasted saddle of kidney- and mushroom-stuffed rabbit, served with gnocchi and a savory sage sauce. (Rabbit is another menu mainstay that Sirio introduced to New York.)

Alternatively, you can order à la carte; the cover stands. We're fond of towers of smoky, peppered salmon (described as pastrami) wrapped around a filling of crispy vegetables and dressed with a honey-mustard sauce for $16, followed by the delicious lamb stew with spring vegetables enlivened by rosemary and orange zest at $27. On the lighter side, there are always a number of entrée salads or vegetable dishes, such as a vibrant $26 chicken curry salad or fresh sautéed porcini mushrooms for $32.

At dinner, plan on spending about $150 for two, including a $2.50 cover. Plan on more if you go for the $70 four-course menu degustation. Whatever the cost, if you're a bouillabaisse fan and it's on the menu, order it along with a young mesclun lettuce salad for $12.50. Otherwise, we start with a pasta or risotto, like the $18.50 lobster risotto made crunchy with shredded green cabbage. Then it's a toss-up between the black sea bass enrobed by a potato crust on a bed of braised leeks in a red wine sauce or sautéed mignonettes of beef with baked shallots and a gratin of vegetables. Both cost $32.

No meal at Le Cirque is complete without dessert. It's not hyperbole to rank Pastry Chef Jacques Torres as the best in town. His work is always inspired and sometimes influenced by his guests. We've never forgotten the time we spent most of our lunch trying to figure out the identity of the distinguished gentleman sitting on the banquette next to us. We couldn't place him until he was presented with dessert — a pastry pyramid filled with alternating layers of chocolate and raspberry mousse. Only then did we realize he was I. M. Pei. Ten points for recognizing Jacques' clue.

If you'd rather be a spectator than a participant in the game, ask for a table in the sweet little bar, where it's quieter, thanks to a glass room divider. While you're somewhat removed from the fray, your visit to Le Cirque is still good for an extra turn in the city's drop-that-restaurant-name game.

HOURS:    11:45 A.M. to 2:45 P.M. and 5:45 to 10:30 P.M., Monday through Saturday.

CREDIT CARDS:    All major.

# *Les Celebrites*

155 West 58th Street                                    (212) 484-5113
in the Essex House between
Sixth and Seventh Avenues
New York, NY 10019

Seldom has there been such truth in advertising as there has been for this restaurant, touting its 14 tables as the most sought-after in town. They are — and have been since the fall 1991 opening, when the restaurant community gasped at the audacity of Les Celebrites' flagrant opulence in the face of plummeting prices and less-is-more decor. What, they wondered, could the Nikko organization, the owners of Les Celebrites' parent Essex House hotel, be thinking when they introduced a restaurant flaunting an $85 menu along with an à la carte selection commanding $75 a head, with a (very) modest consumption of alcohol, before tax and tip? Smart, apparently.

The sheer sumptuousness of Les Celebrites is irresistibly seductive. Burnished mahogany walls set off the decorative symphony that is the room's rich mix of fabrics and colors. Curving tapestry-covered banquettes wrapped around gilded columns form the room's centerpiece, but it is the startlingly illuminated paintings which draw the eye. A rotating collection of the work of amateur artists like Elke Sommer, Phyllis Diller, Billy Dee Williams, Gene Hackman, Van Johnson, and Peggy Lee — they are the source of the restaurant's name. They're also pretty good, worthy of the ornamental competition provided by the specially commissioned Bernardaud Limoges china and Christofle flatware.

The danger of such a sensuous room is that it can overwhelm the food. There is no possibility of that here. Indeed, almost as if to remind you that this is a serious restaurant and not merely a decorator's fantasy showcase, a wall panel slides back to reveal Chef Christian Delouvrier's kitchen. The nightly unveiling elicits appreciative gasps from even the most worldly-wise of diners — including David Frost, David Bowie, and Iman. Of course, the fact that they have already had a taste of the treats to come in the guise of an amuse bouche, such as crab tossed with lemongrass in olive oil, encourages their supportive audience demeanor.

As the star of the show, Christian seldom disappoints, either as the chef who led the renaissance in the city's hotel dining at the Parker Meridien's late, lamented Maurice or as a prima donna. If in the unlikely event you are dissatisfied with your food, we suggest you not make a fuss despite the hefty price tag. Christian does not take well to criticism. He has been known to confront diners who have had the temerity to complain. And it's not easy justifying your taste to an enraged culinary artiste! Mercifully, we've never had even the tiniest quibble with a meal here, which usually starts with one of Christian's trademark dishes, a "burger" of sautéed duck foie gras on a bun of Granny Smith apples for $22.

We've also found the tart of raw tuna coated with sesame oil and framed by an emulsion of tomatoes, garnished with yellow and green peppers, unforgettable at $18. It, like many of Christian's dishes, is a marriage between East and West, reflecting his classical French training and the time he spent studying the cuisine of the Orient. The $31 crisp-skinned salmon steak entrée is another example of Christian's cross-cultural cooking, with its Oriental spice-seasoned sauce and divine leek compote.

More conventional, but no less impressive, is the rack of lamb with mashed potatoes and a salad of green and white beans for $33. And it may seem incongruous to order beef stew in so formal a setting, but Christian's rendition garnished with carrot confit and roasted cepes is properly regal at $31.

Desserts, the artwork of pastry chef Andre Rennard, are equally superlative. Always suckers for synergistic flavor combinations with semisweet chocolate, we love the $11 candied orange peel tart served with a bitter chocolate sherbet and the dark chocolate mousse infused with mint for $12.

And the service? Close to clairvoyant. It seems as if you need only think about another glass of water or another piece of bread and it miraculously appears, thanks to a team approach on the part of the waitstaff. If "your" waiter is otherwise engaged, another keeps a watchful eye on your table and will sprint across the room to refill your wine glass.

No wonder Les Celebrites' 54 seats are almost always occupied. To make sure you get one of them, call a month in advance — or six weeks if you're aiming for a Friday or Saturday night.

HOURS:     6:00 to 10:00 P.M., Tuesday through Thursday; till 10:30 P.M. on Friday and Saturday.

CREDIT CARDS:     All major.

# Lespinasse

2 East 55th Street                     (212) 339-6719
in the St. Regis, between Fifth
and Madison Avenues
New York, NY 10022

It's common knowledge among chef groupies that Gray Kunz is a master of the East-meets-West cross-cultural cuisine of the moment. They know the impish redhead is a native of Switzerland who spent lots of time in the Far East during his association with the Peninsula Organization. What they probably don't know is that the Oriental influence extends beyond his artful use of exotic ingredients. Gray has a fairy godmother in the indomitable Gloria Chu, the former doyenne of Fu's and the woman he calls "aunt." It was Gloria who held his ambitions in check when Andre Soltner approached Gray about joining him in the kitchen of his legendary Lutèce as heir apparent.

The offer seemed the chance of a lifetime, but Gloria told Gray he risked being forever overshadowed by Andre's legacy and that he might never emerge to become the superstar his talent promised. She convinced him that another opportunity would come along. It did, and as far as we're concerned the folks at ITT-Sheraton owe Gloria — big time. Thanks to her, Gray was available for the signature restaurant in their flagship hotel, the St. Regis. Since opening day, Lespinasse has been heralded as one of the city's most important, ground-breaking eateries, and Gray's toque is ablaze with stars.

Admittedly, there are those who've threatened to lay siege to the restaurant to free Gray from its grandiose Old World formality. Lespinasse is the room everyone loves to hate (including Gray), despite the undeniable comforts of its widely spaced tables, thick rugs, and thronelike Louis XVI-style armchairs. It's just so boring in all its monochromatic gilt-detailed splendor. We're sure the 17th-century salon of namesake Madame Jules de Lespinasse had a lot more personality!

Fortunately, the charismatic quality of Gray's cooking animates the room. Even the service, which started out as overbearingly stiff, has developed a sense of humor while remaining exemplary. Waiters now good-naturedly explain Gray's often-complicated dishes that are loaded with a dizzying array of ingredients — without a hint of their former condescension. And, all things considered, the prices are not as serious as the room suggests, especially at lunch when the $40 fixed price is a relative bargain.

Appetizers we have exulted over include tangy pickled sardines complemented by a savoy cabbage salad and sour cream, and a compelling fricassee of mushrooms served in an enchanting little silver casserole and spooned over a rosemary and shallot risotto. And we can still taste the just-hot-enough mustard-horseradish sauce that gave the sweetness of a fork-tender marinated beef short rib a little bite. Likewise the mellow orange sauce that topped potato-crusted salmon. There was barely room for a rich chocolate mousse and an almond-studded pear tart awash in a Syrah wine sauce, but we made do!

Dinner runs about $60 a person, if you ignore the wine list. But that's getting harder and harder to do since Victor Taylor took on the managerial chores. The former sommelier of the late, lamented Quilted Giraffe is putting a lot more emphasis on the wine service here, trying to effect "a marriage between Gray's food and the wine list."

Explore the relationship by sampling the revitalizing capon-flavored bouillon dressed up with winter savory and lotus seeds for $9 or sumptuous roasted sweetbread casserole in a Madeira and truffle sauce at $15. If you opt for the former, follow it up with the hearty glazed osso bucco in a zesty apple cider and juniper sauce. The seared filet of halibut rubbed with an arresting dill and cumin blend is an appropriate light companion to the sweetbreads. Both cost $27. There's also an opulent four-course tasting menu at $67 and a vegetarian variation for $51.

Surprisingly, for all the hyperbole lavished on Lespinasse, reservations are not particularly hard to come by. An early morning call will usually secure one for lunch or dinner that day.

HOURS:     Noon to 2:00 P.M., 6:00 to 10:00 P.M., Monday through Saturday. Closed Sunday.

CREDIT CARDS:     All major.

# *Lutèce*

249 East 50th Street                    (212) 752-2225
New York, NY 10022

Most of us are instinctively resistant to change. For an internationally famous, universally admired French chef of a certain age, the very thought of it is anathema. So, when Andre Soltner, the revered chef-proprietor of Lutèce, announced that in the interest of ensuring the continued success of the restaurant (read updating), he was adding a couple of partners, it came as a shock to the city's foodies. After all, Lutèce is a real culinary shrine for those seeking masterfully prepared traditional French cuisine. For years it was considered the city's best restaurant. While its status has never been seriously challenged, a group of imaginative young chefs have generated praise for their diverse approach to cooking and have proven tough competition for Andre. And David Bouley's eponymous restaurant has taken top-toque honors. Hence Andre's decision to add the talents of chef Pierre Schutz (one of those same whiz kids) and the charm of maître d'Tony Fortuna to the Lutèce legend.

Their role was to effect an evolution (rather than a revolution) that would position Lutèce more firmly in the contemporary restaurant scene and ready it for Andre's retirement. It did not work out. Andre Soltner is Lutèce! Yes, he is still in the kitchen. Andre, as Mr. Congeniality, still visits as many tables as possible with advice about what to order; his wife Simone still greets guests at the door and decor-wise Lutèce remains a cutely quaint anachronism.

There's the minuscule Parisian bar complete with mural and the coffee shop's cheerful garden room blooming with rather unstable-looking trellises. There's a slightly jerry-rigged look to the room, an impression strengthened when you look up (way up) at the corrugated metal ceiling. As far as we're concerned, the ambience quotient improves considerably once you reach the top of the creaking, winding staircase.

Upstairs are two quite lovely, considerably more formal rooms, both small — a Gobelin tapestry dominates one; a marvelous antique copper still serving as repository for a magnificent floral display, the other. Despite the inequities in the decor, there is no vertical pecking order here. No seating location defines your relative importance — no Siberia. It's simply a matter of which room you prefer. Oddly enough, there are those who swear by the downstairs. We would never dream of sitting anywhere but upstairs.

Wherever you sit, we guarantee the food and service will be superb, worth every penny of the $38 and $60 fixed prices. You can't go wrong with either one. Dining at Lutèce is an event of the highest order, one that should not be constrained by a busy schedule. Don't go for lunch. Go for dinner and plan on spending the evening. Andre et al. expect it. An 8:00 P.M. reservation means that the table is yours for the night.

While there is a printed menu, those in the know eschew it in favor of Andre's recommendations. If he mentions lobster-filled ravioli as an appetizer or caviar on a concoction of sour cream, shallots, and vodka served in an eggshell, order it. He's very sensitive to his charge. "I know Lutèce is like an institution. We are keeping key dishes that people expect here and trying some new things." Among the former, the more classically Lutèce dishes, are the extraordinarily succulent herb-seasoned braised baby lamb and the fork-tender venison in a savory sauce as main courses. For an absolutely unforgettable experience, there's always the $78 tasting menu: eight courses selected for your delectation by Andre, in his considered opinion the best of what his kitchen has to offer. While its specifics are in constant flux, the categories always include pre-appetizer, soup, appetizers, sherbet, entrée accompanied by complementary vegetables, salad, and two desserts.

Naturally, the wine list does justice to Andre's exemplary Alsatian cuisine, dishes like foie gras in brioche, timbales of escargots, medallions of veal with morelles, and sweetbreads sautéed with capers. It is also, for the most part, expensive, but even in the recession-ridden, price-conscious 1990s, no one begrudges the lack of bargains here.

It is a sign of the times, though, that the once-obligatory month's wait for a reservation is no longer. Andre sighs that "those days are over," meaning the go-go 1980s of the unlimited expense account. Now, while he still accepts many a booking six weeks in advance, it is "sometimes" possible to get a table with only two or three days' notice. Of course, it's always easier to get an early dinner reservation, at about 6 or so. You may feel a tad rushed because your table will definitely be required again, but it's preferable to missing out on the Lutèce experience altogether.

HOURS:     Noon to 2:00 P.M., Tuesday through Friday; 6:00 to 10:00 P.M., Monday through Saturday.

CREDIT CARDS:     All major.

# *Mesa Grill*

102 Fifth Avenue                              (212) 807-7400
between 15th & 16th Streets
New York, NY 10011

You could hear a pin drop at the annual James Beard Foundation Awards. Debra Ponzek, Montrachet's 1992 "Rising Star Chef of the Year Award" winner, was about to announce the name of her successor for 1993. Would the foundation finally give three-time nominee Bobby Flay his due? Debra opened the envelope with all the flourish of an Academy Award presenter and smiled. Bobby leapt to his feet and was halfway to the stage before she actually uttered his name. You see, Bobby knew that smile; the 1993 Rising Star Chef of the Year was married to the 1992 awardee at that time.

This story is cute and precedent-setting, but Bobby's reputation as a major New York chef had been assured two years before this momentous occasion, with the 1991 opening of Mesa Grill. He succeeded where others had failed in elevating the big, colorful restaurant above disappointing clone-of-Arizona 206 status. Bobby put a new twist on Southwestern cuisine with his adventurous use of chilies in an abundance of tones and tastes. In fact, Bobby says it takes two full-time people to deal with the amount of slicing, dicing, roasting, and toasting required by the quantity and variety of chili peppers he uses in his dishes.

The setting for Bobby's pyrotechnics is saturated with color — clay reds, sage greens, and sunset oranges. One wall is lined with a banquette covered in a red cowboy print that reminds you of the Roy Rogers or Dale Evans Halloween costume you wore as a kid. That and the green walls may remind you of elementary school, but the industrial-looking fan-cum-light fixtures and soaring columns definitely lend 90s drama to Mesa Grill.

There's something inhospitable about the look of the place, a flaw softened by the efficient and friendly service. Unfortunately, not even that helps with the uncomfortable chairs or the annoyingly high noise level. Never mind. One taste of appetizers like the $10.50 zucchini and corn quesadilla graced by smoked tomato salsa, and avocado relish or the grilled rabbit and goat cheese enchilada with a plate-lickin' ancho chili sauce mellowed by mushrooms at $10.75 and all is forgiven.

Not usually given to ordering steak outside of an establishment devoted to it, we can't resist the grilled black angus here for $24.50 because of the sauce that comes with it. It's tomato- and brown sugar-based, energized by horseradish and red chilies, and is emblematic of Bobby's magic formula of imagination, fun, and a whole lot of fire. The same goes for the spicy black grape sauce that dresses the tender pan-roasted $23.50 venison. Even roasted chicken is charged-up, rubbed with red chili oil, and served with fresh sage sauce for $19. Bobby's forte at balancing compelling flavors is also showcased by the entrées' accompanying dishes — potato-corn taco with the steak; horseradish potatoes with the venison; and smoked pepper-studded couscous with the chicken.

If you're uncertain about spending $45 a person at dinner on food that may be a little too hot for you to handle, go for lunch. The prices drop considerably, and you can explore the excellent shopping afforded by the neighborhood's trendy emporiums. You can't go wrong with the cornmeal coated catfish sandwich with a green chili aioli substituting for tartar sauce at $13.75. We also like the intriguingly different lamb chili with black beans and avocado salsa for $13.50.

The bottom line is that if you have any aspirations for becoming a certified foodie, Mesa is not to be missed.

HOURS:     Noon to 2:15 P.M. Monday through Friday; 11:30 A.M. to 3:00 P.M. on Saturday and Sunday; 5:30 to 10:30 P.M. nightly.

CREDIT CARDS:     All major.

# Montrachet

239 West Broadway                    (212) 219-2777
New York, NY 10013

There was a time when making the trek to Montrachet was something of a voyage into uncharted waters, one certain to stump even veteran cab drivers. When it opened in 1985 as Drew Nieporent's vision of a "simple and unpretentious" restaurant presenting high-quality food at low prices, its TriBeCa location (a function of Drew's limited funds) was way off the fine dining map. No longer, because thanks to Montrachet's homesteading, TriBeCa has become a dining destination. Even novice, non-English-speaking cabbies know it well.

Of course, Drew never dreamed he was redefining the restaurant landscape. Seven weeks after its opening, *The New York Times* gave Montrachet three stars, unprecedented in those days for such a modest establishment. "I'm not talking about the food quality," says Drew, "I'm talking about the decor and price structure. Back then, three stars meant $50 per person. We were offering a prix-fixe menu of $16!"

The monopoly long enjoyed by fancy, expensive mid-to-upper East Side establishments in the multistar sweepstakes was broken. Thanks to Drew, other young, talented restaurateurs could adopt their generation's approach to more informal dining and still be taken seriously by food critics.

Of course, nearly a decade later the days of the $16 menu are long gone. And you should know that even then that was the least expensive of three fixed-price options. Today, you can choose between $28, $38, and a five-course tasting menu at $60, which in the three-star scheme of things remains reasonable. Or you can go the à la carte route from a deliberately small menu; Drew keeps it that way to "guarantee quality and interest."

We don't have a Montrachet mantra. We've done it all ways, and it's a matter of budget and appetite each time we visit. Regardless, chef Debra Ponzek never disappoints, with cooking that draws inspiration from Provence. With her tendency toward bold seasonings and creative use of lots of herbs and light sauces, she has a special flair for game and fish — a fact *all* the menus reflect. Among Debra's appetizer repertoire are a gleaming carpaccio of scallops seasoned with lemon, olive oil, and herbs and a gutsy grilled quail salad with mixed vegetables at $10 and $13 à la carte. Her cold vegetable terrine laced with her treasured herbes de Provence is a perennial summer favorite, appearing on the higher-priced menu d'hotel or à la carte at $11. And we always find it difficult to resist the creamy $22 hot foie gras of duck glazed with a shallot sauce and seared just enough to sport a brittle crust.

In fact, if there is any part of a duck that Debra doesn't do wonders with, we haven't had it. Be it roast duck or grilled duck breast, if it's on any of the menus, try it. Otherwise we like the striped sea bass with roasted peppers and lemon and the grilled saddle of lamb accompanied by a lively vegetable chutney ($25 and $28). Not surprisingly, Debra passes our test of a *real* French restaurant with flying colors — the $19 roast kidneys, served with fava beans and a sherry vinaigrette, are superb.

For dessert, pastry chef David Blom takes over. Even the now ubiquitous crème brûlée remains special here. But we love David's way with one of our favorite flavor combinations, banana and chocolate — a rich bittersweet chocolate tart is topped with sugar-glazed bananas and vanilla ice cream.

Given the name, it should come as no surprise that the wines are also exceptional. While the cellar specializes in French wines, especially Burgundies, there is a large selection of often unconventional domestic vintages as well. The staff, in their signature basic black, have a good sense of which wines best complement which dishes. And if you or they are really stumped, there is always the impeccable judgment of sommelier Daniel Jones.

Indeed, until recently the only element of Montrachet not worthy of kudos was the decor. It was on the stark side. In the preferred front room, pale aqua-gray walls met plum-colored banquettes; in the back, they met the floor. Now, abstract art from Garner Tullis's neighboring gallery adorns them in both rooms and the banquettes have been trimmed with eye-level mirrors, which has improved the star-gazing immensely. You can watch Jeremy Irons, Barbra Streisand, Dustin Hoffman, and Robert DeNiro watch themselves and each other. They all seem to be standing the test of time. And so does Montrachet.

HOURS:      5:45 to 11:00 P.M., Monday through
            Saturday; noon to 3:00 P.M. *only* on Friday.

CREDIT CARDS:   American Express.

# *Natalino*

243 East 78th Street                (212) 737-3771
between 2nd and 3rd Avenues
New York, NY 10021

71 West 71st Street                 (212) 875-1078
between Columbus and Central Park West
New York, NY 10023

Natalino, the East Side version, has long been to neighborhood dining what Lutèce is to destination restaurants: a paragon. Of course, at first glance there would seem to be no basis for comparison. Lutèce serves up high-level traditional French cuisine, while Natalino's kitchen is classically homestyle Italian. Then there's the price differential. Sixty dollars buys dinner for two, *with* a bottle of wine at Natalino. The same amount is the fixed price of a single dinner sans beverage at Lutèce.

But there are some striking similarities. Both are long-running, family-owned and -operated successes where ambience runs a poor third to food and service. And at both establishments, reservations are imperative. At Natalino, it's an issue of size as much as anything else. There are only thirty-two seats, every one of them in constant demand by the denizens of the restaurant's prosperous neighborhood seeking relief from overpriced, affected food. None of that here. There's nothing pretentious about Natalino—no condescending waiters, presumptuous wine stewards, or drop-dead decor. There is just uncompromisingly good food and friendly service. There's not even a bar, so the well-heeled patrons aren't asked to cool those heels there. Actually, despite Natalino's popularity, there's very little waiting anywhere. Owner Frank Davi is a stickler about never taking a reservation unless he's quite sure it can be honored in a timely fashion.

While Frank and son Natalino, along with daughters Margaret and Grace, generate the familial atmosphere in the minuscule dining room, wife and mom Frances creates the cuisine. She cooks up a storm with some aid from son Vincent (the youngest) and a lot of help from her assistant Jesus, who seems like a member of the family because he's been with the Davis so long.

By keeping it all in the family, Frank is able to hold prices down. Appetizers are either $6.95 or $7.95, while all the pastas are $9.95, except the spaghetti with olive oil, garlic, and anchovies— it's only $8.95. And Frank's still making enough of a profit to support the expansion of his business. A West Side Natalino's opened in June of 1993. The spin-off is a larger, more spiffed-up version of its parent (complete with small bar and outdoor garden), but the food and service are identical. There are enough Davis to work at both restaurants, and the menus are the same. At both, Frances's flair for chicken is showcased. Try the chicken and sausage sautéed in olive oil with marsala and mushrooms for $16.95.

Veal is another Natalino hallmark, always succulent in part due to Frances's finesse and Frank's early career as a butcher—he knows what to look for when he buys. The $16.95 Veal Chop Natalino is superb. It is pounded paper thin, dipped in egg-moistened bread crumbs, then lightly fried and topped with sautéed raddichio, endive, and arugula.

Although the menu is concise and easy to decipher, many regulars at the original Natalino, like neighbors Neil and Leiba Sedaka, don't even bother looking at it. They leave the ordering up to Frank or Natalino, both of whom have an uncanny ability to size up an appetite. It will probably take a while for them to establish such a rapport with their clientele at the new location, but we're confident they'll do it.

HOURS:    5:30 to 10:00 P.M., Monday through Saturday. Closed Sunday.

CREDIT CARDS:    All major except American Express at the West Side location.

## *One Fifth Avenue*

1 Fifth Avenue                          (212) 529-1515
at 8th Street
New York, NY 10003

As dining becomes an increasingly dramatic experience, the producers and star of Gotham Bar and Grill pushed things a step further toward blurring the distinction between restaurant and theater—they rehearsed their latest show, One Fifth Avenue. It seems Gotham founders Jerry Kretchmer and Richard Rathe, in partnership with the I. M. Pei of cooking, Alfred Portale, had been looking to start a new venture for quite some time. When they heard the old Greenwich Village standby One Fifth was available, they grabbed it. Then, faced with a fully operable restaurant, they decided to give their notion of a piscatory palace a tryout. For two months of previews, they served "simple summer seafood" to an appreciative neighborhood audience, before closing for another two months in preparation of One Fifth Avenue's premiere.

In addition to allowing them to refine their concept, the rehearsal enabled Alfred to bring former Gotham protégé Kerry Hefferman up to snuff as chef de cuisine for the new establishment (though the kitchen now is headed up by Chef Gary Robins). Furthermore, it allowed both fish fanatics time to research the best possible ingredients. "The way we have guaranteed a supply of the safest, freshest, and most interesting types of fish and shellfish is by developing sources, some exclusive to us, that we rely on," maintains Alfred. In addition to strengthening their contacts at the Fulton Fish Market, Alfred journeyed to Maine to network with the local fisher folk. He commissioned divers in Bass Harbor to handpick scallops for the restaurant, and a number of boat-bound old salts now fish exclusively for One Fifth Avenue. While the culinary artists were securing their supplies, interior designer James Biber set about casting the transformation of space in a more contemporary light. Long considered one of the city's classic restaurant interiors, purists are still grumbling about his removal of most of the art deco remains of the ocean liner *Caronia* which had graced One Fifth. But the handsome mahogany curved bar remains as a romantic connection between the two dining rooms, as do the *Caronia's* beautiful porthole wall sconces. In fact, the bar, illuminated by a highly stylized wall of glowing bubbles etched into a black mirror, is the most inviting physical element of the refurbished restaurant. Biber wanted it to recall an exotic aquarium or a moonlit sea, and he succeeded. Elsewhere, a tonal mosaic motif on the walls and floor, given an edge by chrome panels, is less than hospitable.

Fortunately, the warmth of the very professional staff quickly dispels any disappointment with the surroundings. They put you in a good humor to savor the wonderful tastes that are coaxed from the precious seafood.

If the Village is on your agenda, you can't do much better than One Fifth Avenue for lunch. Try the $14 sautéed skate — the recently discovered fish du jour of so many other places has been one of the highlights of Alfred's repertoire for years. Here, its delicacy is enhanced, rather than drowned, by brown butter laced with the tartness of capers. Lobster salad rolls, seldom seen in such a cosmopolitan environment, are priced according to market and authentically served with coleslaw and french fries. We also get a kick out of the smoked salmon "bacon," lettuce, and tomato sandwich, gimmicky but good at $13.50.

At dinner, don't miss the pyramid of shellfish appetizer labeled Le Plateau; the heaps of periwinkles, sea urchins, oysters, clams, and shrimp presented with a mignonette sauce will transport you to the coast of Brittany. Priced according to market, there's plenty for two. Even so, we've been known to explore more territory in our musings by ordering the $10.50 cataplana, a Portuguese specialty. The winning combination of clams, sausage, onions, and garlic steamed in a domed copper vessel takes us back to the harbors of the Algarve — especially when we start dipping One Fifth's excellent bread into the rich broth. (And was it our imagination or was one piece really shaped like a dolphin?)

Should you have particularly happy memories of the French Riviera, try the bouillabaisse, as authentic a rendition beyond the Mediterranean's shores as we've ever had for $24. We also love the striped bass layered with fennel and potatoes in a garlicky sauce punctuated by Moroccan olives at $24.50. As for the $24 grilled yellowfin tuna, we can't attest to its provenance, but we can tell you the two-inch-plus steak is nicely complemented by a velvety red wine sauce.

Happily, we discovered that One Fifth Avenue takes another cue from Portugal by offering a nice selection of ports, at exceptionally good prices. So we usually end our meal with that most civilized of English customs, a glass of port. Now if the menu only offered Stilton....

HOURS:      Noon to 2:00 P.M., Monday through Friday; 5:30 to 10:00 P.M., Monday through Thursday; till 11:00 P.M. Friday and Saturday.

CREDIT CARDS:      All major.

# Orso

---

322 West 46th Street                    (212) 489-7212
New York, NY 10036

Like most producers, Joe Allen wasn't satisfied with one show. Unlike most, he managed to produce two smashes in a row, literally. With his eponymous restaurant a long-running hit, Joe opened Orso right next door in March of 1983, an act which he now describes as "a little bit like shooting myself in the foot." But the wound healed quickly as Orso developed its own devotees; its nineteen tables now play to SRO crowds. Since Joe will accept reservations only a week in advance, if you want one for lunch or dinner on any given day, call by 11:15 A.M. seven days in advance. They don't take calls before 11:00, but by 11:30 or 11:45 at the latest, Orso will be sold out.

What a happy circumstance for the only restaurant we know named after a dog! Orso ("bear" in Italian) was the name of a dog who had the good taste to hang out at the Gritti Palace in Venice, where Joe met him. Joe has equally good taste and visited the world-famous hostelry often, becoming fast friends with Orso. Fond of naming restaurants after those he loves best, Joe had already used his own name—and daughter Julie's didn't seem a proper moniker for an Italian eatery. Ergo Orso, whose picture hangs on the wall to the left, just as you enter.

Looking down from doggie heaven, Orso must be very proud that he's been immortalized by what is one of the very few authentic trattorias in town. Relatively small and decidedly casual, there is nonetheless a sense of elegant spaciousness conveyed by the split-level floor plan and lofty skylit ceiling in the back (read *lower*) room. All tables have a good view of the activity in the open kitchen, which takes up the rear.

Given the varied menu, there's a lot to watch. The antipasti section lists nine selections, to which daily specials are often added, all very suitable for budget-conscious grazing in the $5 to $9 price range. Grilled marinated calamari at $9 is a welcome change of pace from the ubiquitous fried version and is nicely complemented by the $8 cold artichoke, tomato, basil, and onion salad. Top off the meal with one of the small, zesty pizzas—we like the sausage, tomato, mozzarella and parmesan interpretation for $12—and two can forage quite well for less than $30.

For a more conventional meal, thin noodles with olives, capers, anchovies, garlic, and spicy tomato sauce at $14.50 is a good first-course choice. Then it's a tough call between the $18 pork tenderloin with figs, scallions, tomatoes, and marsala, and the $17 spicy sausage with roasted peppers, green olives, and polenta. And Orso is one of the few places where we might opt for chicken— roasted and served with stewed white beans and Swiss chard for $17. All dishes are served on colorful Italian pottery that lends a playful touch.

The menu's the same for lunch and dinner, but the crowd changes dramatically. At lunch, Orso is filled with *New York Times* execs (who apparently have a thing about Italian food—if they're not here, they're at the far grander Barbetta across the street) or Seventh Avenue people like Donna Karan and Geoffrey Beene. Later the eclectic pre-theatergoers assemble. Later still, representatives of the entertainment industry take over. Folks from David Letterman's talk show pop over, as do their cohorts from "Saturday Night Live." Theater greats like Adolph Green, wife Phyllis Newman, and/or partner Betty Comden often visit. William Hurt and Stockard Channing come here, too.

And don't be disappointed if you don't recognize anyone at the table next to you. Take a good look at your waiter, or any other member of the staff, and memorize that face. As Joe points out, literally thousands of aspiring performers have worked at his restaurants, a significant number of whom have gone on to fame and fortune. Remember, today's coat check girl may be tomorrow's recording star—just look at Sonia B. Hawkins, Orso's latest gift to the music world.

HOURS:     Noon to 11:45 P.M.; except Wednesday
           and Saturday, 11:30 A.M. to 11:45 P.M.

CREDIT CARDS:     Visa and Mastercard.

## *Parioli Romanissimo*

24 East 81st Street                    (212) 288-2391
between Fifth and Madison
New York, NY 10028

Located in one of the best residential neighborhoods in New York, Parioli Romanissimo is further distinguished by its luxurious town-house setting. The moment you present yourself at the massive wrought-iron ornamented door, you know you have arrived— arrived at what the urbane owner and host Rubrio Rossi describes as a very private place visited by virtually everyone of a certain (economic) level; i.e, well heeled.

You enter through a tiny bar, where you might be asked to wait a moment or two. Somehow you don't mind, as it gives you time to adjust to your serene surroundings. The stroll through a corridor to the dining room offers a preview of what's to come. You pass a trolley laden with an elaborate dessert display and a fabulous arrangement of 50 or so cheeses.

The original architectural details, intricate moldings, and lovely fireplace, along with the soaring ceilings, lend a sense of quiet grandeur to the dining room. There's an opulent harmony about the atmosphere that makes it very romantic, without being cloying. Even the small garden room beyond the main dining area avoids the decorative pitfalls common to its ilk.

Indeed, Rubrio's exquisite taste is reflected everywhere, from the decor to the courteously formal service to the wine list — the most impressive gathering of Italian wines in the city. It runs quite a gamut, from a California contender in the Pinot Domaine Michel at a relatively modest $28.50 to the current granddaddy of Rubrio's cellar, the outrageously tagged Brunello di Montaleino, Riserva, Biondi Santi 1906 at $2,450. Rubrio maintains that this species is the only Italian red that can stand up to a century of aging, so he's still got a few years left to sell it. He admits, however, that "it's probably more of a collector's item than anything else at this point. But it's here, if anyone wants it." Our guess is that someone will. After all, Rubrio sold a bottle of the 1925 vintage for $4,350!

The cuisine here is to classic Italian what Lutèce, La Grenouille, and La Côte Basque are to French, and it lives up to the wine. The Carpaccio de Agnello, or filet of baby lamb cooked to a turn and served with a cream of red peppers, is a spectacular appetizer; the stuffed baby clams baked in wine and garlic are a proud paragon of their genre. Both cost $14.50.

All of the pastas (ten when we last visited) are well orchestrated. But since no half portions are allowed, we usually share one — the creamy wild porcini mushroom risotto for $26. That way we have plenty of room for the main event, generally culled from the chicken or veal offerings. The $29.50 Pollo alla Romano — chicken morsels sautéed with wine and artichokes — is a favorite with its seductive blend of textures and flavors, as is the tender, cheese-stuffed veal chop sauced with truffles at $39.50. When we're feeling especially compatible, we've been known to enjoy the succulent roast rack of veal, $66 for two.

As for dessert, one of us can never resist a $12 slice of the sinful-beyond-belief chocolate cake, while the other always dives into the cheese trolley for $12.

It's dinner only at Parioli Romanissimo, Tuesday through Saturday. There are only about seventy prized seats, so you'll have to call a week in advance as do Diane Sawyer and Mike Nichols, who adore "our" risotto. They're in good company — Jackie Onassis,

Larry Tisch, Betsy Bloomingdale, and "members of the Bush family" are fans too. We assume Rubrio means the George Bush family, but we had already exercised all of our feminine charms to get that much information out of him!

The menu changes two or three times a year. In season, be sure to order the fresh venison, pheasant, or partridge. During any season, your meal will be topped off by a plate of chocolates and cookies, with Rubrio's warm compliments. As a result, you feel as if you've been entertained by a close friend (who has a dynamite chef) in the sanctity of his own home. Guess what? You have!

HOURS:        6:00 to 11:00 P.M., Monday through Saturday. Closed Sunday.

CREDIT CARDS:   All major.

## Tagliolini with White Truffles

### Ingredients

    1 1/2 cups soft sweet butter
    1/4 cup minced white truffles
    1/4 cup grated parmigiano cheese
    Salt to taste
    1 pound tagliolini
    1/2 cup heavy cream
    Thin slices of white truffles

### Preparation

1.  Prepare truffle butter. In a food processor, combine 1 1/2 cups of soft sweet butter, 1/4 cup of minced white truffles, and 1/4 cup of grated parmigiano cheese. Process until smooth and creamy. Set aside.

2.  In a large pot, bring 4 quarts of water to a boil. Add salt to taste. Add 1 pound of tagliolini and cook just until tender. Drain. Toss well to eliminate as much water as possible.

3.  Transfer tagliolini to a larger skillet, add truffle butter and 1/2 cup of warm heavy cream. Mix well and top with a generous amount of thin slices of white truffles.

# Park Avenue Cafe

100 East 63rd Street                    (212) 644-1900
at Park Avenue
New York, NY 10021

Where are the outdoor tables, the unstudied informality, and the neighborhood prices usually associated with a café? Certainly not at this Park Avenue site, former home to two other large, ambitious restaurants—Perigord Park and the late, lamented Hubert's. Granted, compared to its predecessors, the Park Avenue Cafe is casual on the decor front: bare wood floors stripped of their carpeting; folk art, rather than gold leaf-adorned walls; green squared-off lamps that look like they should be hanging over pool tables in place of Venetian glass wall sconces; arrangements of dried wheat instead of flowers; and half-open blinds where elaborate window treatments once shut out the outside world.

However attractive and comfortable Park Avenue Cafe's American craft museum atmosphere may be, it is a tad disingenuous. Somehow we feel compelled to dress for a place where the signature dish is priced at $29.50. Even the Park Avenue denizens who can afford to consider it their neighborhood restaurant don sports jackets and Chanelesque suits.

Getting back to that signature (make that trademark) dish. It is the Park Avenue Cafe swordfish chop, "invented" by Chef David Burke when he noticed that the area behind a swordfish's collarbone yields a cut of meat complete with bone that looks like nothing so much as a veal chop. Grilled, the mountainous chop serves up tender and juicy, accompanied by pasta tossed with broccoli and sun-dried tomatoes with herb-endowed olive oil. It also comes with a numbered tag, which entitles you to register in the restaurant's "swordfish book" for an annual raffle on the anniversary of Park Avenue Cafe's opening. Last year, the prize was a trip to Paris, so if you have a soft spot for swordfish, don't miss the chop. It normally only appears on the dinner menu, but if you ask nicely, you can usually get one at lunch as well.

One Park Avenue Cafe hallmark (if not trademark) you can count on at both lunch and dinner is the bread basket. Big deal?! Here it is: a heaping assortment of housemade baked goodies including peppery corn sticks, yeasty Parker House rolls, and potato-studded baguettes. But that's not all. David, known for his playful presentations since his days at another *faux* café (as in River), makes it a veritable picnic with apples, baby carrots, tangerines, scallions, radishes, walnuts, and a nutcracker.

The ready availability of the swordfish chop notwithstanding, we prefer lunch over dinner here. The front dining room (accept no substitution) benefits from cheerful natural light and is less boisterously crowded than in the evening. And the prices on the short menus (one of the elements that is classic café) are significantly lower, by as much as $6.75 for the wild mushroom hash. Testimony, perhaps, that fish is David's real forte?

Salmon seared with a cracked-pepper crust mounted on ginger-sauced vegetables is a winner at $26.50, as is red snapper perched on a bed of sautéed potatoes and peppers for $25.50. Among the appetizers, the scallion-laced tartares of tuna and salmon, layered with caviar and crème fraiche is an $11.50 knockout. Whatever strikes your fancy, be sure to order the sensational wild mushroom hash as a side dish. At $6.50, it comes in a miniature cast-iron skillet and serves two.

For dessert, the housemade ice creams and sorbets at $6.50 are first rate, and the milk chocolate crème brûlée for $8.50 is superb.

As final proof that this is a "café" that meets the standards of the city's most affluent zip code, reservations are a must. Manager Kevin Dillon does his best to accommodate, but be prepared to be flexible about time, especially at night.

HOURS: Lunch: 11:30 A.M. to 2:30 P.M., Monday through Friday; noon to 2:30 P.M. on Sunday. Dinner: 5:30 to 10:15 P.M., Monday through Thursday; 5:30 to 11:00 P.M., Friday and Saturday; 4:30 to 9:00 P.M. on Sunday.

CREDIT CARDS: All major.

# *Patsy's*

236 West 56th Street        (212) 247-3491
between Broadway and Eighth Avenue
New York, NY 10019

The name most often associated with celebrity pasta pilgrimages in the theater district is a misnomer. The story goes that when

Pasquale Scognamillo, a native of Naples, passed through Ellis Island on his way to the American Dream, the processors misconstrued his first name. It's a good story and not an uncommon one, but historians contend that name changes so often attributed to misunderstandings at Ellis Island really occurred later because the immigration officials copied names directly from the ships' manifests. In any case, Pasquale became Patsy, and he and wife Concetta opened their first eponymously named restaurant at the corner of 49th Street and Eighth Avenue in 1944.

Several years later they moved to 56th Street, next door to the current site, and they finally settled into what their son Joe ironically describes as the "new-building" thirty-nine years ago. Despite the moves, there's been a continuity about Patsy's that few businesses, let alone restaurants, can claim. Knowing that he wanted to follow in his father's footsteps, Joe started working in the kitchen after school at the age of nine. He eventually relieved Patsy as chef and sent Papa out to the dining room to take care of front-of-house chores. A generation later, Joe's son Salvatore has taken over the kitchen, while Joe plays genial host to a clientele "80 percent of whom I know by name."

No wonder. They've been coming here for decades as part of Patsy's multigenerational theme. On any given night, Joe can point to one or two of the downstairs dining room's nineteen tables occupied by families, often fathers and sons and even grandsons. That is not to say the restaurant is a male preserve. One look at "Patsy's Wall of Fame," adorned with signed publicity stills of *Everybody* who has been anybody since 1940 or so, including Rosemary Clooney, Ann-Margaret, Farrah Fawcett, Donna Mills, and Patti La Belle, is enough to dispel that notion. But the no-nonsense decor and food seem to hold a particular fascination for men.

In fact, if the Smithsonian Institution ever wanted to showcase a classic 50s restaurant, this would be it. Patsy's, so comfortably familiar, with all those celebrity photographs; turquoise leatherette chairs; and white, molded ceramic bud vases decked out in red carnations, looks like a set from "Happy Days." And the menu is one that would bring a smile to the Fonz's face. When was the last time you saw cannelloni in meat sauce and chicken livers cacciatoria, at any price, let alone at $15.75 and $16.75 respectively?

Not often enough. Still, Patsy's also accommodates current tastes without the pretensions of many more contemporary Italian eateries. Grilled portabello mushrooms drizzled with achingly sweet olive oil were a recent appetizer special at $9.50, and one might see Salvatore's rendition of grilled salmon glazed by a spirited mustard sauce, seared on the outside and barely cooked on the inside, for $22.75.

One of our favorites among the more old-fashioned fare is the $19 chicken scarpariello, a hearty dish of chicken pieces on the bone sautéed in garlic, basil, and parsley-infused oil with mushrooms, peppers, and potatoes. Any of the veal chops — à la Milanese, Siciliano, or pizzaiola in the $26 neighborhood — are moist and flavorful, but we especially like the stuffed version, laced with marsala for $28.

Its location and four-course $28.50 pre-theater menu makes Patsy's a natural if you're Broadway-bound. Unlike many other theater district restaurants, however, Patsy's remains busy right through showtime. Dinner reservations for either before or during theater performances are a must, but, since Patsy's is not on the food faddists' circuit, a call early in the day usually secures a table.

If bargains beckon you more than Broadway does, try Patsy's prix-fixe lunch at $19.50. There's a choice of soup or salad, followed by seven entrée options like veal with peppers and shrimp parmigiana, each served with generous portions of potatoes and vegetables. Then it's ice cream and coffee. Not geographically far (though a world removed in tone) from the chichi 57th Street corridor, lunch at Patsy's is an ideal break from a day of shopping.

You should also consider Patsy's as the site of a West Side cocktail rendezvous. There's always a congenial person or two at the snug little bar, but it's never crowded. You will get a warm welcome from Joe, a generous well-made drink at a fair price, and more than likely a gander at somebody you recognize. And don't forget to say hello to our pal and Patsy's fixture, the affable Joe Francis. He's there so often, a plaque on the wall declares that a corner of the bar is his!

HOURS: Noon to 10:30 P.M. Sunday through Thursday. Till 11:00 P.M. on Friday and Saturday.

CREDIT CARDS: All major.

# Petrossian

| | |
|---|---|
| 182 West 58th Street | (212) 245-2214 |
| at Seventh Avenue | Boutique (212) 245-2217 |
| New York, NY 10019 | Fax (212) 245-2812 |

In 1920, two young Russian brothers introduced caviar to the Western world. Sixty-four years later, their sons wrapped it in an intriguing art deco package — an exceptionally beautiful restaurant — and presented it to an appreciative New York.

After fleeing to Paris in the wake of the Russian Revolution, Melkoum and Moucheg Petrossian discovered that their respective legal and medical credits from Moscow University would not be recognized by schools in their adopted city and that they would have to start their training all over again. Even more disturbing, their beloved caviar was unheard of in the City of Light. Yet with so many Russian émigrés descending on Paris, there was certainly a demand. They determined they could fill the void and make a living if they could import the precious eggs. They struck a deal by phone with the new Russian government, which involved loading a suitcase with every franc they could get their hands on and depositing them at the Russian Embassy in Paris. Then they waited. It was more than two months before they got the first shipment that assured them the Russians were honoring the deal.

It's a deal that has held ever since, despite the breakup of the Soviet Union. Petrossian is the exclusive agent for Russian caviar in France, the United States, Canada, and Switzerland. Furthermore, Petrossian is the only firm allowed to actually participate in the Caspian Sea sturgeon catch. They choose their caviar lot by lot as it is caught and oversee the preparation of the eggs. As a result, Petrossian has a well-deserved international reputation as purveyor of the world's finest caviar.

The store Melkoum and Moucheg founded on the Boulevard de Latour Mauborg has been a mecca for connoisseurs of caviar, smoked salmon, foie gras, and other delicacies since the 1930s. The restaurant and shop their sons, Christian and Armen, established in New York is similarly revered.

Unapologetic practitioners of living the good life, the Petrossian boys have created an environment celebrating that fine art. To enter Petrossian is to enter into ravishing decadence. We're told Christian and Armen instructed architect Ion Oroveanu to design "the most elegant, frivolous, unique place in the world." Art-Decoed as it is to the nth degree with polished pink and gray granite, burled walnut, gold-capped columns, bronze sculptures, etched mirrors by Erté, mink-trimmed leather banquettes, and a snail-shell chandelier originally made for Mme. Lanvin, we'd say he succeeded. When he first visited Petrossian, the late Erté gave it his imprimatur of design extravagance by declaring, "This is me!"

No doubt Erté was even more at home once he sat down at one of the luxuriously appointed tables (china by Limoges, custom-designed flatware by Christofle) and contemplated appetizers designed to warm the cockles of his Franco-Russian heart — whole foie gras, smoked salmon, borscht with crème fraiche, terrine of quail and foie gras with stone fruit chutney, and, of course, caviar. Make no mistake, Petrossian does have a perfectly respectable selection of main course dishes. They run the ingredient gamut from honey-glazed duck salad with shaved fennel to a particularly tasty rendition of suddenly trendy skate featuring a braised savoy cabbage and red onion marmalade to loin of venison with a gratin of potatoes, leeks, and cranberries.

But given the grazing-at-its-grandest quotient of the appetizers, we seldom get past them. And we have been known to satiate ourselves with a meal of caviar. Petrossian serves four kinds: beluga, ossetra, sevruga, and pressed. The first three are named after their parent sturgeons, each of which produces a roe with a distinctly different look, taste, color, and texture. "Pressed" refers to the method of preparation. Eggs that are already broken or too mature and therefore liable to break when packed in tins, as is the norm, are pressed — four pounds of fresh caviar are condensed into a pound of pressed caviar, making a very concentrated product with a strong flavor.

Any of the caviars can be ordered individually, the size of the portion determining the price: $22 for 1-1/16 ounces of pressed caviar, and up to $250 for 4-3/4 ounces of beluga. But we think that ordering the Royal Gourmet, 1-1/16 ounces each of sevruga, ossetra, and beluga with toast points for $110 is the way to go. If that's not quite regal enough for your tastes, take a cue from Madonna and order the Centerpiece Presentation — $500 for 8-3/4 ounces of beluga. Enough to serve five or six, although Her Blondness usually wolfs it down with a single companion.

Yes, Petrossian can be pricey and these prices are subject to change. But it's truly unique, so who cares?! Certainly not Candice Bergen and Louis Malle, Melanie Griffith and Don Johnson, Steven Spielberg and Kate Capshaw, Mike Nichols and Diane Sawyer, and Sean Connery (presumably, in this context, Mrs. Connery too). They're habituées and have probably discovered how to frequently indulge in the hedonistic experience that is Petrossian without breaking the bank.

Taking the restaurant up on its fixed price lunch and pre-theater offers—$29 and $38—is one way. Another is making a meal out of the "teasers," lots of tasty tidbits like roulades of smoked sturgeon with wild mushrooms, truffled foie gras en croûte, and smoked trout wrapped in lettuce: $19 for a small sampling, $24 for a large.

Despite the fact that dinner and after-theater reservations are a must (lunch is less problematical), you can enjoy Petrossian's pleasures on the spur of the moment. Just pop into the restaurant's boutique, and pick up Petrossian products like caviar, smoked salmon, foie, and assorted pâtés—you can even taste before you buy. These days you don't have to be in New York to buy or taste. A phone or fax order will dispense any of their estimable comestibles anywhere in the world. Furthermore, the Petrossians' American presence has been expanded with shops in major Bloomingdale's and Neiman Marcus locations.

HOURS:  Daily 11:30 A.M. to 3:00 P.M. and 6:00 to 11:30 P.M.

CREDIT CARDS:  All major.

# P. J. Clarke's

| 915 Third Avenue | Reservations (212) PL9-1650 |
| New York, NY | Front Room Phone (212) EL5-8857 |
| 10022 | Back Room Phone (212) EL5-9307 |

P. J. Clarke's—the bar, the restaurant, the institution—is so "New York" that the legendary crustiness of its waiters was recently featured in a commercial for a major airline. Since 1864 or 1892, depending upon whom you talk to, P. J. Clarke's has occupied this dear little bit of prime real estate at the corner of Third Avenue and 55th Street. In fact, the site is so prime and the institution so cherished that a highly unusual deal was struck in 1967. P. J. Clarke's property was sold to a giant development company but was allowed to retain its sacred and independent status. A new forty-five-story skyscraper was designed and built around the tiny building.

Since Clarke's is open 365 days a year until 4 A.M., stopping by for a little sustenance in the wee hours is a New York tradition. The $5.80 hamburgers are required eating, grilled on an open fire, thick and juicy. Of course, there are other delectables on the blackboard menu: a respectable steak for $15.90, chicken pot pie (just like Mom's) for $10.90, a generous $7.10 spinach salad, and state-of-the-art corned beef and cabbage for $8.70. (Odd prices are a Clarke's trademark.)

There's nothing odd or cutesy about the decor, though. It's good old-fashioned, no-nonsense, turn-of-the-century American bar, with the patina that only decades of smoke can produce — the pressed tin ceiling may once have been a real color. Now it's a sooty, indescribable brown. Likewise the bar, which some claim to be mahogany — it's been transformed to a black hulk. Only the white tile floor gleams.

Clarke's owes its unprecedented ongoing success to the fact that there really was a P. J. Clarke who built the business and gave it his personal stamp. Patrick Joseph "Paddy" Clarke, a native of County Leitrim, Ireland, started working on the premises in what was then termed a "saloon" in 1904. When the owner died in 1920, Paddy took over and remained in charge until his death in 1948. During his tenure, Clarke's became indelibly engraved on the American imagination as the quintessential bar in Billy Wilder's classic film *The Lost Weekend*.

Typical of the timelessness and tradition associated with Clarke's, Paddy's nephew Charlie acted as manager until his recent retirement. He was replaced by Jack Sterling, a Clarke's veteran of 35 years, and a relatively new recruit, Leo Wilson, who has only been around for the last two and a half decades! So even though Paddy's immediate heirs sold Clarke's soon after his death, its heritage has been carefully preserved.

You see, they were smart enough to sell it to Daniel Lavezzo, who already owned the building and operated an antique business in what is now Clarke's large rear dining room. Dan moved the antiques to the second floor and added the dining room. The

Lavezzo family has been part of the Clarke's scene ever since. Dan, Jr., is the current owner but retired, and his son, Dan III, is usually around making sure everything is as it should be, such as the purchase of fresh meat, fish, and vegetables every day (there are no freezers here, except for one reserved for bags of ice cubes). He also makes sure those little white pads are on each table at lunch, part of another tradition. This one was instituted by Dan, Jr., when he discovered that one of his waiters was illiterate. The poor fellow was trying to do his job by memorizing the orders, but his memory wasn't too terrific. Lots of customers were unhappy about getting something they didn't order and not getting something they did. Rather than fire him, Dan solved the problem by declaring that henceforth all orders were to be written on those little white pads by the guests, who presumably would get it right!

Indeed, we hear that some of those orders have been real literary tomes. After all, Clarke's is home away from office for the publishing, journalism, and advertising crowd. There are tales of people who have conducted their business from the back room — phone messages really are reliably taken and transmitted here — and the bar bills are considerably less than the cost of midtown office space.

Over the years, regulars have run a broad spectrum from Jake La Motta to Jackie Onassis, indicative of the unique, special quality about Clarke's. There's something satisfying about it for virtually every taste — even yours!

HOURS:        11:00 A.M. to 4 A.M., daily.

CREDIT CARDS:        All major.

## Primavera

1578 First Avenue                    (212) 861-8608
at 82nd Street
New York, NY 10028

We're always delighted to come across a bar as small as Primavera's; in our experience, it usually means we won't have to languish there waiting for our so-called reservation. Primavera is no exception to this unwritten rule. After all, owner Nicola Civetta has devoted his life to the fine art of sumptuous *dining*, not drinking. The trick here is to get the reservation in the first place.

It requires calling several days in advance and speaking directly with Nicola or mâitre d'hotel Paolo, AKA Paul.

Now, when we say that Nicola has devoted his life to fine dining, we don't say it lightly. At the tender age of fourteen, he entered hotel school in his native Italy to study cooking and restaurant management. From there, he went on to work in a number of top-rated establishments in Switzerland, Germany, France, and England before descending on American shores in the early 70s. In New York, he put in some time as a captain at Regine's, where he refined his ability to deal with the ultra-chic crowd that now calls Primavera its own. This crowd includes Mike Nichols, Jack Nicholson, Anthony Quinn, Richard Avedon, Paul Simon, and Bill Cosby. Nicola comments that "they" (meaning everyone who's anyone) "end up here eventually."

They luxuriate in Primavera's comfortable formality defined by the rich wood paneling and muted lighting. There's a soothing purity about Primavera. Marbled columns and unassuming oils are the principal decoration, set off by the unadorned white linens; the smooth, clean lines of sparkling crystal; and the fresh-yet-minimal flower arrangements on the tables. Much of the decor is authentically Italian. The paneling, windows, doors, and bar were handmade in Italy, then shipped to New York for installation under the watchful supervision of their designer, Caronne, the renowned Italian architect.

Italian craftsmanship aside, the Italian cooking of a relaxed, contemporary nature is the real star here. The menu is relatively standard, but the familiar dishes are executed with flair, as exemplified by that ubiquitous, all-too-often pedestrian menu staple, fried calamari. Here its tasty potential is realized. Even better, Nicola presents it as a complimentary welcoming dish.

Genial captains apprise you of seasonal delicacies like the grilled Italian wild mushrooms that are a specialty or the truffle dishes Nicola features from late September to early January. Pasta with white truffles is a fabulous, if costly, appetizer at "approximately" $39.50. Because the truffle market tends to be on the volatile side, the price may change. As a main course, it'll run at least $69.50, but Nicola cautions that only the nouveaux riches in Italy would ever order such a dish as an entrée.

Baby eels with oil and garlic are usually on the menu but not always available. They, too, are priced according to the market.

But you can count on Spiedino alla Romana, fried mozzarella on bread topped with an anchovy sauce ($14.50), a great choice as a starter. Or you might want to begin with Bill Cosby's favorite, Penne all' Arrabbiata, for $14.50. Sometimes when Bill craves this spicy red-sauce dish in the privacy of his own home, he sends his driver over for an order or two. Nicola doesn't really encourage takeout, but how do you say no to the Cos? And he often makes his request more palatable by sending along a gift of his own chef's special homemade bread.

For entrées, we've been seduced by the robust $25.50 risotto with wild mushrooms, the thinly sliced beef with rosemary and arugula for $29.50, and the spinach-stuffed veal roll covered by prosciutto and a light cream sauce at $28.50.

We've wondered if "50" is Nicola's lucky number. With the notable exception of the $32 roasted baby goat (a succulent though browned-to-perfection house specialty), almost everything on the menu is $x$ number of dollars and 50 cents.

You can happily rack up all those half dollars every night at Primavera, even on Sunday when many other fine restaurants are closed. For that very reason, Sundays here tend to be a madhouse from 7:00 to about 9:30 P.M.. This is definitely a night for regulars, so book your first Sunday supper reservation as early as 5:00 P.M. in order to get one.

HOURS:      5:30 P.M. to midnight, Monday through
            Saturday. From 5:00 P.M. on Sunday.

CREDIT CARDS:     All major.

## Primola

1226 Second Avenue                    (212) 758-1775
between 63rd and 64th Streets
New York, NY 10021

We checked the dictionary, and it seems primroses don't have to be yellow. What a relief! We'd been worried that Franco Iacobiello and Giuliano Zuliana had made a dreadful mistake on their menus. The rose that dots the $i$ in Primola (Italian for primrose) is decidedly hot pink. It had bothered us until we turned to *Webster's*.

However, the seeming incongruity of a pink primrose is about the only disturbing trait of this charming restaurant. Light, contemporary, and casual with its bleached floors and Bentwood-style chairs, it's an unusual hybrid — part power-people place, part neighborhood niche. Monday through Thursday it belongs to the politicos, financiers, and socialites. On the weekends, the locals take over.

They all come for Franco's tasty renditions of Italian favorites. Many followed him from his former gastronomical triumph: the popular Elio's. A native of the Adriatic coast of Italy, Franco has developed a distinctively delicate touch with his specialties: pasta, fish, and veal.

We particularly recommend the risottos — one infused with fresh seafood, the other with spinach at $19.50 and $18.50 respectively. There are eleven more exquisitely prepared pastas to explore, but don't get bogged down with them. In season, Primola flies in a Mediterranean fish called branzino. A white fish reminiscent of sea bass, it's prepared with fresh herbs, garlic, and balsamic vinegar. Priced according to the market, Franco's branzino is bellissimo.

Other favorites worthy of your consideration are the juicy roast loin of veal with three kinds of mushrooms and veal Abruzzese — scalloppine layered with proscuitto and peas in a hearty veal-stock sauce. Both cost $19.50.

When he opened Primola in 1986, Franco wanted to make sure the rest of the restaurant staff would perform as well as those in his kitchen. So he made Guiliano, another Elio veteran, his partner. Guiliano juggles the neighborhood crowd and the power set with equal aplomb. He does a terrific job of pleasing everyone, despite being handicapped by the the fact that the front room isn't equipped to handle all the people who want to sit there. The back room tends to be quiet — too quiet for the likes of Dustin Hoffman, Clint Eastwood, Ronald Perelman, Joanna Carson, Barbara Walters, and Polly Bergen.

With dinner reservations hard to come by and requiring a couple of days' notice, lunch is a good introduction to Primola. It's easier to get a table, less hectic, and a bargain to boot. Fixed-price luncheon menus range from $15 to $20. À la carte, a full lunch or dinner easily runs $60 a head, with a moderately priced wine.

It occurs to us that Franco and Guiliano could justifiably add the Italian word for "path" to Primola. After all, theirs is a restaurant that certainly encourages actions of pleasure and self-indulgence — Webster's definition of "primrose path!"

HOURS:          Noon to 3:00 P.M., Monday through
                Friday; 5:00 P.M. to midnight Monday
                through Saturday; until 11:00 P.M. on
                Sunday.

CREDIT CARDS:   American Express, MasterCard,
                Visa, and Diner's Club.

# The Rainbow Room

30 Rockefeller Plaza                    (212) 632-5000
50th Street between Fifth and
Sixth Avenues
New York, NY 10112

When the Rainbow Room opened in 1934, it set the standard by which all of New York's other glamorous rooms would be measured. Conceived as a "formal skyscraper supper club," its double-height windows afforded heretofore unappreciated views of the city to the three terraced levels of seating. The soaring domed ceiling was lit by a rainbow of colored lights, and a revolving dance floor 32 feet in diameter delighted New York's elite, who adopted the Rainbow Room as *the* place to dine and dance. Over the years, some of the stardust wore off. Among other disappointments, the dance floor stopped moving.

But a massive $20 million renovation that saw the space razed and cleared right to the outer walls changed all that. The Rainbow Room has been restored to all its original Deco glamour, right down to vintage costumed "cigarette girls," who (being politically correct) now hawk teddy bears.

Given his hand in the success of a number of the city's similarly high-profile establishments (The Four Seasons, Windows on the World), it's not surprising that Joe Baum was the creator of the reincarnated Rainbow Room. He is immensely proud of his role in returning it "to New Yorkers as their spot to dine, dance, and romance." While some have quibbled that Joe produced a restaurant with more style than substance, grumbling that the food and service are not what they could be, no one denies that the setting is the city's most intoxicating. The restaurant occupies the entire eastern end of the 65th floor, and the views to the north, east, and south seem endless during the day. At night, the lights of the city and beyond — way beyond — dance into the room, creating an undeniable air of romance.

There's simply no place else like it in the world. And though an evening here will climb to $100 a person with cocktails and wine, we think it's money well spent. The entertainment value alone is worth it. In addition to the views, the people-watching opportunities are unparalleled from tables set up to afford great sight lines to the dance floor, which once again revolves. When you're not tripping the light fantastic, there's usually someone on the floor worth keeping an eye on and musing about.

People dress up here, and we've seen some amazing outfits — as many fashion victims as plates. We won't place them in either category, but we've spotted Regis and Joy Philbin and their pals Frank and Kathie Lee Gifford, as well as Robert Duvall gliding across the floor.

As for the food, it's just fine. No question about what to start with — Oysters Rockefeller, of course, at $15. For even richer tastes, try the steak tartare "iced" with sevruga for $25. The $30 chopped veal loin immersed in sautéed artichokes and morels is an appropriately festive main course. We've also been favorably impressed by the sautéed halibut resting on an island of Belgian endive in a sea of red shallot and chive sauce for $27. This is a dessert kind of place, a necessary indulgence to prolong the evening and keep the table as long as possible. So go for it — baked Alaska for two, spectacularly flamed at your table for $18, washed down with a $9 glass or two of Piper-Heidsieck Extra Dry.

Early- and late-evening meals are available, too. With the relatively bargain-priced $38.50 pretheater menu you run the risk of missing out on the dancing, assuming you really are going to the theater. Otherwise, you can stick around and pay the $15-per-person music charge that gets tacked on to every bill after 6:30 P.M. Monday through Thursday; Friday and Saturday it goes up to $20. The three-course dinner includes selections like chilled shrimp with a zucchini chutney and spiced salmon tartare for appetizers, followed by mustard-glazed salmon or a delicately seasoned lump crab and swordfish cake.

The supper menu, available after 10:30 P.M., features a cobb salad and a fruit-garnished cheese platter, as well as a number of grilled entrées. But unless you stick to the lighter fare, there's not much in the way of late-night economy here. You're still looking at $75 a person, including the music charge. Because it's so special, people flock to The Rainbow Room. Since reservations are mandatory, be prepared to spend some time making them. Calls are answered by a disembodied voice asking you to wait "until the next available operator" can take your call. Momentarily you wonder if you dialed an airline instead of a restaurant. Once you get to a real person, be prepared for a shock. You'll be told they'll be happy to take your reservation for six weeks hence. Talk about planning ahead!

But if you find yourself in New York unexpectedly and are just dying to go, test the mettle of your concierge with a request for a reservation—or place a last-minute call yourself. There are always cancellations. Alternatively, you can almost always get a taste of the Rainbow experience on Sunday afternoons for brunch. Call first—their Sunday schedule is flexible. And you can always sample the *complex* called the Promenade, which stretches along the south face of the building with lower Manhattan spread out below. In addition to being a dynamite spot for drinks, it serves little meals like a hamburger or grilled swordfish sandwich (both $12). And you can create an instant cocktail party with either the "Orient Express" or "A Taste of Mexico," $25 spreads of ethnic hors d'oeuvres. No reservations necessary, but there can be a line pre- and posttheater.

The final Rainbow option, not including a number of rooms available for private functions, is Rainbow & Stars. It's a jewel of a 90-seat cabaret presenting established stars like Rosemary Clooney, Maureen McGovern, and Karen Akers. Lately Rainbow & Stars has also enjoyed considerable success with reviews saluting the music of such great composers as Irving Berlin, Rodgers and Hammerstein, and Julie Styne. Designed to look like a good old-fashioned nightclub, the room has a fabulous view to the north. But here, the view plays second fiddle to the entertainment. Rainbow & Stars envelops its performers, creating an instant bond between the stars and their audience.

There are two shows a night, one at 8:30 P.M. and another at 10:30 P.M., each with a $35 cover but no minimum. If you choose to dine, the corresponding dinner seatings are at 6:30 P.M. and 9:30 P.M. As in The Room, there are dinner and supper menus, with similar selections and prices. Given the sense of occasion we always feel at Rainbow & Stars, we like the caviar sampler platter for $25; somehow it goes with the silver lamé tablecloths sprinkled with glittering stars and sparkling jewels. Predictably, reservations are very necessary, but usually obtainable, especially at the beginning of a run before the rave reviews hit the paper.

Everything about The Rainbow Room, the Promenade, and Rainbow & Stars evokes images of another era without feeling like a monument to that possibly more glamorous time. Rather, the Rainbow complex today is very much alive, creating memories for a whole new generation, but only if they have cash or an American Express card — no other card will cut it.

HOURS:        5:30 P.M. to 1:00 A.M., Tuesday through Saturday. Sunday, Brunch: Noon to 2:00 P.M.; Dinner: 6:00 to 10:30 P.M.

CREDIT CARDS:        American Express only.

## *Rosa Mexicano*

1063 First Avenue at 58th Street        (212) 753-7407
New York, NY 10022

Josefina Howard is a woman with a mission. She wants people to recognize the intricate color, flavor, and variety (over 3,000 native dishes) that is the cuisine of Mexico. She's gone a long way toward her goal with the unqualified success of Rosa Mexicano, which she opened in 1984. It is her response to New York's dearth of authentic Mexican food. And she's about to go one step further with the establishment of a culinary institute in a 17th-century palace she bought for that purpose in a small town an hour north of Mexico City.

Josefina's obvious passion for her mission is all the more interesting when you consider that she's not even Mexican. She was born in Cuba, raised in Spain, and spent her early adulthood in New York before moving with her American husband to Mexico. She spent 34 years there and fell in love with the food, which she found "beautiful and moving like art."

Upon her return to New York in 1979, Josefina first tackled New Yorkers' misconceptions about Mexican food with a café specializing in *real* tacos — soft tortillas filled with charcoal-grilled meat. She often had to mollify first-time customers with a patient explanation that the hard taco shell, so popular in America, was unknown in Mexico. She went on to refine their appreciation for the art of Mexican cuisine as the head chef of the now defunct Cinco de Mayo before hitting her stride with Rosa Mexicano. It is truly her own creation—from design (she was a successful interior decorator in both New York and Mexico City) to dessert. And it sparkles with her presence as she darts among tables, apprising guests of the day's "goodies," specials that allow her kitchen to experiment with the ideas her frequent trips to Mexico inspire.

The subtly dramatic decor—black slate floor, pink and plum tiles, copper-hooded open grill, rustic wood furniture—provides a fitting backdrop to Josefina's special brand of showmanship. Order the guacamole and you'll know what we mean. Starting with fresh avocados, it's prepared at your table at lightning speed by a waiter delivering a running commentary, while soliciting your preference for mild, spicy, or hot. Served in the molcajete, three-legged mortar made of volcanic rock, in which it is made, Rosa Mexicano's guacamole is a rich, chunky mixture and enough for two at $9. This is not to say the tasty $9.75 ceviche or the roasted and pickled green chilies-filled sardines for $5.75 are not worthy of consideration; it's just that the guacamole is a must. And it's likely that your appetite will be further whetted by complimentary hors d'oeuvres—sausage-stuffed quesadillas or cheese-laden nachos—passed by one of Josefina's affable staff like the tall, dark, and handsome Ramon, who has been with her since the opening.

As if that weren't enough of a treat, the last time we stopped by, two shot glasses fueled by a curious concoction arrived with our margaritas. We weren't sure whether to drink them, dip something in them, mix them with our drinks, or throw them over our shoulders! Fortunately Josefina was on hand to give a name to them—esquites—and to explain the delicious blend of corn, chilies, and epazote (an herb Josefina maintains may soon outstrip cilantro as the herb du jour) sold in Mexican street stands is eaten with a spoon. It occurred to her that they would be great as a chef's offering for the restaurant.

As usual she was right, very right, which is why we get especially excited about the specials here. Always unusual, they are just as consistently superb. Take the red snapper awash in black olive, caper, onion, and tomato sauce for $20.50 or the shrimp crepes caressed by an eloquent sweet and spicy sauce at $22. The first conjures up images of Provençal; the second resembles nothing so much as heaven. Neither is likely to coincide with your vision of Mexican fare. Indeed, the menu notes that "Because Rosa Mexicano presents classic Mexican cuisine, some of the popular Americanized dishes often associated with Mexican food are not included on our menu."

That suits most people just fine. The restaurant is always crowded and reservations are most definitely necessary. Be sure to ask for a booth up front or a table in the back room. The often raucous bar crowd tends to overflow around the freestanding tables in the front room, making for cramped dining.

As forthcoming as she is about her Mexican mission, Josefina is surprisingly circumspect about her clientele. While she admits that she feeds a number of the celebrities and socialites who inhabit her Sutton Place neighborhood, she declines to be specific. We did spot man-about-town David Koch and we know that English couturier Victor Edelstein, one of Princess Diana's favorites, spends much of his westward-bound trans-Atlantic flights perusing a Rosa Mexicano menu, plotting his first meal on American soil. Less inclined than we are to risk the specials, he is generally torn between two dishes that showcase the kitchen's special flair with mole sauces — *enchiladas de mole poblano* and *enchiladas de pato*. For the former at $15.50, tortillas are dipped in a rich sauce of ground chilies, scores of spices, and unsweetened chocolate; filled with shredded chicken; then topped with more mole sauce, sliced onions, and crumbled cheese. The latter version sells for $17.50 and features a mole sauce, made green by ground pumpkin seeds, embracing tortillas wrapped around shredded duck and topped with cheese and cream.

Be forewarned, once you've dined at Rosa Mexicano, it's unlikely you'll ever eat at your neighborhood taco stand again.

HOURS:     5:00 P.M. to midnight, daily except Thanksgiving.

CREDIT CARDS:     All major.

# Rosa Mexicano's
## Chile Chocolate Truffles and Pumpkin Seed Praline

**Ingredients**

1 1/2 pounds semisweet chocolate broken in pieces
10 tablespoons unsalted butter
1 3/4 cups heavy cream
6 tablespoons Kahlua
1/2 teaspoon vanilla
1/2 teaspoon *chile de arbol* powder
1 cup pumpkin seeds
2/3 cup sugar
1/4 cup water

**Preparation**

1. Melt chocolate in a double boiler.
2. Stir continuously. Add butter a tablespoon at a time.
3. In two or three additions, gradually stir in cream. Add Kahlua and stir. Add vanilla and chile powder and stir.
4. Let chocolate mixture cool in refrigerator.
5. Toast pumpkin seeds in heavy skillet, shaking continuously. They will crackle and pop. Transfer them to a nonstick or lightly oiled baking sheet.
6. In a small, heavy saucepan combine and stir sugar and water. Bring to a boil to dissolve. Boil vigorously until mixture begins to darken, caramelizing.
7. Immediately pour the caramel over the pumpkin seeds and allow to cool and harden completely.
8. Remove from sheet and break into pieces. Blend until coarsely ground.
9. With a teaspoon, scoop out chilled chile chocolate mixture and roll in hands to make small balls.
10. Roll balls in ground pumpkin seed praline.

# The Russian Tea Room

150 West 57th Street                         (212) 265-0947
New York, NY 10019                        (800) 262-4RTR

A focal point for the famed and famished for nearly seven decades, The Russian Tea Room is a bona fide legend in a city where "in" restaurants fall out of favor with the speed of the Concorde. The RTR (as it's known to regulars) really did start out as a tea room in 1926. Founded by members of the Russian Imperial Ballet who had fled to America during the Bolshevik Revolution, it was a meeting place for Russian émigrés, serving only ice cream, pastries, tea, and sympathy. The end of Prohibition in 1932 signaled a transformation. The soda fountain became a bar specializing in more than twenty varieties of vodka from around the world, and the RTR started serving full meals.

After World War II, a group of investors led by Sidney Kaye took over the restaurant. In 1955 Sidney bought out his partners and devoted himself to preserving RTR's exceptional Euro-Russian charm, while adding his trademark touches like keeping the Christmas decorations up year-round.

When Sidney died in 1967, he left the restaurant to his widow Faith Stewart-Gordon with the stipulation that she have three months to decide whether to keep it or sell it. Faith, a former actress, says it was a difficult, even frightening decision, but she took the plunge. She has since then successfully applied her show business flair—including adding a popular cabaret series and establishing the ingenious Caviar Club—to the management of one of the country's most famous dining establishments. Indeed, for Faith, "The Russian Tea Room is a form of theater. It's like being on stage all the time."

It's an exuberant green-walled, red leather-boothed, pink tableclothed- and art-adorned stage often filled with stars of the highest magnitude. The small booth in the bar at the front of the restaurant, as well as the first three tables along both walls, have traditionally been reserved for the movie moguls and Broadway biggies who regularly transact business here. This tradition was immortalized in *Tootsie* by Dustin Hoffman's in-drag confrontation with director Sydney Pollack at the RTR.

The last few years, however, have seen those tables not quite so star-studded. The RTR's box office had been eroded by that most deadly of reviews, "tourist trap," engendered by high prices, mediocre food, and lackadaisical service. Not one to allow the legacy with which she had been entrusted to die, the indomitable Faith went on the attack. She hired Paul Ingenito (an American Place veteran and graduate of the Larry Forgione school for celebrity chefs) to revamp the kitchen, updated the menus with more contemporary fare at better value, and put a renewed emphasis on service. Much to the relief of many of its fans, the RTR is once again *boffo*.

Paul's knack for RTR staples such as borscht, chicken kiev, and beef stroganoff has gotten raves from RTR habitués Danny de Vito, Tony Randall, Candice Bergen, and Mikhail Baryshnikov, while his ventures into non-Russian territory—sautéed gulf shrimp with a sassy saffron risotto in a light leek and tomato broth, for instance—lend new gustatory excitement to RTR's unique blend of dazzle, deals, and dynamism. The recently instituted fixed price three-course menus—ranging from a $22.50 lunch to the $67 Dinner à la Russe, which begins with a one-ounce serving of sevruga caviar—have also been well received as alternatives to the à la carte route. But don't expect Woody Allen to give up his beloved blini for these (relative) bargains. He never fails to start his meal here with the RTR's superior buckwheat version slathered in two ounces of red salmon caviar with sour cream for $28.75.

As befits a restaurant which serves more caviar than any other in America (2,647 pounds in 1992), you *can* line your blinis with beluga, ossetra or sevruga—$65.50, $54.50, and $49.75 for one ounce respectively. No doubt purists would rather take advantage of the RTR's Caviar Supreme, one ounce each of sevruga and ossetra minus the contamination of blinis and sour cream, for only $65.50. Indeed, with a couple of Caesar salads at $9.75 and/or the heavenly $6.95 borscht, we've called it dinner.

Consequently, we've been invited to join one of Faith's latest innovations, the RTR Caviar Club, which means we can get selected caviars at special prices and are invited to seasonal caviar dinners, featuring the new catches served in both classic and contemporary presentations. You can join too; just ask for an application.

Without filling in the blanks, you can enjoy the benefits of another sort of club, the cabaret at the RTR. It's upstairs in what used to be called Siberia until the likes of Liza Minnelli and Shirley MacLaine started hanging out there to catch some of the best acts in town—Liliane Montevecchi, Karen Akers, Joel Silberman, and David Staller. They hold center stage on Sunday nights. Mondays are devoted to the truly unique American Society of Composers, Authors, and Publishers' "Singers and Songwriters" series, wherein cabaret's boldest and brightest songwriters present their latest material. Both nights, shows are at 8:00 and 10:30 P.M., but the price of admission is different. The cost is $23.50 per person plus a $10 drink minimum on Sundays, and a $15 music charge plus a $10 minimum on Mondays.

A special cabaret menu helps you take care of the minimum. There's a $25 fixed-price offering featuring a choice of soup or salad, followed by entrée selections such as steak frites or roasted filet of salmon on a carpet of sautéed Swiss chard in red caviar sauce, plus dessert. Since we like our cabaret late, we like our food light. We usually opt for splitting the assortment of seasonal Russian hors d'oeuvres called zakuska for $12.50 along with the sensational $19.75 Cabaret Club—smoked salmon with cucumber and onion salad on five-grain bread.

The kitchen's renaissance and the ebulliently timeless atmosphere, coupled with the electrifying anticipation of you-never-know-who-you-might-see now ensures that the Russian Tea Room will not suffer the fate of the Soviet government whose very existence spawned the restaurant in the first place.

HOURS:       11:30 A.M. to 11:30 P.M. daily.

CREDIT CARDS:       All major.

# San Domenico

240 Central Park South                    (212) 265-5959
between 7th and Broadway
New York, NY 10019

When it comes to restaurants, Tony May has the Midas touch, as restaurateur and promoter. He has conceived and launched a number of successful establishments, deploying his right-on public relations instincts to make them hot—magnets to food fanatics and potential buyers. In fact, Tony's modus operandi has often been to sell just before the heat starts to cool, the visually provocative Palio being a case in point. With San Domenico, however, he seems to be in for the long haul.

It could be that this perception is fueled by San Domenico's flame, which has remained white hot five years after its 1988 debut; this despite the departure of founding celebrity chef Valentino Marcatilli for his native Italy and the defection of the celebrated manager, Bruno Dissin, to Cipriani. For anyone but Tony, these could have been crippling blows. After all, it was Valentino's two-Michelin-star San Domenico in Imola, Italy, that was Tony's inspiration for its Central Park South namesake. And Bruno, a world-class hand-kisser, has quite a following as the result of his thirteen years as Le Cirque's meeter and greeter.

Tony managed to replace them both, without losing one iota of San Domenico's popularity or prestige. Indeed, long-time occupiers of San Domenico's burnt orange leather chairs, such as Anthony Quinn, Luciano Pavarotti, Oscar and Annette de la Renta, and Brooke Shields didn't seem to notice, while new fans such as Jodie Foster and John F. Kennedy, Jr., couldn't care less. There was much more of a hue and cry when Tony replaced San Domenico's trademark pumpkin-colored linens with white tablecloths and napkins. Moreover, the awards just kept coming. In 1992, *Food & Wine* named San Domenico as one of the country's top twenty-five restaurants and *Passport to New York Restaurants* made it one of its twelve five-star winners.

San Domenico continues to exemplify Tony's vision of it as a "luxurious and comfortable environment where one can relax amid warm colors and great art, while enjoying wonderful food and wine." These days it also embodies Tony's master stroke of making even the city's most expensive restaurants accessible to the masses with bargain fixed-price menus tied to the year. It was Tony the promoter, in cahoots with dining poller Tim Zagat, who put together a consortium of restaurateurs to promote $19.92 three-course lunches during that year's Democratic National Convention in New York. The program generated a maelstrom of publicity, proving so successful (San Domenico went from an average 45 lunches a day to 120) that it was extended indefinitely. At some participating restaurants, $24.92 dinners were added. Annually, January 1 means a penny increase.

Of course, it is one of the ironies of New York that a lunch here just shy of $20 is deemed cheap. But, when you consider that a midday meal at San Domenico could easily run $45 *without* an alcoholic libation, there's no denying the value. In deference to Tony's PR genius, we go the fixed-price route at lunch. A typical menu starts with a salad or raw vegetables tossed in an herb-infused olive oil followed by pasta with broccoli in a tomato sauce and a fresh fruit tart for dessert. What a pleasure to enjoy the autumnal serenity of San Domenico—terra cotta floors, dappled ochre walls brought to life by colorful paintings by Italian artists, and window sills distinguished by dramatic dried wheat arrangements—without stretching our budgets, our waistlines, or our schedules!

Dinner is another story altogether. As the evening's principal entertainment, we like to take full advantage of the well-documented talents of current chef Theo Schoenegger. His is an aristocratic cuisine in the best Northern Italian tradition. Witness the antipasti, such as crisply sautéed sweetbreads tossed with baby greens in garlic oil or the tender baby octopus on a Mediterranean reef of tomatoes, olive, and capers, both at $12.50. Among the pastas, a large, soft egg-filled ravioli drizzled with a sublime truffle butter is a knockout at $21. And spaghetti with tomato sauce, the most pedestrian of dishes elsewhere, takes on a homemade hauteur here for $16.50.

As for main courses, there are a number of carne and pesce selections, as well as daily specials. Generally speaking, Theo's skills are better exercised by meat and game, possibly the result of his upbringing in the Italian Alps, where he learned to cook at his mother's restaurant. The sautéed goose liver surrounded by three treatments of onions, instituted by Theo's predecessor, continues to be a stunning dish in terms of flavor and price. At $42.50 it may carry the city's highest entrée price tag! A black olive sauce is the surprisingly welcome complement to the $26.50 breast of duck, and breast of pheasant is made particularly savory by a light juniper berry sauce for $29.50.

The wine list of nearly 700 labels means you're bound to find one to suit any meal. If you're in doubt, refer to the section which matches certain bottles with specific categories of food.

Dessert? There are several choices, but they are not the house's strong suit. And who needs them after such a richly satisfying meal?

HOURS:        Noon to 3:00 P.M., Monday through Friday; 5:30 to 11:00 P.M., Monday through Saturday; from 5:00 P.M. on Sunday.

CREDIT CARDS:      All major.

# Sarabeth's Kitchen

423 Amsterdam Avenue          (212) 496-6280
between 80th and 81st Streets
New York, NY 10024

1295 Madison Avenue          (212) 410-7335
at 92th Street
New York, NY 10128

Popularly known as "the breakfast queen of New York," Sarabeth Levine and her kitchens produce the things of which very sweet dreams are made. In 1981, while others were entering the power breakfast sweepstakes, Sarabeth and her little Upper West Side bakery began carving out more modest early morning territory. She quickly gained a citywide reputation for her fresh-baked breads, muffins, cookies, and cakes, as well as her delicious orange-apricot marmalade.

Sarabeth credits the marmalade, based on a 200-year-old family recipe, with launching her business. As demand for it and her baked goods grew, so did her interest in expanding her repertoire. She began serving light meals at the bakery. The few available tables were soon overbooked by a clientele eager for her reasonably priced, ingenious concoctions. Sarabeth and husband/partner Bill Levine decided it was time to expand. They set up an East Side kitchen on Madison Avenue and moved to a larger location on the West Side.

A warm and fuzzy feeling comes over you when you enter Sarabeth's Kitchen on Amsterdam. Is there anything more wonderful than that fresh smell of something baking? All of the baked goods are made here, though the rest of the dishes are prepared to order where they are served. You see, Sarabeth is a woman with a fetish for fresh and perfect. You can depend on her food being both.

You can also count on your appreciation of all those fresh smells not being distorted by smoke. Sarabeth doesn't allow any smoking in any of her restaurants (a third opened in the Whitney Museum in 1991). She never has and never will.

Both the Amsterdam and Madison Avenue restaurants are open for breakfast, lunch, tea, and dinner, featuring light American fare with a European touch. For breakfast, you can't beat the novel pumpkin waffle dripping with sour cream, raisins, pumpkin seeds, and honey for $8 or the cheese blintzes with sour cream and apple butter for $8.50. At lunch, there are a number of interesting sandwiches like the roasted vegetable number — mouth-watering layers of eggplant, tomatoes, zucchini, and arugula on focaccia with hummus playing the role of mayonnaise. It's a $9.50 winner. We are equally smitten with the rigatoni with fresh ricotta cheese crowned by grilled tomatoes, fresh chicken sausage, zucchini, and watercress for $10.75.

At dinner, the tablecloths go on and the lights get dimmer, but the cheerful, informal atmosphere remains. While both restaurants have a pretty, pleasant country kitchen look, embellished by paintings of rural scenes by friends of Sarabeth and Bill, the East Side location tends to attract a slightly dressier crowd than the West Side site. But then, that's the East Side versus the West Side. The menus reflect the difference too — shorter, marginally more sophisticated, and definitely more expensive on the East. We like the greater selection and better prices on Amsterdam.

Try the grilled salmon with couscous, sugar snap peas, and a tropical fruit salsa or the chicken pot pie just like grandmother used to make. Both are $15 bargains, and there are three entrées on the menu priced at only $10!

At either location, any day of the week, you'll find more than a sprinkling of actors, some famous, most not. Sarabeth's low-key, no-muss, no-fuss approach makes her kitchens a haven for them. We also expect they appreciate the touch of fantasy supplied by the Mother Goose theme that turns up here and there in the decor.

Reservations are accepted for dinner. For any other meal, stand in line like everybody else. While you're waiting, you can scan the shelves of bakery products and condiments to decide what Sarabeth goody you're going to take home as a souvenir. We recommend any of her award-winning preserves, all completely hand-made and minus fillers, additives, or preservatives. However, we find a 16-oz. jar of Apricadabra—a blend of apricots, pineapple, and currants—particularly useful. At $9, or the blood orange at $10, is a great glaze for chicken, turkey, duck, or pork.

HOURS:          8:00 A.M. to 10:30 P.M., Monday through
                Friday; 9:00 A.M. to 11:00 P.M. on
                Saturday; 9:00 A.M. to 9:30 P.M. on Sunday.

CREDIT CARDS:   All major.

# Sfuzzi

58 West 65th Street                    (212) 873-3700
between Columbus and
Central Park West
New York, NY 10023

Once, this otherwise likable outpost of a growing national chain of moderately priced Italian restaurants suffered from an attitude problem—the result of too much success too soon. Immediately upon its 1988 opening, it was embraced by a young, hip, and celebrity-studded crowd. No longer. The crowd's still there (at least after 8:00 P.M., when the older types clear out). This is, after all, Madonna's neighborhood haunt. But the "And exactly who are you?" approach to reservations and seating has been replaced by solicitous friendliness. Thanks to General Manager Kenyon Price, Sfzuzzi has, as *New York Magazine* recently noted, "mastered the warmth of the desk."

These days when you are told the restaurant is full—especially during pretheater hours when it's advisable to book three to ten days in advance, depending on what and how much is playing at Lincoln Center—you don't have to take it personally. What's more, you'll be thanked for your interest and invited back or be given the option to take one of the small high-topped tables in the bar. Don't dismiss this alternative out of hand. The three-course $29.95 menu (available throughout the restaurant) is a well-priced dandy, and the chairs are actually more comfortable than the Paris bistro caned ones in the dining room.

Don't be put off if, when you call ahead for pretheater, you're encouraged to take a slot somewhat earlier than the perennially popular 6:30. Kenyon has developed a system of staggered reservation slots starting at 5:00, so that all the takers of Sfuzzi's 150 seats don't arrive at the same time. Take the time given and count yourself lucky that you got it and that Kenyon is so concerned about avoiding anxiety-provoking logjams at the desk and coat room.

For what amounts to a second seating after 8:00 P.M., you might be asked to wait a bit at the bar. Normally that's one of our pet peeves, but not here. The bar action is generally ferocious. Even if you don't care to partake in the mating game, it is fun to watch.

And fun is what Sfuzzi is all about. It starts with the decor, an amusing blend of high-tech minimalism and Roman archeological dig. Antiqued columns stop short of the flat back ceiling sprouting a bumper crop of industrial-looking hanging lamps. Brick walls take on an incandescence from rheostat torches shedding light on fragments of painted friezes, à la Pompeii.

Since the loose translation of Sfuzzi is "fun food," the amusement continues with the menus. You can't help but giggle (at least the first time) at the first item on it, Frozen Sfuzzi. Almost too cutely described as "Un-Bellini-Able," they're made with sparkling wine, peach schnapps, and "secret ingredients." Consequently, they're slushy, refreshing, and predictably strong. In keeping with the fun factor, Frozen Sfuzzis come in small, medium, or ridiculous proportions — a "goblet" of them serves twelve.

On the food front, the fun starts with the fresh focaccia placed on the table, sans butter. Instead, Sfuzzi serves a delightful, not to mention healthy, dip of extra virgin olive oil, enlivened with pepper, shallots, basil, and garlic. In and of itself, the focaccia makes a fine appetizer, but it's a shame to pass on the $7.25 fried calamari accompanied by a spicy marinara and a creamy aioli sauce. We also like the chunks of roasted portabello mushrooms tossed with asparagus in a tomato vinaigrette for $7. And you can't go wrong with any of the pizzas, which are just right for two as a first course. Take a tip from us and ask them to toss some dried tomatoes on the $14.50 smoked chicken pizza with caramelized onions, goat cheese, and rosemary.

"Specialties," more familiarly known as entrées, include grilled salmon in an interesting basil citrus sauce with properly al dente haricots verts and crispy, garlicky potatoes at $23.50 and a romano cheese-encrusted chicken breast on a bed of linguini with a zesty tomato basil sauce for $19.50. The $22 veal scallopini enhanced by wild mushrooms, caramelized onions, and marsala is also good. And there's a selection of pastas ranging in price from $13.50 to $16.00.

But if you're here for the fun, stick with the starters—the pizzas, the Frozen Sfuzzis, and the star-gazing. Yes, that's William Baldwin at the bar. And there's George Michael holding court in one corner, while Tom Cruise and Nicole Kidman are billing and cooing in another. Isn't that Prince Rainer, Prince Albert, and Princess Caroline being spirited out the back way to avoid prying paparazzi? You bet.

Of course, should you get too enamored of the Frozen Sfuzzis, it won't matter much what you eat or who you see. You'll be too busy soaking up the fun, just like Mr. and Mrs. Liebman, the most regular of regulars who show up every Monday night at 8:00 P.M. "just like clockwork," says Kenyon.

HOURS:        11:30 A.M. to 3:00 P.M., daily; 5:00 to 11:00 P.M., Sunday through Thursday; and 5:00 to midnight Friday and Saturday.

CREDIT CARDS:    All major.

# Shun Lee

43 West 65th Street                      (212) 595-8895
between Columbus and Central Park West
New York, NY 10023

When Michael Tong's lawyer suggested he take a look at a space on the Upper West Side as a possible site for the expansion of his Shun Lee dynasty, Michael's first thought was, "No way." Back in 1980, when north of Central Park South might as well have been north of Newfoundland as far as dining destinations were concerned (with the notable exceptions of Café des Artistes and Tavern on the Green), his was a perfectly reasonable reaction. Then Michael, the man who redefined Chinese restaurants in America by introducing Szechuan cooking in his establishments, remembered an ancient real estate proverb—"location, location, location." The one in question was half a block from Lincoln Center. He reasoned that all those people flocking to the center's cultural attractions would welcome a first-class Chinese restaurant just steps away.

Michael was right. Just try to get a last-minute pretheater reservation here, despite the fact that the restaurant shuns the early evening special prix-fixe menus so popular elsewhere. "Limited menus make no sense in a Chinese restaurant. They go against everything Chinese food is about, the communal sharing of lots of choices." We couldn't agree more, as we habitually plunge into a plethora of appetizers including ethereal steamed dumplings, celestially delicate grilled scallops served in their shell with meaty ribs glazed by a caress of honey, and hacked chilled chicken in a vivacious sesame sauce ($6.25, $7.25, and $10.25).

There have been times when we've topped off the appetizers with the stellar $4.50 hot and sour soup and called it lunch, late-afternoon snack, dinner, or supper. Shun Lee is unusually accessible for any of the above, open as it is daily from noon to midnight. Then there are the occasions when we forge ahead into a menu peppered with decidedly extraordinary choices. The sweetbreads stir-fried with scallions, black mushrooms, and water chestnuts in a hot Szechuan sauce are a special favorite for $16.50, as is the sliced Norwegian salmon sautéed in rice wine with ginger, scallions, water chestnuts, snow peas, and Szechuan pepper at $18.50. The $18.75 fresh goose liver and boneless duck with onions and leeks in a zestfully light sauce is another novel choice.

Should you rather tread on more familiar territory, the orange-flavored beef and Peking duck ($16.75 and $35.00) are models of their ilk. In any case, you will be served by energetic waiters who epitomize Michael's commitment to service. "I think, these days, it's 60 percent of a good restaurant experience. And it can be divided into three parts — a warm greeting at the door, a genial escort to the table, and an efficient waiter." Rest assured that you, along with Michael Douglas, Barbara Walters, Robert Redford, Dustin Hoffman, and Mike Wallace, will get all three at Shun Lee.

Whatever the formula for a restaurant as successful as this one is, decor enters the equation somewhere. At Shun Lee you are treated to drop-dead drama. Papier-mâché monkeys cavort over the bar, which opens into a black dining room delivered from being funereal by pink linens; theatrical lighting; and undulating, bright-eyed dragons serving as crown molding. Ask for one of the cavernous booths, the secluded privacy of which is another reason for Shun Lee's high celebrity profile.

But don't count on catching a glimpse of many "names" during the hectic pretheater hours when the restaurant is overrun with well-heeled Upper East Side chic to Greenwich not-so-chic types on their way to the opera. Wait until what amounts to a second seating after 8:00 P.M., when the pace relaxes and Shun Lee takes on the more casual aspects of a neighborhood restaurant, right down to regulars in jeans. In fact, Michael maintains that 40 percent of his clientele partakes in a Shun Lee experience on a weekly basis, either in the restaurant, in the lower-priced dim sum Shun Lee Cafe next door, or via takeout. Clearly Michael has reason to be grateful that he took a walk on the wild West Side.

HOURS:        Noon to midnight daily.

CREDIT CARDS:        All major.

## Sidewalkers

12 West 72nd Street                    (212) 799-6070
between Central Park West and
Columbus Avenue
New York, NY 10023

They *do* walk sideways—crabs, that is. This is the home of the "Maryland Crab-Bash," the only such outpost of the land of pleasant living worth visiting in New York City. If you've never bashed the shell of a steamed Chesapeake Bay crab to get at the sweet, succulent meat inside, don't miss this place. It's an experience you'll never forget and one to which you're likely to become addicted.

But it's an addiction with rules. First and foremost, call ahead to inquire about the size of the crabs being offered. If they only have mediums, dine elsewhere—they're too small, too little reward for all the work. Assuming they have large ones at $19.50 per half dozen or jumbos (priced according to market), make a reservation for your party—invoking rule number two of going with friends as this is a great group activity—and a reservation for your crabs. Figure on a dozen jumbos or large ones for every two people. Otherwise, you're likely to get there and be relegated to the unsatisfactory mediums.

Upon being seated at a table swathed in paper, address rule number three by ordering a pitcher of beer, whether you're a beer drinker or not. It's the most refreshing chaser to the spicy bay seasoning that encrusts the bright red crustaceans. If you're really hungry, you might also ask for an order of tender Long Island steamers. There are more than enough for two at $15.95.

When your waiter appears with a tray heaped with crabs, which are rather unceremoniously dumped onto the middle of the table, the fun begins. Armed with a wooden mallet, nutcrackers, and a knife, and protected by a plastic bib, you attack. If you're unfamiliar with the finer points of crab bashing, any of the pleasant young staff will gladly show you the ropes and assure you of the validity of rule number four—you *will* make a colossal mess. There's no avoiding it. Relax and enjoy the opportunity to eat with your hands, sucking seasoning off your fingers, and tossing the bits and pieces of shell over your shoulder into (hopefully) one of the buckets stationed near every table. This brings us to a subset of rule two: Sidewalkers is the optimal first-date setting. The participatory nature of the bashing exercise provides endless conversational gambits, while the innate seductiveness of food is magnified by the obligatory licking of fingers and lips.

What's more, despite very bright lighting, there's a curious sense of privacy here. Everyone is so *involved* in creating his or her own mess that no one is likely to take notice of your affairs, so to speak. Even the large numbers of usually fastidious Japanese who frequent Sidewalkers get down and dirty. (The restaurant was used as a site for a very popular Japanese TV movie—a love story—making it a must on any itinerary for tourists from the land of the rising sun.)

To accompany the crabs, we order the chunky homemade coleslaw for $2.75 and the sweet potato fries at $2.50. For those too timid to beat their food, the menu features lots of more-accessible offerings, including a large selection of fresh fish broiled, sautéed, deep fried, poached, or blackened—that changes daily depending upon availability. Passable, but there are better places for seafood.

The crabs are really the attraction here, worth braving the almost seedy-looking entrance corridor and bar to gain access to the two large, cheery, though somewhat startling, dining rooms. There's a garish quality to the sharp contrast between burgundy walls and gleaming white decorative moldings, not to mention the equally bright white embossed ceilings. But once settled, the conviviality of the atmosphere washes over you. Who cares about decor when Sidewalkers delivers so much good food and fun?

HOURS:          5:00 to 11:00 P.M., Monday through
                Saturday; 4:00 to 10:00 P.M. on Sunday.
CREDIT CARDS:   All major.

# Sign of the Dove

1110 Third Avenue                          (212) 861-8080
at 65th Street
New York, NY 10021

"Whatever you do, just don't call it romantic," pleads Henny Santo, the fetching doyenne of an institution that for much of its thirty-odd years has oscillated between being beloved and berated. Sorry, Henny, we can't resist; we just can't find a better word to describe The Sign of the Dove. The restaurant is currently riding high in the beloved column, thanks to a 1986 overhaul that saw the refinement of its effervescent decor and the installation of Andrew D'Amico in the kitchen.

It *is* romantic — brazenly so — in rosy brick arches with wrought-iron filigree, lustrous stone floors softened by Oriental rugs, whimsically stenciled walls, and wondrous explosions of flowers. Large mirrors lend a sense of relaxed spaciousness, as do the tall windows and the motorized vaulted skylight ceiling that opens (weather permitting) to the elements. And we love Henny's successful ploy to differentiate the rooms by assigning each their own fanciful china service. Indeed, the Dove (as it is known to afficionados) is drop-dead gorgeous, which has been the good and the bad news since Henny's brother-in-law, Dr. Joseph Santo, opened it in 1962 as a neighborhood grill.

There was a long stretch during which that's all it was — gorgeous and romantic, a well-advertised magnet to tourists. Those who knew food went elsewhere. No longer. These days the Dove is as much a treat for the palate as it is for the eye. Consider soft shell crabs in a soy-based sauce, their sweetness tempered by Chinese sausage and fermented black beans at $16 at lunch and $22 for dinner. It's typical of Andrew's distinctive dishes, which redefine robust flavors with a deft delicacy.

Like most of the city's multistarred young chefs, he mixes and matches international influences, his essentially Provençal menu supplemented by tastes of Thailand, Italy, Morocco, India, and even America. A grilled scallop salad is dressed with red pepper oil and sesame seeds; sautéed sweetbreads sit on a corn fritter; and grilled salmon is rubbed with cumin and served with couscous. Still, Andrew's menus are familiar enough not to deter the meat-and-potatoes crowd that sustained the restaurant before he took over.

Consequently, people of all culinary persuasions are flocking to the Dove. Reservations are necessary, even at lunch when common sense would dictate that its too-uptown and too-East location would take it out of the running. A fixed-price alternative to the à la carte luncheon menu helps, as does the cachet of the company of former first ladies and current royalty.

Still, we prefer Sign of the Dove at night, when it's at its romantic best. Again there's the choice of the fixed-price or à la carte menu — $45 or $55 for the four-course former. Otherwise, if you steer clear of the $140 three-caviar presentation (as in beluga, ossetra and sevruga), plan on close to $50 per person for three courses, before you dive into the far-flung wine list.

Caviar mavens that we are, we've been known to split the more pedestrian but equally delicious $25 gateau of smoked salmon layered with salmon roe and sour cream, or the cornmeal blinis with salmon, whitefish, and sturgeon caviars for $20. Our taste for seafood satiated, we move on to landbound treats like the grilled tandoori marinated duck accompanied by grilled scallions, lentil pancake, and chutney at $26. Or we might order the beef filet braised in a rosemary-permeated broth and graced by sautéed foie gras for $30.

Having stated our preference for nighttime dining here, we should tell you that the Dove is also a favorite weekend brunch destination — especially during fair weather, when a sidewalk café is added to its many charms. Any time of year, though, we're practically addicted to Andrew's version of eggs Benedict — poached eggs with country-smoked pork loin and herb hollandaise for $16.

Finally, we would be remiss if we didn't bring up the subject of the Dove's bar. As you may know, we bristle at the suggestion (read directive) that we wait in the bar. In all fairness, that seldom happens here, but when it does we don't mind because it's just as gorgeous (and romantic) as the rest of the restaurant, not to mention entertaining. There's generally a talented pianist in residence. And, if we're truly famished, we can nibble at Andrew's delectable, well-priced bar food. Actually we've voluntarily spent the entire evening in the bar on more than one occasion!

HOURS:            Lunch: noon to 2:30 P.M., Monday through
                  Friday; from 11:30 A.M. on Saturday and
                  Sunday. Dinner: 6:00 to 11:30 P.M.,
                  Sunday through Friday; from 5:30 P.M. on
                  Saturday.

CREDIT CARDS:     All major.

# Snaps

230 Park Avenue                              (212) 949-7878
at 46th Street
New York, NY 10169

Spawned by Aquavit in June of 1992, Snaps takes a more informal approach to Scandinavian cuisine. As the playful pup to its more sophisticated parent, even its name is derivative. "Snaps" is Swedish slang for aquavit. As far as we're concerned, it's also Manhattanese for a stylish eatery in a very unexpected place. Park Avenue is hardly restaurant row, even in this office district. Consequently, Snaps snapped up a thriving lunch business from professional people eager for new dining options. Don't count on dropping in; you need to call at least a day in advance to get one of the 95 seats. It's equally popular with those seeking a drink and company after work.

   That's why we like it for dinner, after 7:00 when the bar crowd has thinned out from underneath the abstract Viking long boat poised over it. The menus are the same (although the prices are rather inexplicably increased by $1 across the board) but the personable waitstaff has more time to explain the subtleties of cod roe, Västerbotten cheese, and lingonberries. Such ingredients aside, the infectiously enthusiastic maître d' Otto Krupka is quick to point out that P. J. Gustafsson's kitchen is not exclusively dedicated to typical Scandinavian fare. Take the chicken draped in

Gorgonzola sauce and roasted peppers for $18 or the calf's liver crowned by a lively mixture of bacon and capers. And you should; they're both exceedingly good.

But don't eschew those dishes that smack of sparkling fjords and the midnight sun. A crispy, warm potato pancake serves as a bed for a stack of gravlax and crème fraiche. It's so rich that you can split it as an appetizer at dinner for $8 (call it lunch for one for a dollar less at midday). The $9 matjes herring is just as silken as it can be, while the very strong Norwegian cheese known as Västerbotten acts as a refreshing palate cleanser to a pile of boiled Swedish shrimp redolent of the layers of flavor produced by those cold northern waters and served whole (you peel 'em for $9).

Then there are the $8 open-faced sandwiches: rich pumpernickel hidden by smoked venison layered with horseradish and crème fraiche, or cold veal steak with jelly and pickled cucumber. They act as a very satisfactory entrée, if you are feeling budget-conscious, but our hands-down main event favorite is the savoy cabbage rolls. Stuffed with beef, rice, and onion, they are served in an elegant veal stock-based sauce made sweet by Swedish molasses. Not to worry; a side dish of lingonberries adds just the right amount of bitter for a perfect balance ($16).

The same goes for just the right blend of sweet and tart that make the $8 lemon pie the best of the desserts.

Indeed, balance is the hallmark here. The menu adroitly juggles Scandinavian and what maître d' Otto calls "eclectic American," while the decor is equally successful at trading off sleek and comfortable. The boxy lines of the former Goldome Bank have been obliterated with curves and niches, the lofty ceiling brought down to earth by a vaguely Oriental-looking crosshatch of decorative beams. The expected informality of light-toned wood is offset by the grandeur of heavy cream and yellow floor-to-ceiling drapes emboldened by striking navy blue figures. Again, they evoke Oriental images, but they could just as easily be old Norse. Even the wine list is nicely balanced — it tops out at $130, but there are twenty choices at $25 or less.

However, there is something slightly askew at Snaps: the dessert prices. They are decidedly on the high side, mirroring those of the appetizers. Then again, perhaps it's an accounting maneuver to make up revenue on those who, given the fat content typical of both ends of the menu, choose one or the other.

Nonetheless, in an age of boisterous bistros and tiled trattorias, Snaps is a remarkably civilized alternative.

HOURS: Noon to 3:00 P.M. Monday through Friday; 5:30 to 10:30 P.M., Monday through Saturday. Closed Sundays.

CREDIT CARDS: All major.

# Sparks

210 East 46th Street                (212) 687-4855
between Second and Third Avenues
New York, NY 10017

When you've had it with froufrou sauces and food too preciously presented for words, when some inner primeval force cries out for good, old-fashioned, basic red meat, head straight for Sparks. Do not pass Go; do not collect $200, although you could probably use it to dine properly at this venerable chop house.

For almost thirty years, brothers Pat and Mike Cetta have been serving up some of the best properly aged and oh-so-very prime meat in town, not to mention respectable seafood and monster lobsters. Admittedly, other members of the special breed of New York steak houses are older and more famous, but for our 75 bucks a head (standard for a full meal with a modest wine at any of them), none is better. And Sparks has enjoyed higher visibility ever since a reputed gangster was gunned down out front. Now, don't let that put you off. You should consider the late gentleman's patronage an endorsement of Sparks's quality—mobsters are notorious for their appreciation of fine food.

Given its proximity to the UN, rest assured that most of your fellow diners will be respectable, possibly international, and even cute—Matt Dillon and Nicholas Cage are regulars. And Sparks is strongly endorsed by the advertising crowd to whom image is everything—they don't have to worry about seating protocol here. The two large dining rooms share equal status, both benefiting from the truly superior art on the walls—all from the Hudson River School and all signed. Of course, you'll have to look closely for those signatures, because the light is on the dim side. We've complained to the Cetta brothers that it would be more flattering if it had a pink instead of amber glow, but they laugh and claim it

looks soft enough to them. Theirs is, after all, a deliberately substantial establishment, nothing the least bit prissy about it — from
the massive portions to the large, comfortable red leather chairs.
Nor should there be.

Any meat lover worth his or her salt would feel ridiculous con-
suming one of Sparks's "about a pound" $29.95 boneless prime sir-
loin steaks in a room in a pastel palace. Steak houses should have
a masculine air, and Sparks is no exception. Still, unlike some of
its competitors, women are not treated like second-class citizens.
Mike and Pat know that women can hold their own when it comes
to eating and running up sizable tabs. Ours is invariably hefty
since we can't resist working our way through the familiar menu —
*all* the way through.

Generally, we start with the broiled lump crabmeat and bay
scallops delicately flavored with white wine and garlic for $12.95,
and the $11.95 shrimp cocktail (a steak house cliché made special
at Sparks by the sweetness of the large shrimp and the uncluttered
tanginess of the sauce). Then it's on to the inevitable question — to
steak or not to steak. The three double-cut, extra-thick lamb chops
for $29.95 are a tempting alternative to the sirloin. Then there are
those amazing lobsters, starting at $48 for 3 to 3 1/2 pounds worth.
Larger ones, up to 4 1/2 pounds, are usually available although not
priced on the menu. They're like yachts: if you have to ask how
much they cost, you can't afford them.

Whichever way we go, we order the above-reproach $3.95 hash
browns, and we know people who save room for the pretty terrific
New York cheese cake at $5.50. In a rare example of restraint, we
usually settle on whatever fruit is in season, in the $4.75 to $8.50
neighborhood. We've also been known to beg for a slice of Roquefort
(on hand to top the "steak fromage") to accompany one of their
outstanding port wines.

Indeed, no discussion of the merits of Sparks would be complete
without a mention of the extensive wine list, universally recognized as one of the city's best. The dessert selections alone would
put most other wine lists to shame with 22 sauternes, 25 ports, a
number of Reislings and a Madeira or two. As for wines complementary to lunch or dinner entrées, the world's best vineyards are
represented. Tours of the cellar aren't usually offered, but maybe
they'll make an exception if you order #800, the Pauillac Château
Lafitte Rothschild 1970 for $250. If you choose the $475 bottle of

St. Julien, Château Leoville Las Cases 1945, *demand* the grand tour. Should you be inclined to stay seated, lean toward the lower end of the list, starting at $18.

Speak to Rami or Walter about dinner reservations and be forewarned that from 7:30 to 9:00 P.M. is the busiest time, requiring a call a good five days in advance. Can't make plans that far ahead? Then be prepared to settle for earlier or later. To get a table for lunch, speak with Mike's son Steve. But don't bother to speak to anybody on Sundays — Sparks is closed.

HOURS:        Noon to 3:00 P.M., Monday through Friday; 5:00 to 11:00 P.M., Monday through Thursday; till 11:30 P.M. on Friday and Saturday.

CREDIT CARDS:        All major.

# The "21" Club

21 West 52nd Street                    (212) 582-7200
between Fifth and Sixth Avenues
New York, NY 10019

The name may say club, but the establishment never has been. When it first opened on New Year's Eve 1929, it was a speakeasy. Consequently, the only people admitted were those known personally to the management, specifically to Jack Kriendler and Charlie Berns, who had owned a succession of such operations at various locales throughout the city. So if you consider Jack's and Charlie's friends a club, then yes, indeed, "21" was one.

Over the years it has carved a niche in the social fabric of the city unlike any other restaurant. Regulars of "21" lend new meaning to the word — some people practically live here. The stories of childhoods spent at "21," of romances begun and ended, deals done and undone, chance meetings (both fortuitous and not), engagements, weddings, births celebrated, and deaths mourned are legion. We know one young lady who even claims to have been conceived at "21."

Naturally, with so many people feeling so proprietary about "21," there was a fair amount of grumbling when the founding families sold out to Marshall Cogan in 1984. The grumbling got worse when he closed the restaurant for extensive renovations and reached a crescendo when he reopened. It just wasn't the same old "21." Marshall had gussied it up, both the decor and the food. Since human nature is resistant to change, people were suspicious. But the fancier food proved to be pretty tasty, especially after Michael Lomonaco got hold of the kitchen. Michael's approach to modern American cooking with its comfortable, confident, and multiethnic style updated the menus. He even managed to improve upon such staples as the famous "21" hamburger, chicken hash, and sunset salad. And now that the new gloss has worn off a bit, all is forgiven.

All three sections of the bar room (formerly numbers 21, 19, and 17 West 52nd Street) once again overflow with notable regulars like Félix Rohatyn, Jamie Niven, Dixon Boardman, Ralph Destino, Don Hewitt, Robert Tisch, Rand Araskog, and Pete Rozelle — a heavy-hitting, man's-man crowd. Moreover, a new, younger group is embracing "21" as well, standing three-deep at the bar and taking advantage of the user-friendly prices of the "21" Club Supper served after 10:00 P.M. Do they know the bar has always been considered prime seating territory, or are they just attracted to the enchanting collection of toys covering the ceiling? Actually those toys represent America's corporate culture, bearing the trademarks of companies that have long supported "21" via the expansive expense accounts of their top executives.

The second and third floors are devoted to a series of private dining parlors, including the aptly named Remington Room, sporting the restaurant's museum-quality collection of the artist's work. It's perfect for dinner for 20 or 21. There's plenty of room for larger functions on these floors, too; just describe your needs to the Banquet Department.

As in life, as much as things have changed at "21," just as much remains the same. The staff is full of familiar faces. Pete Kriendler remains to remind patrons that Kriendler and Berns *were* "21." Harry and Shekhar still man the door. Vice President Bruce Synder continues to preside from his vantage point next to the stuffed horse, while Walter of the twinkling eyes, gorgeous silver hair, and infallible memory still acts as mâitre d' in the bar.

The 52nd Street site of "21" and the well-priced prix-fixe menu make it a prime destination for dining before or after the theater. Served from 5:30 to 6:30 P.M. and after 10:30 P.M., the $37.50 dinner consists of three courses, with several choices for each. We've found that crunchy vegetable pancakes topped with walnut-flavored crème fraiche, followed by pan-seared salmon on a crispy potato nest blanketed by a zesty basil oil and garlic rouille, and topped off a by a trio of homemade sorbets, puts us in just the right mood for an evening of culture.

But if dining at "21" is the evening's principal amusement, we never fail to order the first-rate steak tartare of black angus for $30. It's such fun to watch the waiter prepare it tableside. The superb $26 sunset salad — chopped tongue, cheese, and assorted greens mixed at the table — is equally entertaining. We also recommend Chef Lomonaco's take on chicken pot pie — his is lobster based and comes with scrumptious tarragon-infused buttermilk biscuits for $39. As for appetizers, the crabcake is an $18.00 knockout. The bottom line? Expect to spend about $150 for a complete dinner for two (marginally less at lunch, depending on the bar tab).

The "21" Club — it's a certified New York institution that, like the city, has served so well for so long and continues to evolve, thrive, and throb.

HOURS:     Noon to 2:30 P.M. daily (except Saturday); 5:30 to 11:30 P.M. every evening. Closed Sunday.

CREDIT CARDS:     All major.

# The "21" Club Crabcake Recipe*
### (Serves 4 as an entrée or 8 as an appetizer)

### Ingredients
1 pound fresh jumbo lump crabmeat
1 sweet red pepper
1 sweet yellow pepper
2 cloves fresh garlic
2 fresh jalapeño chili peppers
3 tablespoons mayonnaise
2 tablespoons bread crumbs
1/4 cup chopped cilantro leaves
2 tablespoons "Old Bay" brand seasoning
Salt and freshly ground pepper to taste

* Recipe courtesy of Michael Lomonaco, Executive Chef, The "21" Club.

Reserve 1/2 cup additional bread crumbs for coating

1/4 cup olive oil for pan frying

## Preparation

1. Carefully clean the crabmeat of all shell fragments, but do not crumble the lumps of crab themselves.
2. Cut the sweet peppers in half and remove the seeds.
3. Cut the peppers into a small dice, sauté in 1 teaspoon olive oil, and set aside.
4. Chop the fresh garlic cloves into a fine dice or crush in a garlic press.
5. Clean the jalapeño peppers of their seeds and dice these finely. (Be sure to wash your hands well after handling chili peppers, as their juices can be quite irritating to the skin and eyes.)
6. Mix the crabmeat with the sweet peppers, garlic, jalapeño, chopped cilantro leaves, and mayonnaise. Add the seasoning powder, salt, and pepper and refrigerate for 20 minutes before continuing.
7. Using an ice cream scoop, form 8 equal-size balls and, using the palm of your hand, pat them into a disklike shape similar to a hockey puck. (This is the basic form of the crabcake)
8. Sprinkle the reserved bread crumbs onto your work area and press the cakes into this, one at a time, to coat evenly on all sides.
9. When the cakes are completed, heat the olive oil in a sauté pan until just before it begins to smoke.
10. Add the crabcake carefully, but do not crowd the pan. Cook them in two batches if necessary.
11. When they are well browned on both sides, remove the crabcakes from pan and keep them warm. This cooking process does not take a long time to complete and should not be done too far in advance.
12. When you are ready to serve the crabcakes, a small salad can be served on the same plate, along with some mayonnaise flavored with ground chili paste, mustard, or horseradish.

# Zarela

953 Second Avenue                    (212) 644-6740
between 50th and 51st Streets
New York, NY 10022

Almost everyone develops a reliable formula for chasing away the
blues—shopping, eating, and drinking are three popular options.
For two out of three, when we are particularly overwhelmed by
life's traumas, we head straight for Zarela Martinez's house party
on Second Avenue. As chef-hostess, the vivacious Zarela has been
holding court at this eponymous fiesta of a restaurant since 1987.
Always crowded, always loud (indeed bordering on raucous
thanks to the potency of the city's best frozen margaritas), Zarela
the restaurant is an infectious blend of relaxed, just-this-side-of-
tacky decor and spirited yet sophisticated cuisine. It never fails to
rouse us out of a serious funk—a cure that starts with the genuine
welcome of Zarela herself or that of her equally attractive daughter Marissa. But don't let the warmth of their smiles and sparkle
of their dark eyes dazzle you into accepting a table in the ground
floor dining room. It doubles as the heavily trafficked bar. Talk
about Margaritaville! Hold out for the marginally more civilized
room upstairs—if for no other reason than to have the opportunity
to inspect Zarela's first-class collection of Mexican artifacts
mounted on the stairwell. The animated music of a trio stationed
on the landing makes Zarela slightly more desirable for dinner
than for lunch. Be advised, however, that the restaurant's already
modest prices are somewhat lower at midday, and that main
courses at lunch are accompanied by vegetables, which at night
take on an à la carte status.

Once seated under a canopy of colorful piñatas and foil paper
letters spelling Zarela, you are presented with a long, laminated
menu as garish in its green and red glory as the surroundings. The
selection of appetizers is almost as large of that of the entrées.
While the fried calamari and guacamole ($7.95 and $5.95 respectively) are more than acceptable renditions of these staples, take
advantage of Zarela the chef's flair for more inventive interpre-
tations of Mexican classics. Choose the tangy snapper hash cooked
with tomato, scallion, and jalapeno at $8.95, for instance, or the
subtly sweet but very flavorful corn, crab, and poblano chowder
for $5.95.

Regulars like Mary McFadden rave about the $16.95 fajitas as a main course, succulent grilled skirt steak oozing with its tasty marinade and served with salsa guacamole and flour tortillas. But again, we tend to opt for the more original dishes which give you an inkling of why the Reagans tapped Zarela to cook for Queen Elizabeth at their California ranch. Tuna marinated in a rich mole sauce and then seared rare is a special favorite at $15.95. Another winner is the tender pan-fried liver marinated in the unusual but successful combination of pickled jalapeño juice and Worcestershire sauce. Topped with slabs of crisp bacon and a mound of sautéed onions, it makes a hearty meal for only $11.95. Just be prepared to stand your ground if, like we do, you want your liver on the rare side. More than one of Zarela's well-meaning waiters have tried to convince us you shouldn't eat liver rare. Nonsense! But at least we know there are no natives of France masquerading as Mexicans in their midst.

Whatever you order and however you order it, don't skip the opportunity to sample the baked rice with sour cream, white cheddar cheese, poblanos, and corn as a side dish — $3.50 for a small portion, $5.50 for a large one. As for libations, ignore the token wine list and stick to Mexican beer or the killer margaritas. And, contrary to our usual policy of skipping dessert in Mexican restaurants, we always indulge at Zarela. Pastry chef Ed Bonuso makes the additional calorie intake more than worthwhile with such concoctions as maple and spice pumpkin cheesecake served with maple-walnut sauce and clove-scented ice cream. If that isn't enough to give you a sugar and fat high, how about chocolate pecan and Kahlua pie topped with vanilla ice cream and Mexican chocolate sauce?

All desserts are $5.50 and are a fittingly festive end to a mood-altering meal at Zarela.

HOURS:  Noon to 3:00 P.M., Monday through Friday; 5:00 to 11:00 P.M., Monday through Thursday, to 11:30 P.M. on Friday and Saturday; 5:00 to 10:00 P.M. on Sunday.

CREDIT CARDS:  American Express, Diner's Club, and Carte Blanche.

# CHAPTER FOUR

# A Sudden Yen for...

*Something for every taste, every mood, every moment*

Just about any whim can be satisfied at virtually anytime in New York. From Carnegie Hall to Cobble Hill, there's some place that will provide nearly anything for any occasion, be it for one person or a thousand — for a price, of course. The price can be pretty steep. But how do you put a price on that perfect pâté, those fabulous flowers, the consummate caterer, the ennobling entertainer?

A little bedtime snack and a bouquet to cheer you up after a hard day up and down the Avenue? A little soirée for eight hundred in the Temple of Dendur? New York's got something for every taste, every mood, every moment. There's no need, ever, to do it yourself in New York. Certainly there are untold numbers of restaurants, but you don't have to be consigned to a fate of always eating out. There are purveyors of fine prepared foods that can be carted to hotel or home for an evening's repast. Or you can have your meals delivered. Or you can throw up your hands altogether, sit back, and let a capable caterer along with the new breed of florist called "party designer" plan your evening's entertainment.

This most entertaining of cities is set up better than any other *for* entertaining — for pampering yourself, those business associates you want to impress, *and* the friends whose company you want to enjoy. The variety is endless, the means to satisfy a sudden yen boundless. So jump into that bottomless pit of opportunities to spoil yourself and others, for a new idea, a new twist, a new angle — *only in New York.*

# PURVEYORS OF FINE FOODS

## *Dean & DeLuca*

560 Broadway                                    (212) 431-1691
at Prince
New York, NY 10012

Like the Statue of Liberty, Dean & DeLuca should be on everyone's list to visit, at least once. Chances are, though, you'll want to go back again and again. If you're into food, you can't help but be seduced by this most epicurean of gourmet food stores.

(If you're not in a shopping mood, you'll find the same great food served at the store also available at Dean & DeLuca's six very European espresso bars. With locations in Greenwich Village, Soho, the theater district, Rockefeller Center, Wall Street, and the Guggenheim Museum, Dean & DeLuca offers a reasonably priced selection of coffees, pastries, sandwiches, and salads.)

Like us, however, you probably will want to go to the source. Inside Dean & DeLuca, the displays are like jewelry — beautiful and tempting. The prices are like jewelry, too — some costume, some precious.

In the precious category, we found a fabulous smoked Mediterranean swordfish at $40 a pound. As for costume, there was an exceptional serrano-style ham for $14 a pound, just one of twelve different types. Dean & DeLuca's own $15-a-pound country pâté is perfect for hors d'oeuvres. Their cob-smoked bacon at $6 a pound makes breakfast a feast.

Pasta? These folks know a lot about it, in all possible colors and configurations — squid-ink-black linguini, green spinach fettuccini, and red tomato linguini or fettuccini, with at least ten more varieties to choose from. Breads? The fantastic display with forty or so different kinds dominates the middle of the store. Whether you're thinking picnic or formal dinner party, you'll find just the right loaf. We especially like the Russian health bread at $3.60, but it's hard to pass up the sourdough rye at $5. As for the baguettes, we've been known to grab one and munch as we shop!

If cooking is not your forte but your palate demands good food, head for the prepared goodies, truly a feast for the eye. There is a tremendous selection of appetizers, entrées, vegetables, and salads worthy of your best entertaining efforts or as a solitary treat.

Wild and wondrous condiments line shelf after shelf — all sorts of jams, honeys, mustards, oils, and vinegars, including every flavor recipe that *Gourmet* or *The Silver Palate Cookbook* has ever thrown at you.

A candy counter caters to the sweet tooth, and dried fruits and nuts encased in enormous jars satisfy the health enthusiast. And, oh, by the way, there is a case full of staples like milk, eggs, and butter, lest you forget this is a real market.

Baked goods are well represented, particularly by the scrumptious Russian spiced coffee cake with nuts, raisins, and sour cream, which serves twelve to fifteen and sells for $25. But the cheese department is truly outstanding with over 250 different kinds — from a single creamy brie at $7 a pound to a rare Corsican sheep-milk cheese covered in rosemary at $20.

When you enter Dean & DeLuca, you are surrounded by breathtaking arrays of fresh fruits and vegetables, along with huge baskets of onions and potatoes. You're tempted, indeed almost dared, to fondle each and every one of them, so we suggest you head straight to the back of the store and slowly work your way forward in a civilized manner. Let the classical music soothe you into a state of making sensible choices — otherwise you'll walk out of here with all sorts of things that look too good to pass up. Dean & DeLuca is a temple of impulse buying. You really shouldn't enter without a list. We can't tell you how many fascinating but totally useless gadgets we've bought from their extensive housewares department.

As you might assume, Saturdays here are a madhouse, with upwardly mobile types and more than a smattering of notables from all over the city wandering through. Fortunately, Dean & DeLuca is open from 8:00 A.M. to 8:00 P.M. Monday through Saturday and from 9:00 A.M. to 7:00 P.M. on Sundays. We highly recommend visiting during the middle of the week, unless you're more interested in people-watching than in shopping.

# Manhattan Fruitier

| | |
|---|---|
| 105 East 29th Street | (212) 686-0404 |
| between Park and Lexington | Fax (212) 686-0479 |
| Avenues | |
| New York, NY 10003 | |

Jehv Gold, without his erstwhile partner Lee Grimsbo, is busier than ever creating his exquisite, stylized gift baskets and center-pieces resembling Old Masters' still lifes. He's even opened a Los Angeles location at 310 North Vista; (213) 938-4122. So colorful, so inventive, so intriguing, the baskets in particular have become the gift currently in vogue with many a Condé Nast editor. Other visually artistic people like interior designer William Diamond and hair stylist Frederic Fekkai find them equally appealing.

The East 29th Street location is a workshop dedicated to filling telephone orders, but you can drop by to have a word or two with Jehv; we highly recommend it. It's a real treat to perch on one of the barstools and chat with him—if he's not overly occupied—while he constructs his wondrous creations. You're surrounded by the beauty of glorious fruit and soothed by the sound of classical music.

Prices start at $50 and go up to about $200, depending on the exotic quotient of the fruit used. Custom concoctions can cost up to $500. The world is Manhattan Fruitier's supplier—apple pears from Asia, blood oranges from Sicily, finger bananas from Ecuador. Jehv is even connected to small growers with just a few trees devoted to the most special strains, like the Esopus Spitzenburg apple, Thomas Jefferson's favorite.

You have the option of picking up your fruit fantasy or having it delivered for a $10 charge in Manhattan. Delivery further afield can also be arranged, but not too far. In the interest of freshness, Jehv sticks to a hand-deliverable radius. If you don't happen to be within that radius, Jehv can now ship three new selections around the country. He does quite a bit of it, in fact. The Traveler Box, which comes in two sizes ($75 and $100), contains a collection of dried and preserved fruits and candies, including dried cranberries, Australian ginger root, lychees, mango, licorice root, and pear wafers. Each is individually wrapped in craft paper, tied with a wax linen string, and delightfully packaged in a beautiful pine box. The Fresh Fruit Box is filled with flowers, greens and, of course, fruit. It, too, comes in two sizes ($65 and $100). Also available is a classic assortment of chocolate, truffles and grenache, some filled with fruit-flavored liqueurs, packaged in a redwood box tied with a French silk ribbon and finished off with a gold wax seal ($25 or $40). All can be shipped around the country via Federal Express, and Jehv passes along just the freight charges, no markup.

To complement the fruit in the baskets, Jehv often includes tasty tidbits like biscotti imported from San Francisco, chocolates handmade locally by Lawrence Burdick, or New York cheddar cheese sticks by John Macy. All encourage breaking into and nibbling on the arrangement, which otherwise seems just too pretty, just too perfect to eat.

Give Manhattan Fruitier at least a day's notice on your order. In turn, you will secure an ornamental, edible item which, once consumed, will leave behind an indelible impression.

## Murray's Sturgeon

2429 Broadway                                    (212) 724-2650
Between 89th and 90th Streets
New York, NY 10024

Talk about specialty shops! This may be one of the most specialized; it is certainly one of the best. For the most part, people line up in this long, narrow space for just two edibles — sturgeon and salmon (although the delicious homemade salads shouldn't be ignored). Since Harold Berliner retired, Murray's has been owned by Ira Goller, who runs it the same way it's been run for the last forty-six years — like an old-fashioned smoked fish store.

Only the prices have changed, and not by much. In fact, the salmon, imported from Norway and smoked in New York, is still priced at $36 a pound. The sturgeon, which comes from Canada, costs $41.96 a pound (or $10.49 per quarter pound). They also have white fish, sable, and a large selection of herrings. And, you get good old-fashioned advice along with the good old-fashioned quality. Murray's customers come in weekly for their smoked-fish fix. They're so addicted that when they're out of town, many have it shipped overnight by UPS or Federal Express (there is nothing stopping those who insist on the best quality). Murray's still adds no markup for shipping. You just pay the freight charges.

So who's keeping Murray's so busy that they're open every day from 8:00 A.M. to 7:00 P.M. (till eight o'clock on Saturday evenings)? Just about everyone who ever enjoyed bagels, lox, and cream cheese for brunch. That includes Isaac Stern, Itzhak Perlman, Barbra Streisand, Dustin Hoffman, and Tom Cruise. Henry and Stacy Winkler and Marvin and Barbara Davis regularly have fish shipped to them in Los Angeles. Apparently, even in L.A., there's no place quite as special and specialized as Murray's!

# Orwasher's

308 East 78th Street                (212) 288-6569
between First and Second Avenues    Fax (212) 570-2706
New York, NY 10021

An East Side fixture since 1916, Orwasher's does bread and does it better than anyone else. Every roll, muffin, and loaf of bread is made from scratch on the premises, right below the tiny storefront, in the same brick ovens built by Abram Orwasher seventy-three years ago.

Two generations later, grandson and namesake, Abram, still insists that absolutely no artificial flavors, additives, or preservatives are used. Abram refuses to make bread any way but the old-fashioned way. He won't allow the conditioners used by most bakeries to make dough rise faster or even the mechanical equivalent of speeding the process with steam boxes. At Orwasher's, the dough rises naturally, at its own pace, in time-honored wooden boxes.

Certainly it would be a lot easier to employ modern methods and mixes, but that would never suit the palates of the likes of Gene Shalit and Itzhak Perlman, who count on Orwasher's for their daily dose of bread. On Saturdays you might run into Henny Youngman here. Time-Warner stocks Orwasher's' bread in its corporate dining room—as do dozens of other businesses, including law firms like Strook & Strook. But, whoever you are, you're likely to find lines during the 7:00 A.M. to 7:00 P.M. (Monday through Saturday) business hours. Leonard Bernstein used to send his butler!

Given its 10021 location, "the best zip code" in New York, all the importance attached to making everything from scratch, and its upscale clientele, you might think Orwasher's' prices would be high. Wrong! Basic rolls run 45 cents apiece, a loaf of bread $2.50 a pound. Then there are rye breads for $1.55 a pound and cinnamon raisin at $2.70 a pound. Muffins—blueberry, bran (with or without raisins), corn, banana, walnut, and the ubiquitous oat bran—range in price from 75 cents to $1.20 each. All of the salespeople are great, especially Elizabeth Nemeth who has been there for twenty years.

Of course, you can spend more (but only in cash, since no checks or charge cards are accepted). Have Orwasher's bake up a loaf for a special occasion—a heart for Valentine's Day, pumpkin bread for Thanksgiving, or a three-color wreath for Christmas made with rye and dark and light pumpernickel, or even challah. Speaking of which, challah loaves can be done in any size, even up to three tiers—that's ten pounds!

Off the rack or custom designed, Orwasher's bread is quite simply first-rate. And you really don't have to stand in line to sample it. Orwasher's now ships all over the United States for overnight or 48-hour delivery—and whatever you order still arrives fresh. Plus, Orwasher's products pop up at all the best places in Manhattan—from Avery Fisher Hall to Zabar's, from Dean & DeLuca to Tavern on the Green, from Bloomingdale's to the Rainbow Room, and everywhere that quality and value are truly appreciated.

# William Poll

| 1051 Lexington Avenue | (212) 288-0501 |
|---|---|
| at 75th Street | Fax (212) 288-2844 |
| New York, NY 10021 | |

Rumor has it that William Poll's Nova is sliced so thin that you can read *The New York Times* through it. But then, what would you expect from an establishment that's been practicing the fine art of salmon slicing since 1921? Self-proclaimed "first in gourmet luxuries and catering," William Poll's is still in the capable hands of the founding family. Stanley Poll is the third-generation owner. Although he doesn't relish mentioning specifics, Stanley's devotees are household names. A famous Palm Beach hostess turns to Stanley every time she plans a dinner party. After preparing everything, he packages it beautifully and sends it off with a courier on the first plane to West Palm on the morning of her party.

A tad extravagant? Perhaps, but William Poll's legions are very loyal folk who don't count their pennies, but do count on the unwavering quality of the food. Many are particularly fond of Stanley's dear little finger sandwiches that show up at all those chic teas. The wonderful hors d'oeuvres are another draw. Most are frozen, so you can stock up at home for that impromptu party, then just pop them into the microwave or oven. A tray (about twelve to fourteen pieces) of such bite-size appetizers as papillons—flaky strudel filled with goodies like chicken and chestnuts, spinach, cheese, or mushroom and bacon—costs about $15.

William Poll's dips are also great to keep on hand. The sun-dried tomato with olive oil, sour cream, and secret seasonings is sensational. The eggplant in olive oil and wine vinegar is another good choice, as is the relatively new jalapeño dip which is not too spicy and has just enough tang. Our favorite is called Fromage—a mixture of several French cheeses, laced with brandy, dill, olive oil, and assorted spices. All the dips range from $7 to $10 for a half-pound container, and, according to Stanley, each will serve as many as eight for cocktails.

If you prefer to entertain on a more lavish scale, spoil your guests with William Poll's rich, velvety foie gras imported from Perigord and Strasbourg. Depending upon the current state of the dollar, it costs about $125 for a ten-ounce block and yields an unforgettable taste sensation.

Stanley will gladly discuss his new range of fresh dinner entrées (altogether more than sixty). You can choose from boneless leg of lamb stuffed with artichoke, paella, baby back ribs, chicken breast stuffed with morels or wild rice, and blackened ginger filet of salmon, among many others. The shepherd's pie is unbelievably popular—he sells several hundred a week. All are $15 per serving and include a side dish like fresh roasted vegetables, mint-rum potatoes, or sweet brandied onions. Then there are the whole smoked hams and turkeys. Salads? The list seems to go on forever. Stanley estimates he sells at least one hundred pounds of chicken salad alone every day! Desserts run the gamut from chocolate chip cookies to baklava. And the new chocolate soufflé comes frozen; it rises in the oven so you can serve it piping hot.

Don't forget that William Poll stocks virtually every packaged gourmet condiment imaginable. Check out the new line of vintage French sardines — they're aged and dated, like wine — and the white asparagus packaged in a jar, no less. We went crazy over the Roquefort crepes, a snack biscuit from France. Stanley told us that the thirty cases he ordered before Christmas to last for months were gone before New Year' Day.

Remember, too, that anything prepared or sold here can be delivered anywhere in Manhattan for a $20 minimum fee.

But if you really want to treat yourself to the essence of William Poll's long-standing popularity with the rich and famous, order one of Stanley's beluga caviar sandwiches for $125. There is one gentleman who picks them up to take with him on the Concorde. (Stanley, in fact, has a tremendous number of clients who take out sandwiches for their flights.) The caviar is served on white bread without a trace of sour cream, egg, or onion; it is a purist's delight. Stanley won't say exactly how much caviar is carefully placed (so as not to break the eggs) on that plain old white bread. "Enough," he laughs, "that you certainly won't go hungry."

# Word of Mouth

1012 Lexington Avenue         (212) 734-9483
at 72nd Street            Fax (212) 737-1637
New York, NY 10021

Kitchens just aren't what they used to be. A professional cook is, unfortunately, no longer standard equipment. Still, you can pretend there is a wizard in your home if you avail yourself of the services of Word of Mouth. With over fifty entrées, and over one hundred pastas, salads, and desserts to choose from, this place gives a whole new meaning to the term *takeout*. You even have to adjust the way you order. Nothing (except desserts) is sold by the piece or the item; everything is by the pound. Basically, a pound feeds one person piggishly, two people moderately.

Owner/chef Christi Finch splits her time between overseeing the kitchen, which is in full view of her customers, and nurturing her new baby. The 28-seat café Word of Mouth opened in March of 1992 right above the store at the same address. But it has its own phone number: (212) 249-5351. The bistro fare allows Christi to show off her stuff on a plate, rather than from a box. You'll find things like omelettes, scrambled eggs with grits, blintzes, French toast, ricotta pancakes, Word of Mouth's signature chicken salad, polenta with wild mushrooms, fresh pastas and salads, sandwiches, and more. You might run into celebrities such as Sigourney Weaver during breakfast, lunch, or dinner (served from 8:00 A.M. to 6:00 P.M. weekdays) or brunch (from 9:00 A.M. to 6:00 P.M. Saturdays and 10:00 A.M. to 5:00 P.M. Sundays).

Sigourney is also a regular downstairs, where you'll see people like Joan Lunden looking to try the new recipes Christi constantly offers. Even regulars find it virtually impossible to work their way through the menu. There are always new dishes to be tried and savored. Christi follows the seasons to ensure the freshest ingredients — chicken corn chowder is a special summer treat. And she takes holidays into consideration too. Traditional delights show up at Passover, Rosh Hashanah, Thanksgiving, Chanukah, Christmas, St. Patrick's Day, and the Fourth of July.

We know of one chic lady who, despite the fact that her husband is in the restaurant business, relied upon Word of Mouth for sustenance throughout her pregnancies and the early years of raising her family.

While you wouldn't know it by the number of limos lined up outside, Word of Mouth does deliver, between 10:00 A.M. and 6:00 P.M., with a $15 to $25 delivery charge. That tends to keep people from having lunch for two delivered, which is exactly Christi's purpose. She's after bigger game — a luncheon for the working committee of your favorite charity or a corporate affair, for instance. And you can take all the credit for being a virtuoso in the kitchen for a lot less than it would cost to keep a cook. Entrées start at about $9 a pound; salads range from $6.50 to $15 for some of the exotic seafood varieties. Divide that delivery charge by twelve guests and it becomes downright negligible!

If it still rankles, take heart in the fact that Christi's staff will help you into a taxi with your order. So with Word of Mouth at your disposal, there is no excuse for not entertaining right in your own home.

# Zabar's

2245 Broadway                                    (212) 787-2000
at 80th Street                              Fax (212) 580-4477
New York, NY 10024

There's just no other place like it. Zabar's is a real trip, an overwhelming assault on the senses — the aroma of fine coffees and cheeses, the sight of food and housewares covering every square inch of floor and ceiling space, and the sound of hordes of crazed people shouting "Here!" as their long-awaited number at the smoked fish or prepared-foods counter is called.

On Saturdays and Sundays, a visit is likely to leave you black and blue. New Yorkers are mighty aggressive shoppers and those are the days they come from all over to shop Zabar's. They come for the amazing variety — the breads (more than sixty kinds), the cheeses (over five hundred), the coffees (better than thirty thousand pounds sold each week), the wall of cured and smoked meats, the feast of prepared foods, the stacks of condiments, the "mezzanine" sporting every kitchen utensil known to man. Oh, yes, and the prices are terrific, as in bargain!

In fact, the pre-Christmas caviar price war between Zabar's and Macy's is an eagerly anticipated annual event. Neither establishment gives any quarter, both lose money, but get lots of publicity and lots of traffic in the process. We think no one gets more of a kick out of it than Stanley and Saul Zabar's affable partner, Murray Klein. He calls it "a tradition" and his eyes light up at the very thought of the yearly fray.

Actually, Murray gets pretty excited about everything here. No wonder — all those cash registers lining the front of the store never stop ringing, Monday through Friday from 8:00 A.M. to 7:30 P.M., till 10:00 P.M. on Saturday, 6:00 P.M. on Sunday. No one walks out of Zabar's without buying something, be it a 40-cent French bean cutter or a $1,000, four-pound tin of caviar. Just in case you do escape without a single purchase, you can satisfy your Zabar's cravings via mail order. Their catalog, chock-full of gadgets and goodies, circulates to over six hundred thousand Zabar's fans around the world. Despite the obvious emphasis on numbers and diversity, Zabar's is no slouch when it comes to quality. The smoked salmon is flown in daily. The coffee is roasted on the premises. Zabar's truly represents exceptional value and consequently has become a beloved institution. Rumors of a sale to David Leiderman of David's Cookies fame prompted a line of customers at the "cash only" checkout line to chant spontaneously, "Don't sell!" One shopper told a *New York Times* reporter that "the entire West Side is having a nervous breakdown over this."

Zabar's dates from 1934, when founder Louis Zabar rented a fish counter in a grocery two doors down from the current location. The business grew to a four-store empire, which sons Stanley, Saul, and Eli later consolidated into the one and only Zabar's. In 1964, Eli was bought out (eventually heading east to establish E.A.T. on Madison Avenue), and Murray Klein, who began his career as a delivery boy at Zabar's, was brought in as partner to tap his marketing creativity—witness the caviar war and his battle with Cuisinart. In 1975, Murray was selling their then-revolutionary food processor for $135, while department stores were charging $180. Murray was selling a lot of food processors, getting a lot of publicity, and making competitors very angry. Bowing to pressure, Cuisinart cut off the supply. Murray retaliated by suing, generating still more publicity. The suit was settled out of court.

As testimony to Zabar's' stature, consider the fact that when Murray donated a dinner for twenty catered by Zabar's to a City Meals on Wheels benefit auction, it sold for $10,000—or $500 a person! Then there's the transplanted New York woman, now a Chicago matron, who couldn't imagine her son's bar mitzvah done without platters from Zabar's. No problem—Murray sent out everything she needed by courier. For years, *New York Times* managing editor Abe Rosenthal and metropolitan editor Arthur Gelb, en route to Albany for the annual legislative correspondents' dinner and show, would stop in and load up with brown bags full of Zabar's specialties. After the performance and late into the night, the likes of Nelson Rockefeller and John Lindsay would feast on the *Times* and Zabar's. And there's a quote from Leonard Bernstein in the catalog, describing the whitefish as "a symphony of delicacy and succulence."

Woody Allen, that chronicler of New York tales, uses Zabar's to cater meals for his cast and crew when filming. He's joined in his admiration for this greatest of the city's food emporiums (not a market like Dean & DeLuca or Balducci's—no fruits or vegetables) by Neil Simon, Lauren Bacall, Barbra Streisand, Walter Matthau, and even Jerry Lewis.

They all know it's ridiculous to have to fight their way through the crowds and wait in endless lines to be served, only to wait in more endless lines to check out. But oddly enough, at Zabar's it's all part of the fun and part of the folklore.

There are some vestiges of civilization in this endearing madhouse. We appreciate the fact that if hunger strikes, you can have them make you a sandwich and retire to their little café next door for some of the best cappuccino or espresso in town. There you can sit quietly, amusing yourself by drawing pictures in the sawdust on the floor with your toes and pondering your next purchase. Ah, bliss!

# Zito's Bread

259 Bleecker Street                                    (212) 929-6139
between Sixth and Seventh Avenues
New York, NY 10014

We've all tittered self-consciously at the double entendre phrase "a bun in the oven." Somehow the vulgar overtones evaporate when it's applied to Josephine Zito, who gave birth to son Julius in the back room of the bakery she and her husband, Anthony, founded in 1924! Having interrupted the family business with his debut, Julius has devoted his life to it, as have his three brothers, Vincent, Charles, and Jimmy. Julius's son Anthony and Charles's son, Charles, Jr., also work here, representing the third generation of Zitos dedicated to the fine art of baking—lots of baking.

The original brick ovens, still fueled by coal as they were when they were built, are full 24 hours a day with Zito's' preservative-free products. The result is mouth-wateringly fresh breads that keep this tiny shop crowded with patrons seven days a week. Of course, the neighborhood has long relied on Zito's; rumor has it that Charles Zito has been forced over the years to transfer his flirtatious attentions from generation to generation, from mother to daughter, even to granddaughter. But Zito's' domain stretches far beyond the Village. They supply decidedly uptown restaurants like The Palm and Elaine's as well as the small mom-and-pop places. And some of the world's most famous descendants of Italian heritage beat a path to Zito's' door — Lee Iacocca stops by on weekends when he's in town, and we hear Robert DeNiro is addicted. Ol' Blue Eyes, Frank Sinatra himself, has his Zito's bread delivered to him at the Waldorf Towers, while Ed Koch picks up his own — but then he always did. (Yes, we know he's not really Italian, but the former hizzoner has, at one time or another, claimed faithful allegiance to every ethnic group.) Mayor David Dinkins, by the way, has his delivered.

A loaf of Zito's' delicious white bread costs $1.25, 22 cents for a roll. Whole wheat comes as loaf, baguette, or roll — $1.35, $1.50, and 22 cents, respectively. They also make a wonderful Sicilian bread, which resembles your basic white variety, but the dough is worked longer (by hand, of course) to give it a thicker crust. Dusted with sesame seeds, it comes in several shapes, sizes, and prices, from $1.20 to $1.75. A special focaccia is made just once a week. Get there by 2:00 P.M. on Saturdays or you won't get it — as fast as they make it is as fast as it sells.'

Zito's is open Monday through Saturday from 6:00 A.M. to 6:00 P.M., Sundays from 6:00 A.M. to 1:00 P.M. But if you plan to shop on Sunday, make plans to get here early — they're usually sold out by noon.

# CATERERS

## *Glorious Foods*

504 East 74th Street             (212) 628-2320
between York and the river      Fax (212) 988-8136
New York, NY 10021

There are those who believe a party without Glorious Foods is not worthy of being considered a party. So many, in fact, have come to this religion that the firm grossed close to $15 million last year, and founding partner Sean Driscoll finds his biggest challenge is making sure Mrs. *X* isn't served the same food night after night at a series of different events. The enormity of the problem is evident when you consider that, on any given night during "the season," Glorious Foods might be handling as many as seven parties. Their sixteen chefs, directed by Jean Claude Nedelec (Sean's partner since 1984), are under constant pressure to come up with innovative menus that live up to Glorious's well-deserved reputation for excellence.

Many of the East Coast's most memorable events have counted on that reputation. When the Guggenheim Museum reopened, Glorious Foods did a week's worth of parties, serving an average of two thousand people a night. Karen LeFrak called on them when she chaired the 150th Anniversary Ball for the New York Philharmonic at the Museum of Modern Art, where they've also catered several movie premieres and lots of corporate shindigs. They produced the Statue of Liberty's centennial dinner on Liberty Island in New York harbor, and although they have not (yet) been called upon by the Clinton folk, they were responsible for one of the presidential dinners at the Bush inaugural in Washington.

They now have their very own dining facility which accommodates seventy people just a stone's throw up the street from their offices on East 74th. It's nondescript, but that's intentional — you can dress it up any way you like, just as Annette de la Renta did when she threw a birthday bash for Brooke Astor with a guest list that was a true who's who. There's a twenty-person minimum for lunch or dinner and it'll run $200 to $250 a person including wines and liquor.

As large as the company has become, employing an army of well-trained waiters (150 full-time and 500 part-time) and fifteen administrators in addition to those sixteen chefs, it had humble beginnings. It all started when Sean began cooking in his kitchen for private dinner parties. His imaginative food drew raves and word quickly spread. Before long, he was in business and the firm has continued to grow. At this point, chairpeople of major events are advised to engage Glorious's services six to nine months in advance. Smaller affairs should be booked at least eight weeks ahead. Still, as with all things in life, there are no hard and fast rules. Don't be shy about calling Glorious at the last minute — the date just might be open. And if you're one of the many faithful, Sean will make every effort to accommodate you.

Of course, there are tremendous demands on his time. Don't be put off if you're assigned to one of Sean's executive staff to plan your party—Jay Jolly, Stephan Baroni, Don McCoy, David Dill, and Bettina Felder. They're as talented and resourceful as Sean, having been with him for years. Tap their expertise when it comes to flowers, music, and decorations—they won't steer you wrong.

A glorious Glorious dinner will hit your budget at the $150-to-$250-a-head level, more like $50 to $75 for cocktails and tidbits. That does include service, and bear in mind that the price includes what amounts to an assurance of the social acceptability of your soirée—particularly important, even crucial, for those aspiring to climb society's treacherous ladder. But don't start that climb between December 23 and January 8. There is rest for the weary, if they work for Sean Driscoll. At the height of holiday party frenzy, he closes Glorious's doors. He can well afford to!

## Great Performances

287 Spring Street                    (212) 727-2424
New York, NY 10013

We all know who to call when it comes to ghostbusting, but who are you going to call when you need help—help in the kitchen, in the dining room, at the bar? Perhaps you're having a few friends in for a little cocktail, nothing elaborate. A call to Word of Mouth or William Poll takes care of the hors d'oeuvres, but what about serving them? You can't serve and tend bar at the same time. Call Great Performances. They'll take care of everything.

Great Performances is also a full-service catering company. In fact, they have produced a terrific video featuring some fifty wonderful Manhattan party sites, including some you might not have thought about, like the Puck Building, the New York Public Library, and the Central Park Zoo. It's on sale for $24.95 plus shipping and handling, but if you're a regular client, you can see it free in their offices.

But while we have attended some perfectly marvelous affairs catered by the company, it is still their provision of very attractive, most accommodating, and extremely professional temporary staff that we count on.

Liz Neumark founded Great Performances in her living room in 1979 with a $1,700 investment. At first she focused only on securing waitressing jobs for women in the visual and performing arts who needed to supplement their incomes. Through regular workshops, Liz taught them how to serve, present, and garnish food; tend bar; and maintain their composure in the midst of the chaos that is often the backstage of a party. In less than a year, business was booming. Nearly fifteen years later she has a staff of over five hundred and an enviable client list, including Coca Cola, Lord & Taylor, Bristol Meyers Squibb, American Express, the New York Stock Exchange, and Seagram's.

Great Performances will send over as many of their well-trained staff (those workshops Liz started a decade ago continue to be mandatory) as you need. Outline the occasion for them and they'll even define your staffing requirements for you. There's a five-hour minimum per person at $25 an hour.

Since most of the Great Performances staff really are performers, they are to a man, or woman, good-looking and well-groomed. They always show up with clean, pressed uniforms—tuxedos for the men and white blouse, black vest, and skirt for the women. They also come equipped with their party kits, useful items like corkscrews, sharp little knives, and peelers. Most importantly they arrive with smiles on their faces, which seem sincere and never diminish under the most trying circumstances. And, boy have we tried them. There was the time we kept running out of ice; worse, the elevator was broken. Kevin, the bartender for the evening, didn't once balk at climbing six flights loaded down with ice. He had to do it three times.

So who are you going to call when you need to put on staff for the day, afternoon, evening—Great Performances, that's who.

## Sylvia Weinstock Cakes

273 Church Street                    (212) 925-6698
New York, NY 10013          Fax (212) 941-9862

Who says that being an exemplary housewife is not good training for a career outside the home? Certainly not Sylvia Weinstock. She took her talent for baking and turned it into a booming business.

It all started when she found herself with some extra time on her hands during weekend trips to her family's ski house on Hunter Mountain. While her husband and kids were off skiing, Sylvia entertained herself by baking. As her repertoire and skill grew, she began baking for local restaurants. Recognizing her own potential, she forsook her part-time career as elementary school teacher and apprenticed to various pastry and dessert chefs in the city's finest restaurants.

In 1980, when Sylvia was finally ready to go out on her own, she quickly assembled a client list that included such institutions of culinary excellence as the Pierre, the Carlyle, the Rainbow Room, and the Metropolitan Club.

Sylvia's cakes are instantly identifiable by their flawlessly delicate floral decoration — handmade sugar peonies, tulips, roses, and daffodils that look as though they'd been plucked from the garden. Someone once even mistook a Weinstock cake for the centerpiece!

But her expertise stretches well beyond flowers. Sylvia takes great pride in being able to recreate just about anything in edible form, including a Faberge egg for the people who owned a real-life version. It was an exact replica, down to its relative value — the edible egg was covered in 24-karat gold leaf!

Sylvia's creations titillate the tastebuds as well as the eye. And, oh, those tastes — so many and in every combination imaginable. All of Sylvia's cakes are made to order, so you can have absolutely anything your little heart desires as long as you are prepared to spend at least $300.

Plenty of people are — Barbara Walters, Jane Fonda and Ted Turner, Donald Newhouse, Anna Murdoch, Adrien Arpel, and virtually any bride worth her sugar. In fact, there is one school of thought that holds a wedding just isn't legal if it doesn't include a Sylvia Weinstock cake. Ted Kennedy, no doubt, believed that. So did Whitney Houston. Her wedding cake was a masterpiece, rising five feet high and decorated with thousands of sugar violets and sugar baskets filled with sugar flowers. Made of lemon yellow cake and a banana-strawberry whipped cream filling, it featured five tiers. When the glamorous Marti Sarlie married "bachelor about town" Jerry Kravat, it was Sylvia's cake they cut. Sylvia reportedly created a $15,000 cake for Laura Steinberg's wedding to Jonathan Tisch, but she will neither confirm nor deny that figure. She is the very soul of discretion, a quality very much appreciated by her already overexposed clientele.

What may not be so appreciated is her very downtown location. We suspect, in fact, it's about as far below 57th Street as many of her patrons have ever ventured. But venture they do. Sylvia insists on it, just as she insists on an appointment. Talk to Sylvia about the kind of party you are planning and she will help you select colors and the appropriate flowers. Of course, the cake will perfectly reflect the spirit of the occasion. Keep Sylvia in mind for anniversaries, birthdays, holidays, and even business occasions. Even with a staff of seven, Sylvia produces no more than twenty cakes a week — each is so elaborate and time-consuming. Moreover, timing is crucial, as they are prepared only a day before your event to ensure freshness. So once you have determined a date for a special occasion, be sure to book Sylvia first. And don't worry if it is slated for out of town. Sylvia routinely has cakes delivered by driver to Washington, D.C., Boston, and territory in between.

Planning a wedding farther afield? Sylvia will hand-carry all the components of the cake on a plane and assemble them at your site. Granted, she'll charge you for airfare, hotel, and expenses, but consider the alternative — the shocking notion of a wedding not sanctioned by a Sylvia Weinstock cake.

# FLORISTS

## *Philip Baloun Designs*

340 West 55th Street                    (212) 307-1675
between 8th and 9th Avenues      Fax (212) 582-1552
New York, NY 10019

There may be no greater testimony to Philip Baloun's talents than all those mentions in Suzy's column about his "unique," "glorious," "extraordinary," "spectacular," "dazzling," and "memorable" decorations. After all, Suzy has been chronicling the world's great parties for more years than her official picture indicates and is not easily impressed. But Philip's parties have a theatrical quality that excites even the most jaded on the social circuit. You see, this boy from Chicago hit town in 1979 with aspirations of becoming a big-time director. Few fill their dreams so spectacularly. He's made the big time with clients like Laura Pomerantz, Cecile Zilkha, Carrol Petrie, Carolyne Roehm, the Metropolitan Opera, Chanel, and the New York Philharmonic. And he's certainly a director — though his stage is more often a ballroom in a hotel or a tent stretched over a plaza than a Broadway theater.

In the tranquil environment of his magnificent apartment filled with Oriental urns and screens, Philip creates memories. And although unquestionably available for intimate parties at home, he has made headlines for his extravagant extravaganzas.

For the 1993 Metropolitan Opera opening night, celebrating the twenty-fifth anniversary of Luciano Pavarotti and Placido Domingo singing at the Met, Philip covered all of the seventy-five dining tables in ivory chintz damask centered by 12-foot topiaries fashioned out of ivy-covered grape vines, embellished with Casablanca lilies, hydrangea, and dendrobium orchids.

Recently, for a New York financial wizard's 60th birthday, Philip filled the famous pool at The Four Seasons' restaurant with live trout. He even furnished a fishing boat!

He's a master at lavish weddings. When Abigail Koppel married The Limited's Leslie Wexner, Givenchy designed the dress, Marvin Hamlisch entertained, Glorious Foods cooked, and Philip decorated. Enough said? Frankly, no, because what Philip did was incredible. Guests arrived via the New Albany (Ohio) Wexner estate's mile-long driveway lined with six hundred candle-lit luminarias. Three tall portals in the entry hall were flanked by fifteen-foot-tall columns bedecked with roses, delphinium, Queen Anne's lace, and Casablanca lilies. Fireworks followed the ceremony, after which guests promenaded through a burgundy silk moiré-walled canopy into the dinner tent which Philip transformed into a real room with ivy-covered walls surrounding twenty tall Palladian-style lattice-mirrored windows. Burgundy carpet covered the floor, which matched the velvet slip-covered chairs tied with silk tassels. High overhead hung five enormous candlelit chandeliers dripping with white lilies and orchids. Inside the house, Philip created a disco with four fifteen-foot towers of flashing lights. Those who weren't too exhausted partied well into the wee hours, and breakfast was served in the dining room, candlelit by Philip, who spent ten days in New Albany before the wedding getting ready for the big day.

The cost for such opulence? Philip's much too discreet to be specific. But "average" budgets for private functions might easily cost $100,000, while charity affairs may run from $10,000 to $25,000 or more. By the same token, that modest-sized dinner at home might just as easily hover in the more comfortable $1,200 to $3,500 neighborhood. Remember, Philip is a planner of parties, not just a decorator of them. And a very detail-oriented planner at that. He's concerned with every visual element, "from the colors of the plates, to how the napkins are folded, to when the candles will be lit." While Philip's certainly capable of last-minute miracles, it's not unusual for him to spend six months planning an event. And the source of Philip's inspiration? It comes from everywhere or anywhere, even the hostess. In fact, especially the hostess. He's a stickler for making sure a party's atmosphere is a mirror reflection of the hostess's taste and style. While he's a star in his own right, he's not in the business of foisting his personality on your party—although you probably wouldn't mind since he's a good-looking charmer. Self-deprecating too. He claims not to be a peer of his high-profile clients, and in fact ruefully maintains that he's not in a league where "I can afford to go to my $1,000-a-plate dinners." This, despite the fact that he puts together some two hundred soirées annually.

# Renny

159 East 64th Street         (212) 288-7000
between Lexington and     Fax (212) 288-7105
Third Avenues
New York, NY 10021

Renny, Renny, Bo-Benny, Banana-Fana-Fo-Fenny, Me-Mi-Mo, Menny, Renny! Apologies to Shirley Ellis, but we couldn't resist. You hear the name so often, always alone. This master of the floral arts does have a last name (Reynolds), but no one seems to have used it since he first burst on the scene with his heavenly design of Bill Blass's penthouse terrace in 1974. Ever since, Renny has been on the tip of a lot of tongues when it comes to decorative flora, flowering, and otherwise.

While his dramatically romantic 1880s mansion serves as both home and shop, where you can pop in for a bountiful bouquet as long as you've got the $45 minimum, Renny is not just a florist. He prefers to be considered a party designer. And indeed, one room in the house is reserved as sort of a staging ground; where his ideas for an event's look come to life. When he's ready to present his plans, he makes it easy for even the most unimaginative clients to visualize them by arranging the room with his envisioned decor.

It may be that veterans of world-class entertaining like Brooke Astor and Anne Bass don't need this particular service, but they do need Renny. Indeed, they wouldn't dream of having a party without him, whether it's one of Anne's chic little dinners at home for twenty-four or one of her charity functions for hundreds. When Anne chaired the France Dance, Renny turned the National Academy of Design into an eighteenth-century French chateau. He also created, literally, a forest for a Bass birthday bash, with trees and leaves "growing" from everywhere including the tables and the ceiling.

Corporations depend on Renny too. For Compaq Computers, he transformed the Manhattan Center into a space-age fantasy as the backdrop for a presentation of their latest computing innovations. Fantasy is Renny's specialty. His recent "Child's Garden of Delight" design was centered around an alphabet theme, appropriate certainly for the New York Public Library location, with letters decorating each of the forty-five tables. Like this party's theme, you can count on Renny to come up with everything from *A* to *Z*.

He'll create tiny bits of fantasy for your more private parties in the form of a glorious centerpiece or other decorative touches for about $500. And while one of his extravaganzas, like a dinner dance for 2,000 at the armory, might cost upwards of $70,000, he can work wonders on considerably less, say, $2,000 for something quite grand.

Renny, himself, is a delight to work with. There's nothing pretentious about this man despite a client roster that includes David Geffen, Richard Avedon, Norma Kamali, Alan Alda, and *Vanity Fair*'s Bob Colacello. Claudia Perelman absolutely adores Renny, as does husband Ron ever since Claudia overwhelmed him with Renny's work. For Valentine's Day she had Renny sneak into Ron's office and cover every square inch of it in red flowers — *Revlon* red, of course.

Now an author (as if he isn't busy enough!), Renny has received great acclaim for his tome *The Art of the Party*, published by Viking Studio Books ($45). Filled with entertaining and design tips and lavish illustrations, it's available directly from Renny or at bookstores.

If Renny's ever likely to relax, it's down on his Pennsylvania farm. Check out his "backyard," featured in Kelly Klein's coffee-table book *Pools*.

When you get a sudden yen for one of his lovely orchid plants (a specialty) or refined arrangements, and Renny's not available, ask for the delightful Robin Bergland. She's a marvelous purveyor of the Renny magic.

# Robert Isabell, Inc.

410 West 13th Street                    (212) 645-7767
New York, NY 10014

Calling Robert Isabell a florist is like describing Michelangelo as a painter. Truly, Robert is a creator of environments — environments that play host to many of the city's most lavish parties. None is more elaborate than the spectacular Steinberg/Tisch wedding, which is rumored to have cost tycoon Saul Steinberg millions. *W* speculated that the flower bill alone (read *Robert's bill*) ran into the hundreds of thousands.

In twenty-four hours, Robert transformed the Metropolitan Museum of Art with fifteen thousand tulips imported from France, countless Casablanca lilies, innumerable sweetpeas, and myriad lilies of the valley. Garlands swagged across walls draped with softly glowing white muslin (cleverly lit from behind). At least that's what the gushing (and impressed) press reports claimed. Robert is decidedly circumspect about what he really did, and his lips are absolutely sealed about what it cost. You see, the Steinbergs are among his best and favorite clients. The divine, but by all reports down-to-earth, Gayfryd gives him interesting and lavish assignments, like the bash for husband Saul's fiftieth birthday.

Robert transformed the Steinbergs' beach house on Long Island into an ocean front Versailles with hundreds of flickering lights in terra-cotta pots, identical twins impersonating twins in the swimming pool, and dancers and banner wavers in period costumes. To celebrate Saul's status as a collector of "Old Masters," Robert decorated the tent stretched over the tennis court to resemble a seventeenth-century Flemish eating-and-drinking house. The walls were hung with photographic reproductions of Saul's art collection, while tableaux featuring posed actors re-created some of the world's greatest paintings — perhaps some of Saul's future acquisitions?

A tad much for your taste? Keep in mind that Robert adjusts his style to his clients. He's a master at reflecting his clients' personality in the decor of their parties. He can grasp your most outrageous fantasy and produce it visually.

Although he will put together a single arrangement and charge a minimum of $125, that's not his interest or his forte. He'd much rather create and execute a design theme for your next dinner party. It'll probably cost $1,000 to $3,000, but it's likely Robert will custom-design the linens. He'll definitely produce a dramatically beautiful setting for a memorable meal.

There'll be flowers, of course, in exquisite color combinations that complement the decor of the room. Some will be arranged in pieces from his fabulous collection of containers — perhaps an eighteenth-century English porcelain or something contemporary in glass or silver designed by Richard Meier. Candles might take the form of dozens of twinkling votives or long, slender tapers set in dazzling candelabras. And in addition to the centerpieces, he'll do arrangements for the entrance hall, living room, and even the powder room.

When Caroline Kennedy got married, Jackie enlisted Robert's services. When he does dinners for Giorgio Armani, the look is contemporary, sleek, and simple. Many of Bergdorf's special events benefit from his exceptional touch, and the too-chic-for-words Royalton Hotel relies on Robert's creations to lend a little warmth to its public spaces.

Like Jackie, his clients are secure, sophisticated women, who often dare to do the unexpected. They want to add a touch of the theatrical to their parties, and they know that with Robert in charge they'll get rave reviews. They also tend to be married to very rich men.

# CHAPTER FIVE

# Shopping

*If it's not here, it doesn't exist*

S ome visitors to New York couldn't care less about what room
they'll stay in, or at what hotel. (We're not among them.) The
reason: They plan to use the room only when the shops are closed.
We're fairly certain they use their rooms from midnight to 5:00
A.M. but wouldn't swear to it on a stack of Bibles. This *is* the city
that never stops.

The point is this: whatever you are looking for, New York has it.
Grecian antiquities, Egyptian artifacts, the latest fashion state-
ments from Paris or Milan, and every book you ever thought of
reading—in hard cover, paperback, or both. There are endless perfumes, sensual lingerie. There are neckties so gaudy you wouldn't
give them to the cousin you hate, and watches so costly you'll think
you're buying a suit.

The designers, artisans, and craftspeople from around the world
make sure that the New York stores have their wares because, to
paraphrase the song, "if it makes it here, it will make it anywhere."
If you could merge Rodeo Drive, Via Condotti, Michigan Avenue,
The Ginza, and the Avenue Montaigne—but wait a minute—New
York already did that and labeled the result 5th Avenue and
Madison Avenue. Even the shop-till-you-drop fanatics have never
been able to investigate all the tantalizing boutiques, shops, custom clothiers, department stores, jewelers, and cosmeticians that
line those two thoroughfares and the cross-streets that link them.

With *Only in New York* in hand, you'll manage to sort out the very best from the also-rans.

It's not surprising that the city that's become the world capital of everything from cuisine to finance to the arts has also become the world's shopping bazaar. And in true bazaar fashion, there is room for some judicious bargaining here and there. Don't try it at Tiffany's (they invented the unassailable price tag) or at any of the larger stores. But at some of the smaller ones, especially those featuring big-ticket items like jewelry, there may be some room for negotiation. It ain't Istanbul, but it's worth a try.

# FOR MEN
## *Arthur Gluck, Chemisiers*

37 West 57th Street                    (212) 755-8165
between Fifth and Sixth Avenues    Fax (212) 758-0627
Room 403
New York, NY 10019

For thirty years, since long before gentlemen "dressed for success," Arthur Gluck's has been doing just that — dressing gentlemen with that smooth, expensively tailored look that gives anyone wearing one of his shirts a little edge at the bargaining table. We've no doubt that the perfectly comfortable fit of Arthur's shirts has helped get, and keep, such power moguls as Lew Wassermann, Lee Iacocca, and Henry Kissinger where they are today.

Although Arthur himself is semiretired, his associate Michael Spitzer, who has worked alongside Arthur for years, is running things as ably as ever and has maintained his quality. Like Arthur, Michael operates on the theory that shirts are a very personal matter, magnifying the individual's appearance and personality. He, too, spends a great deal of time with new clients, discussing personal preferences. He presents fabrics in all conceivable colors and patterns from his vast inventory — bolts and bolts of the finest imported cottons, broadcloths, and silks. He sets the collar according to the customer. Narrow styles are suggested for oval faces; wider styles are recommended for round faces.

Careful measurements define neck size, the slope of the shoulder, and posture. A pattern is created that will ensure a flat, wrinkle-free front and just the right amount of collar and cuff showing under the jacket. If your schedule requires, fittings can be arranged in your hotel suite or office.

With all this time and attention, it's not surprising that Arthur Gluck's sets a first-timer's minimum order of six shirts. Two fittings will usually be required, and it takes eight to ten weeks for the order to be completed (six weeks in the slow season). Prices start at $180 and go up from there. But new cuffs and a new collar can be yours for just $60, and you have a brand-new shirt. A tuxedo shirt may run $250 to $300.

Once past the hurdle of the initial order, there is no minimum, but Michael says that most of his clients buy sixteen to twenty shirts a year. No wonder so many—clients and shirts—turn up on the world's "best-dressed" lists!

If you're concerned about the proper care and feeding of these precious shirts, you should know that Arthur Gluck maintains its own laundry service. Prices start at $8 for a "basic" shirt and range upward, depending on fabric and style. Silk shirts should go to a good dry cleaner, but if they lose a button, call Michael. He'll send a replacement right over!

## Beau Brummel

421 West Broadway                    (212) 219-2666
at Spring and Prince Streets
New York, NY 10012


1113 Madison Avenue                  (212) 737-4200
between 83rd and 84th Streets
New York, NY 10021

In 1958, it occurred to Sol Laxer that what Forest Hills in Queens needed was a men's store combining the quality and variety found in Manhattan with a convenient neighborhood location. Twenty-five years later, he decided what Manhattan really needed was a store like the one he owned in Queens, catering to a neighborhood and dedicated to high-fashion quality. Given the success of Beau

Brummel's foray into the city's store wars on the Upper West Side, he was right.

Sol is now retired, but his partner Avram Goldman is still going strong and Beau Brummel's new president is Steve Gutman, who has been with the firm since 1988. Together they mix up the Beau Brummel formula, aimed at the twenty-five to forty-year-old customer, that has worked so well.

The Columbus Avenue store was consolidated into the other two Manhattan locations, which both cultivate a calm, serene atmosphere, enlivened by fun, jazzy music, and the complimentary serving of assorted libations. The salespeople are all young, impeccably groomed, and very informed about their primarily Italian collection. Indeed, Italian fashion is considered Beau Brummel's specialty, though French, Japanese, and German lines are represented too. In fact, there's always an exciting mix of merchandise, thanks to Avram, who began his career more than twenty-five years ago as a stock boy at the Forest Hills store. He understands his young, mostly professional clientele and provides them with the latest fashion trends, tempered by good taste.

Suits featuring a wide-shoulder, narrow-hip silhouette sell for $495 to $1,200. Shirts go for $55 to $265. Jackets range from $400 to $900. And sweaters average about $225. Beau Brummel is definitely for the man who appreciates the finer things in life, as long as he can afford it. Regulars include such diverse personalities as Branford Marsalis and Axl Rose. Jerry Seinfeld is also a client both on- and off-camera.

Service has been the firm's trademark since its earliest Forest Hills days. There was a time when they could guarantee same-day alterations, but no longer; they're simply too busy and good tailors are too difficult to find. Still, you can generally count on less than a week, and they will make every effort to schedule fittings at your convenience. They'll open early, stay late, or send the tailor to your home or office. In any case, alterations are, of course, free.

The Soho West Broadway location is, so far, the largest, and in deference to the neighborhood carries slightly more avant-garde clothing than the other New York-area stores. So stop by if you're feeling especially bold. And if you're feeling more "Madison Avenue," you know what to do.

# *Brooks Brothers*

346 Madison Avenue                    (212) 682-8800
at 44th Street
New York, NY 10017

Of course, you know that Brooks Brothers put the "tradition" in traditional men's clothing, but did you know that it is the oldest specialty retail men's store in the United States? Not only that, Brooks Brothers was probably the first company to manufacture and sell ready-made men's clothing. No wonder the word *venerable* comes to mind with this most conservative of stores.

The company and the traditions it stands for have withstood the test of time with flying colors. Today, as it has for generations, Brooks Brothers outfits men in quietly classic clothes that project an unassailable image of good judgment and practical taste. Indeed there are many scions of America's oldest families who have never known another clothing shop—from their first knickers to their first blazer to their first pinstripe.

President Clinton wears Brooks Brothers clothes bought for him, we're told, by Hillary. George Bush has been a client for years, as have been a number of his Republican predecessors. Gerald Ford chose to wear a Brooks Brothers morning coat and ascot for his historic meeting with the late Emperor Hirohito of Japan. On what turned out to be a considerably less happy but more historic occasion, Abraham Lincoln wore a Brooks Brothers suit to Ford's Theater to see a play starring John Wilkes Booth. Abe Rosenthal of *The New York Times* began shopping for his suits off the rack. As he moved up the editorial ladder, he moved from ready-made to custom. Fittingly, Brooks Brothers is strolling distance from such pantheons of the establishment as the *Times*, the Century Club and the *New Yorker*, the Harvard, Yale, and Princeton Clubs, and, of course, the New York Yacht Club.

Although it's true that the store's signature soft-shouldered, three-button suit hasn't changed much since it was first designed toward the end of the last century, it has slowly evolved. The "sack suit" of twenty years ago, while identical in "look," is modern by fit and technological standards. And it's a little like the club tie. Those who are truly members of the Brooks Brothers Establishment can still recognize each other by the oddly placed buttonhole square in the lower half of the lapel. This suit was considered novel when it first appeared and it still is — but it's only one of a number of innovations the store has notched in its all-leather belts down through the years. It was, for instance, Brooks Brothers that introduced the deerstalker to the United States, as well as the Shetland wool sweater, and the first wash-and-wear shirt. Furthermore, the camel-hair polo coat is attributed to the store, as are Indian cotton madras clothing and lightweight summer suiting. Its soft slippers and supple leather shoes are all from the best British and American booters.

Most notably, John E. Brooks, grandson of founder Henry Sands Brooks, invented that staple of the businessman's wardrobe, the button-down shirt, as the result of a trip to England in 1910. While watching a polo match, he noticed that the collars on the players' shirts were anchored by buttons to keep them from flapping in the wind. Upon his return to New York he suggested that Brooks Brother make such a sport shirt, which slowly evolved into a dress shirt and the company's best-selling item. In a tribute to the ample girth of most captains of industry and government, it's never given in to tapering, and its tent-like style perseveres. Button-down and otherwise, Brooks Brothers shirts sell for $48 to $65. They are displayed in such a way as to make it easy and comfortable to make your choices about collars and patterns. Complementary ties run the price gamut of $18 for cotton knit to $58 for silk.

As for suits, we recommend the Own Make selections, tailored and produced by Brooks Brothers' own manufacturing facilities. Wardrobe separates are available from $395 to $495. Top-of-the-line Super 100s run from $595 to $895. And there's always the made-to-measure or special order option — their salespeople have been here for decades. They know their merchandise and they know the general profile of their customer. Discuss your needs with them and trust their judgment to know what's best.

They'll outfit you very correctly, sportswear to black tie. Indeed, a young gentleman's purchase of a Brooks Brothers tuxedo is considered a rite of passage in some circles. Prices range from $495 to $595 for formal wardrobe separates, not including all the paraphernalia that goes with it, which of course the store carries, right down to the proper shoes and socks. As for the latter, with black tie a Brooks Brothers salesperson will lobby for a nonribbed, over-the-calf sock.

Secure in its refined gentility, the store's subdued wood paneling and lithographs of old New York City make you feel confident and secure. There's a comforting aura of aristocracy about the store's trademark known as the "Golden Fleece." Adopted as Brooks Brothers' own in the 1850s, it's a modified version of the insignia used by the famous order of knighthood known as the Golden Fleece. Today, it appears in their advertisements, on their packaging, on certain merchandise, and in the decor. It's quite enchanting—and somehow a reminder that this is one store in which you can be absolutely sure you won't be taken or fleeced!

## Davide Cenci

| | |
|---|---|
| 801 Madison Avenue | (212) 628-5910 |
| between 67th and 68th Streets | (212) 628-5911 |
| New York, NY 10021 | Fax (212) 439-1650 |

Even if you're a habitué of the original Davide Cenci, which opened in 1926 in Rome, don't you love the idea that you can now find the same unique combination of classic style and Italian flair right here on Madison Avenue? And with an expanded range of merchandise as well as a new third floor in the store, run by Davide's grandson David Cenci, there's now even more to love.

With two windows in the front now rather than one, the store's look is much more dramatic; the lighting throughout is particularly spectacular. Unique details like the lush hand-finished mahogany display cases and the wrought-iron bannister enrich your experience as you stroll through the store, enjoying the soothing classical music and finding whatever you want. This is a true gentlemen's haberdashery. There are suits—custom-tailored and off-the-rack—a glorious array of sweaters, Italian dress and sport shirts, formal wear, casual wear, jackets and coats, ties, pajamas, robes, slippers, underwear, socks, shorts, shoes, and leather accessories.

Their suits have that sleek Italian cut, with enough panache to satisfy the more daring, yet classic enough for conservative tastes justly slightly to the left of Brooks Brothers. The top-of-the-line handworked suits run from $1,250 to $1,700, or more if you have them made in Italy rather than in the New York store's workrooms. Either way, plan on two fittings and at least five weeks for delivery.

Most of the sweaters are from Italy. The Cenci family has scoured their native land for resources and has identified several fine manufacturers who knit designs exclusively for them. Scottish products are also represented, but they are in the very distinct minority. In fact, the only other non-Italian items in the store are the loden coats from Austria.

Lightweight summer sweaters, perfect for cool mountain evenings or midnight walks on the beach, sell for $175 to $400. Warmer winter weights range from $225 to $1,700. Naturally, our favorite was of the four-figure variety, but then it is a reversible eight-ply cashmere cardigan, solid on one side, patterned on the other.

There's row upon row of dress and sport shirts to match with the sweaters, all of Italian origin and very much a part of the Cenci tradition. It seems Davide Cenci began his career in Rome as a custom-shirtmaker. At his grandson's establishment, you can get a sense of what launched Davide Cenci's international reputation by purchasing one of the firm's ever-so-elegant hand-finished shirts — $180 and up. Their handsome standard line of shirts starts at about $115.

We couldn't help but notice their beautiful tweed cashmere sport coats (about $1,500) and a great line of country/weekend clothes, including cord pants from $160 to $195 and pleated-front jeans for $150. You can top these with wonderful leather and shearling coats in exceptional colors from rich taupes to cognac and brandy, or classic black if you prefer.

Ties run anywhere from $85 to $105, and they have terrific leather accessories ranging from key chains and credit card cases to beautiful wallets, from $45 to $600. There are great-looking Italian handfinished shoes from A. Testoni, for $295 to $425, and these are exclusive in New York to Davide Cenci.

David and his young, congenial staff are very adept at pleasing their clients. They keep extensive files on each, so they can guide the building of a coordinated, practical Davide Cenci wardrobe. And David takes great pains to ensure that his gentlemen are looking their very best. When a new batch of sweaters or shirts arrives, he'll call those whose cards reveal they might be in need of a fashion boost.

Of course, once you've become a part of the extended Cenci family in New York, you're automatically embraced by the Italian contingent. David's dad Paolo and uncle Germano hold court in their large Rome store, where you can really expand your Cenci collection, and their brother Giacomo has a store in Milan. But if an Italian sojourn is not in your immediate future, don't be dismayed or feel cheated. The Cenci selection on Madison is even better suited to American tastes, extensive enough to satisfy all but the most extreme shopping habits.

# *Maurizio — Custom Tailors*

18 East 53rd Street                                    (212) 759-3230
between Fifth and Madison
5th Floor
New York, NY 10022

Tony Maurizio, a tall, slim, perpetually tanned native New Yorker, is the very image of the elegant men he's been dressing to such perfection since 1947. Tony is the reason Henry Kissinger, Alan King, Steve Lawrence, and Nelson Rockefeller, Jr., always look so well groomed. They made their way to his beautiful, clublike, wood-paneled showroom years ago and never dream of going anywhere else.

Tony's suits begin at $3,000 and go up from there. Naturally, they are made of the world's finest fabrics, English wools and Italian silks. They are constructed by hand. And each of Tony's four tailors has been with him more than twenty-three years.

Custom tailoring is a marathon, with an initial visit to choose fabrics and take measurements, at least two more fittings, and four to five weeks of waiting for the finished garment. But it's worth every bit of it. Remember the old saying that clothes make the man? The fact is, you look different in a custom-made suit; you stand taller, walk straighter, feel better, secure in the knowledge that all those inevitable flaws in your profile are cleverly disguised by custom tailoring. Everything is considered, everything muted — the slight paunch, the less-than-perfect posture, even the bowed legs.

Whether it's a cashmere sports jacket for $3,000, a $4,000 three-piece tux (the two-piece version is $3,500), or a heavenly cashmere overcoat for $5,000, Tony pays a lot of attention to your neck measurement. He maintains that the most important part of a jacket is the way it hugs the neck, which crucially affects the balance. If the neck doesn't fit properly, the rest never will.

Fit, of course, is the name of Tony's game — from $850 silk slacks to $4,000 topcoats. In fact, Tony became so renowned for the extraordinary fit of his clothes that the wives of his customers began clamoring for his services. So now he will outfit very special ladies with blazers for $2,200, skirts for $800, and his trademark pleated trousers with cuffs and three-quarter-inch self-belt for $750.

Whether you're a gentleman or a lady, owning a suit (or pant-suit) from Tony Maurizio is a sign of good taste and an indication that you have most definitely arrived.

# *Paul Stuart*

Madison Avenue at 45th Street      (212) 682-0320
New York, NY 10017                 (800) 678-8278

Sociologists claims it's human nature to resist change. That all-too-human discomfort with innovation may have a lot to do with the ongoing popularity of Paul Stuart. Nothing much has changed here since Ralph Ostrove opened the store in 1938. It occupies the same site and it's run by Ostrove's son-in-law Clifford Grodd, whose vision has made Paul Stuart what it is today: a bastion of good taste in gentlemen's (and ladies') furnishings. Credit Grodd for that signature Paul Stuart look — the unusual colors and fabrics, the distinctive button treatments, the cuffed trousers, the natural shoulder for men, the bow ties and braces, the pleated pants.

Paul Stuart is a store where a man can feel comfortable knowing he's not going to make a mistake. Walking onto any one of the three selling floors is a little like slipping into an old, comfortable shoe; a feeling of well-being envelops. Things can be counted on here — things like quality, since everything is made exclusively for Paul Stuart; selection; and service.

We know any number of nattily attired men who swear by the custom-shirt department, which features traditional style with just the right touch of flair. The shirts range from the orthodox to whatever your heart desires. You can, indeed, design your own shirt; they have a variety of collars, cuffs, and fabrics to mix and match. If you don't know exactly what's best for you, trust the sales staff to help. Their competence in coordination insures that you'll always look smart. There's a four-shirt minimum order and a lead time of four to six weeks.

Appropriately, just across the aisle, the tie department provides an enormous selection of the perfect accessory for the perfect Paul Stuart shirt. From silk paisleys to knits, from neat prints to stripes, not to mention the ubiquitous club, the ties are constructed to form an always-fashionable three-and-a-quarter-inch column and cost between $39.50 and $89.50.

Jewelry, socks, underwear, and an extraordinary array of sweaters complete the first level's complement of exceptional merchandise. And they have such a sensible system—one salesperson can help you throughout your tour of the floor. When it's time to go upstairs to investigate the suit situation, he'll guide you and introduce you to your next escort. Our favorite first-floor fella is Louis Agront.

The oversized, rather grand wooden staircase leads past a mezzanine reserved for women's sportswear and business attire, to the second floor devoted to suits, sport coats, trousers, and overcoats. The natural-shoulder look sets the standard. You can get "off the rack" suits, of course, but regulars like David Halberstam, Phil Donahue, Spalding Gray, the "L.A. Law" regulars, and a whole pack of Wall Streeters, go for custom-made, costing around $2,000 depending upon design and fabric. Plan on three fittings and a six- to eight-week wait. If you're hard-pressed for time, they'll even arrange to have a fitter visit your hotel, home, or office to ensure tailoring perfection.

For the up-and-comer, they're introducing a new suit called the Stuart Classic for $588. Match it with their wonderful shirts and ties as well as cap-toe, or wing-tip, or lace-up shoes in calf or suede.

If you've no time, or patience, for shopping altogether, consider the expert services of Paul Stuart's personal shopper, Maureen McCormack. She can assemble an outfit—suit, suspenders, shirt, tie—or an entire wardrobe and dispatch it to wherever you are or wherever you're going. She'll even keep track of important birthdays and anniversaries, select the proper gift, and have it delivered in time for the celebration.

Prefer to do your own shopping from your own turf? Paul Stuart's beautifully produced catalog will come in handy. Distributed twice a year, mid-March and mid-September, its mailing list bears witness to the store's sophisticated international clientele — Japan, France, England, Saudi Arabia, Switzerland, Hong Kong, Italy, Venezuela, Colombia, and more are represented in droves.

To join the ranks, just call Paul Stuart's toll-free 800 number. There's a one-time $5 sign-up-charge, but the catalog is free thereafter, and you won't want to miss things like their great selection of enamel-on-vermeil cuff links done in stripes, polka dots, plaids, and harlequin patterns ($245).

House charge accounts are available. They're especially useful for some of Paul Stuart's more luxurious items, like the absolutely divine navy blue cashmere topcoat, with hand-stitched lapels and collars, lined in Chinese weasel. (Naturally, at $4,300, the lining is removable.)

For a dose of sheerly frivolous pleasure, guaranteed to lend a little Fred Astaire debonair dash to even the most conservative investment banker, pick up a $124.50 black walking stick topped with a sterling silver crown.

If you subscribe to the theory of clothes making the man, make sure Paul Stuart makes your clothes. You'll be assured of presenting an image of affluence, success, and impeccable taste.

# Uma-Reddy, Ltd.

| | |
|---|---|
| 30 West 57th Street | (212) 757-7240 |
| between Fifth and Sixth Avenues | Fax (212) 956-5243 |
| Suite 6E | |
| New York, NY 10019 | |

What do you get when you cross an Italian perfectionist and an Indian charmer? In this case, you get a perfectly tailored custom-made suit. Italian Nino is the tailor and pattern-maker. He oversees the six tailors and two seamstresses, while Indian-born Uma Reddy is in charge of quality control and sales — sales to exacting clients like investment banker Benjamin Lambert, businessman Joseph Israel, the Metropolitan Opera's Bruce Crawford, and theater impresario Jimmy Neiderlander. They value the flattering fit and classic cut, made stylish with just a dash of flair.

Uma-Reddy uses nothing but the finest woven fabrics from England. Suit prices start at $2,600, though cashmere can run to $3,600. For sport jackets, plan on $1,800 to $2,100; slacks range from $455 to $600. One of their last-half-a-lifetime overcoats runs about $2,400.

Clients earn "regular" status by ordering an average of four to six suits a season. Each takes about six to eight weeks and requires two fittings. New clients, of course, need to be measured and should figure on at least eight weeks before hanging a new suit in the closet, as they'll need three fittings.

To set off that suit, see Uma's wife Kantha Reddy, who now runs Rosa Custom Ties on the same premises (phone: 245-2191). You can choose from the thousands of Italian or Swiss silk swatches, and, they'll make a custom pattern to your exact specifications. Priced from $75 to $125, your tie will be handmade. There is no minimum—you can buy one or one hundred ties from Kantha, which Uma told us some people do. "I wish I could do as well as she!" he proudly confides.

Uma keeps a file on each client's suit purchases, with swatches. He knows exactly what they need, because he knows what they already have in their wardrobe. So he welcomes last year's suit, in need of a few alterations due to gain (or loss) of weight, like an old friend. Of course, there's never any charge for such services. Nino and Uma are even so fond of their handiwork that they happily encourage clients to bring in their suits for pressing. It's done by hand here—so much better for the shape of the suit than the machines and steamers the neighborhood cleaner uses. They just want to make sure nothing happens to embarrass you—or them—when you're wearing a Uma-Reddy.

# *William Fioravanti, Inc.* — *Custom Tailors for Men*

45 West 57th Street          (212) 355-1540
4th Floor
New York, NY 10019

You've arrived. You're the Chairman of the Board, the President, or the CEO. Your first call should be to William Fioravanti. Be advised, however, that a call earlier in your career might have helped hasten your climb up the corporate ladder. William is, after all, at the top of that same ladder when it comes to custom tailors for men. Of course, Bill works only by appointment. He deals with only one client at a time in his understated wood-paneled showroom, where for a quarter century he's been dressing some of the world's most powerful men.

The Fioravanti look is fitted with a broad shoulder (the better to bear all those burdens?) and executed in soft, sensuous fabrics of mostly British origins—100 worsted wools and 150 worsted spun cashmeres. Naturally, the silk linings are Italian, exquisite in rich solid tones or lively prints, depending upon your preference.

For years there have been few things finer than one of Fioravanti's fashions in cashmere. A two-piece suit runs about $4,850, and a top coat will set you back $4,750. But these days, thanks to Cheil Industries, the Korean company that invented it, there is an even finer fabric in Fioravanti's stable. It's "out of this world," says Bill, "something we call, in the trade, a 1-PP—it means that each strand of yarn is literally as fine as the hair on your head. So it allows the weavers to make something even better than cashmere!" A suit made from 1-PP costs $5,750.

If you can settle for slightly less than the best, "regular" wool suits are $3,750. Slacks hover in the $950 neighborhood, and sport coats start at $3,150—a bargain when you consider the $3,850 price tag of one made up in the 1-PP cloth.

Whatever the fabric, being outfitted by Bill requires some advance planning. For one thing, no matter how large your initial order, he'll only cut one piece, which he'll work until you're both happy. Then, and only then, will he proceed with the rest. And getting to that happy phase is a lengthy process because Bill is so meticulous about creating the absolutely perfect fit.

It starts with a first visit, when Bill spends a lot of time chatting with you about your life-style, so that he can get a handle on the kind of clothes it requires. He bases his recommendations upon the nature of your business, the number of homes you maintain, the amount you travel, and the places you frequent. Once you and he have come to an agreement on your needs, he works with you to pick the appropriate fabrics. Finally, he sets about taking your measurements, which may take half an hour or so. He's very precise and the measurements are very detailed. You won't see Bill or daughter Raquel, who's been with him since graduating from Fordham University, till at least three months later, when you come for the first fitting. The second fitting takes place two to three weeks later, the final one about a week after that. We're talking a minimum of four months. If you need clothing for fall, see Bill by June as do his high-profile clients (who we're told very much appreciate our *not* naming names). Like that anonymous group of who's whos, you'll know that all the time and effort was justified the first time you put on a Fioravanti suit. The fit is fantastic—the shoulders straight, the back flawless, the lines clear and uncluttered.

Bill can do the same for ladies, perhaps in deference to Raquel and wife Olga, who also works with him. But he doesn't do it often. It's a matter of talking Raquel into it and then relying on her to convince her father. When they do decide to honor a special request from a woman, they produce very tailored, very ladylike suits for $4,150. We beg for the slacks, even at $1,150. And we're negotiating for a couple of drop-dead cashmere coats.

We want to feel as if we've arrived too. Fashions by Fioravanti make such a statement because they don't just cover a body, they adorn it.

# FOR WOMEN

## *Chanel*

5 East 57th Street                    (212) 355-5050
between Fifth and Madison Avenues
New York, NY 10022

Sometimes in a world of quilted handbags, little black dresses, gobs of chains and pearls, cardigan suits, white collars and cuffs, and blazers and black-tipped sling-back shoes, it's hard to believe that the woman who first introduced them, first popularized them, is no longer with us.

Coco Chanel, or just Chanel: the name is so often invoked when fashion mavens speak of true style and elegance. She revolutionized the way women dressed in the 20s, liberating them from long skirts and constricting styles. Today, her signature is more prevalent than ever, thanks to the inspired interpretation of Karl Lagerfeld (whose designs for other labels are far superior to his own). The number of Chanel copies in every price range is testimony enough to the continued importance of the house that Coco built.

If you'll settle for nothing less than the real thing, then head for this glamorous store with its full range of Chanel products. It may not be quite as large as its Rue Cambon parent in Paris, but it's every bit as chic—all done up in beige, black, and cream, with gleaming mirrors, brass, and chrome as accents. You find yourself hesitating at the bottom of the baby-grand staircase, looking up just in case you might catch Coco's ghost about to descend.

The cosmetic center near the entrance carries all the Chanel products that you can find at other counters. Beyond, you'll find men's ties for $105 and a marvelous selection of silk scarves. The classic 40 × 40 goes for $255, even more for the 56 × 56 versions, which make great beach or pool cover-ups. The $500 oversized wool challis lends a special Chanel touch to what otherwise might be an ordinary suit or dress. And speaking of accessorizing with Chanel, who can resist some of the classic costume jewelry first made fashionable by Chanel? A basic go-anywhere gold-and-pearl clip runs about $130. Glitzier and larger evening earrings go for closer to $585. To decorate your waist, day or evening, collect the archetypal "C" chain belt, which varies slightly every season, but always sports the hallmark Chanel medallion. It's priced from $700 to $1,300, depending on the thickness of the links and the length, defined as how many times it can wrap around.

Upstairs are the clothes that exemplify Coco's fashion edicts — "Nothing goes out of style more quickly than a fashion, while elegance is for all time." "A dress that is not comfortable is a failure. To be elegant is to wear clothes that permit you to move easily, gracefully, comfortably." "A woman can often be over-dressed, never over-elegant."

In Chanel, you'll never be over-dressed or over-elegant, but you will pay a not-inconsiderable sum for such self-confidence. Two-piece suits start at $3,000, and prices can go as high as $14,000 for a truly glamorous evening gown. Chic little day dresses fall into the $1,600 to $3,000 category. For evening, a classic black satin might cost about $2,000, but we can never resist the slightly more elaborate concoctions with just the right amount of beading for closer to $3,000.

The shoes and bags that have become so much a part of the landscape are here too. And here, you can be sure they're the real McCoy (or real Chanel). A basic black pump with the hallmark stitched toes runs about $425. An elegant little silk evening slipper with a tiny sparkling sequined bow or some jet beading falls into the $400 to $550 range and complements almost any ensemble. Then there's *the* bag, complete with quilted leather and gold chain threaded in leather. They come in all shapes, sizes, and colors with a similar variety of inventive closures. But start with the time-honored black shoulder version for $1,375. For travel, you'll like the Chanel duffle at $900 and perhaps a well-constructed cosmetic case for $470. This is the principal store of Chanel's eleven free-standing U.S. boutiques. As such, it can draw from the stock of any of the others. If colors or sizes available here don't quite suit, ask for the manager or the assistant managers. They will conduct an all-out search. They'll also make sure your packages are delivered, while expert repairs are made on any (perish the thought) defective merchandise. And if you're in desperate need of something Chanel, but just can't find the time to stop by, call Brigitte and she'll send it over. She's used to such requests from sophisticated international clientele, including a fair number of French, Germans, and Japanese. Each of those languages, by the way, is spoken in the store and all of the multilingual staff carry beepers. If you can't seem to find your favorite salesperson, ask and she'll be instantly summoned.

Who exactly are Chanel clients? It's almost easier to say who *isn't* wearing a piece or two of Chanel. And, with the two Premiere and Mademoiselle collections of gold and diamond watches ($1,500 to $46,000), the ranks of Chanel devotees are bound to swell even further. Besides, now that the store is open seven days a week all year, there's even more time to shop Chanel.

## Fendi

720 Fifth Avenue                    (212) 767-0100
at 56th Street
New York, NY 10019

Fendi — in the U.S. the fabled name was most often associated with furs and fragrance, until those five fabulous sisters opened their U.S. flagship store: a 20,000-square-foot, three-floor Roman palazzo, showcasing everything that is Fendi — $2 body lotions to $20 leather pocket agendas to $200,000 sable coats.

Rumor and retailing common sense has it that this is just the beginning of the Fendi conquest of America. Naturally, though, New York had to be first, never mind that it meant ending the long and successful relationship with Bergdorf Goodman, once the only place in the city where you could get those fantastic Fendi furs.

And what they've done to that space! Roman arches, columns, marble floors, and parchment-covered walls transport you to another time and place. The superb lighting bestows a lustrous jewellike quality on every piece of merchandise. That same lighting caressing the beautiful grain of light wood with dramatic black accents lends a certain serenity to the store, which makes shopping very pleasurable indeed. What's more, the specially recruited and trained staff doles out genuinely warm Italian hospitality. Their goal is to make clients feel welcome and valued, not intimidated. The lovely, spacious dressing rooms and the presence of the sisters themselves (on a rotating basis) add to your sense of *dolce vita*.

The main floor houses the Fendi fragrances, men's and women's shoes running the gamut from classic to high-fashion styles, and a vast assortment of small leather goods — including limited edition handbags that were formerly available only in Rome. The second floor is devoted to men, who even have their own label here — Fendi Uomo. Predictably, it's a sensuously luxurious line, heavy on the cashmere. Each season brings great new pieces for the fellows, and they'll always find a range of sporting accessories including golf bags and racquet covers.

There's a new line of sunglasses, starting at $160, and a fabulous new bed and bath line with comforters, sheet sets, towels, and the like, which we definitely like!

But despite these temptations, we tend to make a bee-line for the second floor, home to women's clothes and the fur salon. Here many Americans are getting their first look at the handiwork of a third generation of Fendis — Fendissime, created by the Fendi sisters' daughters and nieces, Maria Teresa, Sylvia, and Federica. It's a complete line of clothes, furs, and accessories designed for the young and the young at heart. And, of course, it is here that you will find the Fendi ready-to-wear, the result of a most successful collaboration with Karl Lagerfeld that dates from 1965. He consistently does the Fendis proud, and indeed helped put them on the international fashion map with the creation of the famous double F logo.

And then there are the furs — those oh-so-fabulous furs, the result of years of experimentation and research lead by Paola Fendi. She and her team of craftsmen have changed the nature of fur from a precious but stiff material into one that is light, soft and above all easy to wear. They have done so by developing new tan-

ning and dying methods and innovative ways to cut and construct
fur. While we're generally overwhelmed by the wondrous selection
of their work here, we have been known to zero in on the exquisite
cashmere scarves and shawls trimmed in fur — about $1,200 and
$4,500 respectively. The shearlings, made surprisingly light by a
special process, and the fur-lined raincoats have also captured our
attention.

The Fendis' approach is to create an aura of enticing, sophisticated femininity (or masculinity) in all they design. There is an
elegant, witty, even humorous quality to their creations. After all,
these are the girls who dared to make fur fun, dramatic, and surprising. The same qualities infuse everything bearing their distinctive trademark, from jewelry, watches, and handbags to luggage
and evening wear.

The likes of Georgette Mosbacher and Nan Kempner get a kick
out of the Fendi style, and we know why. Just ask about the custom
services. You'll find that at Fendi, you can get just about anything
you want.

# Givenchy

954 Madison Avenue                     (212) 772-1040
at 75th Street
New York, NY 10021

There was a time when it seemed every woman in the whole world
wanted to look like the young Audrey Hepburn. Doubtless, one of
the reasons was that she always looked so incredibly elegant, yet
girlish and coquettish, partly due to her on- and off-camera wardrobe by Hubert de Givenchy. Was she his muse? Perhaps. But one
thing is certain — it is all but impossible today to think of one without evoking images of the other.

So naturally, Audrey still pops into your mind as you cross the
refined and graceful threshold of Givenchy's boutique. In wonderfully comforting and familiar surroundings, he offers his myriad
ready-to-wear clothes and accessories. The boutique's merchandise
covers the whole gamut — day to evening wear, suits to sports
separates, cocktail dresses to ballgowns. There are coats and
raincoats to cover the suits, capes to shelter bare shoulders exposed by evening clothes, and shoes, gloves, and jewelry to set off
everything. And sunglasses, there are even sunglasses.... And then,

of course, what would you expect from the only freestanding Givenchy boutique in all of the good old USA?

The divinely chic and sophisticated Yuta Powell presides over this empire. We're most fond of Monsieur de Givenchy's versatile cashmere capes, with their generous ruffles that are so flattering to the face. He remains the master of classic clothes with a sense of humor and a touch of fantasy. For evening, he's got a fabulous new woolen angora coat trimmed with velvet for $2,000. It functions like a cape but sits fitted on the shoulders so you can throw it over anything, and it works great for traveling.

Dressy cocktail dresses start at $2,100 and go up to $4,500. For a really glamorous evening, you'll want a long beaded chiffon gown, which might run as high as $5,000. And, we finally found the perfect raincoat (we've been searching for years). With a cape-like form, it's reversible and lined in wool flannel ($1,750).

Givenchy also remains very much involved with his business. You might catch sight of his tall, elegant presence here. He directly oversees the operation of the boutique, often making the trip from his native Paris to check things out.

For new clients, the big question is: Where do you begin? Yuta says you needn't try to build a whole wardrobe in one fell swoop. Start with the impeccable Givenchy suit, really a value at $2,100. Blouses run $900 to $1,000 and generally pick up the suit's print or the color, but more exaggerated for that magnificent effect. Next, you'll add a sweater, then pants, and later a cape, and you're on your way. When you're ready to start, call Yuta or Veronica (who's been here for ages and knows everything there is to know about the extensive choices). They'll set up an appointment to put you together — head to toe. Naturally, it's quite an investment, but you know that Givenchy's women count on him to design timeless clothes. He doesn't disappoint; you'll be wearing your new wardrobe for years, never feeling dated.

Timing-wise, we've found the best time to shop for fall is during the months of July and August. Look for spring clothes in the dead of winter. (What else is there to do in January and February?) Once you become a regular, you can get even further ahead in your planning by ordering from the photographs Yuta always brings back from the Paris shows. She'll call the minute she returns. Let's see now, that means you can deal with fall in March and spring in October!

Whichever schedule you follow, the boutique's excellent fitters will have ample time to adjust your new duds to perfection. They're so good, they can even improve considerably on nature, hiding a nasty little figure problem or two. There are a lot of big names in the fashion business, but very few class acts, very few who understand and respect their clientele. Hubert de Givenchy is a notable exception. He knows they expect the best and he delivers.

## *Helene Arpels*

470 Park Avenue                                    (212) 753-1581
between 57th and 58th Streets
New York, NY 10022

The perky green-and-white striped awnings beckon. They summon you to wander into the small, pale blue salon of the tall, slender Madame Helene Arpels, designer of the city's most comfortable, chic, and pricey shoes.

Her absolutely smashing footwear is complemented by a few select pieces—clothes, handbags, and accessories. She has an exquisite black silk/satin belt, delicately decorated by black jet beading, which sells for $750. It'll spruce up that old reliable standby, the little black dress. For further drama, you can cover it with any one of a selection of beautiful evening capes, priced at around $1,900. We were particularly taken with the transparent chiffon number dotted with velvet flowers. Then there's the butter-soft three-quarter leather and suede jacket with a small band of black fox at the collar and a detachable hood. It turns ordinary slacks and sweater into a couture costume for $3,400. Her lovely handbags start at $500.

But enough of this. It's still the shoes that are the real draw at Helene Arpels. And what extraordinary shoes they are. She has a pair of lizard pumps dotted with a few hand-sewn rhinestones, tri-colored in platinum, silver, and pewter for $1,900. Perhaps a pair of alligators would be just the thing for that dear little Givenchy dinner suit—light and delicate in a dramatic combination of brown, rust, and black at $3,200.

Well, maybe you don't need quite so much gator. You can soften the look and the price with the purchase of a shoe crafted in alligator and suede for around $2,600. For evening, the hand-embroidered silk slippers can be either high- or low-heeled. They come in a rainbow of conventional colors, or can be colored to match an uncommon shade for $1,900. Special orders take about four weeks.

At these prices, you'll be pleased to know that Helene provides an extra pair of heels, so you can actually wear these puppies on the streets of New York with impunity. The first grate that seizes your heel will not be cause for any ill-considered revenge.

Of course, the heel issue evaporates when it comes to Helene's luxurious suede loafers, the ultimate in comfort and a favorite with clients for more than forty years. They come in any color or skin you might want, with a broad price range — leather and suede for $550, lizard for $900, ostrich for $1,500. The ultimate? In crocodile, these casual little loafers will cost $2,700.

Naturally, one does not wear Helene Arpels shoes in inclement weather. One does, however, don her signature rain boots, which also happen to be the least expensive item (at $275) in the store. Rubber-soled patent leather, they're trimmed in red, black, or taupe leather. Devotees tend to have a pair of each.

Helene's fans hail from all over the world. Hers is a very personal business. She told us of many clients who, after wearing a particular pair of shoes for fifteen years, come in requesting the exact same style to wear again — and again! She showers clients with attention and embraces them with her philosophy that life is beautiful, especially if it includes some of her beautiful things. Eternally elegant clients like Nancy Reagan, Gloria Vanderbilt, Barbara Taylor Bradford, and Betsy Bloomingdale wholeheartedly endorse that hypothesis.

But we think you're not a true believer until you order one of Helene's caftans. All hand-beaded, each takes two years to make, once Helene has designed it. The price — not a penny less than $13,500. Only those seeking the most beautiful of lives need apply.

## Henri Bendel

712 Fifth Avenue                    (212) 247-1100
between 55th and 56th
New York, NY 10022

The Bendel story basically begins in 1896, when Henri Bendel set up a little hat shop on East Ninth Street. His clientele appreciated his personal service (he made a point of learning each customer's name) and attention to detail. As business prospered, he added perfumes, then custom-made clothes. Soon he was in the market for a larger location and in 1912 opened the first store on what was then the residential 57th Street. Situated literally in the backyard of families with names like Vanderbilt and Whitney, Henri Bendel began to cater to the crème de la crème of New York society. Bendel's reputation as a store for the carriage trade developed over the years to near epic proportions. The introduction in 1957 of the innovative "Street of Shops," a series of individual boutiques on the main floor, created a sensation. As designers' names became household words, Bendel's was in the vanguard of securing exclusive arrangements with some of the world's top couturiers, and the store elevated window dressing to an art form. Fashionable New Yorkers made it a point to study Bendel's windows to find out what was new and exciting. Bendel's was the most special of specialty stores, always the dependable source for something intriguingly unique.

Then came the merger and acquisition mania of the 80s. Even Henri Bendel succumbed, ending up as the crown jewel in retailing wizard Leslie Wexner's empire — The Limited. But if there were doubts about Bendel's future, they've been put to rest. Under the leadership of dynamic Susan Falk, who succeeded marvelous Mark Shulman as president and CEO, Henri Bendel New York has truly become a flagship, moving into space four times larger than its former location. Now, three fabulous new Bendels are thriving, in Chicago, Boston, and Columbus.

Lots of what was familiar at the former 57th Street site has been transferred to the new setting, while some old Bendel traditions that for a while had been lost in the shuffle have reemerged. The elegant Bendel's brown-and-white-striped shopping bags continue to be a souvenir of your visit, thank goodness.

Despite the profusion of French stone and Italian marble, entering the foyer of the new Henri Bendel is like entering a private home — which is exactly the idea. Bendel's fashion-savvy, sophisticated, international clientele likes to shop in an intimate environment. They appreciate the store's division into a series of seemingly self-contained small shops, rather than departments.

There's the main floor Montana Fifth Avenue boutique, with jewelry and cosmetics nearby. Bendel's is one of the purveyors of

Canadian Mac cosmetics and skin-care products. The range of colors, developed for Mac by internationally acclaimed makeup artist Frank Toscan, is enormous.

A grand staircase beckons you to the second floor. Of course, the elevator is also an option, but the stairway provides a great bird's-eye view. You might spot Barbra Streisand, Cher, Teri Garr, Kelly McGillis, or Linda Gray from your perch.

As for the rest of the store, rely on Bendel's for the latest fashion finds. We're just crazy about the sportswear by Todd Oldham, Claude Montana, and Anna Sui. And their "New Createurs" offers the latest European and American designers.

If you're hungry, stop for lunch or cappuccino at Salon de Thé run by French chef Guy Pascal in the second floor atrium. Afterward, stroll into Frank McIntosh's fabulous tabletop department. And, for the well-heeled, the Susan Bennis/Warren Edwards shoe salon is on the fourth floor, filled with incredible shoes, most of which are exclusive to Bendel's.

So, despite the changes, the years have been good to Bendel's. As far as we're concerned, the store's mystique seems to be very much intact. We are sure that Henri would approve.

# *J. S. Suárez*

26 West 54th Street (212) 315-5614
between Fifth and Sixth Avenues
New York, NY 10019

These days it's so embarrassing to be seen in public without a tote bag screaming Chanel, Hermès, or Bottega Veneta slung over your shoulder. It's equally embarrassing to explain their price to husbands, lovers, or mothers (especially mothers) who think a purse is meant to be utilitarian, not an indication of your economic and social standing.

There is a solution, a compromise between fashion sense and common sense, provided by José Suárez. At J. S. Suárez you can purchase that status bag, minus the status label, at one half to one third the price. And with the exception of Hermès, it really is the same item, having been produced by the same manufacturer responsible for the authentically labeled version.

As for the Hermès look-alikes, they're definitely copies, but who can tell? The classic Kelly bag with the shoulder strap in leather is only $379. It comes in ostrich, lizard, and crocodile as well; prices vary. You can also have the "Hermès" trim bag for a fraction of what the original Hermès cost.

With the largest — and least expensive — collection of ostrich, lizard, and crocodile bags in the country, J. S. Suárez features some exquisite generic bags, from the smallest clutch to the largest tote, starting at well under $1,000. Elsewhere, you couldn't touch any one of them for less than $1,800.

José won't reveal the names of any of his customers and neither will his son Matthew or his daughter Ramona, who are usually here as well. They know their business is built on illusion. Their customers would be horrified to be identified as such. After all, the whole point is to convince the world that the Chanel on their shoulder is the real McCoy.

# La Lingerie

792 Madison Avenue                    (212) 772-9797
at 67th Street
New York, NY 10021

You'll find whatever milady desires, or whatever turns her fella on, in this tiny shop jam-packed with intimate apparel. From flirtatious bras and teddies to glamorous nightgowns and robes, La Lingerie's ladies can help you assemble a seductive wardrobe meant for your (or his) eyes only.

Almost everything in the shop is made of silk or cashmere (or both). Ungaro and Valentino are well represented, including the latter's wonderful robes. Look for the long or short cashmere version in several different colors for about $1,000 or the silk-lined embroidered style for about $1,500.

For the bride, La Lingerie is sheer heaven — all those coquettish bras and panties for her trousseau. The beautiful beaded lingerie cases make for perfect honeymoon packing. For approximately $150, you can choose from a collection of Art Deco-style Koos cases, covered with pearls and patches of suede.

They also now carry antique christening gowns in the $750 range. Apparently, you're never too young to start shopping at La Lingerie.

# *Laura Biagiotti*

4 West 57th Street                    (212) 399-2533
at Fifth Avenue
New York, NY 10019

Although *The New York Times* dubbed Laura Biagiotti "The Queen of Cashmere," one glance inside her magnificent 57th Street store makes it clear that this appellation only begins to tell the story. Located in the prestigious Crown Building, the first Biagiotti boutique in this country features sportswear, swimwear, jewelry, fragrances, cosmetics, sunglasses, watches, handbags, scarves, a range of accessories, and a vast line of ready-to-wear clothes. You won't even see the cashmere collection until you get to the second floor.

Biagiotti was born in Rome, and although she obtained a university degree as a literature/archaeology major, she was, no doubt, groomed for fashion by her mother Delia, a tailor/designer. She garnered raves beginning with her first collection in 1972 and today lives and works just miles from her birthplace in an 11th-century castle that she and her husband/business partner reconstructed stone by stone in 1980.

Not content with stores in places like Rome, Milan, Venice, Athens, Seoul, and Tokyo, Biagiotti outdid herself for her U.S. debut. Working with Italian architect Piero Pinto, she devised surroundings whose design — in keeping with her other stores — is reminiscent of a private home's comfortable surroundings. (Don't miss the impressive Rene Gruau painting of the Biagiotti castle on the main level.) Hardwood floors, beautiful antique and modern Italian furnishings, an inviting couch or two, and lovely trompe l'oeil murals truly enhance your visit. Fashions are displayed discreetly to encourage browsing so that the rich and famous who shop here can do so in privacy and relative anonymity.

Biagiotti's exquisite taste is in evidence throughout. It's all there: dresses, jackets, suits, tunics, skirts, cardigans, and pants. We love the "stars and stripes" that decorate her new Harbour line as a salute to the flagship U.S. store. Another favorite is the Sweetheart line's bell-shaped dresses in knee- or ankle-lengths. Don't miss the 15-ply silk dresses and tunics in fishing net and rigging color tones from the appropriately named Rope line.

Biagiotti's designs are not without whimsy. The Mermaid line, for example, includes apron waistcoats and ankle-length dresses made of iridescent sequins, and taffeta silk shorts in pale pink, yellow, and mint green. But fear not if that doesn't appeal, for Biagiotti is widely respected for her practical fashions and you're sure to find lots to like.

The Manhattan store is the only place in New York where you'll find Biagiotti's Roma and Venezia fragrances. Roma comes wrapped in a marvelous marble-like package, paying homage to the Eternal City. We loved Venezia's intense Oriental scent; its green and gold package is noteworthy as well. Both fragrances cost around $50 to $60.

Biagiotti's signature eyewear averages $145, and her watches, which feature crystals containing dried flowers or petals, range from $300 to $500.

Upstairs, the cashmere selection is excellent and endless. You'll find all kinds of sweaters, from round neck to V neck to polo-style. There are selections for men, too, in colors ranging from classic greens, blacks, and whites to pastel yellows, pinks, and blues. There are also wonderful leggings, skirts, scarves, and shawl-like blankets. We had to have the snow-white cashmere jeans for $600; most pieces here are priced from $400 to about $3,000.

After a visit to the Biagiotti boutique, we always find ourselves feeling very grateful that when faced with the choice between literature, archaeology, and fashion, Laura opted for the latter.

# Maud Frizon

19 East 69th Street                              (212) 249-5368
between Madison and Park Avenues
New York, NY 10021

Just about everything in the relocated Maud Frizon salon has changed, except for the quality of the shoes and the dramatic manner in which they are displayed. The move from East 57th Street coincided with a company decision to concentrate on a well-rounded collection of women's shoes and a few accessories. So, gone are the pantyhose and stockings, the luggage, the children's line, the lower-priced Maud Frizon Club, and even the custom-order service.

But black granite, black marble, mirrors, and natural wood still surround you as you browse, and you can still sink into one of the extremely comfortable black leather chairs to try on any of the shoes Maud designs annually for her two collections. It's likely something will appeal to your sense of shoe style. If not, Maud would be the first to tell you to look elsewhere. She believes shoes are a very personal thing; they should be a reflection, and extension, of the wearer's personality. If you're of a feminine, romantic frame of mind and have a sense of humor, Maud's shoes with their distinctive look are for you. Whether it's the curve of the heel or the flounce on the side, every pair announces it was designed by the ever-creative Maud. A basic black pump is never all that basic from Maud Frizon, nor should it be at $225 and up... and up!

Not all of each 200-piece collection is available in the store at any given time, but, like Shirlee Fonda, Liza Minnelli, Lois Garner, and Mary Tyler Moore, you'll likely find what you need. Ranging in price from $200 to $575, there's a large selection of casual, dressy, and business-wear. We were taken with the $375 wedge sandal and the raffia-and-leather pump for $295. We also like her suede boots in a broad range of colors for $425 to $525.

There is still a versatile selection of bags for $300 and up, including some wonderful satin overnight cases for $475.

We can't resist a visit to see what Maud has been up to, even with the selection reduction. With her style, it's okay. As they say, less is more.

# Rene Mancini

655 Madison Avenue                    (212) 308-7644
between 60th and 61st Streets
New York, NY 10022

If you're a Chanel devotee and you think there's something familiar about Rene Mancini's shoes, give yourself a gold star for your good eye. Back in the 1950s, the late Frenchman originated what became known as the two-toned Chanel-style shoe. Today, the Rene Mancini legacy lives on through the Paris-based company that bears his name, now run by Rene's daughter Claire Mancini. In addition to their own lines of fine shoes for women, available at their Paris and New York stores, they also continue to design for couturiers ranging from Givenchy to Hanae Mori.

You'll find the Manhattan salon a delight. Its soothing beige walls and gorgeous decorative Italian glass show off the equally gorgeous shoes to their best advantage. Though the shop appears small because it's narrow, it is actually about 600 square feet, quite enough space to display daytime styles of all kinds (priced in the $390 range) and a great selection of evening shoes (which start at about $420), plus evening bags (mostly around $625). They'll likely have what you want, whether you prefer your heels low, medium, or high. And of course they stock samples of their handmade atelier line, from which you may choose your heart's (or foot's) desire. And if you see something you like but want it done just a bit differently, by all means speak to Manager Tony Amato or any of his pleasant staff. Forty percent of their business is special orders, so don't be shy about asking them to make something just for you. Custom orders usually take about five weeks; they start at about $675 and can go as high as $2,000 for crocodile.

Speaking of crocodile, we saw a terrific pump in a variety of colors for $1,695, made from what Tony assures us is the finest skin on the market. We also liked the high-heeled silk shoe with satin toe for $390. It comes in black or blue and is available with a gold leather or gold lamé toe as well. Pay special attention to their wonderful patterned platform shoes, too.

On any given day, you're likely to run into Rene Mancini regulars like Lee Annenberg, Barbara Taylor Bradford, or Danielle Steele. Like us, they've discovered that all they have to know about shoes is that the Mancini people know about shoes. It's that simple.

# Sylvia Pines — Uniquities

1102 Lexington Avenue                    (212) 744-5141
at 77th Street
New York, NY 10021

While there's no telling what treasure you might unearth in this small shop delightfully cluttered with Victorian, Art Nouveau, and Art Deco goodies, be sure to concentrate on plowing through the amazing collection of unique and antique purses. Remember mother's intricately beaded evening bag? Sylvia's got hundreds, from $55 to $500. She's also amassed a huge selection of French Deco purses glittering with marcasite. Starting at about $475, some go for as much as $2,400.

In the twelve years that Sylvia Pines has been stocking her small space with treasures like antique-looking glasses, charming silver picture frames, and a splendid selection of Art Deco and Art Nouveau jewelry, she has developed a special affinity for beautiful day and evening purses of a certain age. She even has a bag hospital of sorts. If cleaning out the attic of the family manse yields a purse or two in need of repair, Sylvia can probably handle it. She'll either fix it herself or send it to one of her excellent sources for refurbishing.

Sylvia's penchant for purses is contagious. As regular browsers, we became addicted... and collectors. Besides being unique fashion accessories, they make very respectable objets d'art suitable for strategic display — a Uniquitous addition to any decorating scheme.

Credit cards (Visa, MasterCard, and American Express) are now accepted. As Sylvia says, "don't leave home without them."

# *Ungaro*

803 Madison Avenue                              (212) 249-4090
between 67th and 68th Streets
New York, NY 10021

No one, but no one, designs sexy feminine clothes like Emanuel Ungaro. He is truly the master of the seductive fit, using every trick in the book to accentuate and define the female body. Ungaro claims to love women. It shows in his designs.

Considered the master of prints, his silks, especially made for him in Milan, are extraordinary — for their sophisticated floral patterns and their bright, radiating colors. But they're not for everyone. We suspect Ungaro counts few wallflowers among his clientele. Rather, his women are secure, self-confident types, who enjoy making entrances in his statement-making clothes.

Of course, these days there are plenty of women who fit the Ungaro profile — women like Marisa Berenson, Morgan Fairchild, Jackie Onassis, and Joanna Carson. Some even make a habit of collecting his designs, happily and comfortably wearing them for years, secure in the knowledge that, for them, the feminine approach to dressing is always in style.

His Madison Avenue boutique, part of what has become a multi-million-dollar fashion empire, is always busy with browsers and buyers alike. Manager Carol Vargas oversees the action, dispensing advice when asked but never offering it unsolicited. She knows her clients are contemporary, decisive women who know what they want. In this case they want Ungaro's tailored no-nonsense but nonetheless provocative suits, which start at about $1,800. The wide shoulders and other elements of the fit do wonders for slimming the waist and hips. His signature dress silhouettes with lots of draping or shirring through the bodice are even more form-flattering. Almost liquid in the way they undulate along womanly curves, they're definitely not for everyone from a figure point of view. Usually constructed in his famous silk prints, they seldom constitute business attire but are dynamite for social luncheons and cocktail parties for $2,000 or thereabouts.

As for evening clothes, think grand, glorious, and about $3,500. Of course, there's also sportswear by Ungaro—slacks for $500 to $900, sweaters starting at $600. They bear his distinctive style, but for our money you're better off sticking with the suits, dresses, and evening gowns since that's where he really excels.

We do, however, have two exceptions to that rule. Try both of his fragrances (approximately $200 an ounce). Diva, dedicated to French actress Anouk Aimee, the great (and very public) love of Ungaro's life, is romantic, seductive, and daring. His new Ungaro scent is more subtle. Both are marvelous—but then what else would you expect from one of the very few designers whose clothes inspire passion, both literally and figuratively?

## *Vera Wang Bridal House, Ltd.*

| | |
|---|---|
| 991 Madison Avenue | (212) 628-3400 |
| at 77th Street | Fax (212) 628-4410 |
| New York, NY 10021 | |

| | |
|---|---|
| *Vera Wang Made-to-Order* | (212) 879-1700 |
| 25 East 77th Street | |
| in The Mark | |
| New York, NY 10021 | |

There's something about wedding clothes that brings out the best in people—and the worst. That's why we love Vera Wang, whose full-service bridal boutique offers enough personal attention and sophisticated fashion savvy to make everyone happy.

With impeccable credentials that include eighteen years at *Vogue* as a senior fashion editor and two years at Ralph Lauren as a design director, it was a natural when Wang recently added Vera Wang Made-to-Order to her repertoire. You probably remember Sharon Stone's stunning satin outfit at the 1993 Oscar ceremony—it was a Wang, one of many exclusive evening gowns Vera offers via her second retail operation.

But let's talk weddings first. Vera's inspiration for the bridal business came during preparations for her own wedding several years ago (a splendid affair for 400 at The Pierre). She had discovered, to her dismay, that personal service combined with a full range of merchandise befitting her style were nowhere to be found, not even at department stores or at bridal shops. Like every good entrepreneur, she was determined to explore this untapped niche; thus, Vera Wang Bridal House, Ltd., was born.

She offers a high-fashion sensibility not normally associated with the word "bridal." You'll find help creating a truly coordinated style for that very special day—everything the wedding party's distaff members could want, from dresses, shoes, matching kidskin gloves, and custom-designed veils and garters for the bride to her new Vera Wang Bridesmaid Collection. She'll suggest (or custom-design) accessories for the attendants, and you can count on her, too, for help with attire for the rehearsal dinner, the reception, traveling clothes, or whatever you need. Vera really does it all, including advising the groom and creating the ring-bearer's pillow.

Vera has been a big hit from the night of her opening party, when Bobby Short entertained and Sylvia Weinstock, queen of wedding cakes, baked one that matched the salon's cream-and-gold decor. Though diminutive in size (and usually dressed in black), Vera is packed with enough energy to run her thriving businesses. That's why, no doubt, she's designed wedding dresses for such high-powered types as Gregory Hines' daughter Daria, and Victoria Strauss, wife of Max Kennedy (Ethel's son).

Located at the corner of 77th Street, the scene itself of many magnificent weddings, Vera's stylish bridal salon is stocked with designs by such fashion-forward types as Victor Edelstein of London, David Fielden, Vicky Tiel, Michael Kors, Mary McFadden, and Donna Karan, as well as those of traditional wedding specialists like Priscilla of Boston, Eva Forsyth, Jim Hjelm, and Paul Diamond. Vera's own designs are available through her Vera

Wang Bridal Collection, or you can have her create something that's one of a kind, just for you. Once you select your wedding dress, you'll be whisked across the street to the Vera Wang Styling Center in The Mark, next door to Vera's Made-to-Order salon. All three of her salons, by the way, are reminiscent of a fine European fashion house, with the feel of a private home that particularly serves to soothe those prewedding jitters.

We fell in love with one of her bridal made-to-orders, a pale pink gown with a strapless bodice, multilayered silk tulle skirt, and a silk tulle collar that doubled as a hood, held at the shoulders with tiny satin rosebuds (approximately $5,500). Another very pretty gown, for about $8,400, was an off-the-shoulder white satin-faced silk organza number whose neckline and hem were trimmed with bright yellow silk satin. We also saw some lovely suits, afternoon tea dresses, and even some skin-tight minidresses.

Whatever your taste, your age, or your size, Vera will take care of you. You'll need to book your first appointment at least three months before the wedding, particularly for anything that's custom-made, and plan to spend anywhere from $1,500 to $25,000. Bridesmaids' dresses are priced from about $250 to $400. Be sure to let them know if you're from out of town so they can have everything you want to see ready to show. And don't fret if you don't see Vera herself the first time; she's trained her staff of twenty-seven to handle your every need. Everyone you see is very good at what he or she does.

But even if there are no wedding plans in your future, fear not. You'll love the Vera Wang Made-to-Order Collection, which made its debut in 1991. It contains primarily cocktail and evening dresses, whose mood is inspired by Vera's version of that bygone era when Audrey Hepburn and Grace Kelly defined a certain kind of femininity and flirtatiousness. Viewed only by appointment in the suite at The Mark, designs range from about $6,000 to $10,000. Although the collection, of course, changes from year to year, we were delighted with a piece from a recent spring/summer line, a long ballerina gown with a gold-corded lace strapless bodice sprinkled with diamonds and a skirt made from layers and layers of white silk tulle. And as are her wedding fashions, the Made-to-Order styles are created to suit a range of tastes. Figure skater Nancy Kerrigan is a client, sharing with Vera not only a love of great clothes but also a love for the ice — Vera was a finalist in the 1969 Junior United States pairs championships.

Vera's skills are quite endless, ranging from entrepreneur to businesswoman, fashion designer, and trendsetter. And with the increasing popularity of her work, it's probably accurate to say that while she spent the first half of her career *at Vogue*, she gets to spend the second half *in vogue*.

# *Walter Steiger*

739 Madison Avenue                           (212) 570-1212
New York, NY 10021

Monday through Saturday from 10:00 A.M. to 6:00 P.M. is the time to shop for soft, sensuous shoes at Walter Steiger. The diminutive boutique imitates its luxurious products. Here, soft black leather couches line gray carpeted walls supporting a burgundy lacquered ceiling that surveys the rather seductive scene.

Manager Antonia Trimarchi is a fountain of footwear knowledge and can direct you to the perfect pair. All of the shoes are designed in Paris by Walter Steiger and manufactured in his Italian factories. With Antonia's guidance we found Walter Steiger's dear little shoe boot with its leather cowboy heel for $225. A best seller, year after year, it should be a staple of every woman's wardrobe.

Likewise the classic Walter Steiger walking shoe — arguably the world's best — sporting a one-and-a-half-inch stacked heel that defies destruction and redefines comfort. It comes in every color of the rainbow (and then some) for $275. Then there's his take on the timeless Dorsay pump, cutout on both sides. Available in myriad materials, you can assemble a complete day-to-evening wardrobe in just this one design — from a sturdy leather rendition with the traditional wooden heel to a dainty all silk moiré number. Prices start at $235 and go up, way up, depending on style and fabrication. For any of the Walter Steiger evening shoes, like a beautiful pair of black silk sling-backs encrusted with gold-trimmed rhinestones at the bottom of the instep, count on a minimum of $325.

While his shoes are available at many fine stores throughout the United States, this is the only freestanding Walter Steiger shop in the country. This is the one place that you'll find the complete collection, which explains why so many sophisticated ladies from out of town drop off their luggage at the nearby Mayfair Regent or Plaza Athénée, then make a beeline for the store. They just can't wait to see what they've been missing elsewhere.

# FOR MEN AND WOMEN

## *Barneys New York*

| | |
|---|---|
| Seventh Avenue and 17th Street<br>New York, NY 10011 | (212) 929-9000 |
| 660 Madison Avenue<br>at 61st Street<br>New York, NY 10022 | (212) 826-8900 |
| 225 Liberty Street<br>New York, NY 10281 | (212) 945-1600 |

Barneys New York may be the official title, but for seventy years it's been just plain "Barney's" to New Yorkers who enthusiastically embrace its unique formula of diversity, value, quality, and service. Now that the self-described "largest specialty store in the world" (as opposed, we suppose, to Macy's, the world's largest department store) has expanded to three Manhattan locations, Barneys is poised to conquer the world. Whether you're in Chestnut Hill, Massachusetts, or Tokyo, Japan, there's a Barneys nearby. With nearly twenty throughout the United States and more to come, these are ambitious plans indeed for an organization that until 1988 had essentially one location. But then what would you expect from the enterprising Pressman family, who have parlayed a $500 investment into a multimillion dollar business?

It started in 1923, when at his wife's suggestion, Barney Pressman pawned her engagement ring for $500 to cover the cost of renting a space on lower Seventh Avenue and stocking his first forty suits. He quickly established a reputation for providing quality clothing and service, despite a discount pricing policy. Today, the shop that Barney built houses an inventory of more than forty thousand suits and employs thousands, including about two hundred in-house tailors. And it is decidedly no longer discount oriented.

Under the leadership of Barney's son Fred, his wife, Phyllis, their two daughters and two sons, along with the sons' wives (we did say it was a family business), Barneys has moved into the ranks of the upscale—skirmishing with Bergdorf's and Saks over designer exclusives, while developing a somewhat avant-garde or cutting-edge attitude. In the process it has expanded its dedication to men's clothing and furnishings to include boys' wear, gifts, silver, china, antiques, jewelry, and women's clothes and accessories. And in fact, in 1986, Barneys transformed six turn-of-the-century brownstones adjacent to the men's store into a 70,000-square-foot store for women, bringing the total square footage of the original Barneys to a staggering 170,000. But that's small potatoes when compared to their new 250,000-square-foot Madison Avenue store, the largest store built in Manhattan in sixty years. Positioned at the gateway to Madison Avenue's prime lineup of designer boutiques, the new branch treats men and women as equals insofar as space and amount of merchandise is concerned.

We heartily recommend an outing to the new store as well as to the 10,000-square-foot World Financial Center location, where every March and September they bring over Britain's best tailors to provide custom made-to-measure services for men. But, truth be told, our heart remains with the original location.

Inspired by the Parisian department stores of the early 1900s, the women's emporium is classic yet modern. A sky-lit atrium with a sweeping marble stairway forms the nucleus of the interior. Each floor encircling the staircase reflects the character of its merchandise in an elegantly intimate setting. And each of the six floors benefits from the natural light provided by the brownstones' original windows, as well as Art Deco and Wiener Werkstaette pieces along with custom fixtures crafted in Europe.

The women's areas range from lingerie and cosmetics to two floors devoted to clothing for the professional woman. But you don't have to carry proof of your "ladies who lunch" status to venture to the upper floors sporting names like Beene, Chanel, Zoran, Lagerfeld, and Mugler. But healthy bank balances or unlimited credit are helpful. Prices are indeed special, creeping into five figures in some instances. On the other hand, the "professional clothes" are as well priced as they are diverse—Donna Karan,

Perry Ellis, Ralph Lauren, Calvin Klein, and Byblos, to name a few. The Barneys New York collection has become very important for the working woman, too.

Professional or not, you can take advantage of the personal shopping expertise of the divine Louise Maniscalco. If you're more of a do-it-yourselfer, you'll do it better here than in most stores with such a large selection. The salespeople can travel with you, gathering merchandise along the way for you to try on all at once. In fact they're so accommodating that once you're in the dressing room, they'll send down for the proper shoes for each outfit if you desire.

If you're a bargain hunter but not trouper enough to endure the indignities of most operations regularly offering that elusive commodity, head for the CO/OP. It's a complete store, part of the total complex just past the women's regions, featuring the best in contemporary clothing for women — cosmetics, shoes, accessories, and activewear, as well as sportswear from the likes of Basco, Anna Sui, Gaultier, and Liza Bruce. Prices stay around the $500 level here, but the collections are just as tightly edited as they are in the rest of the store. Barneys knows its female customers — women like Claudia Schiffer, Demi Moore, and Julia Roberts — whether they're in the market for $15 bath soaps or a $5,000 evening gown.

Of course, Barneys is equally well acquainted with its male clientele. After all, they built the business in the first place (as the world's largest *men's* store, Barneys had nothing to do with women until it added a *department* in 1976). Originally dependent upon American manufacturers' close-outs, Barneys expanded its purchasing horizons, not to mention pricing policy, and in 1968 became the first men's store to feature European designers. Five floors were designated "international," encompassing the city's most complete selection of designer men's fashions.

In 1976, Barneys introduced the designs of Giorgio Armani to America, demonstrating its on-going commitment to discovering and developing new, innovative talent. Today, that policy means Barneys carries sport coats by Byblos, sweaters by Romeo Gigli, and suits by Comme des Garcons. For more traditional tastes, much of the second floor is filled with clothing of the reliable British variety — suits, double and single breasted, by Gieves & Hawkes and Oxxford. The bespoken suitings of H. Huntsman & Sons and Kilgour, French & Stanley are also represented.

Made-to-measure shirts are just one example of the American furnishings that occupy the main floor. Rainwear, outerwear, and the boys' department fill the lower level, as well as Le Café serving breakfast, lunch, tea, dinner, and Sunday brunch. While we wouldn't necessarily make a special trip just to dine here, the charming garden setting does provide a pleasant respite from the rigors of shopping. And the kitchen serves food far superior to that of most *department* stores — we can't think of a single specialty store kitchen to compare with it!

# Bergdorf Goodman

754 Fifth Avenue                        (212) 753-7300
between 57th and 58th
New York, NY 10019

*The Men's Store*
745 Fifth Avenue                        (212) 753-7300
between 57th and 58th Streets
New York, NY 10022

Although in the last decade, Bergdorf Goodman has had as many ups and downs as its elevators, we are delighted to declare that troubled times are over. Following a successful stewardship by Carter Hawley Hale's Ira Neimark, Bergdorf's is now run by the Neiman Marcus Group's Burton Tansky. The once-haughty store has been transformed. Tansky, Bergdorf's chairman and CEO, and eminent Ellin Saltzman, senior vice president and fashion director, are dedicated to presenting the newest fashion trends to a clientele that includes not only the ladies who lunch but the ladies who work as well. With its continuing commitment to providing featured designers with generous space, attention, and exposure, adoption by Bergdorf's is every fledgling designer's dream.

Bergdorf's reputation for excellence was built by Edwin Goodman, who entered the field of women's tailoring in 1899 at the age of twenty-three as an apprentice in the firm of Bergdorf and Voight. When Mr. Voight died two years later, Edwin became a partner in the new firm of Bergdorf Goodman. Buoyed by Edwin's flair for fashion and his insistence on impeccable workmanship, the firm's business flourished, enabling him to buy out Mr. Bergdorf upon his retirement. Under Edwin's sole leadership, business continued to grow, with the city's leading socialites becoming frequent visitors to the store's sumptuous West 32nd Street quarters, which resembled those of the great couture houses of Paris. By 1914, Edwin was in need of more space for Bergdorf Goodman. He moved the store to 616 Fifth Avenue, where the entrance to the Rockefeller Center Gardens is located today. But another move to even larger quarters was still to come. When Edwin heard the great Vanderbilt mansion on the corner of Fifth and 58th was to be razed, he determined that its site overlooking the beautiful fountain of the Pulitzer Plaza and Central Park beyond was perfect for Bergdorf's future and final home. The building now occupied by the store was completed in 1928.

Actually, there was another move in store for Bergdorf's, which took place in 1990 when the men's departments became The Men's Store across the street in the former F. A. O. Schwarz location. You won't find any toys here, just grown-up stuff like sportswear by Perry Ellis and Valentino, marvelous sweaters by Joseph Abboud, ties and shirts by Turnbull & Asser and Charvet. Predictably with Bergdorf's fashion-forward attitude, suits seem to be heavy on the Italians with lots of Armani and Valentino. To Boot offers a small shoe boutique, and Sentimento has an outstanding collection of antique cuff links. Don't miss the tie rotunda with its great assortment featuring the best of the best, including Ferragamo, Hermès, Bottega Veneta, Chanel, and on and on.

Meanwhile, women will continue to take advantage of Bergdorf's philosophy of showing complete, though carefully edited, collections, rather than just a few pieces here and there. A number of the best American and European designers have entire boutiques within the store — Calvin Klein, Donna Karan, Geoffrey Beene, Ralph Lauren, Michael Kors, Isaac Mizrahi, and Bill Blass represent the Americans. From across the Atlantic, Bergdorf's features Saint Laurent, Chanel, Ungaro, Ferre, Armani, Versace, Lagerfeld, Valentino, Gaultier, and Montana. But there's nothing carved in stone about the list. A mediocre to bad collection or two and a formerly favored designer can find him or herself out of Bergdorf's good graces. Saint Laurent and Montana have only recently been reestablished within the store.

While fashion is the driving force at Bergdorf's, it's not just clothing fashion. The seventh floor presents an eclectic host of fashionable treasures for the home. There's an antique shop supplied by its parent emporium from Kentshire, England. The best of Frette, Pratesi, Bischoff, and Cocoon line the shelves of the linen department, which contains more manufacturers under one roof than anywhere in the world. Exquisite crystal and china sparkle here too, casting pretty patterns on the selection of contemporary gifts.

Cafe Vienna on the seventh floor beckons for lunch, tea, or a light snack, but the more popular meeting and eating spot seems to be the new and always-crowded Cafe on 5ive on the fifth floor (natch), which has been completely redone. You'll find it more contemporary and more modern with clothing, accessories, shoes, and cosmetics from Anne Klein II and Adrienne Vittadini, among others.

Of course, though shopping at Bergdorf's is considerably more civilized than at some stores, you still might want to take advantage of the personal shopping service offered by Mary Kavanaugh and her staff. They work by appointment and will either gather merchandise for your review or guide you through the store. But, once you've ensconced yourself as a regular client, you can call Mary with a description of your needs and she'll have an appropriate selection of merchandise sent to your hotel, office, or home.

As talented as Mary is, we never use her service when we're in the market for accessories here. It's just too much fun strolling through the spectacular array on the main floor — you find whole collections of bags, belts, scarves, and jewelry from the likes of Paloma Picasso, Chanel, and Donna Karan, plus bags and jewelry by Judith Leiber. Here too you find some of Bergdorf's famous exclusives like Angela Cummings's fine jewelry and hats by Philip Treacy.

The unique jewelry of Barry Kieselstein-Cord is another exclusive knock-out here. His stunning signature muted gold pieces have a vaguely medieval yet distinctly contemporary look. Barry has a flair for setting precious and semi-precious stones to their best advantage, and his sterling belt buckles have become intrinsic to any truly chic wardrobe. As you consider how your credit cards will react to the attempted purchase of the gold necklace of large rectangular links studded with emeralds, you might run into Barry's much-photographed wife, muse, and business partner, Cece.

But she's only one of the rich, famous, and beautiful people you might find yourself standing next to at Bergdorf's. Candice Bergen strolls over from her Central Park South aerie. Cher stops in as do Anne Bass, Anne Johnson, and Nan Kempner. Obviously, it's not difficult to spend a fortune here and many happily do so. But Bergdorf's can be enjoyed without spending a dime. Consider it an exhibit of much of the best the world has to offer, displayed in luxurious surroundings. Wandering through Bergdorf's can be an educational, and free, experience.

## *Billy Martin Western Classics*

812 Madison Avenue            (212) 861-3100
at 68th Street
New York, NY 10021

Although Billy Martin has gone off to that big baseball diamond in the sky, his memory lives on at Billy Martin Western Classics. And the store is famous now not only for the best bunch of Western boots this side of Texas; it also recently tripled its size to accommodate a smashing selection of Western wear.

But let's start with the boots. Doug Newton (Billy's original partner), president Colette Nerey Morgan, and VP Carroll Watts commission special designs from bootmakers all over the Lone Star State. Sophisticated and stylish yet decidedly Western, the boots here are anything but prosaic. The same goes for the clientele — Bruce Springsteen, Elizabeth Taylor, Arnold Schwarzenegger, Bruce Willis, Eric Clapton, Alec Baldwin, and James Taylor come here to satisfy their cowboy fantasies. And whether you're a celebrity or not, you'll get lots of attention from the staff of twenty-seven. They'll work with you to pick just the right heel, the perfect toe. They'll also arrange for a custom-made number if by chance there is nothing here that quite suits you — but that's unlikely. This down-home store is chock-full of boots in every fabrication you can possibly envision — from calfskin for $395 to lizard for $595 to alligator for $3,200 and everything in between, including ostrich and hippo skin.

The appropriately Western assortment of men's and women's clothing fills out the rest of the store, including many items exclusive to Billy Martin. They sell lots of denim work shirts, of course, in a range of different colors including a great $175 number with sterling silver and turquoise buttons. Suede skirts ($250 to $650) come short, straight, full, or with fringe in colors good enough to eat — chocolate brown, cranberry, cognac, and mustard — as well as the garden-variety black and navy. Besides the full line of leathers, suedes, buffalo skin, and deerskin, there are cottons and wools, too. Don't miss the belts and belt buckles, particularly the striking sterling silver buckles made by artists hailing from Santa Fe.

So whether you're dressing up or down, do take a look at Billy Martin Western Classics. You'll like what you see.

## *Bloomingdale's*

1000 Third Avenue            (212) 705-2000
New York, NY 10022

Self-proclaimed as the most famous store in the world, Bloomingdale's is that and more — much more. In fact, it's ten floors and one city square block of more. And all of it is a far cry, literally and figuratively, from the tiny "Bloomingdale's Hoop Skirt and Ladies' Notion Shop" that brothers Joseph and Lyman opened in the late 1860s. But almost from the beginning, the brothers Bloomingdale demonstrated a daring retailing style incorporating constant change that would become the Bloomingdale's trademark.

Their first store took advantage of the rage for the hoop skirt ignited by Empress Eugenie. As that craze faded, they opened the East Side Bazaar, offering a wide variety of ladies' fashion — a bold move in an era of very specialized shops. In the 1880s, as the popularity for bicycling made the fashionable bustle impractical, the Bloomingdale boys were among the first to recognize the fact and adapt their styles accordingly. And by 1886, they changed the face of retailing forever, opening their new store at 59th and Third. Always the pioneer, Bloomingdale's stood alone on the muddy field punctuated by tenements and railroad tracks that was then the Upper East Side — all other stores were below 34th Street. But Joseph and Lyman attracted shoppers — brought by their use of the latest technology, plate glass, and cast iron, to create large open spaces brightened by natural light and filled with a vast array of merchandise. They were enticed by innovative window displays, themed rather than crammed with a potpourri of products that was the custom of the day. Joseph and Lyman supported their window's themes with special promotions inside the store — the forerunner of today's famous country and state promotions.

Business was good, very good. And Bloomingdale's embarked on an expansion program. By 1929, it had acquired the entire block it occupies today. But it was the 60s and 70s that really put Bloomingdale's on the world map. The country themes and other promotions were so lavish, so exciting that there was an air of theatricality about the store. It became "Bloomies," a destination, a place to go, a Saturday afternoon diversion, an adventure—so much more than just a store. Indeed, rumor had it that Bloomingdale's was New York's second biggest tourist attraction after the Statue of Liberty. The store was always mobbed.

It still is, and frankly we find it a little overwhelming. All those people with all those accents (foreign and otherwise) and all that attitude. The only way to cope is to retreat periodically to one of Bloomingdale's' five restaurants to get away from the maddening crowds. Our favorite is the sixth floor's Le Train Bleu, evoking the tranquil, romantic atmosphere of a nineteenth-century dining car. On Saturdays, the restaurant serves an elegant champagne brunch starting at 11 A.M. A full luncheon menu and cocktails are available from noon every day, except Sunday when Le Train Bleu is closed. Afternoons, from 3:30 to 5:00 P.M., you can pop in for a light snack, and supper is served until 7:30 P.M. on Thursdays when the store is open until 9:00 P.M.

For more casual dining there's 40 Carats, featuring food on the self-consciously healthy side—creative salads, vegetable casseroles, and frozen yogurt. Then there's the Showtime Café on the seventh floor, with its cafeteria-style, albeit rather elegant, service. As if all that weren't enough, Bloomingdale's boasts an Espresso Bar, a continental-style coffee and wine bar that also sells delicious muffins and croissants fresh from the store's bakeries. The Tasting Bar, with its selection of inventive soups, salads, and sandwiches, completes the Bloomie's dining scene, but not the food story here.

There's a whole food department, which puts many so-called gourmet stores to shame. The collection of delicacies, both foreign and domestic, is huge—106 different coffees alone are available, along with innumerable vinegars and oils laced with every conceivable flavor. Bloomies-made baked goods and candies abound as do freshly prepared entrées that require only the warming touch of the microwave to captivate the palate. Like every other department, it is an embarrassment of riches.

Indeed, we find the only way to shop the store sensibly is to let someone else do it for us. When we're in the market for a couple of wedding gifts, a powder room overhaul, or a getaway weekend wardrobe we head straight for the fourth floor and At Your Service. Director Sylvia Spitalnick oversees a platoon of personal shoppers, dedicated to ferreting out just what you're looking for, even if you're not quite sure what it is. They'll cover the whole store from housewares to furs, selecting appropriate items along the way. Then they'll set you up in a spacious dressing room where you can review the loot in leisurely privacy. Sip some coffee or tea while you sort through it all—enjoy a light lunch while you're at it. Indeed, spend the whole day.

For truly special Bloomies' assignments, however, we've come to rely on Hope Golden at Hope's Corner. She accomplishes personal shopping miracles, like getting the buttons changed on the otherwise divine Ungaro suit or accessorizing to perfection that stunning Oscar de la Renta gown. Call her directly at extension 3375.

Gentlemen, don't despair, Bloomingdale's is also equipped to handle your needs with At His Service. Run by Cathy Newman, this department does it all—from putting together a wardrobe for a young buck about to take Wall Street by storm to keeping track of special occasions for an older buck's wife or girlfriend (or both). Cathy keeps extensive files on birthdays and anniversaries. One call to her at extension 3030 and Cathy will make sure the right gift in the right size will go to the right person to celebrate the right occasion.

Our final tip for coping with the Bloomingdale's experience is to check into the Estée Lauder spa. You can take a mini-vacation here by indulging in the Day of Beauty—five and a half hours of pampering for $175, including manicure, pedicure, body massage, facial, makeup lesson, and application, not to mention lunch. Even if you don't have that kind of time, you can take advantage of this oasis of calm in a sea of madness by dashing in for any one of those services.

In all fairness, though, we should note that the rah-rah days of retailing are over. Under the continually inspired stewardship of Chairman Michael Gould, Bloomingdale's has taken up the banner of renewed concern for the customer and service. So the sales staff numbers almost two thousand and the store has been reconfigured to make shopping easier and more comfortable. Each fashion floor offers accessories that complement its merchandise. Consequently, if you're buying a Chanel suit on the fourth floor you can be secure in the knowledge that just the right shoes, handbags, hats, scarves, and jewelry (Chanel and otherwise) are within only a stone's toss away.

Bloomingdale's continues to adapt, to evolve just as it has for over a century. The store that discovered Ralph Lauren, Perry Ellis, and Norma Kamali continues to seek up-and-coming designers. It's brought Sonia Rykiel, Kenzo, and Fendi ready-to-wear to America, and Bloomingdale's continues to shop the world for incredible variety. You can spend as little as $1.25 on a muffin (lemon, zucchini, pumpkin, cinnamon, apple, blueberry, or even chocolate) or untold sums on fine jewelry. And the whole scene, driven as it is by Gould's bold approach to merchandising, display, and advertising, continues to titillate even those whom you might expect to be somewhat jaded — the likes of Jackie Onassis, Liza Minnelli, Diana Ross, Isabella Rossellini, even Queen Elizabeth. They have all been intrigued by the institution that is Bloomingdale's.

## Bottega Veneta

635 Madison Avenue                    (212) 371-5511
between 59th and 60th Streets
New York, NY 10022

It's so refreshing — an upscale European emporium of leather goods and accessories that doesn't believe in splashing its initials all over the merchandise. Bottega Veneta feels your own initials, if you are so inclined, will suffice as testimony to your good taste and the size of your bank account.

They've built their twenty-one-year-old business around connoisseurs of quality, subtlety, and elegance. Born in Northern Italy, the company began with handbags, briefcases, and luggage and has subsequently expanded to large, luminous, exotically printed scarves, a selection of unusually good-looking ties, jewelry, classic mix-and-match sportswear separates for men and women, and, in the head-to-toe mode, shoes.

They've also branched out from their leather roots in the handbag and luggage arena with a luxury sport line — coated canvas and leather called Marco Polo. A large soft-sided thirty-inch suitcase costs about $960. If you want to make a real statement while traveling, go for the massive $8,500 steamer trunk. Should you suffer a serious reversal in your fortunes, you can always live in it!

You won't want to overlook the trademark Bottega Veneta woven leather handbags, all made by hand in the company's Vicenza factories and priced from $300 to over $1,000. They also make divine crocodile and lizard bags, with prices that are best described as "on request"!

The New York store is the company's flagship; as the largest of the eight U.S. outlets, it has the biggest selection — the entire collection is showcased here. However, even in this light and airy space, not everything can be displayed. So if you see something that strikes your fancy, but the color doesn't quite suit, be sure to ask. Manager Genevieve Overholser has gone to Beverly Hills, but the new manager, Rachel Weiss, will find it for you, either from stock or from one of the other stores.

If she's busy with the likes of Harrison Ford, Donald Sutherland, Bette Midler, Steve Martin, Diana Ross, or Glenn Close, look for Robert Brown. He's just as knowledgeable as Genevieve and is a whiz, too, at putting together that very special order.

# Burberry's

| | |
|---|---|
| 9 East 57th Street | (212) 371-8050 |
| between Fifth and Madison | (800) 284-8480 |
| New York, NY 10022 | |

Okay, so you probably figured some guy named Burberry invented the raincoat favored by yuppies and other dressed-for-success types. But we bet you had no idea that Thomas Burberry was, even more importantly, the inventor of waterproof clothing. Born and bred in mid-nineteeth-century rural England, he noticed that shepherds' gear seemed to keep them comfortable in the region's often wet weather. Upon closer inspection, he realized the close weave kept the moisture out.

Armed with this knowledge and his natural bent for improvement, he set about experimenting with the weave using other fabrics, especially cotton. The result was gabardine — a waterproof fabric that is cool and comfortable because air passes through it. Burberry's coats made of gabardine were a vast improvement over their chief rival, the hot, rubber-lined mackintosh. By 1888, Burberry had developed a loyal clientele, many of whom were avid sportsmen like himself. He was advertising hunting and fishing garments as well as clothing "suitable for India and the Colonies." He also sold tennis, golf, and archery wear.

In 1899, with the help of his two sons, he moved the business to London and began to wholesale his wares to retailers throughout England. Still, for the longest time, there was no real name for his best-selling coat, which Burberry simply described as a "slip-on." It was left to King Edward VII to name the garment. He would say, "Get me my Burberry" when he wanted his favorite coat. The appellation caught on throughout his kingdom and, eventually, the world.

But it wasn't until World War I that Burberry created his signature piece — the trenchcoat. At the onset of the war, Burberry designed a new variation of his gabardine coat and proposed it as part of an officer's formal uniform. It was especially produced to deal with the conditions of trench warfare. Today, as the trademark of such stars as Alan Ladd and Humphrey Bogart, it has become a universally recognized symbol of adventure, drama, and intrigue.

Despite America's love affair with the trenchcoat, Burberry, a public company since 1920, didn't stake out any U.S. territory until 1978, when Barry Goldsmith opened the New York store. While there are now sixteen others across the country, the New York store remains the largest, with four floors of selling space.

The first floor of this little bit of country-house Britain, so lovingly tended by Barry, houses men's furnishings — shirts, ties, and sweaters. The shirts have that distinctive Burberry point of view, particularly those with wide, bold stripes and white collar and cuffs for $60. As for the ties, they're in a class by themselves. Burberry's buyers head for Como, Italy, home of the world's finest silks, to secure exclusive patterns. Prices of silk ties range from $65 to $80, depending on the weight of the fabric.

The best of Burberry's sweaters are, of course, cashmere. And you can be sure they are made of the best quality cashmere. Buyer Mark Sussman goes to the Scottish mills to personally select the colors, shapes, and styles. Prices start at about $275.

On the second floor you'll find the classic raincoats, as well as suits. You'll also probably find store manager Michael Bishop. Like his boss, Barry, he is British and a Burberry veteran. He's also one of the most customer-oriented retailers we've ever met, another Burberry trademark. Worldwide the company's staff is invariably charming, good-looking, and impeccably dressed. Even royals like Charles and Andrew seek their advice when it comes to Burberry specialties, like the practicality of a detachable lining in a raincoat. Depending upon the state of the lining and the style, the coats sell from $395 to $1,295.

Have something dressier in mind? How about an elegant cashmere topcoat, priced from $895 to $1,795 depending upon the style? It comes in black, navy, gray, and vicuna, but they tell us navy is by far the most popular. Top it off with a white silk scarf for $145 and you're set for a black-tie evening. For the blackest-tied of formal affairs, you might want the ultimate scarf—silk on one side, cashmere on the other ($195 to $295).

Suits run from $585 to $800, and the Burberry blazer deserves a mention. It's a year-round item that's a best-seller and is priced well at $385.

The third and fourth floors are dedicated to the ladies. An extensive collection of sweaters includes styles ranging from cotton wool at $85 and to the finest Scottish cashmere for $600. We love the double-breasted serge blazer ($995) with matching skirt, pleated or straight ($295), and trousers ($335). The colors change from season to season, but you can always get navy or black, and they're hand-tailored with mother-of-pearl buttons (gold for the navy). These are top sellers and you can think of them as a great investment — they'll last seven to ten years!

Ladies' trench and top coats come in a multitude of colors and designs. Still some generalizations can be made. They're cut fuller these days to go over suits, and they're longer in length. All in all while fashionably styled, they are more practical than they've ever been.

The classic trench raincoat with removable lining and collar comes in colors like tan, red, and black and remains a favorite at $695. But we prefer the long, sleek look of the cashmere blend Chesterfield for $1,425.

Like us, you'll fall in love with the store, the clothes and, certainly, those wonderful English accents. Together they make up that marvelous Burberry's mystique.

# *Cashmere Cashmere*

| | |
|---|---|
| 840 Madison Avenue | (212) 988-5252 |
| at 69th Street | |
| New York, NY 10021 | |
| | |
| 595 Madison Avenue | (212) 935-2522 |
| at 57th Street | |
| New York, NY 10022 | |

Cashmere — the word itself is so sumptuous that you want to say it more than once. We like to think that that's why these special stores bear their double name. And the abundance promised by that moniker is borne out by the bountiful selection they offer. In two New York locations (and one in Chicago), Cashmere Cashmere stocks its shelves with row upon row of cashmere and cashmere-blended clothes for men and women.

Cashmere is probably everyone's favorite fabric. Indeed, it is the softest in the world. Alas, it is also the costliest due to the immense demand and limited supply. Less than five million pounds are produced annually versus five billion pounds of wool. That's because cashmere comes from small mountain goats whose location in China's Himalayas is so remote that herdsmen venture to their habitats but once a year. The soft fleece which grows under the thick outer coat of coarse hair is laboriously removed by combing the goats by hand. You can understand cashmere's high price when you consider that one goat makes just four ounces or so of high quality cashmere fleece per year, and it takes a year's fleece from three to four goats to make just one sweater!

If you're a math whiz, you might want to take a stab at calculating just how many goats are represented in the Cashmere Cashmere stores literally filled with the stuff. We aren't so inclined, but rest assured that it must be hordes, because you can find almost any article of clothing made of cashmere here. There are hooded sweatshirts, warmup outfits, T-shirts, tights, and biking shorts, plus sweater sets, tunics, dresses, slacks, capes, jackets, slippers, gloves, caps, scarves, shawls, mufflers, and blankets. Everything is sized small, medium, or large and you'll find most merchandise suitable for men or women.

Owned by Dawson International, P.L.C., the largest cashmere company in the world, Cashmere Cashmere was acquired in 1987 from its founder Adriana Mnuchin to allow Dawson to showcase its own fabulous Scottish cashmere. The 57th Street store attracts primarily tourists and international travelers, while the 69th Street location caters to Upper East Side residents and businesspeople, so the merchandise varies slightly from one to the other. Both stores, however, are warm and inviting, with wood paneling, taupe tones, and marble-topped tables. Their muted shades allow the merchandise to beautifully brighten the interior.

And if there's anything more wonderful than cashmere's soft touch, it is its vibrant colors. Cashmere Cashmere develops this to ⁙ ⁙⁙ ⁙ antage by grouping colors with like colors in rainbow ⁙ ⁙ find a range of reds, from light pink to deep crim- ⁙⁙ctrum of beige tones, and so forth, folded on shelving or attractively hung.

Selections range from classic styles to 90s-look fashions, and prices vary quite widely as well. Cashmere blends are, of course, less expensive than the 100 percent variety. You can find all-cashmere accessories for under $100—a pair of gloves runs $95—but almost everything else costs more. A muffler runs $195, slippers go for $200, and their fabulous big-seller, short-sleeve T-shirt is $275. Pricewise, it's all uphill from there. But don't miss the beautiful suede and cashmere blankets, which run about $3,000.

We love the sweaters, which come in any style you can imagine. They start at $250 (for blends), and they've got a wonderful new dark-colored line inspired by European tapestries.

And as costly as cashmere is, it is also very durable and relatively easy to maintain. Dry cleaning is de rigueur, unless you prefer to handwash, in which case Nilda Ruiz, who manages the "uptown" store, and Melissa, who oversees the other, will advise you to use Lavant soap.

However you end up cleaning your garmets, buy them, by all means. Don't miss a chance to envelop yourself in the sensuousness of deluxe cashmere at Cashmere Cashmere. After all, you wouldn't want the efforts of those hardworking Himalayan herdsmen to go to waste!

# *Charivari*

18 West 57th Street                    (212) 333-4040
between Fifth and Sixth
New York, NY 10022

Few enterprises have a flagship store and several branches all in one city. But then no one would ever accuse Selma Weiser of being conventional. Quite the contrary, the robust red-haired dynamo has made a retailing phenomenon out of being decidedly unconventional from merchandise to merchandising, decor to advertising.

With more chutzpah than resources, Selma opened her first store on Upper Broadway in 1967. She chose the name Charivari because, in old French, it means "uproar." She hoped to create one by concentrating on the cutting edge of fashion, on new young designers. She succeeded, having introduced Issey Miyake in 1974, Yoji Yamamoto in 1983, and a host of others in between. Fueled by Selma's eye for innovation tempered by quality and a strategy of stocking a strong core of updated but basically classic and versatile merchandise, Charivari has grown into a six-store miniempire.

Charivari enthusiasts like Barbra Streisand, Carly Simon, Kelly McGillis, Diane Keaton, and Diana Ross know that each store has a distinct character, merchandised for a specific clientele with a neighborhood orientation. One Charivari store will likely not have the same offerings as another. Buying is indeed a family affair, handled by Selma (CEO), her son Jon (president), and her daughter Barbara (executive vice president). There's a lot to buy for: an "International Designers" store at 72nd and Columbus, a moderately priced casual clothes "Sport" location at 79th and Amsterdam, an avant-garde "Workshop" at 81st and Columbus (which won a Coty Award for innovative retailing), a career-oriented "Women" store on Broadway at 84th, the newest "Women's Designers" store on Madison Avenue at 78th Street, and, of course, the 57th Street "Best of Charivari" flagship.

The 57th Street store is the largest and most dramatic with its soaring foyer and stunning staircase. There's an Oriental economy to the decor which allows the clothing to double as the principal decoration. Indeed, it has won several design prizes for its creator, Japanese architect Yojeda.

There's an exhilarating quality about the atmosphere intensified by the upbeat music and the enthusiasm of the young, singularly attractive staff (mostly actors and Fashion Institute of Technology students). Charivari shuns the trendy, seeking instead to offer the work of "designers with integrity...who give value in the form of the strength of an idea, and the beauty of fabrication and styling," according to Barbara. That includes designers like Dolce & Gabbana, Gianni Versace, Jean Paul Gaultier, Claude Montana, Thierry Mugler, Romeo Gigli, Azzedine Alaia, Barbara Bui, Prada, Complice, Rifat Ozbeck, Paul Smith, and Giorgio Armani. Large portions of their day and evening wear collections are represented. What's not in stock can be seen on video monitors that run tapes of the collections' original presentations in Paris, Milan, New York, London, or Tokyo.

There's also a large selection of wearable, moderately priced private-label basics, and Charivari carries a terrific selection of accessories including uniquely theatrical jewelry that the Weisers buy from sources all over the world.

Despite its size — over 6,000 square feet — and diversity of merchandise with prices starting at a little over $100 and peaking at about $5,000, the store makes a cohesive fashion statement. It flows and in the process upholds Charivari's fashion-forward, somewhat avant-garde, and definitely daring image — an image that is also effectively reinforced by very distinctive advertising.

The ads are created by Kirschenbaum & Baum, and whether it's the "Never coming to a mall near you" campaign or the more recent "Wake us when it's over" series, they are arresting enough to catch your eye. One of our favorites from a few years ago depicted a woman in a striking, oversized brocade coat resplendently trimmed in fringe. Dangling high above the harbor, with Manhattan spread out beneath her, she is rather tenuously connected by one hand to the top of the Statue of Liberty. The headline reads, simply and succinctly, "Charivari. On the edge." That, we believe, just about says it all.

# *Emporio Armani*

110 Fifth Avenue                              (212) 727-3240
at 16th Street
New York, NY 10011

There's never been any doubt about Giorgio Armani's design genius. His development of the Emporio Armani concept, essentially lower priced and more accessible, proved his business acumen as well. With the 1981 opening of the first Emporio right across the street from his Milan headquarters, Armani firmly established this worldwide fashion empire by expanding his audience. Originally, "for kids who can't afford Armani" and stocked with fast, faddy goods often made out of remnants swept up from the atelier floor, Emporio Armani has evolved into a purveyor of a vast array of fashion (dressy clothes and sportswear), accessories, and even goodies for the home. The common thread is a distinctly sleek Armani look with a mass appeal in design and price.

This handsome Fifth Avenue branch of what has become a chain of 109 boutiques is the first in the United States. Designed to incorporate many of the building's original Stanford White touches, the fifteen-foot-wide red brick window bays and chestnut wood floors, the store also displays some amusing touches — wood sculptures of bras, panties, and ties, along with an air-conditioning unit shaped like the Emporio's eagle logo, spreading its wings across the ceiling. There's a very spirited, young-at-heart atmosphere about the decor and the merchandise, reinforced by the upbeat music, that is drawing hordes to this new Armani outpost.

You enter into the accessories area — sunglasses to jewelry to luggage and everything in between. We were taken with the new eyewear collection, priced from $150 to $175. Their soaps, in sets of three for $35, make the perfect gift for your weekend host. The natural pads of handmade papers with pigskin covers are another terrific choice at $45.

The men's department stretches along the right side of the store, from front to back. Suits range from $700 to $900 and Armani's signature loosely cut sports jackets are available from $525 to $700. For more casual dressing, there's a large selection of comfortable sweatsuits in a variety of colors and patterns.

Jeans for men and women occupy their own significant space here. We love the classic five-pocket, straight-cut style for $78, with either button or zipper fly. It's always available, but there's a new jeans collection designed every season, so you can choose a more fashionable model for $180. Jackets, matching and otherwise, range from $160 to $220. And there's a line of T-shirts and stone washed cotton tops to complete your Armani jeans look.

Or almost complete it. To be thoroughly Armani, dive into the rather spectacular collection of underwear for men and women.

From dull to daring, it's all here, along with bathing suits and a great line of coordinated robes and towels.

Trousers for women range from $160 to $350 and jackets are about $500. We particularly like the classics in a variety of fabrics and colors, from $450 to $550.

In fact, about the only thing we don't like about Emporio Armani is the decision making — there's just too much to choose from!

# E. Vogel — Custom Boots to Measure

19 Howard Street (212) 925-2460
between Broadway and Lafayette
New York, NY 10013

Right smack in the middle of Chinatown sits a little shop left over from another time and place. For four generations, since 1879, E. Vogel has been making boots, specializing in those meant for riding, English-style. The smell of leather fills the tiny showroom, where you're likely to meet some member of the Vogel family: President Dean Vogel, his cousin Jack Lynch, and his father Harold who is semiretired but still active (he runs the trade shows and horse shows that they do).

They make and sell over three thousand custom shoes and riding boots a year. Shoes cost $650 for the first pair, $550 for the second. Boots range from $525 to $975 and slide into the stirrups of the U.S. equestrian team and most foreign riding teams — and of Cliff Robertson, Sigourney Weaver, Sly Stallone, Tatum O'Neal, Bo Derek, and Jackie Onassis, too.

Vogel boots make them all look very smart atop their mounts. Remember, it's the rider's boot that tends to be at eye level for those left on the ground. So from a vanity standpoint, properly shod feet are just as important to the rider as they are to the horse.

For showing, dressage, and eventing, Vogel recommends French calf leather because of its lightweight softness, suppleness, and fine grain. Perhaps most importantly, it "shines up beautifully." It seems domestic leathers, while more rugged and long-wearing, aren't quite as pretty; they're better suited to polo, fox hunting, and cross-country hacking.

Of course, all of Vogel's boots and shoes are made right here. The leather is cut on the first floor. It's taken up the creaky stairway to the third, where the uppers are sewn together. The second floor reeks with the smell of glue; that's where the soles arc cemented to the uppers, rather than sewn. Dean Vogel maintains that gluing yields the strongest possible shoe.

Once measurements have been taken, you'll wait up to sixteen weeks (sometimes less, depending upon how busy they are) for the finished product. Remember, everything is "bench made," a careful, time-consuming combination of handwork augmented by some machine operations.

But it's worth the wait and the work. Vogel's boots and shoes are the product of good old-fashioned American craftsmanship and enterprise. It's almost your patriotic duty to buy them. As Dean says, "There aren't many of us left."

## Gianni Versace Uomo

816 Madison Avenue                          (212) 744-5572
at 68th Street
New York, NY 10021


*Gianni Versace Donna*                          (212) 744-5572
817 Madison Avenue
between 68th and 69th
New York, NY 10021

Versace has done so well in New York that there are now two stores on Madison Avenue, one for the gents and one for the ladies. Designed by the Milan architects who do all the Versace stores, both are dominated by granite, steel, and glass, and each houses the most complete selection of Versace clothes in the country.

For men, Versace's sophisticated, fashion-forward prêt-à-porter carries price tags that spell "made to order" for many other designers. His signature silhouette for men — the jacket more classic now, not as broad shouldered, and the pants not as full, though still pleated — runs $1,800 to $3,000 for a suit. Those distinctive sports jackets in bright colors can be had from $1,400 to $2,200. Slacks sell for $400 to $800. Shoes, socks, belts, and even ties are available in a broad range of prices, though it would be difficult to categorize any as modest. And while the goods change from season to season, customers like Luther Vandross, Phil

Collins, Rod Stewart, and Elton John know they'll always find a selection that runs the gamut from sportswear to formalwear. For women, the look tends to be extravagantly, exuberantly sexy — and expensive. Suits range in price from $2,000 to $7,000, blouses from $600 to $2,300. For evening, there's nothing for less than $2,000, and several elaborately embroidered numbers approach the $12,000 mark. Look for Versace's new Medusa-head logo carried throughout the collection on everything, beginning with buttons. And be sure to talk to Lori Santoro, Versace Donna's engaging manager, about the wonderful sportswear, swimwear, and the full line of accessories, priced from $100 to $2,000, including belts, costume jewelry, beautiful print scarves, handbags, fragrances, and a new line of watches, both gold-plated and solid gold.

As for what Versace calls couture for both sexes (read *more* expensive prêt-à-porter executed in better fabrics and benefiting from handwork finishing), expect to pay a minimum of $3,000 per suit. Made to order, it takes at least seven to ten weeks and may make you feel closer to Versace disciples like Diandra Douglas, Candice Bergen, and Elizabeth Taylor.

In the "if you have to ask how much it costs, you can't afford it" category, there's his Atelier line. These are absolutely one-of-a-kind outfits designed and made exclusively for those who dare to venture into this rarified territory beyond couture. It means flying to Milan to be measured by Versace's specially trained team; it also means joining the ranks of Cher and Jane Fonda, who have already done so.

The delightful Afrodita Badescu at Versace Uomo is the person to call if you have any special requests, if you need something sent over on approval, or if you want to stop by before or after hours. Don't be hesitant or shy about it. With a clientele like this, she's heard it all!

# *Giorgio Armani*

| 815 Madison Avenue | (212) 988-9191 |
| at 68th Street | Fax (212) 472-8795 |
| New York, NY 10021 | |

It's fitting that a former art gallery houses what was, before the advent of Emporio Armani, Giorgio Armani's flagship in the

United States. Armani's designs are, after all, works of art. Indeed, they are displayed as they might be in a gallery — each design occupying its own space, hung facing outwards instead of sideways, with nothing in the rather spartan decor to distract the eye from its beauty. Waxed black steel forms square frames around the clothes, and soft museum-quality light bathes them. Actually, since this store features the upper end of Armani men's and women's wear, while Emporio Armani and the A/X Armani Exchange cater to a broader market, we still prefer to consider this *the* Armani store in town.

It's certainly more intimate that its sister stores, although it recently grew from three to four floors. The first and second floors house women's clothes, accessories, fragrances, and shoes, with ready-to-wear below and evening above. Armani's masterfully tailored looks will literally suit you. His jackets are really fantastic, starting at about $1,300. Simply cut in fabrics that move with the body, they are a particular favorite with Lee Radziwill. (She is Armani's spokesperson, which we find to be rather odd; but then if he's happy with her, why shouldn't we be?) Blouses begin at around $800, trousers are in the $850 range, skirt suits start at $2,000 and pantsuits run about $2,300.

Armani's evening wear follows the seductive look of his daytime outfits, but is translated into even softer dressing, and ever softer fabrics. Plan on spending at least several thousand for a cocktail dress, more for an evening gown, and $9,000 and up for any of his exquisite beaded pieces.

Keith Scott oversees the third and fourth floors devoted to men's wear — clothes with a full complement of furnishings, accessories, shoes, and leathergoods for those who appreciate a highly styled yet Italian look, fully cut and decidedly unconservative clothes. Often from the theater or the arts, Armani men tend to be some of the more successful inhabitants of those worlds. They don't bat an eyelash at sports jackets starting at $1,350 or trousers from $450 to $550. Suits are around $2,000, while basic dress shirts hover in the $200 to $300 range.

There's a subtle richness about Armani's designs, which is reflected in this store where you can indulge in a total Armani look. We think the Emporio and the Exchange are fun, but this is fashion.

# *Gucci*

685 Fifth Avenue                                    (212) 826-2600
at 54th Street
New York, NY 10022

It all started in 1906, when Guccio Gucci began tooling the finest leather saddles money could buy. It almost ended a few years ago, when Guccio's son, Dr. Aldo Gucci, ran afoul of the law over a little matter of several million dollars in tax fraud. Now that unpleasantness is behind Gucci. The government is satisfied and a new consortium is in charge, bent on reinstating Gucci's reputation for unparalleled quality and service. The results are quite evident in the New York store; the selection of bags, suitcases, leather accessories, shoes, scarves, clothes, jewelry, and decorative home items befits a world-class organization, all under the direction of Senior Vice President and Creative Director Dawn Mello. And the staff assembled by store manager Paula Pronsky is knowledgeable and helpful. The attitude problem that beleaguered Gucci for so long—snobbish salespeople who made you feel as if they were doing you a favor even speaking to you—has been banished.

Customer service is now the byword. Maurizio Gucci (Aldo's nephew and worldwide chairman) has seen to that. He instituted a training program for the entire sales staff, which ensures that they are familiar with their merchandise and stresses the importance of customer satisfaction.

You'll find the classic Gucci loafer, as well as an extensive collection of other stylish shoes for men and women in leather and other fine natural materials, on the store's first floor. Nearby are gifts ranging from clocks and selected pieces of china to a wonderful array of silver including things like pens, pins, shaving brushes, and much more. You'll also find small leather goods and handbags, some made of precious skins like crocodile and ostrich, for equally precious prices. You're encompassed by that rich aroma reminiscent of the leather interior of a brand-new Jaguar. Should it become a bit too rich, head for the perfume counter. Gucci 3 is for the ladies at $120 for a half ounce. For the gents, Gucci makes Nobile, four ounces at $50.

Watches are a big draw at Gucci. Sometimes you literally have to line up to purchase their bracelet watch. Gold-plated, it comes with twelve interchangeable bezels in different colors to coordinate with any outfit and sells for $195.

Of course, you don't need us to tell you about Gucci's scarves and shawls; they're legendary with their spectacular, colorful, and instantly recognizable signature prints. Prices start at $195.

The clublike atmosphere of the second floor flatters the merchandise — men's Gucci-designed and Italian-made clothes, from sportswear to suits. Women are catered to on the third floor. Again, there is a complete collection, active wear to cocktail dresses.

The fourth floor houses the gift department with crystal, silver, and china. You'll also find Gucci's splendid luggage here — a set suitable for jet-set living runs about $2,000.

It seems as if there's a little something for everyone at Gucci, much of it acting as testimony to the shopper's good taste with the identifying stamp of the Gucci stripes, logo, or crest. All those "Gucci-isms" are internationally recognized and respected, which explains the store's popularity with the United Nations set. When the UN is in session, Gucci is awash with foreign dignitaries and their families, but they're not the only status-conscious shoppers here. You're just as likely to run into Bill Cosby, Frank and/or Kathie Lee Gifford, Whitney Houston, Paula Zahn, or Christie Brinkley.

They all come for their Gucci fix and a dose of the warm Italian hospitality that is once again extended by the house that saddles built.

# Hermès

11 East 57th Street                              (212) 751-3181
between Fifth and Madison
New York, NY 10022

When Thierry Hermès first opened a harness shop in the Paris of 1837, we wonder if he ever imagined that the firm bearing his name would one day dress not only horses but royalty and that it would be the producer of *the* status accessory for men. Doubtful. For one thing, he never could have conceived of the World War I carnage that decimated the horse population of France. He could never have dreamed the residential Champs-Elysées filled with beautiful horse-drawn carriages sporting Hermès trappings could be transformed into a commercial thoroughfare ruled by a whole new mode of transportation—the motorcar.

Fortunately for Hermès, his grandson Emile-Maurice was not thrown by these events, which could have proved devastating to the firm. Quite the contrary, he was inspired to set a new direction for the company. Using the material he knew best, leather, he turned Hermès on to the path it has traveled ever since, making handbags, luggage, wallets, and attaché cases for the carriage trade. For the first time, the Hermès signature saddle stitch—visible top-stitching accomplished by two needles—lent a handsome decorative touch to accessories. While Emile-Maurice had changed the course of Hermès's future, indeed assured that it would have a future, he adhered to the basic tenet of the company, which remains the same today: "Leather, sport, and the tradition of refined elegance."

Motivated by the worlds of sport and travel, the Hermès collection expanded over the years to include watches, jewelry, clothes, and designs for the home. The first leather agenda appeared in 1930, the first scarf in 1937, and the first ties in 1954.

After a false start (the first Hermès store in the U.S. was felled by the market crash of 1929), and 30 years of a limited American presence maintained by boutiques in stores like Lord & Taylor, Bonwit Teller, Neiman Marcus, I. Magnin, and Bergdorf Goodman, Hermès firmly established its U.S. base in 1983 with the opening of this exquisite 57th Street shop. Here Hermès flourishes with the full range of its exclusive patterns. Designed by architect Rena Dumas (who also happens to be the wife of the current chairman of the company, Jean-Louis Dumas Hermès), the interior has a richly understated, classic look reminiscent of the Faubourg shop in Paris—cherrywood display cases, handcrafted brass trim, Hermès's hallmark "grecques" lighting, and the ex-libris inlaid in brass in the floor. The walls are decorated with artworks from the famous Hermès Museum collection (something else the family can thank Emile-Maurice for) interspersed with photographs of famous clients—a Princess Grace clutching her "Kelly" bag in one hand and a young Caroline by the other; Ingrid Bergman carrying her twin babies and wearing a "Collier de Chien" belt; and Queen Elizabeth, her royal coif covered by a Hermès scarf.

The first floor houses the fragrance counter, home to the delightful Hermès scents for men and women. Men's ties hold court here, too. Even at $110 each, they're scooped up by the dozen, often along with matching pocket squares. Further along is the area devoted to Hermès's famous colorfully printed silk scarves, which, like the tie counter, is always crowded. Sometimes, when a tour bus of Japanese tourists descends on the store, the scarf counter looks like the object of a shark feeding frenzy. Indeed, Hermès scarves at $225 each are to women what Hermès ties are to men—an internationally recognized status symbol. We've never quite gotten over the time we spotted a young lady using one for a sling. How chic.

Leather goods are displayed throughout the store, from the "in" gift of the moment (a $105 case for Post-it notes) to belts, wallets, picture frames, briefcases, and luggage. Plus, you'll find every type of glove imaginable: for golf, for riding, for hunting, for daytime, for evening. Talk about a selection! There's lambskin, suede, pigskin, deerskin, fringed, studded, buttoned, tasseled, embroidered, rabbit-cuffed, with leather horse ribbons, or with saddle nail clasps, to say nothing of the incredibly varied color choices. And a Hermès handbag is a must-have. One of our favorites is the new blazer, striped in navy and white or orange and tan, for $1,525. Check out the famous Kelly (as in Grace) bags, too, which range from $3,100 for a twenty-eight-inch box in calf leather to $13,800 for a tricolor crocodile. And thirty-year-Hermès veteran Claude Gandrille stands by to repair or recondition any of your purchases. He knows just about all there is to know about leather and what can be done with it. Claude will give counsel on any special custom order you might have in mind. He's even been known to put together the leather interior of a private plane and fashion a crocodile bicycle seat.

For men, there's a whole ready-to-wear department complete with suits, sports jackets, dress and sport shirts, sweaters, bathrobes, pajamas (the silk ones are sensational), and underwear. Women will find an equally extensive ready-to-wear selection, but generally we find Hermès accessories more exciting than the clothes. We particularly love the new line of watches with vibrantly colored straps that run about $1,000.

If you're an equestrian, this is definitely the place to be outfitted with a complete line of riding clothing from jodhpurs to raincoats. In fact, you can purchase just about everything you need here except the horse—the saddle, all the tack, crop, whip, and saddle and glycerine soap. No boots, though.

The home designs are another highlight here. What could be softer and more snuggly than a cashmere blanket trimmed in leather? And what could be more practical than the new line of folding furniture by Rena Dumas and Peter Coles, including a stool, writing desk, and chaise lounge, all made of perfect pear wood, impeccably finished with a satin varnish (or ebony trim for the lounge). Each piece is numbered and travels beautifully. Finally, what could be more spectacular than Hermès's beach towels? They look like paintings, since they benefit from the same printing process used on the scarves. The colors of the intricate patterns are incredibly bright and true. Their lavishly large size, 60 × 72, makes quite a statement on any beach.

From horse blankets to beach blankets, Hermès stands for unparalleled luxury, craftsmanship, and quality. If you don't believe us, just read their *World of Hermès* publication, a beautifully produced, brilliantly conceived piece of marketing propaganda. It's bound to convince you.

# Leggiadro

700 Madison Avenue             (212) 753-5050
between 62nd and 63rd
New York, NY 10021

You've bought the perfect dress and the most divine little pair of pumps, but there is something missing, something in-between, which is needed to truly complete the ensemble—leggings. No longer just stockings, today's legwear is an important fashion accessory, and comes in a mind-boggling assortment of colors and fabrics.

Leggiadro offers a vast selection of stockings, pantyhose, tights, and socks in virtually every configuration imaginable from all parts of the globe. More importantly, the store offers the personal service and encyclopedic knowledge of owner Ann Ross. She opened Leggiadro four years ago because she recognized the need in New York for a leg-coverings store with an eclectic inventory, realistic prices, and a view of leggings as fashion.

Ann knows how leggings can make or break an outfit. Open and friendly, she will work with you to find the perfect complement to any style. As you begin to become a regular, Ann establishes a record of your likes and dislikes, what you've bought, and what you haven't yet tried.

When you are in the market for basics, Ann might suggest a pair of Elbeo pantyhose for $10. A German product, they are sheer, yet strong and dependable. They come in umpteen colors, none of which are blotchy, and they don't sag.

The Wolford tights and stockings from Austria make a fashion statement in unusual cotton and wool patterns, especially the opaques, which run $30 to $55. Wolford makes perfectly smashing evening stockings too. They're classic, but with a little bit of pizzazz. Some in lace sell for about $40 a pair.

There are socks galore for men as well as for the women. You'll find stripes, solids, and patterns in cotton and cashmere, too. The hot fashion colors are fabulous!

Perk up a dreary winter day by trying on their bathing suits with beautiful, bold patterns (and matching accessories), priced from $165 to $250.

But legwear is their mainstay, and there's just no comparison—Leggiadro is the ultimate. And if that weren't enough to make it irresistible, Ann Ross makes it such a pleasurable place to shop.

# Macy's

151 West 34th Street               (212) 695-4400
at Broadway
New York, NY 10001

They say there's no place like Macy's. It's our guess that suits the NCAA just fine—another nationally televised Thanksgiving-Day parade would wreak havoc with all those lucrative television contracts. Since 1924, Macy's has presented a seasonal gift of monumental proportions to the city, and, since 1948 via TV, to the nation. It's the annual Macy's Thanksgiving Day parade. Over three thousand Macy's employees and their families are joined by a dozen or more marching bands and numerous themed floats sprinkled with celebrities. But for most spectators, all 37 million or so of them, it's the giant balloons that *are* Macy's Thanksgiving. At least a couple of million spectators line up along Central Park West and Broadway to watch it live, while another 35 million view from the comfort of their homes.

Frankly, we usually opt for the latter. But we have been known to bestir ourselves the night before to witness a part of the annual pageantry that isn't televised—the annual ritual of inflating Snoopy, Superman, and all their balloon pals. "Inflation Eve," as it's known to parade mavens, begins every year at about 6:00 P.M. on 77th Street, between Central Park West and Columbus, adjacent to the American Museum of Natural History. "Oohs" and "Ahs," punctuated by cheers of applause, fill the crisp evening air as the assembled crowd marvels at the spectacle of the balloons being brought magically to life. If you're in town, join the fun. This is truly a cheap (absolutely free) thrill.

Visiting the store responsible for this annual pageant is a thrill too, though it's likely to be none too cheap. With the exception of major appliances, cars, airplanes, and yachts, there's not much you might want or need that the "world's largest store" doesn't have. With nine floors, plus a balcony and cellar level, and occupying an entire city block, Macy's is, according to its brochure, "part theater, part welcoming forum that reflects your lifestyle needs." We can't argue there. Nor can we come up with an answer for the brochure's rhetorical question, "Where else can you find a financial planning seminar, cooking lesson, a fashion shoe, a complete beauty make-over, an interview with your favorite author and Santa Claus—all under one roof?"

In addition to such special events and appearances that keep Macy's hopping, you can dine at any of five restaurants, book a trip at the American Express Travel counter, mail a letter at the post office, fill a prescription at the old-fashioned apothecary shop, have your hair done at the Glemby Hair Salon, get your jewelry appraised, and have your film developed. If you have any time left, you might even want to check out the merchandise—a daunting task indeed; there's just so much of it.

Macy's even has a solution to that "problem" in the petite form of Linda Lee who runs the "Macy's by Appointment" service. From the perfect gift to a complete wardrobe, just give her and her staff of consultants a budget and let them do the work. Of course, it's easier if a girl's got unlimited funds for a new look. They can just pick out a little Armani this, a little Montana that. But Linda and company are equally adept at working with $500, assembling the wardrobe equivalent of soup to nuts, shoes to lingerie to business suit to cocktail dress. They might even throw in a fabulous new fragrance to top it all off. Gentlemen, don't fret. It may cost you a tad more than $500, but they can do the same for you—no matter who you are or where you come from. Seven languages are spoken at Macy's, so somebody's bound to speak yours. After all, there's one universal language called "shop."

Shopped for clothes till you've dropped, or drooped? (Even sorting through all the duds Linda collects can be exhausting.) Dreaming of relaxing at home, only to have the vision dashed by memories of shredding towels and sheets? Stop by the sixth floor and wonder at the selection of bath and bed linens, along with every conceivable accessory. They carry all the designer towels and sheets, lots of Lauren and beaucoup de Buatto (as in Mario, the first of New York's celebrity decorators to successfully license his name), along with the more moderately priced Macy's private label. Upstairs on the ninth floor, you can buy a bed to go with your new sheets as well as furniture for every other room in your home. From classic to contemporary styles, the entire floor is devoted to the enormous array.

If it's your kitchen that needs a bit of sprucing up, head down, all the way down to the basement, otherwise known as The Cellar. Inaugurated in 1976, it has been a major attraction ever since, stocked with much of the world's finest housewares and gourmet delicacies. Here you'll find everything from the latest in garlic presses (and there have been some major improvements) to the most impressive of espresso machines. Foodwise, The Cellar runs the gamut too. There are the ingredients for a fabulous feast in the fresh meats of Ottomanelli and calorie-calculated spa dishes. The Gourmet Gazelle features great smoked fish and caviar. Buy it when Macy's is locked in its annual pricing war with Zabar's!) Then there are the cheeses, the coffees, the condiments, pastas, the baked goods, the candy, the everything necessary for a dynamite dinner soiree—including a Hallmark Shop for invitations and stationery.

Be sure to check out their new Indoor Gardener Shop, even if you don't think you have a green thumb. You'll find vegetable gardens designed for kids, fixings for window gardens of all kinds, and more.

For a real lift, visit the year-round Christmas Shop with ornaments starting at $3.50. Equally sparkling and inspiring is the extensive crystal, china, and silver department on the eighth floor.

Of course, it boasts Waterford, Orrefors, Lenox, Royal Doulton, Rosenthal, and Spode. So you can spend a lot. But you can also spend a little — like $70 for a boxed twenty-piece set of good-looking stoneware.

Likewise for kids, the Littlest Shop carries a full line of imported children's clothes and accoutrements. You can spend hundreds on a lace-trimmed christening gown, thousands on a full layette. But in other areas dedicated to children you can find a christening gown for $36 and play clothes starting at $12. We're particularly delighted with the Gap-inspired Macy Kids and Macy Baby line of sportswear, which includes adorable accessories like matching hats and socks. A little girl's denim shirt from this line runs just $14. Mark S. Handler and Myron E. Ullman III, co-chairmen of R. H. Macy & Company, remain very protective of the Macy's tradition of offering alternatives and value.

This tradition dates from the store's 1858 founding by a Quaker, Rowland H. Macy. As his twenty-foot-wide dry goods store on Sixth Avenue near 14th Street prospered, he became "Captain," trading on the fact that he had spent four years of his youth plying the coast of his native New England on a whaler. A souvenir from those days, a red star tattooed on his arm, became Macy's' symbol.

From modest beginnings — first day's sales were $11.06 — the store grew into a New York fixture, strong enough to survive Rowland's death in 1877, and two successive mediocre management partnerships. The Strauss family, involved since 1874, took complete charge in 1896 and set Macy's firmly on the road to retailing greatness. It was Isidor and Nathan Strauss who engineered the risky but wildly successful move uptown to Herald Square in 1902 — a move that catapulted the store solidly into the twentieth century.

We wonder if the "Captain" could ever have imagined his Macy's as site of the annex to the Metropolitan Museum of Art Gift Shop or home to an Antique and Estate Gallery. Certainly, the assortment of electronics — from telephones to TVs to computerized date books — on the fifth floor would have baffled him. Still, like most men, he could have lost himself here. And certainly he would approve of the extremely knowledgeable staff. You can rely on them to tell you what technology will operate in which part of the world. No more purchasing a nifty little gadget in the

United States, only to discover it won't work at your hunting lodge in Scotland.

And speaking of traveling, there are loads of useful guides in the eighth floor book department, this one among them. You'll also find a good selection of children's books and current best-sellers, along with all those glossy numbers meant to decorate your coffee table.

The acre of Art Deco that is the main floor now includes The Arcade, filled with six pop-culture-inspired shops that change with the seasons and the trends. A few years from now, the Saturday Night Live shop will likely have been replaced, but we have a funny feeling that the Elvis shop — complete with containers of dirt from Graceland's yard (at $15, they sell like hotcakes!) — will live on (as has the King himself) for years to come.

Generally speaking, Macy's is for the busiest among us, who appreciate one-stop shopping. Should we name a name or two, the list would include Busy Persons Cher, Christie Brinkley, and Kathleen Turner. Maybe it should include you, too!

# *Ralph Lauren at 72nd Street*

867 Madison Avenue                    (212) 606-2100
at 72nd Street
New York, NY 10021

Have you ever walked into someone's home and coveted every-thing in sight? Our guess is you'll feel that way when you walk into this crown jewel of Ralph Lauren's empire. And make no mistake, you will feel like you are walking into a home, albeit a *very* grand one, done to within an inch of its life, which is exactly the way Ralph wanted it. He spent five years searching for the perfect location to showcase the Ralph Lauren life-style. He finally settled on the landmark Rhinelander Mansion, built in 1895 to resemble a French chateau of the Loire Valley. Then he spent eighteen months restoring the mansion's architectural in-tegrity and designing the interior to properly present his cre-ations, all of his creations — from clothing and accessories to home furnishings — in their natural habitats. It's doubtful this old house ever looked this good, this opulent in its heyday! You really do want to move right in.

Manager Charles Fagan is "king" of this mansion which boasts a mountain of treasures, from silver-lidded antique perfume bottles to one-of-a-kind sterling charm bracelets starting at $375. There's the Cashmere Bar on the first floor, a plethora of sensual riches if ever there was one. Prices range from $395 to $800. The small collection of men's shoes is nothing short of exquisite, so beautiful they even draw sighs of envy from women. Now, while we're thinking leather, check out Ralph's line of hard leather luggage. It took him four years to get it right. Presumably it was worth the wait. The luggage is certainly lovely, and heavy, and totally impractical unless you charter your own jet to carry it. At $2,050 for a train case and $2,395 for a trunk, it's either that or have plastic slip covers made for it (but don't tell Ralph, he doesn't like reminders of his Bronx beginnings).

It's no secret that the Polo knit T-shirts are terrific, not to mention part of the upwardly mobile uniform. The weathered mesh variety runs $55. In sea-island cotton, they're $145 and both versions come in every color imaginable. Close by you'll find cotton and silk ties for $37 to $70. Oxford cloth shirts are only $55, but pale in comparison to the sea-island cotton versions at $150. They look so chic under one of Ralph's silk robes for $500, or better yet, a cashmere lounger for $1,300.

An imposing wood-paneled stairway leads to the second floor, home to boy's and men's wear along with a magnificent Waterford chandelier. You can impose the Ralph Lauren life-style on a youngster as young as four years old here. For older boys, trousers run from $145 to $275. Seersucker sports jackets can be had for as little as $295. Cashmere jackets go for as much as $1,000. Suits fall into the $750 to $1,360 range, with five labels that differentiate the look.

The men's fitting room was once the mansion's music room and remains a hospitable place. In the morning you can enjoy coffee and croissants while an expert tailor works on you. Later in the day, you might get a light lunch or a glass of wine.

Ladies' clothes, from business suits to active wear, are on the third floor. For the woman who works, suitable skirts, blazers, blouses, sweaters, trousers, and suits occupy a large price range, from $125 to $2,500. You'll also find clothing for active and spectator sports — a little tennis outfit for playing at Wimbledon, as well as a little something to wear while sitting in the Royal Box.

There's also a terrific selection of weekend wear — lots of Western-style jeans for around $65, with matching jackets for $90 and change. In addition to denim, Ralph does great work in suede and buckskin.

Ralph's home collection occupies the fourth level. Twice a year the whole floor is redone, in only five days. It's so complete, so cozy, and so inviting that you feel as if all you need is a toothbrush to settle in. Everything is for sale.

Ralph Lauren, more than a store, is a way of life embraced by an eclectic group of celebrity regulars like Tom Selleck, Bruce Springsteen, Pat Buckley, and Demi Moore. We did say eclectic — Ralph's concept of the American dream is shared by a large and interesting cross-section of this and several other countries, which explains his billions of dollars in sales annually!

# Saks Fifth Avenue

611 Fifth Avenue            (212) PL3-4000
between 49th and 50th Streets
New York, NY 10022

Unlike its four "Big Brother" (Barneys, Bendel's, Bergdorf's, and Bloomingdale's) competitors, Saks started out to be exactly what it is — a large, upscale, high-fashion specialty store. It was the dream store of Horace Saks and Bernard Gimbel, both of whom operated independent retail stores on 34th Street at Herald Square in the early 1900s. The union of the financial clout of these two retailing families allowed Horace and Bernard to purchase a site on upper Fifth Avenue and realize their vision of a store synonymous with fashionable, gracious living. Saks Fifth Avenue opened for business September 15, 1924.

While the name said "Saks," the driving force that would make the store a legend was named Gimbel. With the untimely death of Horace Saks in 1926, his assistant (and Bernard's cousin) Adam Gimbel stepped into the SFA presidency. From the beginning, he displayed a unique flair for a business in which he had relatively little experience — he was only 30 when he assumed his exalted role. To attract greater numbers of affluent customers, he first remodeled the brand-new store in the sophisticated Art Moderne style he had admired at the Paris Exhibition of 1925. He felt Saks should have the appearance of a sumptuous home, stocked with elegant, exciting merchandise. So he hired buyers to scour the earth for the finest goods money could buy, concentrating on suppliers who would guarantee exclusivity to Saks.

The quality and tone Adam Gimbel set has endured throughout the decades. Its relatively recent acquisition by Investcorp, the introduction of a new executive management team, a $300-million-dollar infusion, and a complete store renovation have kept Saks Fifth Avenue at the helm of the retail industry.

The expansion has particularly benefitted gentlemen seeking Saks's impeccable brand of good taste. Always heeding Adam Gimbel's policy of providing men with the same level of quality and service it offers women, Saks has now doubled the space to do it. Dress furnishings are the focal point of the additional square footage on the main floor. Men's sportswear, including the new J.O.E. shop featuring casual sportswear by Joseph Abboud and the A/X Armani Exchange, have taken over the second floor tower. The entire newly renovated sixth floor accommodates the enlarged collection of traditional, European, and private label men's clothing. Men's European sportswear now features Dolce & Gabbana, Moschino, Versace Jeans, and Thierry Mugler, bringing Saks customers the latest in fashion-forward styles. Ralph Lauren has an enormous shop featuring denim and casualwear. Men's shoes have their home in the sixth floor tower, as do the Italian suit collections which highlight the greatest names in menswear.

Of course, women haven't been given short shrift in the remodeling of Saks. The impressive collection of accessories has been made even more awesome — Saks carries the largest collection of Donna Karan hosiery in the city, as well as the largest selection of Judith Leiber's exquisite evening bags. Newly designed Giorgio Armani boutiques for the Black label and Le Collezioni boutiques were unveiled in conjunction with Saks's launch of "scent-sation" Gió de Giorgio Armani. You'll find an impressive Ralph Lauren ready-to-wear boutique on the second floor, and Saks's designer sportswear and ready-to-wear collections have grown tremendously. Selena Blow, Norma Kamali, Issey Miyake, Dolce & Gabbana, and Complice are among their brightest stars.

The third-floor tower extension has enabled the further development of Saks's couture business, with an emphasis on evening wear from the likes of Giorgio Armani, Yves Saint Laurent, Ungaro, Lacroix, Lagerfeld, and Versace. The dramatically luxurious furs of Revillon have new larger quarters here overlooking Fifth Avenue and Rockefeller Plaza. And the bridal department, possibly the city's best, has been expanded to fill much of the remaining space. It features European and American designers of bridal wear with gowns starting at about $2,000. Custom collections with intricate detailing and handcrafted designs begin at $4,900.

Of course, the expansion has benefitted nonfashion areas, too. One long-awaited addition to Saks's customer services is a café-style restaurant—two levels facing Fifth Avenue with fantastic views of Rockefeller Center and St. Patrick's Cathedral. The elegant, subdued decor is rich with wood, marble, and slate, providing a serene respite from the rigors of shopping.

The new state-of-the-art salon on the eighth floor is an alternative retreat. Services for men and women, including hair styling, facials, and beauty treatments by Elizabeth Arden, and manicures are performed by expert practitioners in an architecturally dramatic marble and slate setting. Adding amenities like food service, monogrammed robes and towels, and phones at each chair make each salon visit the ultimate in luxury and relaxation.

The Terme di Saturnia spa on the fifth floor offers complete full-service treatment and skincare programs for revitalization, relaxation, and a more youthful appearance. Services here include massage, facials, waxing, and body wrapping.

But if you're determined to do nothing but shop at Saks, consider joining the Fifth Avenue Club. There's no membership fee for this club (one of the few in this city that can boast such a claim!) and it furnishes executive, corporate, and personal shopping services and more for both men and women. The Fifth Avenue personal shopping services complex employs numerous bilingual associates, so tourists visiting Sak Fifth Avenue always feel right at home.

President Rose Marie Bravo is always on the lookout for goods worthy of a Saks label, striving to bring its customers the best merchandise—exclusively, whenever possible. In fact, Saks now has exclusive arrangements with designers Gordon Henderson and Nancy Heller, both of whom will be producing collections at significant savings to Saks customers. Saks also now has an exclusive Gucci boutique carrying men's and women's accessories, footwear, and ladies' ready-to-wear.

To reach out-of-town customers long after they have left the Big Apple, Saks's private label, Real Clothes, is being made available via the QVC network. We think this is a somewhat surprising (for Saks) marketing technique, but you never know. Bravo believes that this "first" puts the retailer in the front line of the distribution wave of the future. And who are we to argue with success?

# *Susan Bennis/Warren Edwards*

22 West 57th Street                    (212)755-4197
New York, NY 10019

Remember Cher's red silk pumps in *Moonstruck?* They were classic Susan Bennis/Warren Edwards—ravishing and just a wee bit naughty. They're the kind of shoes that turn people into collectors. We don't know if Imelda Marcos ever darkened the door of this perfectly laid-out shoe showcase, but we do know fanciers of fantasy footwear like Demi Moore, Elton John, Tom Cruise, Don Johnson and Melanie Griffith, Bruce Springsteen and Patti Scialfa, Jacqueline Onassis, Ann Getty, and Cher (off camera!) are regulars.

They come for the unique designs, so exceptional that the Metropolitan Museum of Art designated fifty of Susan Bennis/Warren Edwards's styles for inclusion in its permanent collection. Then there is the quality of the footwear and the attentive, personalized service. Susan Bennis and Warren Edwards are a creative dream team. They do it all, from the fashion-forward designing of men's and women's shoes, to directing production in their Italian factories, to creating a catalogue that serves a worldwide clientele.

All their shoes are handmade in limited editions. No style numbers here. Each design bears a name, and the three hundred or so styles that make up each season's collection are only available at this store or through the catalog. Some two hundred steps go into each pair, which go a long way toward explaining the prices: a basic woman's pump starts at $395. There are plenty of pairs priced closer to $1,000; boots kick off at $995 and can go as high as $1,400 a pair.

For men, prices start at about $495 for leather and escalate to $2,500 for alligator. A classic loafer runs about $595, while the not so classic but very cunning tuxedo slipper, with its dear little flat satin bow, is $495. On the more macho side, Susan and Warren have come up with a new signature line of outerwear called Roughstuff. We're talking rubber-soled practicality with flair, for men or women, in the $195 to $350 range.

A word to the wise. Women's shoes tend to run small here. If you normally wear a size 7, you're probably a size 8 in Susan Bennis/Warren Edwards's shoes. Conversely, men may wonder if their feet have shrunk—they'll usually slide into a smaller size in this sunlit salon.

The collection is always a work in progress, but don't despair if your favorite design is no longer in stock. Records of each customer's purchases are kept. So if the pattern is still considered current, a pair of shoes can be constructed from it, if you're willing to wait six to eight weeks.

Staff members like Walter Sommer and Karen Robbins take special pains to familiarize themselves with the latest clothing fashions. So if you've done some serious damage at any of the city's designer boutiques, a call to them describing your purchases is enough to guarantee you the perfect footwear companions. They'll send them right over for you to try on.

With a firm foothold on the upper end of the designer shoe market in New York, Susan and Warren have ventured into a new, more popularly priced arena in cooperation with Neiman Marcus. Their shoes can now be found at Neiman's more high-profile locations, such as Beverly Hills, Bar Harbor, San Francisco, Scottsdale, Houston, Chicago, and Atlanta. Ladies only, though. Gentlemen addicted to the Susan Bennis/Warren Edwards look still have to visit the store or order through the catalog.

## *Tender Buttons*

143 East 62nd Street                    (212) PL8-7004
between Lexington and Third Avenues
New York, NY 10021

As much a museum as a shop, Tender Buttons stands out as a particularly quirky (albeit very successful) enterprise, in a city full of them. And like most of New York's other idiosyncratic businesses, it has a story worth telling. Tender Buttons started in the 1960s with Diane Epstein's routine of replacing the plastic buttons on her clothes with those she found in a rundown little shop at 77th and Madison. One day she found her button source shuttered, allegedly for alterations. Since this reason seemed dubious, "because the place was such a dump," she called the landlord to investigate and was told the owner had died. All the buttons were for sale, so she bought them. Then, because she needed a place to store them, Diane rented the store. Suddenly she was in the button business.

Diane recruited her buttonophile buddy Millicent Safro to help her organize her cache and make it presentable. Tender Buttons—named after Gertrude Stein's *Tender Buttons*, a tribute to insignificant objects—was born. So trifling did Diane and Millicent consider their buttons, they sold them for a penny each. The first year's revenue was equivalent to one day's sales now to fastener fetishists like Candice Bergen, Bianca Jagger, Ralph Lauren, Joy Philbin, Harry Belafonte, Bobby Short, and Donna Karan.

Yes, the penny-a-piece days are long gone, though you can still find buttons for as little as a quarter, as in the old 77th Street shop. Tender Buttons moved to its current location on the ground floor of a brownstone in 1968. The long, narrow space just about accommodates the million-plus inventory which ranges in price from 25 cents to well over $1,000, but doesn't even to begin to address the partners' personal collection of vintage and antique buttons, reputedly the world's largest. Although you get some sense of it from the framed displays that adorn what little of the shop's wall space isn't covered by floor-to-ceiling shelves supporting stacks of button boxes.

The selection is staggering, but staff members like David Gibilie and Barbara Stoj, gluttons for buttons like their bosses, will help you wade through it. They'll show you everything from the buttons that look like little French chairs, favored by Christian LaCroix at $10.50 each, to some in the form of enameled dice for $8, $11, or $15, depending on size. Then there's the extraordinary collection of late 19th-century enameled buttons from $40 to $450 a piece to a marvelous medley from the 1930s. They run $6 to $75 each. A set of almost any has a great gift quotient. And many make terrific earrings or cuff links. Tender Buttons provides conversion services starting at $35 for either. Earrings can be made with clips or posts for pierced ears.

Actually the decorative possibilities of all these beautiful buttons is boundless, as is the imagination of the creators of many of them—Diane and Millicent, who design about half of the stock for both their stores (they opened a second Tender Buttons in Chicago, Diane's hometown, in 1990). Theirs are the buttons you'll most likely pick to replace those you lost on your raincoat or to add even more pizzazz to that new blazer, buttons in the $8 to $25 category. Diane and Millicent find that button buyers, motivated by either practicality or generosity, seldom spend more than $50 a piece. The pricier antiques are pretty much the preserve of the growing number of collectors.

If buttons, no matter how enchanting, don't tickle your fancy, then check out the assortment of antique cuff links, stick pins, and studs. We found a sensational pair of links—a lovely hand-painted English landscape scene "under glass" in carved rock crystal. Truly unique at $3,000. We also liked several sets of English enamels in sterling for around $225.

But back to basics—and to buttons. The store offers the ultimate in decadence: a 14-carat solid gold blazer button set. Available by special order, it takes five or six weeks for delivery, and the price tends to fluctuate with that of gold. Suffice it to say, it will be considerably more than the $400 charge for a very attractive set of brass buttons dating from the late 1800s.

Once curious about where the "tender" in Tender Buttons came from, we've come to accept the salute to Gertrude Stein, but we still think it can be interpreted as a verb. This store certainly does tender buttons!

# T. O. Dey

9 East 38th Street                            (212) 683-6300
between Madison and Fifth Avenues
New York, NY 10016

No part of the human body seems to work so hard and be so neglected as the foot. After all, have you ever even considered the amount of punishment a foot takes every day? Don't you just take your feet for granted, until they rebel and cause you discomfort, even excruciating pain?

Tom Bifulco and brother Gino imagine that's the case. Indeed, they count on it—their business depends on it. Since 1926 their company, T. O. Dey, has treated feet with tender loving care, by custom-making shoes specially designed to correct painful problems. As Tom is fond of saying, doctors often tell people, "Look, you don't need an operation—just go get some custom-made shoes." More often than not, by following doctors' advice, they'll wind up at T. O. Dey.

Tom and Gino didn't found the company (neither did their father, who ran it for twenty-six years before turning it over to the boys), but they have perfected the technique that allows their sixteen cobblers to construct corrective footwear that conceals all the modifications inside the shoes. On the outside, they appear to be simply beautifully, currently styled loafers, pumps, or boots. Whatever your fashion fancy, they can make it—or copy it—while assuring you carefree feet.

It's quite a process they've developed, starting with a pedegraph, an ink impression of the feet in a weight-bearing position. The graph reveals their secrets as to where they may be absorbing too much weight, or not enough. Then measurements are taken and both feet are completely encased in plaster of Paris. Just before they dry, the casts are cut in half so the feet can be removed. Subsequently, the halves are reassembled to form two negative casts. Positive ones are made by filling the negatives with liquid plaster. Once the plaster sets, the negative casts are removed, leaving behind exact models of both feet.

Using the model and the information from the graph, T. O. Dey's master craftsmen literally mold shoes for each foot that can camouflage any peculiarity, even deformity. Most ready-made shoes are manufactured on standard blocks with identical right and left feet, despite the fact that many people's right and left are markedly different. At T. O. Dey's, no two rights and lefts are exactly alike. In fact, each customer's initial casts are kept as a permanent record, allowing reorder by phone or mail. Just choose the style, color, and leather and an absolutely perfect pair of shoes will be yours.

There's always an eight-to-ten-week waiting period, and the first pair costs at least $650. Additional pairs run more in the $500 neighborhood, but can cost as much as $1,500 to $2,500 if special leathers are requested—skins like ostrich, crocodile, alligator, stingray, or snake.

T. O. Dey does repairs, too, and not just the standard fix-me-up. From heel to toe, they can change virtually anything: your shoes can grow larger or wider, your heels can be altered in any way you fancy, your open-toes can be closed (or vice-versa), and your closed-heels can become sling-backs (or vice-versa, again). And if you have, shall we say, full-figured calves, they'll either enlarge your too-tight boots, or custom make you a special pair, riding or regular. Or, if, for whatever reason, you can't wear a standard ski boot, you now know where to go.

Bring T. O. Dey some extra material from that great dress you had made and they'll whip up matching shoes and a handbag like they do every year for about forty of Georgette Mosbacher's outfits. When your luggage (Louis Vuitton or otherwise) needs TLC, they'll take care of it, including fixing the wheels. They restore antique luggage and briefcases, too.

Besides Georgette, their celebrity-studded client roster also includes Prince, Billy Idol, Sylvester Stallone, Liza Minnelli, Tony Danza, Tom Wolfe, Dudley Moore, Steven Segal, and Penn & Teller. Tony Randall and Hugh Downs head up a large group representing more conservative taste. They'd probably be horrified by the notion of Tom and Gino's most novel service. For $350, the Bifulco boys will make shoes for a (very) pampered pup! The practice began with a cocker named Tassels, whose paws had become irritated from walking on salty New York sidewalks.

What's the old adage about dogs and their masters looking alike? If they frequent T. O. Dey's, it's entirely possible their feet can be identically clad, at the very least!

# Yves Saint Laurent Femme

855 Madison Avenue                    (212) 988-3821
between 70th and 71st
New York, NY 10021

*Yves Saint Laurent Accessories*      (212) 472-5299
857 Madison Avenue
between 70th and 71st
New York, NY 10021

*Yves Saint Laurent Homme*            (212) 517-7400
859 Madison Avenue
at 71st
New York, NY 10021

Yves Saint Laurent — YSL; YSL — Yves Saint Laurent. Let's face it, that's all we really need to say about the man who is to fashion what Elvis was (is?) to rock 'n' roll — The King. In fact, he's so imperial that he's gone public. His is the first fashion house to have shares traded on the Bourse, the French stock exchange.

Even before he made that particular fortune, he had invested a considerable sum in the expansion of his United States flagship store on Madison. Although there are three separate entrances, there is really one wonderful store inside, so it's very convenient as you walk from one area to the next. The interior is as elegantly modern and sleek as are his clothes, with black (Saint Laurent's favorite) the predominant color. And he makes it anything but basic, especially when it comes to his classic "Le Smoking" pantsuits — so understated, so mannishly tailored, yet utterly feminine, and oh so comfortable.

Besides a reminder of Saint Laurent's passion, the black serves as dramatic backdrop to the clothes. They almost leap off the walls and look very accessible, inviting you to browse, to touch, to feel. They seem to beg to be tried on, and Saint Laurent has wisely provided some of the city's largest dressing rooms for that very purpose. Once you've slipped into one of his jackets and admired yourself as you privately pirouette in front of the generous mirrors, you're hooked. His jackets and slacks fit to the proverbial *T*.

While he may prefer black, Saint Laurent is a superb colorist, reveling in unusual combinations that work brilliantly together despite their decidedly non-complementary nature. Indeed, a few seasons with YSL will develop your eye for color, giving you new courage on the mix-and-match front. You'll find yourself expanding the horizons of last year's suit by topping the skirt with a new jacket in a richly contrasting hue, or jazzing it up with a blouse in a hot, luminous color.

The price palette is almost as broad as the color. Blouses range from $125 for a T-shirt to $1,200 for a silk evening blouse. Slacks start at about $300 for a cotton pair and wander up to the $1,800 neighborhood for the tuxedo variety. And while you can pick up a little cotton suit for $1,100, an elaborate brocade evening suit can cost you $5,000.

Saint Laurent's jackets and coats, which we absolutely adore, can be had for $1,000 to $3,000. The ante is about $1,500 for his fabulous fur-lined raincoats. Their straight, no-nonsense lines make them ever-so-versatile — great and yet elegantly appropriate for formal evenings.

Everything is arranged in sections — blouses with blouses, slacks with slacks, and suits with suits — making it easy for devotees like Angelica Huston, Mary Tyler Moore, and Nancy Dickerson to shop. Only hats are splashed throughout the store, while the other all-important accessories are located in the bright center boutique that shows them off fabulously. From handbags, gloves, and belts to umbrellas and costume jewelry, they'll complete any outfit. Prices start at $55 and go up from there. The scarves are spectacular, especially the wraparound ones which transform a simple dinner dress into a real showpiece. Handbags range from $150 for the waistbelt style; clutches start at around $300. Everything you'll find here can also make last year's outfit look brand new.

Shoes, located at the front of the women's store, run from $175 to $200 for day shoes and can range up to $265 for a pair of lace evening shoes.

Service, as always, is a byword. Whatever your purchases, the very knowledgeable sales staff keeps a permanent record to help you add sensibly to your YSL wardrobe in the future. Alterations are done on the premises by three talented seamstresses; they'll also alter a piece from a previous collection and there's just a minimal charge for both sets of services.

If you're in need of a real lift, visit makeup artist Louis Philippe. His domain, filled with YSL's complete cosmetic line, perfectly reflects Saint Laurent's fantastic sense of color. Louis will do your makeup and send you out into the world a new woman.

If the world is more (or less) than you care to face with your new countenance, mosey on over to the men's YSL store next door for some world-class trolling. (Gentlemen take note; it's a two-way street here.) The YSL man tends to be every bit as classy as his female counterpart. He's a successful type who wants a European look to his wardrobe, without totally abandoning classic traditions. He loves luxury, savors the feel of superior cloth, and revels in interesting design. He's somebody like John Kennedy, Jr., Harrison Ford, or Harry Belafonte — none of whom have any trouble plunking down $1,200 and up for a suit.

As you wander through the very elegant, contemporary men's store, you'll find everything you want, including blazers, slacks, sweaters, and sportswear. Notice the beautiful display cases and keep an eye out for the over-the-calf socks in sea island cotton for just $26. The ties, from strictly classical to wonderfully whimsical, start at $85.

Susanne Splan manages the women's and accessories stores and also looks after the men's. Sue oversees an incredible three-in-one experience. In fact, one might even retranslate the YSL acronym to Yes, Shop Lots!

# FOR THE HOME

## *Asprey & Company, Ltd.*

725 Fifth Avenue                              (212) 688-1811
at 56th Street                          Fax (212) 826-3746
Trump Tower
New York, NY 10022

Founded in London in 1781 by William Asprey, Asprey & Company has long been *the* source for cultivated gift-givers seeking the elegantly unusual. Fortunately, the Asprey Group has elected to open an outpost of priceless chic on this side of the Atlantic in Trump Tower, whose overwhelming pink marble and brass, alas, clash with the understated opulence of this special preserve.

Mercifully, one does not have to deal with the visual assault and the chaotic masses of the tower to enter Asprey. You can walk in right off Fifth Avenue and, once inside, it may be all you can do to restrain yourself from leaping like a delighted child from one area to the next. There's something special everywhere you look. Asprey's people are dispatched to all parts of the globe, looking for the world's most original treasures: hand-carved animals, boxes and frames, objets d'art made of carved gemstones, scarves, handbags, leather accessories, antique glass and furniture, china, crystal, flatware, and clocks and watches—and that's all just the beginning!

The ground floor Centre Shop is a good place to start exploring. You might find things like a spectacular brooch or 18-karat gold enameled gingham ear clips bordered with cultured pearls. Asprey New York's President Edward Green says his greatest passion is jewelry; it shows in the store's selection.

If your fancy leans toward antique porcelain or silver, there are whole departments devoted to these costly collectibles. They are staffed by erudite and helpful people, like Elaine Werner, an authority on eighteenth-century Viennese porcelain. There are also an antique jewelry department headed by Marilyn Meyers and even a bridal registry.

While browsing, your imagination might be captured by the life-size $12,000 sterling silver gilt construction worker's hard hat, the quintessential gift for the real estate magnate in your life. It comes in a beautiful leather presentation case, as did a similar sterling silver gilt football helmet (complete with blue leather padding), which was sold for $29,750 after the 1992 Super Bowl. Don't worry if you can't live without one of your own (it can, of course, be engraved with your favorite football team's logo or anything else you like). Although Asprey stocks just one at a time, they will make one up for you in their London workshop; it will take three months or so — all handmade, don't you know.

Sometimes, however, you must act quickly at Asprey — their wonderful one-of-a-kind pieces are often there one day and gone the next. When we saw the antique Russian travel bidet made for Princess Xenia Feodorovna, sister of the unfortunate Czar Nicholas II, we thought it would make a magnificent cooler for a bottle of vintage Dom Perignon. Soon after, it was sold for $25,000 as, yes, just that! Not to worry, though, because they now have something even more spectacular — a picnic hamper made by Asprey in 1886 for Empress Maria Feodorovna, Nicholas's mother. Calling it a collector's item is really an understatement. Inside the leather-bound Victorian wicker basket are riches like silver-topped crystal cordial flasks, silver gilt mugs, silver plates and flatware, and other accoutrements for four. Its brass plaque proclaims Empress Maria's cypher, but it can be yours for $50,000.

No visit to Asprey is complete without stopping by Kathleen O'Brien's book department, home to rare first editions and reprints. She also offers the extraordinary service of binding your masterpiece in fine hand-tooled leathers. Asprey maintains two binderies in London. Custom bindings start at about $700, including your choice of endpapers. The book department also conducts searches for the titles and authors missing from their library.

Asprey's new baby department is complete with all kinds of goodies for newborns. We particularly like the six-piece christening set, which comes in a fitted leather case. Inside, the sterling silver mug, napkin ring, plate, cereal bowl, spoon, and egg cup each feature an adorable bunny. At $3,000, it gives new meaning to the phrase "born with a silver spoon...."

Nearby is a beguiling collection of handcarved animals, boxes, and frames in semiprecious stones. We are also enchanted by the $425 silver rocker blotter which makes a wonderful gift, as does a gorgeous set of mother-of-pearl caviar knives for $850. Another gift we love is a sterling silver flashlight. (Being typically English, they call it a torch.) At $850, at least it does include the batteries. And it will surely come in handy wherever you live, from New York (blackouts) to California (earthquakes) to Florida (hurricanes).

Whatever you buy at Asprey, from a set of $5,750 1920s-era rock crystal and diamond studs to a $1 refill for their wonderful leather jotters (notepads), your sales receipt comes on beautiful bond paper. It's just like Asprey to do everything in exquisite taste.

One of Asprey's most intriguing items is available only between Thanksgiving and Christmas. It involves the British tradition of crackers, those brightly colored paper cylinders that, when pulled, break open with a loud crack and reveal a wonderful little gift. They have an incredible selection of festive crackers and gifts to fill them — a champagne stopper for $40, a sterling silver key ring for $145, an 18-carat gold collar pin at $190, or a little enamel box at $95, among other things. It's a delightful tradition to adopt and the best part is that it will keep you coming back to Asprey & Company year after year.

# *Baccarat*

625 Madison Avenue  (800) 777-0100
between 58th and 59th Streets  (212) 826-4100
New York, NY 10022  Fax (212) 826-5043

Before *Baccarat* became internationally synonymous with exquisite crystal, it was the name of a tiny village in the midst of then heavily forested northeastern France. In 1764, the village was part of the domain of a certain Bishop of Metz, by the name of Monseigneur de Montmorency-Laval. Troubled by the burg's unemployment problem, he devised a clever solution. The good Monseigneur petitioned King Louis XV to grant him the authority to establish a wood-burning glassworks. He reasoned that it would put the area's resources to good use, as well as provide work for Baccarat's unemployed woodcutters.

We figure the king was less concerned about the plight of the woodcutters than he was about the fact that, at the time, France did not produce any art glass. Large quantities of francs were leaving the country to import Bohemian decorative glass. The Bishop of Metz's proposal was a way to stem the ebbing tide of funds that were sorely needed in France to deal with the recovery from the crippling Seven Years War.

Whatever arguments swayed the king, he granted the request on October 16, 1764, thereby creating a company that has (so far) survived three revolutions, four invasions, and the patronage of czars, kings, popes, and presidents. Originally a producer of rather simple glass, Baccarat had evolved by 1817 into the creator of elegant full-lead crystal that is still its hallmark. Each Baccarat piece is meticulously made by hand—lots of hands; a goblet may be handled by fifty people during the course of its production. The result is nothing short of perfection—no specks, no ripples, nothing but the luminous sparkle of light dancing on crystal.

The New York Store is designed to show off the artistry of Baccarat, with dark charcoal gray museum-like display cabinets and superb lighting. Light caresses crystal everywhere you look, from the majestic Imperial Eagle priced at $39,100 to a $61 wine glass, perhaps in the Capri pattern, Princess Grace's choice for her stemware. Take a look at Perfection, a timeless design created in 1886. It was Coco Chanel's favorite, an opinion apparently shared by many of her compatriots; in 1933 the wine growers of Bordeaux named Perfection the perfect glass for toasting.

Baccarat's selection seems almost endless, from incredibly beautiful vases and candleholders to ornate clocks and chandeliers. It's absolutely impossible to pick a favorite, but for us, the blue and clear-glass sculpture-like Vecteur line comes close. Also be sure to check out the whimsical "Lochness," a glass sculpture whose four disconnected pieces offer the illusion that the mythical monster swims serenely on your coffee table.

You'll find no shortage of china and flatware either. Baccarat carries familiar names like Cristofle and Puiforcat. There is a

bridal registry, of course. And they handle corporate accounts
as well.

And though there is nothing they do that isn't wonderful, it's
crystal — elegant, pure, gleaming crystal — that is really what Baccarat is all about.

# Bernardaud

777 Madison Avenue        (800) 884-7775
between 66th and 67th Streets    (212) 737-7775
New York, NY 10021       Fax (212) 794-9730

Gorgeous, gorgeous, gorgeous — that's what we have to say about
Bernardaud porcelain dinnerware.

Since its founding in 1863, The House of Bernardaud has maintained a reputation as one of the world's most highly regarded
creators of porcelain, serving royalty and heads of state from Emperor Napoleon III and Russia's czars to the King of Morocco.
Today it is France's largest porcelain dinnerware producer and despite its years, it maintains both feet firmly planted in the present.
Besides being beautiful, Bernardaud porcelain has a consistently
dynamic and contemporary quality, even avant garde, that will
have you wanting each design that you see more than the last.

Although you can find some Bernardaud at Asprey, Bergdorf
Goodman, and Bloomingdale's, we suggest you go to the source
on Madison Avenue, where they carry more than 250 patterns.
Opened in 1990, it's the only Bernardaud Store in the United
States. To make your table picture perfect, the store also carries
crystal and sterling.

Everything you ever wanted to know about porcelain can be
learned at Bernardaud. The owners maintain a historical archive
of their museum-quality work in their Limoges, France headquarters, including those pieces featured in the Cooper-Hewitt's
recent French design retrospective.

The production of porcelain dates back to China more than
twelve hundred years ago. After porcelain was introduced to the
West by Portuguese traders in the 16th century, Europeans sought
to learn how to make it themselves. The secret ingredient, a fine
white clay containing hydrated aluminum silicate called kaolin,
was discovered around 1700. It turned out that the soil in Limoges,
located 200 miles south of Paris, was filled with it, which is how the

porcelain industry came to be centered there and why the city's name is synonymous with quality porcelain.

Since the late 19th century, America has been the largest market for Limoges-produced porcelain and although the industry suffered a lull between World War I and World War II, the introduction of modern equipment led to a revitalization in the late 50s, and it thrives still today. Bernardaud, of course, leads the way. Unlike most companies its age, Bernardaud is still run by its founding family. Chairman Pierre Bernardaud and his son Michel, president, remain intimately involved in their business and are responsible for the firm's design-forward bent. Bernardaud is a member of the Comite Colbert, France's prestigious association of luxury manufacturers who, according to Bernardaud's description, are "committed to the preservation of the 'savoir-faire' of the crafts of artisans." In keeping with this commitment to tradition as well as to innovation, Bernardaud was the first to deviate from the traditional circular plate form. It has square plates with square (rather than round) impressions inside. Its Line Trianne is even more unusual: its round plates feature a triangle-shaped space. And the Line Gemini plate and silhouette are octagonal. The store does, of course, carry your standard round plates as well, but almost every line has something that makes it truly extraordinary, from a nonstandard size to a special use of silversmithery.

Their patterns are equally exceptional, and the Phoebe line seems to include most of our favorites. The one that fascinated us the most is called Metropoles. Each plate contains a collage of landmarks from New York, Paris, Rome, London, Berlin, or Moscow in vivid colors set on a deep blue background. It's $370 for a five-piece place setting, or you can buy just the dinner plate, which contains the design around its border, for $99. The salad plates depict the highlights of each city. We also liked the Paris pattern ($320) whose design incorporates Leger-style nudes (another Bernardaud first), lending an artistic flair to your table. Fruitti Fiori ($320) offers a more traditional look and Borghese ($195), with its bright flowers in mostly warm yellows and blues, looks good enough to eat. The brand-new Corcovado pattern is less expensive at $150 but its undulating motif is no less attractive.

Lest you think we've slighted the other lines, we hasten to include Line Trianne's avant-garde Nil pattern ($195) and Line

Gemini's whimsical Macouba ($170), another of our preferred choices.

Even with its fabulous selection, Bernardaud understands that some people prefer a one-of-a-kind look, which is why they offer "couture" porcelain. Clients for this custom service range from the Sultan of Brunei to Air France to New York restaurants like Bouley and the River Café. It runs $1,300 to $1,400 a place setting, plus 50 percent more for an encrusted monogram, and can take anywhere from two to three months to go from Bernardaud's table to yours. (This service includes a personalized back stamp, too.)

Brides who register at Bernardaud are offered this back-stamping service as well. The stamp says "To celebrate the marriage of...." or "In commemoration of our marriage" plus the names. Bernardaud's bright and articulate manager, Mary Kaye Denning, told us that people these days are even registering for their anniversaries, making it easier on the giver and delicious on the receiver. You can get backstamping at no charge for an order of $1,000 or more, or for a small service charge otherwise. One lucky lady received a new set of china from her husband with "I still adore you" and his signature stamped on the back.

Besides the basic dinner plates, each line offers other pieces like sugar bowls and creamers, gravy boats, soup tureens, salad bowls, coffee and tea pots, and even pickle dishes. They also have the odd strawberry dishes, breakfast trays, and an oversized breakfast cup and saucer big enough for a little pastry or toast. These sell for $112 a set, $48 for the cup by itself, or $64 for the plate.

To complement your china, Bernardaud offers Saint-Louis crystal, which comes in patterns that match some of the Bernardaud selections. Surprisingly affordable, the prices range from $50 to $400 a glass. Fine sterling by Old Newberry Crafters, the last handwrought silver company in America, is available in all kinds of special shapes and patterns. They also carry Heritage silver from England, where a seven-piece place setting, including dessert service, runs $980 to $1,200.

One last thing: Bernardaud has a custom stationery service that offers invitations in foreign languages, should you require them.

But Bernardaud's mainstay is its dinnerware. And because of its extraordinary quality and variety, we remain as passionate about their porcelain as the Bernardauds do.

# *Christofle*

680 Madison Avenue                                    (212)308-9390
at 62nd Street                                  Fax (212) 644-7487
New York, NY 10021

Have you ever been to an embassy dinner and wondered about the
origins of the breathtakingly beautiful silver? We know you've
flown on a Falcon jet or Henry Kravis's private plane, where you've
taken a surreptitious look at the trademark on the blade of your
knife. Or maybe it was the Kluge yacht, the *Virginian?* At any rate,
all of these private retreats of the very rich are outfitted with
Christofle silver. On the *Virginian*, the Christofle collection is particularly extensive — from plate to sterling.

Considered the premier French silversmith since 1830,
Christofle continues to pursue its motto of "one quality: the best."
Christofle created the exclusive silverware used by King Louis-
Philippe, the Emperor Napoleon II, and the Imperial Court.
Known for its timeless, sophisticated designs, the firm's New York
base reflects its reputation. Elegant and chic, the sleek wood
cabinets gleam with Christofle's complete line of sterling, silverplate, goldplate, and stainless steel flatware, as well as china, table
accessories, and gift items.

Manager Helga Calvo knows her silver and can guide you in
your selection. If you're after silverplate, she'll tell you why you've
come to the right place. Christofle revolutionized the whole industry in 1842, when it bought the patent rights to the new process of
applying precious silver and gold onto metal by electroplating.
They might also show you Christofle's latest technological coup —
*les cloisonnés lague de chine.* As executed in the Talisman pattern,
$440 for a five-piece place setting, it combines silver and either
natural sienna, black, blue, or green Chinese lacquer. Christofle
has rediscovered the ancient cloisonné technique, entwining luxur-
iant arcades of shiny lacquer with delicate silver threads.

More conventional sterling patterns featuring Christofle's signature attention to design detail — each fillet, each bead, each
flourish is hand-finished — range from $175 to $325 per place
setting. The simple, pure form of the Albi pattern is vintage
Christofle with its delicate ridge as the only decoration at $195.
More elaborate is the Aria, with its fluted handles gathered at top
and bottom by bands plated with 24-carat gold. As with any

Christofle plating, it is dishwasher-safe, and the standard five pieces sell for $225.

They've expanded (and perfected) their china line, too. You'll find five-piece place settings in colorful patterns ranging in price from $245 to $300.

As you would expect, Christofle has a bridal registry, but with a French twist. Rather than sending the gifts selected by relatives and friends, they send a card. So after the honeymoon, the bride can sort through the cards to weed out the duplicates or items she no longer wants. Christofle will send all the final selections at one time—so much easier than lugging the gifts destined for exchange.

Christofle likes to call its products *French Couture Pour La Table*. We can't argue—a table set with Christofle is the most fashionable we can imagine.

# *D. Porthault & Co.*

| | |
|---|---|
| 18 East 69th Street | (212) 688-1660 |
| between Madison and | Fax (212) 772-8450 |
| Fifth Avenues | |
| New York, NY 10021 | |

They have become such a part and parcel of our lives, it is difficult to imagine that in 1925, when Madelaine Porthault first designed prints for her family's linen business, they were considered a radical notion. Inspired by the Impressionists, the lush florals that she silk-screened onto Porthault sheets were to have a lasting impact on the world's tastes in home furnishings.

Today the firm's colorful products can be found in more than two hundred locations in twenty-four countries, and the business has expanded to include table linens, towels and bathwear, lingerie, children's clothes, porcelain, accessories, and home fragrances. In New York, Porthault occupies a landmark townhouse just off Madison Avenue that shows off their merchandise to its best advantage. A series of rooms has been created to display it in the kinds of settings that might be found in a private home. You'll know just where to put that breakfast set in Porthault-patterned Limoges for $290 and the matching tea cart that will add another $570 to the cost.

No matter how tempting the other products, concentrate on the linens and towels — that is where Porthault made its name for exceptional quality and setting new trends. After all, it was Porthault that first introduced scalloped borders, lace borders, piped toweling, printed toweling, and the coordinated look of matching bed linens and towels.

All the sheets are one hundred percent cotton, woven in the firm's factories in France. There are more then three hundred patterns to choose from, but remember that bottom sheets do not come fitted as a matter of course. However, you can order a fitted bottom sheet for no extra charge — just a little extra time. It will take about three weeks.

Our favorite design is called C126. Lavishly embroidered, a queen-size set with two pillowcases will set you back $4,130. With her taste for expensive luxury, it's no wonder that the Duchess of Windsor (our own dear Wallis Simpson) would sleep only on Porthault sheets. She traveled with several sets, as she just couldn't count on every household she visited to be up to her exacting standards.

Carol Matthau, who's been collecting Porthault sheets for years, probably has every print that they've ever done. Other devotees include Marlo Thomas, both Mesdames Bass, Suzanne Somers, Dominick Dunne, and Eileen Ford.

Porthault's luxurious terry robes (from around $320 to $800) are made 500 grams to the square meter, but if you prefer the lighter-weight version which they make for children (400 grams), they'll do a custom order and it will probably cost around $50 less than the 500-gram version.

Bath towels in prints begin at $160; solids start at $119. Our favorite is the rich, multicolored bathsheet labeled 5426A. The price — $345 — may seem steep, but we think it's worth it. You'll feel like you're wrapping yourself in a Monet.

If you've been buying Porthault towels for years and years, you know that they last for years and years. But you may not know that Porthault will rebind them to perk them up for just a minimal charge.

The small cosmetics bags ($32) are noteworthy, as are the travel-size cases ($50 and $66) and a jewelry case lined in velvet ($28). Their children's wear is adorable — take a look.

Ask for Arlette, who's been there for the last twenty years —

you can practice your French with her. Or see Jane Borthwick, Porthault's U.S. president, who is as charming as she could possibly be. There is nothing Porthault won't do for you; they'll come to wherever you are, from your home to your yacht (or your corporate jet, for that matter). Their designers will work with you and/or your interior decorator to create motifs best suited to your decor.

Perhaps Marc Porthault, the president, who is also Madelaine's son and inheritor of her extraordinary talents, sums it up best when he says, "Porthault is a luxury business. We are a guarantor of French quality and taste."

# Fortunoff

681 Fifth Avenue                          (800) 937-4376
at 54th Street                            (212) 758-6660
New York, NY 10022

Fortunoff, the self-styled "Source," has come a long way from its origins as a little neighborhood housewares store—as far as Brooklyn is from Fifth Avenue. Founded in 1922 by Max and Clara Fortunoff, the company remains a family-run operation with five locations, which most New Yorkers can recite, having been exposed for years to extensive, even aggressive, advertising.

Not that we're complaining. Fortunoff does have a lot to crow about. The Fifth Avenue flagship store opened in 1979 as a veritable four-story testimony to the good life reflected in contemporary jewelry, estate pieces, watches, fine china, porcelain, and silver—lots and lots of silver, with senior vice president Joe Figueroa overseeing it all.

It's silver where Fortunoff truly stands out as a resource. Just ask Jerry Blumert, the resident expert. Ask him anything imaginable about silver and he'll have an answer—it will even be accurate! Silver devotees like Dustin Hoffman, Joan Rivers, Christie Brinkley, and Robert Duvall depend on his advice when they browse for that treasured collectible or for the perfect gift. The third-floor collection of antique sterling Georgian, Sheffield, Victorian, and Tiffany silver is mind-boggling. Arrayed with the enormous selection of modern silver, it's almost overwhelming.

Absolutely overwhelming is the range of flatware—plate, gold-plated, and stainless, not to mention sterling—the largest assortment available anywhere in the world, with more than five hundred patterns from which to choose.

In the spirit of one-stop shopping, you can also pick up crystal and china to accompany the silver. Not surprisingly, the bridal service department is one of the best in the city.

Jewelry is also very important at Fortunoff's. There's an enormous selection of watches, from $30 to $20,000, and the estate jewelry department is increasingly expanding. The first floor, always bustling with activity, glitters with its displays of rings, bracelets, necklaces, and brooches. Many pieces are designed exclusively for Fortunoff and carry price tags that always strike us as more than reasonable. Due to the stores' tremendous volume, Fortunoff tends to offer a lot of glitz for the buck.

Moreover, Fortunoff sticks by its glitz. Everything sold can also be repaired or restored in the second floor service department. With two jewelers, one watchmaker, two hand engravers, one machine engraver, and two polishers, you can have any Fortunoff purchase serviced here for a lifetime.

Still, the most intriguing thing about Fortunoff is its sheer breadth of merchandise, artfully displayed in a 20,000-square-foot arena. From a $25 silver-plate frame to a 30-carat flawless diamond for $100,000, there's something for almost anyone at The Source.

# *Frette*

| | |
|---|---|
| 799 Madison Avenue | (212) 988-5221 |
| between 67th and 68th Streets | Fax (212) 988-5257 |
| New York, NY 10021 | |

Since 1860, Frette has been making the things that household dreams are made of—beautiful sheets, table linens, towels, blankets, and even lingerie. The traditional supplier to European royal families, deluxe hotels, international embassies, and indeed the altar of St. Peter's in Rome, the Italian company has had this outpost on Madison Avenue since 1981.

Recently redone to look like an elegant townhome, it is warm and inviting. After all, there's a working fireplace, beautiful rosewood floors, and antique paintings. Walls are covered by Frette-made tapestries dating from the turn of the century. The lingerie department resembles the most seductive of boudoirs.

While Porthault is renowned for prints and Pratesi for embroideries, jacquards are Frette's great claim to fame. Though jacquards present the effect of a print, the decorative elements are actually woven. Frette mastered the technique in the 1880s with the introduction of sophisticated state-of-the-art machinery and has devoted much of its energy to refining its patterns and designs ever since. Pastels are a specialty, but the color spectrum runs from bold red to trendy black and includes beiges, bones, terra cottas, rusts, and golds.

Using only the finest Egyptian cottons, Belgian linens, and Italian silks, sheet sets—top, bottom, and two shams—sell for $750 to $5,000. We're quite fond of the art masterpiece-inspired patterns based on a detail from, say, a Donatello or a Caravaggio and named eponymously. Very special, too, are the hand-embroidered sets with lace trim. Bachelors will love the extraordinary bronze-tone Aurelia pattern ($600 for a king-size set). If you want a "test-drive," spend the night at The Mark, which stocks only Frette linens.

Their silk sheets come complete with recommended laundry service by a woman named Rosa Duran, who does fine hand laundry in her home. If you live in Manhattan, it will take two to three days and cost just $32 per set (top and bottom sheet plus two shams). Ms. Duran can be reached directly at (718) 617-0806, but if you're from out of town, send your sheets to Frette's manager Rosa Szule; she'll get them to Rosa Duran who will send them directly back to you. (Here we go 'round the Rosa???) Anyway, Frette swears by her.

Their custom business is quite wonderful; they can do literally anything. If you find something you like in cotton but want it in silk, no problem. If you have a custom-size bed, be it round or 9'× 9'(like a Florida client), they can make sheets for you. Or if you want a tablecloth and matching sheets, or a tablecloth to match your china pattern, or a robe/pajama set to match your sheets, just give them the order. They'll coordinate everything Frette can supply for your home, including having your own logo or family crest embroidered on table linens. (For this, ask about machine-embroidery as opposed to hand-embroidery if you want to save a few dollars, and be prepared to wait eight to twelve weeks for delivery.) They can also pick up the patterns in your wallpaper or in the fabrics of your furniture. Whatever your taste in design, Frette can work with it.

Tina Turner and Madonna are among those who count on Frette to make their tables the most hospitable in the neighborhood. Place mats start at $45. Hand-embroidered beauties go for as much as $250 apiece, including matching napkin, while tablecloths range from $250 to $3,000.

Whatever you do, don't miss the towels. Bath sheets run $120 to $500; bath towels are around $60; washcloths go for $20 (ouch!). Be sure to ask Rosa about the European linen hand towels, which are $125 each and, yes, do need to be pressed.

One more thing to see would be the lightweight quilts. They wash beautifully and cost about $550.

We could go on and on, because shopping at Frette can become an addiction. But you've got to experience it yourself. After all, what's that they say about one picture being worth a thousand words?

# *Lalique*

680 Madison Avenue                    (212) 355-6550
between 61st and 62nd Streets      Fax (212) 752-0203
New York, NY 10021

If you were alive at the turn of this century, chances are that, when you purchased perfume, you brought your own bottle to the local perfumery to be filled from large glass storage containers. That all changed — as did the entire perfume industry — in 1907 when Roger Coty asked his friend René Lalique, internationally renowned as a designer of exquisite jewelry, to fashion a label for a perfume he intended to launch. Forty-year-old Lalique, who had started designing jewelry at age eleven and opened his first shop when he was twenty-five, was ripe for an exciting new challenge. Upon deciding that Coty's fragrance deserved something more distinctive than a label, he began experimenting with glass and produced a sumptuous bottle to encase the scent.

Lalique positioned the bottle itself as a vitally important part of any particular perfume's mystique, not only signaling his new career as a glassmaker but paving the way for the perfume revolution in evidence today when we open almost any magazine.

Lalique's expertise and creativity as a glassmaker blossomed as the demand for his bottles and other decorative objects grew. By 1933 his glassware collection consisted of more than 1,500 items, and he had applied his imagination to fountains, furniture, doors, chandeliers, and entire buildings. In fact, the front of the Fifth Avenue Henri Bendel building (commissioned by François Coty) features Lalique's climbing poppy motif—don't miss it as you pass by. Upon René's death in 1945, his son Marc assumed responsibility for design and production. It was Marc who transformed Lalique glass into crystal and who virtually patented the use of an acid-etched finish to enhance decorative elements. Marc's daughter—René's granddaughter—Marie-Claude carries on the Lalique tradition of designing richly decorated glassware, working in René's studio and overseeing the production in the Alsace factory he opened in 1921.

In 1992, Lalique's international reputation was justification enough for the Olympic Games Organizing Committee when its members, setting aside a time-honored tradition of metal medals, commissioned Lalique to create the coveted awards for the XVI Winter Games at Albertville. Made entirely by hand, they were sculpted from pure Lalique crystal set like a gem in an engraved frame of gold, silver, or bronze.

The Madison Avenue shop dedicated to the Lalique family's legacy is tiny, but oh, so sophisticatedly gray—gray carpeting, gray leather banquettes, gray suede walls. The interior was designed and built in Paris. Shipped to New York in large containers, it was reassembled and installed here several years ago as the first store in the United States entirely dedicated to the fine art of Lalique.

Stemware starts at about $65 per piece and goes up to $250. Decanters range from $345 to $1,000. For collectors, there's quite a selection of the 2,000 items currently made by the company, from a $160 perfume bottle to the fabulous $2,825 vase called Bacchantes with its graceful, luminous nude figures.

New to Lalique in recent years is a jewelry line. Earrings, cuff links, tie clips, pins, bracelets, and rings can be yours in a variety of styles, with prices like $150 for a pin and $260 for cuff links. Don't miss the extraordinary silk scarves ($295) patterned with replicas of antique jewelry, or the even-more-extraordinary new Astellia vase ($8,900) — there are only ninety-nine of them in the world.

Serious collectors should sign on to the two-year waiting list for the horse-head sculpture that sells for $18,000. You see, only fifteen are made each year. Directeur Bruce Petricca will be happy to estimate when you can expect yours.

Quite spectacular and precious is the truly awe-inspiring Lalique chandelier in the center of the store. It's called Champs-Elysées. At only $9,600 we'll put it on our wish list. Maybe we could arrange for a waiting list for it too.

## Pratesi

829 Madison Avenue                    (212) 288-2315
at 69th Street                   Fax (212) 628-4038
New York, NY 10021

Pratesi on Madison is the perfect illustration of the pronouncement that you can't judge a book by its cover. Though the building's exterior is truly nondescript, its windows are your eyes to Pratesi's soul. Take a good look—there's no question that you're gazing at some of the most beautifully lavish, yet understatedly elegant, sheets and towels imaginable. And it gets even better when you walk inside.

Business has been so good that Pratesi has taken over the shop next door, which garnered them an extra window and more natural light. As you enter, there's a showcase room to your right whose focus might be on the season's collection, things for men, a terry collection, or some such specialty. It's worth a visit every few weeks to see what they've come up with.

The ground floor at Pratesi is done in subtle tones of gray, dramatically accented by black, to show off the incredible selection of embroidered towels. All the toweling is made of Egyptian cotton, but the design and production is done in Pistoia, Italy. It's all very thick, very luxurious, and costs from $130 to $190 per bath towel, depending upon the elaborate quotient of the embroidery.

The sheets are instantly recognizable as Pratesi with their fine three-line stitch and chain-pattern embroideries. Others have tried to copy the look but are stymied by the subtle delicacy that has been the Pratesi trademark for four generations, transforming an ordinary bedroom into a captivating boudoir. We constantly marvel at their pretty patterns. Our favorite? Probably the pineapple lace in either white or white/cream. They've been making it for years and it's as beautiful today as the first time we saw it. Many of Pratesi's sheets now come in the 370-thread variety. (For those whose grandmothers didn't teach them, the higher the thread count, the more luxurious the feel!) There's an easy-care sheet, with king top sheets running $430 for prints and $590 for solids with trim. Fitted bottom sheets can run anywhere from $250 to $270, and regular pillow cases cost about $150. Other styles will run higher. King-size sheet sets (top, fitted bottom, and two shams) start at $1,080. Add thirty percent if you want to order a special color. In silk, a top sheet will run $2,900, a bottom fitted $1,500, and pillow cases $550. There are king-size sheet sets for around $4,500, too. They're so luxurious that you may never want to get out of bed. Remember that every Pratesi sheet seam (not only the silk) is hemstitched.

If you want to ensure truly sweet dreams, treat yourself to a cashmere blanket. The cashmere is Chinese, only the best of course, but it is woven in Italy. In king size, it will be $3,200. If that's out of the question, consider the $780 fringed cashmere throws which come in everything from bright colors to pastels, plus your basic beiges, bones, and blacks. They're so wonderfully warm and cozy that we've been known to wear one outside, folded in a triangle and tossed over the shoulders!

This year a new collection of blankets and throws will be unveiled from applique lamb's wool blanket to gossamer cashmere batiste, something truly different and very special. For an inexpensive present ask for their oval classic placemats in all the classic prints, for just $20 you'll add a glamorous touch to your table.

Brides register here, of course, for a selection that can run the gamut from $10 cocktail napkins to much more expensive lace table linens whose design is adapted from a Pratesi-made 19th-century royal christening dress. This dress, by the way, is back in Pratesi's possession. Ask store manager Adelaide Goitein (who's a delight!) to show it to you.

They also have bed linens based on this royal design, indeed fit for a royal house. The king top sheet costs $2,200, but before blanching at the prices, remember that Pratesi pieces last at least twenty years.

Don't forget to visit the second-floor garden, always exquisitely planted. Have a look, too, at the terry robes, which range from $330 to $460, and the cotton makeup dusters which are absolutely terrific for traveling or simply as an after-bath wrap.

With each passing year, Pratesi's lines get prettier and prettier. Whatever you need (and whether you need it or not), they have the perfect bed and bath wardrobe to pamper and please you.

# Puiforcat

| | |
|---|---|
| 811 Madison Avenue | (212) 734-3838 |
| at 68th Street | Fax (212) 734-3165 |
| New York, NY 10021 | |

Not that long ago, examples of Puiforcat's mastery of the art of silver craftsmanship were difficult to find in the United States. You'd see the occasional piece or pattern available only in a few selected shops. That unfortunate situation was rectified in December 1988, when this small store opened, dedicated to the artistry and tradition of Puiforcat.

As manager Eva Merritt will tell you, it is a tradition that can be traced to 1820 and to Paris, where Emile Puiforcat established a silversmith dynasty in the Marais district. Originally a workshop devoted to the mass production of industrial silverwork — serving dishes and hollow ware — the house's shift toward the creation of luxury pieces sold directly to a wealthy clientele began a century later under Louis-Victor Puiforcat. He moved the operation "uptown" to the Boulevard Haussmann, where it remains today. He also began to amass a monumental collection of the most exceptional silver designs ever produced.

Much of that collection now belongs to the Louvre, though about a hundred pieces remain with the Société Puiforcat. In any case, the firm retains exclusive rights to the entire collection, allowing it to reproduce a staggering 180 flatware patterns and 10,000 hollow ware designs.

Puiforcat silver continues to be made entirely by hand — each piece individually crafted, each destined to become an heirloom.

Five-piece place settings like the popular Cannes or Annecy are about $1,550. They are representative of the inspired work of Jean Puiforcat, who was the unchallenged master of Art Deco-style silver. He designed the silver for that ill-fated floating temple of Art Deco, the *Normandie*. (She caught fire while docked in New York and sank, courtesy of the New York Fire Department, causing irreparable damage to Franco-American relations. Fortunately, the pattern named (what else?) the Normandie endures.

You get a sense of Louis-Victor's unparalleled collection and the quality of Puiforcat's current craftsmanship in the stylized reproduction of a sterling tea set originally commissioned by an eighteenth-century King of Portugal. With ivory handles, it's priced at $263,000. If they're out of stock, don't worry. It takes only six months for them to make another.

In a more contemporary vein, there's a spectacular Empire soup tureen for $31,105, as well as Puiforcat's concession to modern economics — silver plate. They've translated three of their patterns, including the *Normandie*, into plate, which sell for about $295 per place setting. True to form, while it is not made by hand, the quality is exceptional — heavily coated with forty microns of silver that will last at least a lifetime. And it is hand-finished.

We love their silverplate plates, which run $225. If you want sterling, though, plan to spend close to $4,000. And we highly recommend the small (8" × 10") silver trays; although the sterling runs $2,400, you can manage nicely with the silverplate version (8" × 6") for just $200.

They also have some china patterns, the most popular of which seems to be the Art Deco-style "Variation" at $560 for a five-piece place setting.

Jewelry is another relatively new addition to the Puiforcat repertoire. Crafted in sterling silver with vermeil trim and studded with semiprecious stones, the cuff links, earrings, and bracelets are translations of Jean Puiforcat's dinner and hollow ware designs. They are priced from about $800 to $5,000.

Puiforcat — it is to silver what haute couture is to fashion: the hallmark.

# Schweitzer Linens

| | |
|---|---|
| 457 Columbus Avenue | (212) 799-9629 |
| between 81st and 82nd Streets | |
| New York, NY 10024 | |
| | |
| 1053 Lexington Avenue | (212) 570-0236 |
| at 75th Street | |
| New York, NY 10021 | |
| | |
| 1132 Madison Avenue | (212) 249-8361 |
| at 84th Street | |
| New York, NY 10028 | |

First opened by Sandy Schweitzer some twenty years ago, this ultimate in linen stores has enjoyed considerable expansion in recent years. The second location opened on Columbus Avenue in 1982, a third on Lexington in 1989. Schweitzer Linens has a guileless formula for success—a large and complete inventory, mattress pads to place mats, featuring well-priced quality items. Schweitzer is quite simply the most complete, upscale linen store in the city. It stands out in a market otherwise dominated by specialty boutiques dedicated to one label, usually French or Italian, and department stores committed to domestic brands. But here, be it French, Italian, Belgian, German, Chinese, or domestic, you can find a healthy selection. Florals, stripes, bold patterns, and embroideries, from cotton sheets to damask tablecloths—they have it all, and then some.

You can adopt the look of Porthault, Pratesi, Frette, or your own mix-and-match motif. Schweitzer carries the best, but the prices are lower than you might expect. King-size sheets run from $375 to $600 for a set including two standard shams, usually with button closures.

Schweitzer's big on terry too—American terry, which the family swears is the best. Accordingly, they carry a terrific assortment of towels and terry bathrobes. While it would seem they already feature every color you could possibly envision, if nothing quite matches your color scheme, bring in some sample swatches or paint chips. Schweitzer will custom-color terry merchandise to match. It will take six to eight weeks, but there's no additional charge.

The inventory here changes frequently, so you might consider taking a cue from Princess Yasmin Aga Khan, Yoko Ono, and Liza Minnelli and stop by on a regular basis to see what's what.

# Steuben

717 Fifth Avenue                    (212) 752-1441
at 56th Street                      (800) 223-1234
New York, NY 10022            Fax (212) 424-4240

A bona fide American art form, Steuben glass has been chosen by every president of the United States as a gift of state since 1947, when Harry Truman started the tradition by presenting then Princess Elizabeth with the Sidney Waugh-designed Merry-Go-Round bowl upon the occasion of her marriage to Prince Philip. In 1992, Elizabeth (now Queen) was gifted again with Steuben, this time by

President George Bush who presented a Shakespeare's Flowers bowl during her state visit.

Steuben, a part of the Corning Glass works since 1918, makes some of the finest clear lead crystal in the world. Its works are represented in important museum collections in a number of countries, and are prized for the excellence of their design and purity of form. Steuben is the only major glassmaker that never uses acid polishing. Instead, the company employs a time-consuming hand-finishing technique that gives Steuben crystal its legendary brilliance. Furthermore, there are no seconds at Steuben. Every piece is thoroughly inspected at various stages of production — about one quarter are rejected in this rigorous process and destroyed.

The firm's Fifth Avenue shop boasts the world's most complete collection of present-day Steuben. Its window displays are always arresting, thanks to the talented Mark Tamayo. The store itself is dramatic and compelling, designed to show off Steuben's sculptural, ornamental, and functional glass to its luminescent best.

Don't miss the precious animals collection, known as "hand coolers." The name comes from nineteenth-century etiquette, which dictated that well-bred ladies carry a piece of glass in their palms when attending dances to keep them from sweating — excuse us, we mean perspiring. At any rate, these tiny charmers start at about $150 for a palm-sized, soothingly smooth owl, or a two-and-a-half-inch-wide curled-up cat.

We also adore the snail, the first animal Steuben's artists ever created, for $210. Only three and a quarter inches long, the little creature is a delightful representation of the fluidity of crystal, as is the graceful bouquet vase. Decorative as it is practical, shaped to encourage blooms to cascade over its sides, the base sells for $310.

Coming soon are several new lines, including desk accessories and tableware, by well-known international designers.

Be sure to head for the museumlike back room dedicated to special exhibitions of their engraved and sculptural works, each in its own locked, spotlit case. Prices start in the $2,200 range for a piece descriptively entitled Triangles Two. Should you wish to commemorate a very special occasion with a totally unique piece, talk to Clifford R. Palmer, who arranges all commissions. He will discuss your original concept and then coordinate with Steuben's designers to translate it into a crystal work of art. There's a $20,000 minimum.

If that's not what you had in mind, you can always have certain pieces engraved with a meaningful inscription. Ask store manager Andrea Berta about those services, which generally take six to eight weeks, depending on the time of year. The closer you get to Christmas, the longer the wait. The popularity of Steuben glass as gifts is, after all, not the private preserve of presidents.

# Tenzing & Pema

956 Madison Avenue                              (212) 288-8780
between 75th and 76th Streets
New York, NY 10021

As his two young children became real people, with distinctive personalities and active minds, Simon Abrahams found it increasingly difficult to find them captivating playthings. A certified sighter of trends and no stranger to retail (his Leg Room chain embraced the socks craze and ran with it), Simon figured fellow baby boomers were experiencing the same problem on behalf of their offspring. So he opened a thinking child's toy store named after his youngsters — son Tenzing and daughter Pema.

While the store's slogan is "Presents of Mind," Simon doesn't like the word "educational" associated with its wares. He considers the store's selection of "materials" (as opposed to toys), targeted to children 7 to 12, "challenging."

Arranged by subject — art, history, photography, nature, science, religion, music, literature, and astronomy — the store exudes a shopper-friendly informality that encourages children and adults alike to explore its treasures. It's not uncommon to find people plopped down on the polished wood floor, lost in a fantasy world created by the $3,600 six-foot-tall Renaissance-style doll house or a $7 plastic gyroscope.

We're fascinated by the assortment of colorful globes in an enormous variety of sizes and styles, from clear to musical at $12 to $160. There's even a $165 number that addresses our rapidly changing world by assuming a puzzle form. When a new country emerges, the manufacturer issues an appropriately named and shaped piece.

Equally intriguing are the possibilities for exposing children to the delights of the classics, whether of a literary or musical nature. Shakespeare can be accessed via software for a Macintosh, while a

very entertaining video entitled "Beethoven Lives Upstairs" intro-
duces the composer and his music to new fans for $24. And yes,
you can also find renditions of Will and Ludwig in books and on
tapes and CDs!

For the do-it-yourselfer in your life, there are $85 wooden looms
and $7.50 kits for making cast-metal toy soldiers. They are so
much more satisfying than your basic G. I. Joe, which Tenzing
unsuccessfully lobbied his dad to add to the inventory. Abrahams
told him that was out of the question, but may have appeased him
with the addition of Samurai Dojo, a cardboard punch-out martial
arts studio complete with rubber figures of Buddha and a samurai
master at $29. For another $9.50 each, you can buy extra rubber
swordsmen, as Robin Williams did, along with larger ones on
horseback for $16 apiece.

Harrison Ford and Woody Allen are also customers, although
it's not clear whether they're buying for themselves or for their
children—a distinction that is tough to draw with any of Tenzing
& Pema's adult clientele. What *is* clear is virtually every star in the
firmament, thanks to a $4,000 quartz-powered telescope capable of
tracking any object in the sky. We're saving our pennies for it in an
ingenious high-tech lucite "piggy bank" we got here. It's so smart
that it arranges deposited coins by denomination and is one of
Tenzing & Pema's more popular items at $14. Now if we could just
get it to balance our checkbooks . . . .

# CHAPTER SIX

# Jewelry
*Baubles, bangles, and big bucks*

*O*ne of our dearest friends says her ideal New York day is totally Italian. It begins with lunch: minestrone, linguini alla checca, and cappuccino — and then it is capped with jewelry shopping at Bulgari and Buccellati.

Even if you don't speak Italian or the "Italian" of our friend, you will do well on your quest for the best in diamonds, rubies, jade, emeralds, and all the other high-priced flavors. The lights of Times Square are dim in comparison to the stylish sparkle you will find in the famous Fifth Avenue shops: Van Cleef and Arpels, Winston, Cartier, and Tiffany — or even in the chaotic chic of the 47th Street Chasidim. Once you tour New York's "ice palaces," you will truly appreciate the wisdom of Oscar Wilde, who said, "I can resist anything except temptation."

Designing your own treasures is taking its place alongside these pillars of the jewelry establishment. These small custom houses with original craftspeople and impeccable taste may well become the Winstons of tomorrow. Their locations may be on Fifth or Madison, but their styles are decidedly nonconformist. And they're making a noticeable impact on fashion and style, not to mention jewelry boxes and wallets.

Whatever the origin, though, New York is truly lighting up these days. And all that glitters may only be glitter. Crime stories about New York haven't discouraged the sparkle at the society soirées, but they *have* given a big boost to some of the city's more celebrated costume jewelers. Their work may look real, but cost less—so much so that your bauble bucks will go a long way to outfitting you in fabulous fakes.

# *Buccellati*

46 East 57th Street                    (212) 308-2900
between Park and Madison
New York, NY 10022

Buccellati. The name caresses the tongue; the jewelry and silver bearing that name seduce the eyes.

A family enterprise founded at the turn of the century, the House of Buccellati draws upon a traditional art of gold- and silversmithing that dates back to the eighteenth century. Now run in America by the founder's namesake and grandson, Mario Buccellati II, the company maintains its reputation for innovative creations and excellent workmanship with all design and production still originating in Milan by Buccellati-trained craftsmen.

The company's presence in New York is twofold—a jewelry store in Trump Tower and a glorious space devoted to jewelry and silver in the Buccellati Building on 57th Street.

The frenzy of the Trump Tower seems a universe away once you step into the refined world of Buccellati, into a store designed to evoke the interior of a jewel box—plus fabric-covered walls and a hand-painted ceiling depicting lush foliage. Here you can marvel at the Buccellati signature pieces that employ a jewelry technique pioneered by the firm: texture engraving. Using special tools, lines are engraved in the metal, creating beautiful patterns. They capture and reflect light in a unique way, with the metal adopting a lustrous jewellike appearance. The result is breathtaking, like the intricately patterned yellow and white gold cuff-bracelet with 140 diamonds totaling 9.11 carats and priced at $128,000. There's a distinctive delicacy about Buccellati designs, whether they take the form of an elaborate $81,500 yellow and white gold necklace with nine oval rubellites, forty-two sapphires, and fifty-six diamonds or a sweet $1,750 yellow, white, and rose gold pin fashioned as a thistle and laced with silver.

Like his predecessor Robert Philipson, manager William Feldman is a fountain of knowledge about jewelry, Buccellati and otherwise. If none of his one-of-a-kind pieces quite suits you, rest assured that something can be designed especially for you, to your specifications.

The store's silver store is equally intriguing. The two levels are connected by a dramatic curved staircase. At the base, cradled in the curve, rests a magnificent silver centerpiece. It is cast as a mythological sea setting with Neptune as the central character, and playful mermaids, seahorses, and children surrounding him. The tray, balanced on ten supports, encases a mirror that gives the illusion of a reflecting pool. The centerpiece took three years to complete and is priced at $750,000.

The first floor houses the Buccellati collection of jewelry and the flatware and hollow ware — all twenty-three patterns with prices ranging from $660 to $1,570 for a five-piece place setting are on the second floor. We're partial to Milano at $690. It's contemporary, yet timeless, and graced with classical elements like beading, a combination typical of the Buccellati style in silver and in jewelry. As one family member says, "We have been influenced by Italian Classical and Baroque jewelry and even more by eighteenth-century French and Italian art. We use elements from each to create contemporary style, but we reject practically no influence — be it architecture or even a sunset. After all, some things are universally beautiful. And we are not afraid to incorporate anything in the design and execution of our pieces."

A little of the Italian classic meets contemporary influence in our favorite Buccellati gift item — the $398 champagne opener. Executed in what Buccellati calls Old Italian, it is elaborately beautiful and eminently practical. It not only makes popping the cork a mere twist of the wrist, it even sports a device to cut the wire.

Buccellati — the beauty of the name does the product proud.

# Bulgari

730 Fifth Avenue                              (212) 315-9000
at 57th Street
New York, NY 10019

The name is Greek but the home base of this jewelry dynasty is Rome, where the shop that Sotirio Bulgari opened near the

Spanish Steps with sons Giorgio and Constantino in 1905 was once described by Andy Warhol as the city's "most important museum of contemporary art." Since 1977, New York has had such a minimuseum tucked away in a corner of The Pierre. But the growing demand for Bulgari's life-style jewelry, which works as well with jeans as it does with evening gowns, prompted the current generation of Bulgari brothers, Paolo and Nicola, along with their nephew Francesco Trapani to expand their Manhattan base with this Fifth Avenue store.

Designed by Piero Sartogo, it's essentially an enlarged version of the gem of a boutique in The Pierre—lots of glass, mirrors, chrome, and brass skillfully combined to produce a luxuriously rich, surprisingly warm environment. It's the kind of place that encourages you to come in, relax, and relish the opportunity to fondle beautiful jewelry. The divinely debonair Nicola, who's often on the floor, encourages you to pick up the pieces, hold them up to the light, and put them on. He maintains that "fine jewels are to be enjoyed and experienced," a philosophy that explains their latest venture.

Paolo, Nicola, and Francesco recently introduced Bulgari Eau Parfumée, which combines fine tea aromas with Mediterranean fragrances and is available exclusively in Bulgari shops worldwide. We found it to be quite spectacular, as is the elegant glass bottle with its green nuances, specially styled to represent the contents. Eau Parfumée is really a natural new direction for Bulgari; Nicola says the fragrance was designed for those who select a perfume using the same attention and care with which they select a jewel.

And as you experience Bulgari jewelry, you'll notice certain signature traits. The firm emphasizes the use of colored stones and tends to use yellow gold for settings rather than white gold or platinum. They also have an interesting habit of intermingling gold with steel and other seemingly incongruous materials. And the cabochon cut—rounded and polished rather than faceted—first adopted by Bulgari in the 30s revolutionized the look of serious jewelry, as did their innovative use of semiprecious stones like tourmalines, rubellite, topazes, peridots, amethysts, coral, and turquoise.

The broad range of materials and the Bulgari penchant for the constant evolution of their designs allows for prices that run a very wide gamut, several hundred dollars to well over a million. It's likely that whatever your budget you can find something that suits it. The inventory of their handcrafted jewelry is large and varied, with prices and styles for the young as well as the not-so-young.

An 18-carat gold necklace caught our attention, its heavy carved links accented by steel balls allowing it to rest solidly at the base of the neck. More formal are the six-millimeter pearl necklace laced with amethyst rondelles set in gold, and a stunning gold and diamond collar—large, gold heart-shaped links alternating with oversized links of pavé diamonds set in geometric patterns. For truly important evenings there's a pair of killer earrings of pavé diamonds alternating with baguettes and surrounding two good-sized marquis-cut diamonds. A 7.66-carat flawless oval diamond surrounded by twenty-eight baguette emeralds weighing 4.23 carats makes a perfectly complementary ring. Check with the store for prices; they prefer to discuss them with you directly!

For everyday Bulgari wear, there's a never-ending stream of new styles of modestly priced bracelets, gold and steel woven to embrace aquamarines, pink tourmelines, or amethysts and running about $9,000. They're the sort of pieces you can put on and never take off, as is the new Quadrato watch, available for men ($4,300) as well as women ($3,900). Its squareness presents a classic shape in an entirely new way. The dial is an opaque black, with the Bulgari logo engraved on the side of the watch itself.

Typical of Bulgari, the Quadrato is just as finely finished on the inside as it is on the out, just as beautifully detailed. Indeed, most Bulgari pieces could be considered reversible if it were possible to physically turn them inside out. Knowing Bulgari, they're probably working on it. As Nicola says, "design, design, design. It's everything."

## Cartier

653 Fifth Ave. at 52nd Street          (212) 753-0111
New York, NY 10022

Cartier established its beachhead in America in the best Manhattan tradition. In 1917, Pierre Cartier, grandson of the firm's founder, traded a couple of strings of beads for a five-story Fifth Avenue mansion, now designated a historical landmark by the city of New York and still Cartier's home. Of course, even in the early years of the century, the double strand pearl necklace Pierre

Cartier handed over to Mrs. Morton Plant in exchange for her palacelike home was worth considerably more than the legendary $24 value of the beads used to purchase the isle of Manhattan — $1,200,000 to be precise. Even translated into today's dollars, it would seem that Pierre had as fine an eye for real estate as he did for jewelry.

But it was really his older brother Louis who was responsible for catapulting the family business that began in a small Paris work- shop in 1847 into the firm that Edward VII of England proclaimed, "if they have become the Jewelers of Kings, it is because they are the King of Jewelers." Louis was the first jeweler to work with platinum. He was the first to fashion transformable diadems — crowns and tiaras that could double as necklaces or other orna- ments. Today that may not sound like a stunning innovation, but in an era when the coronation of Edward VII generated orders for 102 royally jeweled headpieces, the notion of being able to wear one's crown on occasions other than those of state was both novel and intriguing.

Louis also put Cartier on the map for timepieces. He was deter- mined to restore the great clock-making traditions that had been lost toward the end of the 18th century. The clocks and watches made under his supervision competed with each other for their beauty, originality, and technical perfection. The best-known example of all three qualities is the Cartier tank watch, designed as a tribute to the American Expeditionary Forces and presented in 1918 to General Pershing and several of his officers. Louis's in- spiration for the now classic design had been a World War I com- bat tank he'd seen the year before.

The other Cartier hallmark initiated by Louis is the animal styles so beloved by the Duchess of Windsor. The sale of her jewels revived the popularity of Cartier's "Great Cats." If you want to jump on the bandwagon, we suggest a breathtaking Cartier tiger necklace. Dazzlingly rendered in pavé canary diamonds and striped with onyx, these one-of-a-kind pieces are so intricate that they take two years to create and run $450,000 and up. Should your favorite have been sold by the time you stop in, you can always con- sole yourself with a $6,100 trinket, the charming 18-carat-gold panther pin with its bright emerald eyes and pert onyx nose.

Or you might consult with salon director Jill King about another of the fabulously jeweled cats, like the platinum and diamond panther brooch with sapphire spots. Indeed, you have to speak to someone about them as the prices are only available upon request. But don't be intimidated by the prospect. The whole staff under Jill's gentle direction is a delight. Each is an expert, dedicated to excellence. Then there's the legendary Cartier service department run by Worthy Bodey, and we can't resist saying she's indeed "worthy" of the honor. She can arrange everything from reloading your pen and opening the jammed lock on your leather attaché case to redesigning the brooch passed on by your great aunt. You'll enjoy thorough assistance dispensed with warmth and humor.

George Raymond oversees the stationery department. It was another of Louis's innovations to develop and carry accessories complementary to precious gems — like original creations in enamel, silver, and crystal, fancy leather goods and distinguished stationery. Certainly, George and his lovely selection of writing papers, cards, invitations, and announcements must be just what Louis had in mind. George is one of the country's foremost experts on protocol, so you can be sure of the social acceptability of anything you order from him.

But the person truly synonymous with Cartier in New York is the firm's U.S. Chairman of the Board, Ralph Destino. Tall, lean, and elegantly handsome, Ralph is an accessible, hands-on executive, always happy to make sure that all your Cartier needs are attended to. He's just as concerned about your satisfaction as he is Elizabeth Taylor's or Elton John's or Lionel Ritchie's. Whether you're in the market for the $7,300 Tank Americaine watch, the latest version of the celebrated classic, or the price-available-on-request white and yellow pavé diamond tiger watch that doubles as an entrance-making bracelet, Ralph wants you to enjoy your Cartier experience.

We always do. It's a pleasure just to wander through the plush store, ogling all the goodies like the new men's fragrance, Pasha de Cartier ($180). Speaking of fragrance, we've discovered a terrific and inexpensive souvenir of our Cartier visits — the divine Panthere de Cartier perfume. For only $235 you get an ounce of wonderful scent in an exquisite refillable flacon that admirably represents Cartier's distinctly elegant, always tasteful art.

# *Ciner Fashion Jewelers*

20 West 37th Street　　　　　　　　(212) 947-3770
between Fifth and Sixth Avenues　Fax (212) 643-0357
New York, NY 10018

Now here's a label to look for—not at their wholesale-only showroom, but at Neiman Marcus, Ciro's on Fifth, and Mariko New York. Ciner makes the most amazing costume jewelry, absolutely indistinguishable from the very real and very expensive thing. In fact, director of sales Jacqueline Rogers takes great pride in the knowledge that "at every Hollywood function, every Washington ball, every East Coast gala, you will see many prominent stars and socialites wearing incredible 'Ciner Designs' that have the look of Winston, Bulgari, Van Cleef, etc."

There's a good reason Ciner jewelry looks so real. The firm, founded by Emanuel Ciner in 1892, operated as a manufacturer of fine jewelry until the 1930s, when the family recognized a growing market for beautiful bargains. They entered the business of fabulous *fauxs* by applying to their manufacturing the same techniques they had employed to make the more precious variety. Today, having recently celebrated the firm's 100th anniversary, Emanuel's daughter Pat and her husband David Hill run the business with their children Jean and Douglas, still insisting that everything be made by hand. Furthermore, each piece is finished with an 18-carat-gold-plated process that withstands the test of time. We know women who inherited their mothers' Ciner jewelry—it looks just as good and is just as fashionable as the day it was purchased decades ago. And Pat assures you that if you ever happen to misplace something, you will likely be able to replace it, as the timeless collection includes pieces that have been in the line for years. They do, of course, frequently add exciting new things, like a fabulous rhinestone dragonfly pin ($350) and a jeweled enamel butterfly pin ($300). We also adore Ciner's black enamel frog, complete with gold bumps and emerald cabochon eyes for approximately $180, depending on the retailer. There's a pavé version closer to $220. Other brooches are multi-jeweled with large cabochon or pearl centers and sell for about $325. At around

$1,300, Ciner's gold and rhinestone collar is a knockout, particularly with a strapless dress or gown.

By our calculation, you could put together a world-class Ciner jewelry collection for less than $10,000. And we guarantee that only you and your bank account would know the difference. Your friends would have to attack you with a loupe, and even then it's doubtful they'd know what to look for. We've graciously accepted any number of compliments on our Ciner pieces from some of Winston's and Bulgari's best clients, while commiserating with them over the cost of insurance and the security risks associated with wearing such serious jewels!

You don't have to wait for your next trip to New York to start that collection, either. Ciner jewelry is sold at fine stores worldwide. Just call Jacqueline and ask her where you can find it in your area—or ask that friend of yours who has been a little coy about the origins of the awesome diamond necklace she's been wearing lately.

# The Gorevic Collection

635 Madison Avenue                          (212) 832-9000
at 59th Street                          Fax (212) 832-1509
New York, NY 10022

The Gorevics have been at it for nearly eighty years; they're into the third generation of specialists in antique and estate jewelry, objets d'art, Russian and Viennese enamels, antique silver, nineteenth-century French animal sculptures, and, of all things, American carousel horses. They also pride themselves on their selection of contemporary Italian designer jewelry. Diversification is a Gorevic byword and clearly sets their firm apart from any other jeweler in the city.

It all started nearly a century ago, when Ferdinand Gorevic left his native Russia for Czechoslovakia, where he opened an antique store. In fear of the Nazi takeover in 1940, he set sail for New York, where he opened the precursor of the current establishment. Eventually, his son Charles and his grandson Roger joined him in the business.

Today, it is Roger and his wife, Cali, who are most in evidence in the store, though Charles makes regular appearances. In fact, you can count on a Gorevic being on duty Monday through Saturday, 10:00 A.M. to 6:00 P.M.

Shopping, even browsing, here draws you into the family. Roger and Cali are more interested in developing a regular clientele, in making new friends, than in just making a sale. For them, it's not a proper transaction unless they feel they can expect to see the buyer again. To help ensure the comfort of their clients, whom they treat more like guests, Roger and Cali even take pains to accommodate youngsters who might have tagged along. A desk in the back is stocked with crayons and paper. The resulting works of art are proudly displayed in a gallery devoted exclusively to the children.

But make no mistake, while friendly and unassuming, The Gorevic Collection is the site of very serious merchandise, serious even when it tickles your fancy with a cherished memory. We were quite taken with the exquisite antique natural pearl "sword" pin for $1,400, and spent a goodly amount of time browsing through the large selection of men's antique cuff links and studs, which range from $500 to $10,000. And while you can spend several hundred thousand on, say, a magnificent European-made yellow and blue sapphire/diamond necklace (over 90 carats), there are also jewelry pieces for as low as $50.

Be sure to have a look at the antique sculptures. If it hasn't sold by the time you stop by, the rare bronze by Antoine Louis Barye, called "Roger Abducting Angelica on the Hippogriff," is something to see ($135,000).

Should silver be your heart's desire, you will fall in love with the Gorevics. The exceptional antique silver collection ranges from the sublime to the ridiculous. You'll find great wedding or hostess gifts like Georgian berry spoons ($150) and French wine tasters ($150 to $5,000), not to mention a $140,000 Paul Storr gilt tankard or a $300,000 Storr soup tureen.

And remember, whether your budget calls for a $450 gold charm by Italian designer Pomellato or that expensive tureen, you will be subject to the added value of becoming a member of the Gorevics's extended family.

# Kenneth Jay Lane

677 Fifth Avenue                           (212) 750-2858
between 53rd and 54th Streets
New York, NY 10022

The story goes that one day Richard Burton walked into the connubial bedroom to find the bed strewn with astonishing baubles. "Priceless" necklaces, bracelets, and rings covered virtually every square inch. He flew into one of his famous larger-than-life rages, certain that the divine Elizabeth had gone on a shopping rampage at Harry Winston or some other store where one can drop millions. It took all of La Taylor's considerable feminine wiles to calm him down enough to listen to her explanation that it was only Kenny Lane's costume jewelry.

*Only* is perhaps a bit of an understatement. Ever since Kenneth became convinced that fake jewelry could be just as beautiful as the real thing and created his first rhinestone-encrusted bangles in 1963, he has been responsible for any number of raised eyebrows and catty comments about where *she* might have gotten *that!* Since he works like a fine jeweler, devising his designs in wax, or by carving or twisting the metals, it can be extremely difficult to identify Kenneth Jay Lane pieces as imitations.

Bows are best-sellers, especially the rhinestone-and-gold version for $95. We fell in love with the rhinestone bow trimmed in black enamel, a Tiffany copy. It'll set you back $250, but the real thing at Tiffany is $100,000, and it'll definitely set minds wondering. The "diamonds" are so bright because Ken has many of the stones he uses made exclusively for him, to his very exacting specifications.

Of course, due to her refreshing candor, we all know about the fabulous fakeness of Barbara Bush's famous pearls (the three-strand choker runs about $500, and, in keeping with the times, you'll also find Hillary Rodham Clinton's saxophone pin for just $30).

So what's stopping you from enjoying that incredibly delicious feeling only exquisite jewelry can bestow? No matter how much of the real stuff you have in the vault, another trinket or two can't hurt. What about a terrific-looking brooch — a charming diamond bow trimmed in gold. At $85 it's the perfect finishing touch for that little Saint Laurent cocktail suit.

Still, the pièce de résistance of the collection is Kenneth's signature multicolored stone belt — a knockout, priced at $875. Self-consciously and deliberately counterfeit, it's fun and flirty. It also comes in an all-rhinestone version, at the same price, for real evening sparkle.

Vice president Michele Doolan is the person to call. She'll assemble a versatile jewelry ensemble for you. Since it's from Kenneth Jay Lane, you'll know it's fake, but it's also definitely fabulous.

# *Marina B.*

| 809 Madison Avenue | (212) 288-9708 |
| between 67th and 68th Streets | Fax (212) 744-6532 |
| New York, NY 10021 | |

There's something familiar about Marina B.'s creations — something about the heavy settings, the massive stones, the use of cabochons and pavé motifs that reminds you of a very distinctive style of jewelry design. Once you realize the *B.* is short for *Bulgari*, it all becomes quite clear.

When Marina Bulgari left the family business to strike out on her own, she had to agree not to use her last name in connection with her new independent enterprise. She may have lost a few letters, but she gained a rather singular period and the freedom to create what *Connoisseur* has described as some of "the most extraordinary pieces of jewelry seen in this century."

In New York, she displays her work in a sleek jewel box of a store designed by Gai Aulenti (who did Paris's Musee d'Orsay) and furnished in black lacquer and brown suede. Simple cabinets lined in white silk are theatrically lit to set off the jewels inside. It's a quiet, discreet place conducive to discussions about major purchases.

If you're interested in trying something on, you'll be ushered to the rear of the store and seated in private. There you will be dazzled by leather tray after tray of Marina's opulent but startlingly modern jewelry. She has taken the traditional art she learned from her father, the great jeweler Constantine Bulgari, and revolutionized it with the use of twentieth-century technology.

What makes Marina B.'s creations so instantly recognizable? Simply the way they fit — a quality not usually associated with jewelry. She likes her pieces to conform to the body; her chokers and bracelets fit like clothes because she's devised a tiny spring implanted in each piece that enables it to cling comfortably to the neck or wrist.

We like the look and the fit of the Onda I (Marina often names her pieces after friends or the person for whom the prototype was fashioned). With diamonds set in 18-carat gold, the Onda I sells for $15,000. More elaborate and perhaps more representative of Marina B. is the choker with the ionized black finish on an 18-carat yellow gold base. Five different patterns in diamonds dance along the surface — more than ten carats in all. It's also part of the Onda series, and costs $28,000.

In addition to her frequent use of "black" gold, Marina has another signature — a heart shape, minus the indentation. One spectacular use is the Caty reversible earring. A tiny hinge makes it possible to flip the casings around the large central pear-shaped sapphire. So the earrings can be worn with onyx surrounds, pavé diamond, or one of each — day into night, night into day. What flexibility!

Perhaps it's such a combination of practicality and exquisite extravagance that draws fans like Sophia Loren, Countess Counselo Crespi, and Princess Yasmin Aga Khan. We're sure the personal rapport Marina establishes with many of her clients is another attraction. She works with them to alter pieces to suit their tastes and to create designs based on their ideas. If you have something in mind, be sure to check her schedule, as she is in town only about four times a year.

In the meantime, treat yourself to a serious look at the magical, unrestrained, even playful jewelry that is Marina B.'s.

# Norman Landsberg

66 West 47th Street            (212) 586-7422
between Fifth and Sixth Avenues
New York, NY 10036

Everyone's most outlandish jewelry fantasy can become a reality at this small counter manned for more than forty years by Norman Landsberg. A veteran of the industry for some fifty years, Norman has developed an outstanding business based on quality merchandise at very competitive prices. The arrival of his two good-looking and extremely knowledgeable sons, Jonathan and Jeffrey, indicates that we can all look forward to the Landsberg touch for at least another generation.

It's a good thing, too. While other counters in this crowded arcade are often deserted, there's always action at the Landsbergs'. Their business has been built solely on referral; relationships with their clients are all-important. As Jeffrey says, "You may have to wait in line here in Landsberg, but then no one here is going to give you a line. The clients know they can depend on our reputation for quality and value—that's why they come back." That reputation is truly comforting in an era of almost daily reports of jewelry scams.

Whether you want to spend a little or a lot, you'll no doubt find something you like. There are handmade 18-carat diamond pieces from $500 to $10,000; earrings range from $50 to $5,000; and bracelets can run $150 and up.

What a relief to know that the bargain here that borders on being too good to be true is true indeed. You see, Landsberg's young designer, Jackie Greenstein, is a treasure. Not only are her own creations divine, but she can re-create anything imaginable. Bring her your ideas. Jackie will do a sketch and price it for your approval. Once given the okay, they'll fashion a wax mold and cast the piece. It's a great way to save lots of money.

Please, let's keep this just between us—Norman Landsberg is a real find, one we don't want to share with just anyone.

# Runsdorf, Inc.

19 West 47th Street          (212) 575-1919
between Fifth and Sixth Avenues     Fax (212) 575-1991
New York, NY 10036

Lee Runsdorf, who runs this little gem of a place, has been in the jewelry business for forty-six years. His family was involved in the trade for four generations before him, and now his daughter Elise, a graduate gemologist, represents the sixth. To compound the family's association with jewelry, Lee's Belgian-born wife, Lucette, hails from a long line of diamond merchants. Her family has been supplying his family with glorious diamonds for ages.

Today Runsdorf's business encompasses estate jewelry, loose certificate diamonds, and closeouts from other manufacturers, as well as their own designs. It operates on both a retail and a wholesale level. While many of the other merchants in the diamond district were trained by this family, the Runsdorfs' business still stands a cut above the rest.

It has a lot to do with the broad scope of their merchandise and their sources. The pieces here are distinctive, starting with unusually detailed gold bracelets for $300. We found a spectacular pair of David Webb earrings for $30,000 and a wonderful Van Cleef Art Deco diamond watch for $25,000, not to mention Schlumberger diamond clip earrings for $4,000. At these prices, they probably cost less here than they did from Webb, Van Cleef, and Schlumberger in the first place!

If you can't deal with the concept of "previously owned," you can enter virgin jewelry territory with a piece made by Lee just for you. He showed us an amazing necklace he had just finished for a client—round diamonds with a total weight of fifty carats and a price of $60,000. Of course, Lee insists on issuing a certificate stating the size and quality of all stones and backed by the Gemologist Institute of America. None of those famous shady 47th Street deals here.

Lee will also search the world over for whatever you have in mind. He recently fulfilled a client's commission with the purchase of a flawless 7.56-carat, $250,000, emerald-cut diamond from Sotheby's in Geneva. He wouldn't tell us who it's for, but we do know that many of his clients appear regularly in the nation's social columns. They come from across the country to take advantage of Runsdorf's extraordinary selection and prices. Many have grandfathers who bought from Lee's grandfather; frequenting Runsdorf tends to be a family tradition. After all, it's one of the oldest established American wholesale and retail jewelry businesses in New York. Why not put a little something from Runsdorf on your family tree?

# Tiffany & Co.

| Fifth Avenue at 57th Street | (212) 755-8000 |
| New York, NY 10022 | Fax (212) 605-4465 |

When you visit this cavernous (by jewelry store standards) emporium, with aisles and elevators swarming with people (3,000 on a slow day, 25,000 on a Christmas-season Saturday), it's difficult to believe that when Tiffany & Co. (then Tiffany and Young) opened in lower Manhattan on September 18, 1837, the first day's sales came to a grand total of $4.98. Today, despite the broad range of merchandise and prices, there's not a single item you can take home in one of their signature robin's-egg blue bags or boxes for that amount.

Charles Tiffany and John Young didn't start out to establish a world-class, let alone world-famous, jewelry store. Rather, theirs was a shop full of stationery and "fancy goods" — fashion and home accessories that had nothing whatsoever to do with jewelry. A couple of years later, a line of paste jewelry was introduced, but it wasn't until the mid-1840s that the real thing was offered — diamonds, not paste. Indeed Tiffany's association with fine gemstones was largely a quirk of fate. It just so happened that in 1848 John Young's annual European buying trip coincided with the final downfall of the French monarchy. By the time he reached Paris, the city was in chaos, overflowing with aristocrats long on jewels but short on cash and desperate to flee the country. With the glut of diamonds on the market, prices dropped dramatically, and John, knowing that partner Charles would enthusiastically approve, took full advantage of the situation, acquiring, among other treasures, a substantial share of the French crown jewels.

Having already experienced the benefits of publicity (his then-novel policy of putting a non-negotiable price tag on every item in the store had made headlines nationwide), Charles leaked the story of Tiffany's priceless acquisitions to the press and the store's identity as a purveyor of fine jewelry was assured. It was reinforced by the development of the six-pronged Tiffany setting that revolutionized the manner of mounting gems — formerly, settings had covered all but the top of the stone. And the Tiffany legend became indelible with the 1877 purchase of the "Tiffany Diamond," a 287.42-carat yellow diamond. Even after being cut to 128 carats it remains the world's largest flawless canary diamond, and a proudly displayed symbol of the Tiffany mystique.

Tiffany today runs the gamut, from a dazzling array of diamonds to Limoges porcelain china and sterling flatware. They have a fabulous selection of exclusive watches, leather bags, even personal stationery. And while you can still pick up less expensive items like cuff links, keyrings, and belt buckles, there are many more, shall we say, high-caliber items in the store's inventory than there were during the darkest period of Tiffany's history, 1979 to 1984, when Avon was in charge.

Charles Tiffany was the first and last Tiffany to preside over the store. Since his demise, it has operated under a succession of owners and managements, none more successful than the current stewardship of William R. Chaney. Under his direction, the store walks the fine line of appearing exclusive with showpieces like an $800,000 pear-shaped diamond ring and a $250,000 eighteen-inch string of iridescent Tahitian black pearls, while not intimidating its large middle-class clientele, who count on Tiffany's for their wedding invitations and classic single strands of cultured pearls, a Tiffany specialty. Avon, on the other hand, had stepped way over the line to appeal to the masses with a preponderance of $7 wine glasses and garden variety engagement rings, displaying very little truly serious jewelry. Tiffany's was, for a while, a place not to have breakfast, or anything else as far as we were concerned.

But all that has changed now, and Tiffany's is once again a worthy destination for anyone trying to unload a thousand dollars a day (before lunch). One reason to stop by is to ogle the work of Paloma Picasso. Her bold, statement-making jewelry, in sterling as well as gold with exotically colored stones like rubellite or citrine, sells for $60 to $70,000, a typical Tiffany range. As a designer whose work is only found here, she follows in the footsteps of such luminaries as Elsa Peretti. Indeed, Elsa remains a popular attraction here — her counter is always crowded, often by the Japanese who seem particularly drawn to her fluid designs that are so very close to nature. You'll recall that Elsa is credited with spurring the development of sterling silver jewelry design and was heralded for her innovative "diamonds-by-the-yard" design — diamonds set in 18-carat-gold chains.

Check out the additions to Tiffany's lush Signature Series, with prices ranging from under $1,000 to over $17,000. The woven gold accessories are particularly apropos for business- or evening-wear, a feature we really appreciate when it's a rush-rush kind of day.

After the main floor filled with cases of precious jewels, our favorite floor at Tiffany's is the second. It's the home of the silver for which we have a particular weakness, as do many other connoisseurs ever since Tiffany started winning international prizes for its designs more than a hundred years ago. In 1867 the firm was the first American silvermaker ever to be awarded a prize by a foreign jury at the Paris Exposition. The rich and intricate English King flatware pattern, first introduced in 1885, has developed a worldwide following. And now, courtesy of Tiffany, 150 place settings of it grace Blair House, the recently renovated official guest quarters of the White House — quite a donation at $480 each.

The other main attractions on the second floor are the spectacular table settings — by far the highlight of the store's otherwise somewhat pedestrian decor. Changed every six weeks (and also adorning the third's china and crystal department), they're always the creation of artists, fashion designers, socialites, interior decorators — persons of note and taste. They're usually worth a visit. Be sure to look for American Garden, a recently introduced collection of sterling flatware and porcelain, designed to "celebrate" America's plants and flowers.

Also new is *The Tiffany Gourmet Cookbook*, compiled by Tiffany's Design Director John Loring, scrumptiously filled with recipes and entertaining secrets from notable hosts and hostesses throughout the world, from Wolfgang Puck to Yves Saint Laurent. For $50, it's a great gift — buy it for yourself! Or send it to a friend–with a personal note on stationery purchased on the second floor. Assistant buyer, Whitney O'Connor, has that department looking very smart indeed.

You can see one of Tiffany's most famous sights without even setting foot in the store — its five windows along Fifth Avenue and 57th Street. Since 1955, Gene Moore has been amusing New Yorkers with his titillating displays. With his ability to reflect prominent issues of the day while complementing exquisite pieces of jewelry, it's impossible to walk by his windows without taking a peek. Once during a city transit strike he decorated the windows with roller skates, pogo sticks, and a unicycle. A water shortage prompted him to feature a fountain merrily splashing gin. And every Easter he creates a new set of windows using eggs in some shape or form — one year, he even scrambled them!

# *Van Cleef & Arpels*

744 Fifth Avenue                                                    (212) 644-9500
at 57th Street
New York, NY 10022

One of the most revered names in jewelry is the result of the union between a Dutch diamond cutter and the French daughter of a dealer in precious stones. Alfred Van Cleef left Amsterdam for the brighter lights of Paris, where he met his wife-to-be and went into partnership with her brother Julien Arpels. In 1906, they opened a salon on the prestigious Place Vendôme (where it remains today), followed by locations throughout France and, in 1929, a New York branch. Van Cleef & Arpels is still family-owned and -operated; presently there are two U.S. locations (Beverly Hills and Palm Beach) in addition to the Manhattan salon, which has called Fifth Avenue home since 1942.

The creative use of rubies, sapphires, and emeralds is the Van Cleef & Arpels hallmark; their designs have a distinctive delicacy. Stones are shown in soft, feminine forms like the fancy yellow and white diamond "Rose" clips created to commemorate Van Cleef's sponsorship of the 1992 Peggy Rockefeller Rose Garden Dinner Dance held at New York's Botanical Garden. Many leading organizations and charities are supported by the firm as a way of expressing their appreciation and giving something back to the communities in which they have experienced success.

Much of that success is due to Van Cleef's 1936 perfection of the "invisible setting." It is exactly what its name suggests, a setting constructed so that none of it, not a single prong, is visible to the naked eye. When you see a flower clip, its petals invisibly set with rubies or sapphires, each cut and fit with such precision that the surface has a velvety look and the setting is completely hidden, you can be sure it's the work of Van Cleef & Arpels.

A spectacular example of the invisible setting, specially created by Van Cleef & Arpels, is called the "Parure Galliera" and consists of a necklace, earclips, and ring, set with 1,717 rubies enhanced by marquise diamonds. A magnificent example of a classic technique matched with a contemporary design, it was created to commemorate a retrospective exhibition at the Palais Galliera of Van Cleef's eight-decade history.

That history includes almost as many sparkling names as jewels. The Duchess of Windsor wore a Van Cleef-designed sapphire and diamond "Marriage Contract" bracelet and clip on her wedding day, and Prince Rainier conferred the title of "Official Purveyor to the Municipality" upon the firm in 1956 when he invited them to create Princess Grace's wedding present. Painter Marc Chagall designed a unique clip as a gift for his wife at Van Cleef's Paris workshop, and ladies ranging from Barbara Hutton to

Queen Sirikit of Thailand to Elizabeth Taylor have adored the Van Cleef jewels with which they've been adorned.

Impeccable, flexible settings are a Van Cleef signature. Imagine a necklace of alternating oval- and emerald-cut emeralds surrounded by round diamonds set in platinum. Not too difficult, but just try to figure how they could make it so that you could wear it as: 1) a double row of emeralds in the front with diamonds continuing in the back; 2) a single row of emeralds all the way around; or 3) a single row of emeralds in the front with diamonds in the back with the shorter row detached and worn as a bracelet. "Upwards of a million dollars," it was snapped up shortly after we marveled at its practicality. But don't worry; typical of Van Cleef artistry, there's bound to be something similar to it, though not exactly like it — each piece is copyrighted and numbered.

The good news is that at Van Cleef you can work your way up to such important pieces and still savor the renowned quality and workmanship. Their boutique on the main floor of Bergdorf Goodman, right next door, features items priced from $1,000 on up. Ask for Nancy. She's a delight and seems to really enjoy helping novices navigate the jewelry roadmap. You'll love the terrific collection of gold and diamond day-into-evening pieces.

In the main salon, ask for our favorite salesman, William Lorenzo. Among other things, he'll show you the unsurpassed collection of floral jewelry, with clips, earclips, and necklaces featuring roses, daffodils, gardenias, and marigolds in stunning combinations of diamonds and colored stones. Take a look, too, at one of our favorite necklaces featuring a collection of brilliantly white oval diamonds with a total weight of sixty-six carats. They're surrounded by pairs of marquis-shaped diamonds with a total weight of thirty-four carats. So now we're talking a one-hundred-carat necklace with a price tag of $1,363,000, yet for all that it is surprisingly delicate, even subtle. But then, what else would you expect from Van Cleef & Arpels?

# CHAPTER SEVEN

# Beauty and Health

*"If Eyes were made for seeing then beauty is its own excuse for being."*
Ralph Waldo Emerson

*"Beauty draws us with a single hair."*
Alexander Pope

*"Beauty calls and glory leads the way."*
Nathaniel Lee

A trend that started in the '80s has exploded in the '90s. Men look in the mirror almost as often as women, and, like women, they see things that could be, should be, and will be improved.

New York is chock-full of places to make women and men more beautiful and more handsome. It can be the hair: a stylish cut, a richer look in the same color, a helping hand to remove or hide those gray strands.

Or it can be a new shade of lipstick, a different eyeliner, a simple gloss, or a complete makeover. New York is one big beauty establishment, with separate doors for men and women. What goes on behind the doors is your secret; what comes out is something to be praised and enjoyed.

Note to male readers: Do not skip this page or this section!

The greatest cosmetic aid is the glow of robust good health, and the city provides many exercise palaces. They come with or without machines. You can walk or jog to nowhere on a treadmill, climb a thousand stairs without ever going higher, or stretch muscles even Arnold Schwarzenegger wasn't sure he had. And if you overdo it, there are masseurs in a dozen different disciplines to make you feel good again.

If you're to shop in the most elegant places and dine in the most fabulous restaurants, then, ladies and gentlemen, you want to look your best. As our old friend, John Keats phrased it: "Beauty is truth, truth, beauty — that is all ye know on earth, and all ye need to know."

# SUPPLIES

## *Boyds of Madison Avenue*

655 Madison Avenue                    (212) 838-6558
between 60th and 61st Streets    Fax (212) 832-0972
New York, NY 10021

It used to be that the front window at Boyds of Madison Avenue was filled with what could only be described as a jumble. Today, that's still true, only there's twice as much jumble because Boyds has doubled its space. So now there are two windows, both filled with a truly world-class selection of cosmetics and perfumes, accessories, hair-care and bath products, costume jewelry and watches, and the occasional fox boa. Cher, Liza Minnelli, Diana Ross, George C. Scott, Tony Roberts, and Jackie Onassis are fans of Boyds, the city's best source of personal hygiene and beauty products.

With more space, there's more merchandise (sporty apparel, eyewear, handbags, optical-quality mirrors) and a variety of added services (facials, manicures, pedicures). Albert Fader, who has owned Boyds for the last fifty-two years, carries an even larger inventory that specializes in things impossible to find elsewhere. With his wife, Carol, Albert frequents the far corners of the earth seeking unusual but quality products. What they haven't been able to buy, they've had made for their private-label line by Europe's finest manufacturers.

Pretty, blond, and vivacious, Carol always looks perfect and is happy to share her beauty secrets with you. She oversees twenty makeup artists, who will retouch or redo your face, in return for a $50 purchase—an easy requirement with Boyds' exceptional products.

Take the terrific German-made line filler pencil; for $13.75 it does a magnificent job of filling all those bothersome little lines around the eye and mouth. Then there's the most incredible collapsible hairbrush, actually capable of brushing even the thickest hair. It slides perfectly into a lady's evening bag (even into Judith Leiber's exquisite minaudière) or a gentleman's briefcase and costs only $9.98.

Ever wonder how Joan Collins's lipstick always seems to sit perfectly on those pretty, pouty lips of hers? Seems Carol introduced her to something called Sealed Lips; once applied, it keeps lipstick adhering to lips through eating, smoking, kissing, or whatever (especially whatever). For $8.75, how can you possibly beat it?

Carol's no doctor, but she swears by Eye Tucks—a $29.95 nonsurgical eyelift that really works. Carol won't say exactly who, but she proudly claims that any number of famous and beautiful faces benefit from its regular use.

Many of those faces also benefit from Boyds' exclusive line of Renoir cosmetics. Boyds' own private label, the Renoir products are first rate and well priced—lipsticks at $14.75, mascara (the late Greta Garbo bought no other) for $14.75, and foundations starting at $23.50.

As for hair, Boyds has everything necessary and accessory— Italian boar-bristle brushes so fabulous that fifty of the nation's best beauty salons work with nothing else, and ornaments—racks and racks, drawers and drawers filled with them.

Needless to say, you'll need lots of time at Boyds—time to sort through all this, to make the right decision. So try confining your Boyds shopping to weekdays between 10:00 A.M. and 1:00 P.M.— they tend to be the least hectic hours. Boyds is open weekdays from 8:30 A.M. to 8:00 P.M., but the early mornings and the afternoons are crazy. Saturdays are nothing short of insane—from 9:30 A.M. to 7:00 P.M.—and so they're now open Sundays from noon to 6:00 P.M.

If your main interest is a makeover, call for an appointment. Facials are $60, manicures $15, and a wonderful pedicure runs $35.

And don't forget the catalog for your favorite supplies, wherever you might find yourself in the world—like so many of Boyds' faithful.

# *Floris*

| | |
|---|---|
| 703 Madison Avenue | (212) 935-9100 |
| between 62nd and | For Mail Order (800) J-FLORIS |
| 63rd Streets | Fax (212) 888-2001 |
| New York, NY 10021 | |

These days, a stroll past any fragrance counter evokes a roll call of show business luminaries like Elizabeth Taylor, Cher, Sophia Loren, Catherine Deneuve, and Dionne Warwick. Another name rich in Hollywood associations had joined this star-studded fragrance firmament—Niven, as in James Niven, son of the late, great English actor David Niven. But rather than cash in on the cachet of his surname, Jamie had taken on that of a treasured institution from Dad's native land—Floris, and transplanted it to the U.S.

Though Floris of London has taken over and Jamie is no longer involved, it was still a smart move. Newer names may temporarily capture the public's imagination, but Floris has truly withstood the test of time. It was established in 1730 by Juan Famenias Floris, who sailed to England from his native Spanish island of Minorca to seek fame and fortune. He secured both with his shop on fashionable Jermyn Street dedicated to perfumes, at that time considered a novelty. Capitalizing on the traditional English love of gardens and possibly on the coincidental descriptive nature of his name, Juan's shop became renowned as a purveyor of floral-scented perfumes and toiletries. Seven generations later, the dynasty he founded still operates the business from the same extended premises at No. 89 Jermyn Street.

Thanks to Jamie, just as suave and debonair as his father, an almost-exact replica of the original shop sits on Madison Avenue dispensing a tranquil breath of fresh English country air. The moment you enter the tiny shop lined with softly gleaming mahogany showcases, your senses are soothed by the seductive scent wafting from the large bowl of English rose potpourri. It can work its magic in your home for $17.50 for four cups or $35 for sixteen.

There are other fragrant home products, like the $15 room spray, but Floris built its reputation on scents for the person. And they remain the specialty dispensed in the unique collection of perfumes, colognes, talcum powders, and bath preparations—for both sexes. Floris caters to masculine as well as feminine tastes and needs. Indeed, men seem to feel uncommonly comfortable shopping in this clubby atmosphere, where the staff is incredibly hospitable.

Here gentlemen can assemble a complete fragrance wardrobe— hand soap, shaving cream, shaving soap (which comes in a wonderful wooden bowl), aftershave, deodorant, hair lotion, talcum powder, and toilet water—all in the classic No. 89 named after the address of the London shop. If No.89 is a little too citrusy, all these products are also infused with a more woody bouquet called Elite. And for the herbophiles, there's a new signature range called J. F. after the founding father.

For ladies, there are thirteen scents with names like Edward Bouquet, English Violet, Ormande, and Wild Hyacinth. Perfumes range from $50 to $90, while the toilet waters fit into the $27.50 to $47.50 slot, depending on size and dispenser. As confirmed devotees of long, luxurious baths, we're especially fond of the various concentrated bath essences. The "bath book" presentation of six for $22 makes a terrific present.

Indeed, manager Andrew Puckering, whose boundless enthusiasm is matched only by his flawless taste, puts together marvelous gift baskets of Floris's wares. The selection, presented either in wicker baskets or "hat boxes," depends on your taste and wallet. They start at $50, but Alex reports he's assembled several for closer to $600 and maintains that the sky's the limit. For Christmas, the gift boxes get into the spirit disguised as sleighs or nutcrackers. They range in price from $150 to $500.

Andrew knows that, as bewitching as Floris fragrances are, service is a great part of the appeal here to clients like Henry Kravis, Blaine Trump, Dominick Dunn, Barbara Walters, Julia Roberts, Liz Smith, Tommy Hilfinger, Carrie Fisher, and Stan Margulies. Consequently, Floris delivers, takes on corporate accounts, and routinely handles large gift lists—from selection, to the insertion of your personal note, to mailing. And if you want to build a basket around some special gift you found elsewhere, by all means send it over to Andrew; he will do it and you proud.

Even if your preference in perfumes leans toward the spicy Oriental scents rather than florals, we highly recommend a visit to this little oasis of British gentility. It's such a refreshing experience.

# *Kiehl's*

| 109 Third Avenue | (212) 677-3171 |
| between 13th and 14th Streets | (212) 475-3698 |
| New York, NY 10003 | Fax (212) 674-3544 |

There's nothing fancy about Kiehl's — no elaborate packaging, no advertising, just simple see-through plastic bottles containing beauty products that lure New York's most fashionable women to the store's less-than-chic East Village location. It's no wonder that this thriving cosmetics business has found the secret to success — it's had 142 years to figure it out!

Founded in 1851, Kiehl's was a typical neighborhood apothecary dispensing homemade preparations — aphrodisiacs, virility cream, and cures for baldness. In 1921 Irving Morse, a trained pharmacist, purchased the store from the founding family and began formulating the first Kiehl-brand products. His son Aaron took over in 1978. A pharmaceutical expert, Aaron had already enjoyed a brilliant career as the developer of the nation's first fluoride treatment and as a pioneer in the development of a drug instrumental in fighting tuberculosis. It was Aaron who conceived of many of what have become Kiehl's most popular products.

Yet another generation of Morses is now in charge at Kiehl's — Araon's striking daughter, Jami, is CEO. She's expanded Kiehl's market by selling their products to Barneys and Bergdorf Goodman and to outlets in Europe and Japan. Training director Charlotte Carlson travels the world, so when you see a Kiehl's product abroad, you can be sure that the sales staff there has learned from the source. Jami's husband, Klaus, the firm's president, is a former professional skier and has added a number of men's and unisex items geared to the needs of the athlete.

Still, the basics of Kiehl's haven't changed much, though they have stopped the practice of custom-blending fragrances, which used to be one of their great claims to fame. Unfortunate perhaps, but Kiehl's does offer 118 different scents, so it's difficult to complain too much.

As for their other claim to fame, there are some 350 Kiehl's skin- and hair-care products, based on a combination of the best homeopathic and herbal remedies, high-quality oils, and other natural ingredients, all mixed with a good dose of modern technology.

On our last visit, we discovered quite a few new items, including the Herbal Toner with Mixed Berries and Extracts ($10.95 for four ounces), an alcohol-free formula made with pure berries, herbal extracts, and natural astringents to tone and soothe. The "Very Unusually Rich—But Not Greasy At All Hand Cream with Sunscreen SPF 8" is a must-have ($9.95 for two ounces), as is the Ultra Protection Moisturizing Eye Gel with SPF 18, formulated especially for those with a skin type that's either "puffiness-prone" or sunscreen-sensitive ($28.50). We're partial to the scented hand and body lotions, particularly the vanilla variety ($8.95 for four ounces), as well as the Herbal Toner ($22.95) for the scalp, which need not be washed out and can also be used in between shampoos to help prevent oil accumulation.

They decline to divulge names of their celebrity clientele, but Calvin Klein has been quoted as a fan and we've run into Anne Archer, Susan Sarandon, and Daryl Hannah, who was fascinated with a tableau of classic motorcycles, one of the many fantastic displays showcased on an ever-changing basis (from planes to race cars). Kiehl's exhibitions often include wonderful 1800s-era artifacts, including some face creams from that period.

If the one hundred percent money-back guarantee doesn't convince you of Kiehl's' quality, the fact that more than one hundred of their products are on permanent display at the Smithsonian's Public Health and Pharmacy Exhibit in the National Museum of History and Technology probably will. And, we're happy to report that they use only recyclable packaging.

In any case, it's unlikely you'll buy anything that doesn't satisfy. The delightful staff, led by manager and chief skin-care consultant, Una Cassidy, is very liberal with its samples. Indeed, Kiehl's actively encourages new customers to try samples before purchasing anything, it helps ensure that each will find the optimum regimen for his or her individual skin, scalp, and hair types. Besides, they know once you've tried their products, you're hooked!

Kiehl's may not be fancy, but it sure is smart!

# LADIES' SERVICES
## *Elizabeth Arden*

691 Fifth Avenue                    (212) 546-0200
at 54th Street
New York, NY 10022

When you breeze through that trademark red door, you enter a whole new world, a sea of calm dedicated to pampering, to improving the tone and pace of your everyday existence — a world created by a feisty little Canadian redhead named Florence Nightingale Graham, who parlayed a jar of cleansing cream into a billion-dollar industry.

Encouraged to follow in the footsteps of her illustrious namesake, Florence attended nursing school during the early years of this century. There she developed an acute awareness of the direct correlation between the feeling of physical well-being, massage, and the maintenance of healthy-looking skin. A chance encounter with a biochemist working on formulating a cream that would soothe and heal skin blemishes led her to seize upon the notion of devising skin creams for cosmetic use. The rest, as they say, is history.

Florence popularized skin treatments that combined the use of massage with that of her cosmetic creams. She experimented with rouges and tinted powders and discovered that she had a flawless sense of color. Her metamorphosis into the world's leading beauty expert — Elizabeth Arden — had begun. It was completed with the opening of the flagship Red Door Salon on prestigious Fifth Avenue in New York City. Today there are products or services on four floors to take care of your every need.

The main floor features a complete selection of Elizabeth Arden cosmetic, treatment, and fragrance products, plus a display of J. Mendel's world-famous furs. The building's eleventh and twelfth floors are devoted to Arden hairdressing, manicures, and pedicures. There are sixteen stylists and eleven assistants, trained and equipped to deal with the most sophisticated haircutting, styling, and coloring.

For nails, a staff of sixteen manicurists is ready to cater to any request, from a polish change to a soothing Spa Pedicure, featuring a moisturizing paraffin treatment.

On the eighth floor, you'll find the face and body departments, where you can indulge in a restorative facial or a Swedish or Shiatsu massage. The twenty-two facialists possess the secrets of what were known as Florence's "magic hands," while the ten masseuses are equally adept at easing away your tensions.

One of our favorite people here is makeup artist Constantine. You'll be amazed by what his little tips can do for your appearance. As he has done for many of New York's smartest women, he will teach you how to (literally) put your best face forward.

. Should you wish to sample all the beauty wonders Arden has to offer, plan ahead and make arrangements to experience either the Miracle Morning for $175 or the Arden Spa Day for $225. As part of the package, you are served a light spa lunch.

The fashion department is gone, which is, in our opinion, no great loss. Elizabeth Arden is now much better focused on Florence Nightingale Graham's original vision of furnishing a sophisticated clientele with a beauty salon they can truly call their own.

# García

| | |
|---|---|
| 240 East 27th Street | (212) 889-3028 |
| New York, NY 10016 | Fax (212) 889-8120 |

Few people are as lucky as García, master makeup and hair artist. This is a man who loves his work — and his work loves him. It has fulfilled his dreams of traveling around the world, meeting and working with all the best people. One of them, the amazing Amalita de Fortabat of Argentina (you know, the cement heiress who had to loan the Argentine government her aircraft fleet for the Falklands War) counts on his services twice a day when she's in town — for daytime and evening looks. She flew him to Venice last year, and for her granddaughter's wedding in Buenos Aires, Amalita imported him for the duration of the festivities.

Likewise, Gayfryd Steinberg made sure García was the director of beauty services for stepdaughter Laura's wedding to Jonathan Tisch. García even did Laura's hair and makeup for her wedding-dress fittings with Scassi, so that the total look could be polished and refined to perfection.

He's done dozens of magazine cover models, including Daryl Hannah for *Town & Country* and Margot Perot for *Harper's Bazaar*, and is in demand by celebrities ranging from Diandra Douglas to Ann Getty.

García will gladly work with you, too, developing your best features and bringing out your personality in the most uncomplicated and attractive way. For $300 in his studio, he'll do your makeup and freshen your coif with hot rollers and comb-out. When he comes to you, it's $400. (His wedding prices depend on how long you need him; they start at $400 and go up from there.) A makeup lesson is $400 at his place or yours, but we think it best that you go to the studio. Everything is at his fingertips there, and it's likely he can spend more time with you. His makeup line, geared for the colors and textures he likes, is quite inexpensive, ranging from $6 to $20. And the best news is that, with typical grace, García has the good sense not to insist you use his line. If you're happy with whatever you've been using, that's okay with him.

Indeed, the only thing difficult about the charming García is getting an appointment with him. Agent and business partner Charles Howard is the keeper of García's schedule. Call him and see what you can work out. You'll be very glad you did.

## John Sahag

| | |
|---|---|
| 425 Madision Avenue | (212) 750-7772 |
| at 49th Street | Fax (212) 750-7494 |
| New York, NY 10018 | |

When you put yourself in John Sahag's capable hands, you'll know you've done the right thing. His beautiful new salon has a completely different look from that of the original East 53rd Street location, but it's just as relaxing. The terrazzo floors, waterfalls, fish ponds, and earth tones give it a real forestlike feel, and this theme is carried out at the stations, each of which is separated from the other with its own treelike divider complete with water spouts and goldfish.

John really is a master, having trained in Paris and free-lanced for the world's leading magazines for years. At 41, he's shed the long, wavy mane in favor of a short, straight cut, but he's as warm as he's always been. Over the years, he's made quite a name for himself. Who else insists upon a consultation before touching your hair? It takes only about five minutes, but you'd better call at least a week before. And who else is constantly booked three to four weeks in advance despite (or maybe because of) a $250 charge for a cut? Should his services be required at your hotel or home, the price tag jumps to a whopping $1,000 (plus travel costs). The regal presence of his greyhound, Baron, usually in graceful repose right next to John's station, adds to the alluring mystique of this establishment dedicated to the perfect cut.

Make no mistake, things are done differently here. John and his seven stylists cut hair *dry*. He likens it to sculpting stone, taking advantage of the natural shape and texture. It takes an hour or two, but the results are worth the time. The cut is custom-designed to suit the hair's inherent qualities and to flatter the face. Look at his success with Farrah Fawcett, Jaclyn Smith, Brooke Shields, Alana Stewart, and Demi Moore.

John feels a sincere and abiding responsibility to such visible heads. He knows how important hair is in defining a woman's total appearance. Laughingly, John claims, "It's probably easier to get into Harvard than it is to get a job here. I'm a fanatic about making sure the people who work for me are really talented and well trained." In fact, he requires a minimum of five years' experience to become an assistant in his salon. Only after serving an apprenticeship with John are the assistants allowed on the floor as full-blown stylists like Eiji, who trained under John for six months. Eiji's been very popular and also serves as the salon's manager; he charges $150 and is booked four weeks in advance.

Mark Schwartz offers another styling alternative at $125. Call him about three weeks before you need a cut. Lello and Mayumi are terrific too, and bargain-priced at $100.

Predictably, John's approach to coloring is uniquely his own. He bases it upon the cut, taking advantage of the shape to illuminate the texture. He applies at least two and often as many as five different shades to give hair a lovely luminescence, comparing the process to properly lighting a carefully assembled decor.

Clearly, John Sahag is not the kind of place most people go for a weekly wash and blow-dry. Still, some can't resist, so John allows his assistants to do the honors at $45 a session. If you insist, by special request and for $65, one of the senior stylists can be engaged for the job.

But why bother? There are any number of places in New York to get washed and coiffed, but few others that can guarantee a cut that's so undeniably you.

# *Leonardo*

(212) 288-8060

Ever wonder who's responsible for the dazzling locks that frame those gorgeous faces staring out from the covers of all those magazines? One possibility is Leonardo, the Venezuelan who emigrated to New York fifteen years ago and has been working hair wonders ever since.

He operates on the "have scissors and hair drier, will travel" principle. Leonardo goes to you — hotel, home, or office. Even at $150 for a wash and blow-dry (including carfare), he's often booked at least a week in advance. He's just so popular.

In fact, there are those who simply cannot live without him. When summering in the Hamptons or at the Cape, many of his clients import Leonardo. Of course, when his services are required beyond the boundaries of Manhattan, he expects his transportation to be provided — limo or private plane will do!

When not keeping tabs on the glamorous manes of actresses and models, Leonardo is often occupied with wedding parties. He has developed quite a specialty — wedding dates are set pending his availability.

Leonardo takes weddings very seriously indeed. He consults with the bride months in advance, considers the gowns and headpieces, and scouts the bridesmaids to determine the most flattering and complimentary styles. The results are gratifying, but costly — $250 for the bride, $150 for each attendant. With a $500 minimum for weddings, you might as well enlist at least two bridesmaids. Weddings, it seems, are very time-consuming, and Leonardo *does* stick around for retouches during the postceremony festivities.

Dream weddings just a dream for the moment — no man in sight? Leonardo to the rescue! Nothing improves your appearance faster or more dramatically than the perfect custom-designed hairstyle. Leonardo can perform the appropriate magic; a complete reworking of your coiffure will cost $175. Consider it an investment in your future!

# Nathan

22 East 62nd Street                    (212) 838-5583
between Fifth and Madison Avenues
New York, NY 10021

Few people are as specialized and talented as Nathan—he does hair color, period. He creates beautiful natural color for some of the chicest heads in New York.

Working in his new ground-floor salon, complete with an all-mirrored private section, Nathan builds on and enhances his clients' inherent attributes—skin tone, eye color, and original hair pigmentation. He shuns fads and trends in favor of a classic genuine look, loaded with glamour.

He's truly a master colorist, having trained under the legendary Rosemary at Kenneth. When she retired, she passed the scepter to Nathan, who now reigns supreme.

His prices start at $175 and up, depending upon what is required. Nathan's special kind of custom highlighting can be a lengthy process. You may spend hours with him and drop several hundred dollars, but it will be time and money well spent. Your hair will look marvelous, making you in turn look sensational. You should expect nothing less than perfection from Nathan, and you'll get it.

Nathan's calm, soothing personality and sympathetic nature are another bonus. A couple of hours chatting amiably with him is a great substitute for a weekly visit to the analyst.

# The Wayne Webb Technique

(212) 472-3119

Mirror, mirror on the wall, who's the fairest of them all? You are, of course. Wayne Webb truly believes that every woman has the potential to be the fairest; she just has to learn how to make the most of what she's got.

With his easy manner and love of beauty, Wayne is indeed the man to do the teaching. Interested in real people with real lives, Wayne teaches you how to master your look and tailor it to your life-style.

Wayne sees just four or five clients a day, and he's very popular, especially with women active on the social circuit. They book him in the afternoon for their evening outings, so he generally reserves the morning for lessons.

The salon is no more, but Wayne will come to wherever you are, including your hotel. A single makeup lesson costs $250, as does a makeup application, which for a new client is almost always a lesson in itself. He won't let you leave without knowing what to do when he's not there.

Before getting started, Wayne will find out how you want to look and how much time you have on a daily basis to devote to that look. Plan to spend about an hour and a half going over what you've been doing and what products you're using. Wayne says that most women call him because they're not happy with how the cosmetics they're using are performing, and he can usually point out how to make them work better. There's never any future charge for questions; just call, and Wayne will be only too happy to help.

Since Wayne knows products better than anyone else, you can trust him. Take him shopping with you for a $100 charge. It's worth it to be able to select the best cosmetics and avoid relying on the "advice" of the salesperson who very likely is pushing certain products to get the commission. No matter what you spend, what you buy with Wayne's help will ensure that you'll accomplish what you want.

He will, of course, do makeup for your wedding. It's $250 for the bride, plus $150 for each individual person, and there's a $500 minimum.

Count on Wayne for trustworthy advice and the finest hand to apply your makeup for any occasion when nothing less than perfection will do. Not only does he want you to look good — he wants you to feel good, too.

# UNISEX SERVICES

## *Georgette Klinger*

| | |
|---|---|
| 501 Madison Avenue | (212) 838-3200 |
| at 53rd Street | (800) KLINGER |
| New York, NY 10022 | |

| | |
|---|---|
| 978 Madison Avenue | (212) 744-6900 |
| at 76th Street | |
| New York, NY 10021 | |

At seventy-eight, Georgette Klinger is a pretty persuasive advertisement for her skin-care regimens and products. You recognize her immediately from her famous ads, featured with her very attractive daughter Kathryn, who's forty. Clearly, for the whole family, beauty is another fine example of the Klinger philosophy. Together they operate an empire of seven salons and over four hundred products with annual sales of about $20 million. No wonder the press often refers to Georgette as the Dean of Skin Care.

Born in Czechoslovakia, she studied skin care in Budapest, Vienna, and Zurich, before opening her first salon over her then-husband's objections. He was afraid people would think he couldn't support her. It became a moot point when the war broke out and they fled to London, but his protests resurfaced after they moved to New York and Georgette started angling to open another salon. She claims she had to sneak out, but through stealth, not to mention hard work, in 1941 she opened a six-room salon at 509 Madison Avenue.

In 1959, having shed Mr. Klinger, she moved to larger quarters at 501 Madison, a location which today sports three floors, with sixty treatment rooms, a hair salon, manicure and pedicure facilities, and serves as many as 250 clients a day. To address what she considers the active urban dweller's need for a scientific, total-care program offering comprehensive services in a private, relaxed setting, Georgette opened a second uptown New York facility at 978 Madison in 1986.

This luxurious sanctum acts as a restorative haven focused on the individual's total well-being—health, nutrition, personalized exercise, and appearance. Consider it a personal retreat in the city, where you can go to take advantage of regimens and treatments specifically designed for you. It's all very nurturing, from the private nutritional counseling by Harvard graduate Dr. Lilian Cheung, to the soothing massage by European-trained experts, to the private exercise instruction. The initial counseling session lasts more than an hour and costs $100. Follow-up sessions are $75. Massages run $58 for 55 minutes and the exercise classes are $60 each.

Georgette is a firm believer in individual treatments, which is why she's developed so many products in her New York labs. She's adamant that every skin is different, and insists on careful analysis by her skin-care specialists before any product is recommended. They are all fragrance-free and sold exclusively in her salons, despite tempting distribution offers from major department stores. Careful records are made of your skin type and purchases. The client files are kept active for three years, after which it's time to reevaluate your skin. So a quick call from anywhere in the world to (800) KLINGER can ascertain your needs, and arrangements will be made to ship your selections to you. Her line also includes a group of skin-care products for men, which she launched in 1972.

"Herbal Essentials," priced from $10.50 to $38, is Georgette's latest line. Formulated using homeopathic principles, it includes nine skin-care products ranging from makeup remover lotion and cleansing lotions to moisturizers and face masks. Always environmentally correct, Georgette devised this mineral-oil-free line with no animal-based ingredients. Like all other Klinger products, these have never been tested on animals and the elegant packages are made with recyclable glass and plastic. An hour-long Herbal Essentials Facial at the salon ($80) does wonders!

Having anticipated the now huge market for preparations for men, she continues to cater to their needs at the uptown salon. There, she's created a masculine, wood-paneled environment decorated in vivid blues and reds. It has a private entrance and consists of a personal exercise room and designated areas for facials, body treatments, massages, hair styling, nutritional counseling, manicures, and pedicures. Indeed, just like the ladies, gentlemen can pamper themselves with a day at Georgette Klinger for $215 including a spa lunch in the solarium. Individual services range from $35 for a pedicure to $68 for a facial.

Prices for the ladies are comparable, although the Deluxe Full Day of Beauty is $275 and facials for females include makeup application. There's even a Full Year of Beauty for $560—six facials, four body massages, an hour-long makeup lesson, and a bottle of Georgette or Kathryn cologne.

Best of all is Georgette herself. She's available and accessible almost all year long. You'll find her at the uptown salon from 11:00 A.M. to 3:00 P.M. and downtown after that until 7:00 P.M. If you're having a special skin problem, call to book an appointment. She really cares, and she's delighted to use her decades of experience to solve your problem. The best part is that she doesn't even charge for her time.

Behind the signature lily of the valley–etched glass doors of every Georgette Klinger salon awaits a cool, calm oasis. It envelops you cocoonlike, separating you from the stresses, the demands of the outside world, and makes you concentrate on some wonderfully decadent, very restorative self-care.

# Il Makiage

107 East 60th Street                                    (212) 371-3992
New York, NY 10022                              Fax (212) 753-2372

Just when you think you've got it all together, fate has a nasty, though often fortuitous, way of stepping in and rearranging everything. Take the case of Israeli-born Ilana Harkavi. She was enjoying a successful life as a professional dancer when a taxi accident ended her career, or rather the career of the moment. Undaunted, Ilana decided to channel her artistic energies in another direction by attending beauty school in New York with the intention of becoming a special-effects makeup artist.

She continued to pursue that dream, working as a theatrical makeup artist in Europe, until fate stepped in once again on her return to the United States in 1971. This time it appeared in a more pleasant form, that of her future husband. Together, they decided to open their own business; Il Makiage was born in 1972.

Ilana and Il Makiage literally lit up the cosmetics industry. At a time when colors were confined to what was tried and true, Ilana experimented with a broad palette, producing an unlimited array.

When hair colorings were mostly chemically based, she introduced natural henna as an alternative, and at a time when interest in skin-treatment products was practically nil, she helped to revolutionize the industry with collagen products.

Today, her products are distributed in more than five hundred fashionably upscale outlets worldwide. The Il Makiage cosmetics line is one of the world's most extensive, with over seven hundred colors (almost double what she offered several years ago), including two hundred eyeshadows, one hundred lipsticks, and ninety nail polish shades—and dozens of new color variations are added each year. Considered *the* makeup artist's makeup, it is very popular with those who march down runways or tread the boards of a stage.

Ilana's Avigal hair colors are still the best-selling henna products on the market. The line's thirteen shades are used in exclusive salons like John Sahag, Vidal Sassoon, Bruno Pittini, and Jacques Dessange. And the homeopathic-based Shoynear skin-care cosmetics use natural liposomes and vitamins to normalize the skin, winning praise for their ability to prevent skin from aging prematurely.

Of course, at the Il Makiage Salon, you can benefit from all of these products, made at Ilana's own factory on Long Island. The salon, Ilana's international headquarters, gives full head-to-toe service—haircut to pedicure, for men as well as women. At street level, you'll find the cosmetics counter, where you may run into supermodels Iman or Linda Evangelista checking out the huge assortment. Or you might see noted makeup artists François Nars, B. J. Gillian, and Heidi Schulze stocking up.

Rooms for the $30 pedicures and $15 manicures are located just beyond the cosmetics, followed by the hair salon, which occupies what once served as a corner of the garden, now glass-enclosed. The greenhouse allows the stylists and colorists to take advantage of strong natural light. What remains of the garden is, during the warmer months, a delightful oasis for the drying of nails and toes.

The lower level is reserved for facials, waxing, and makeup application. Ilana will do your makeup, as she does for Diana Ross, Demi Moore, Marlo Thomas, and Sly Stallone when movie parts require it, for $350. A popular service is the application of individual eyelashes for $50—they last for two to three weeks. Group lessons are given, limited to ten people, on Monday and Thursday evenings from 6:00 to 8:00 P.M. They're only $35, and you get a 10-percent discount on any of Ilana's products.

The salon has another specialty, besides the quality of the products and the expertise of the personnel — conveniently extended hours. It's open from 8:30 A.M. to 8:00 P.M. on Mondays and Thursdays, and from 8:30 A.M. to 7:00 P.M. on Tuesdays and Wednesdays. On Fridays, Il Makiage opens at 8:30 A.M. and closes at 3:00 P.M. in the winter, 5:00 P.M. in the summer, and Saturday is Ilana's day of rest for religious observance. (Isn't it nice that some people can make their lives work and still carry on their spiritual traditions!) That means she's open for business on Sunday from 10:00 A.M. to 6:00 P.M. (except during July and August, when no one in their right mind is in the city anyway). Those highly unusual Sunday hours have bailed us out on more than one occasion. Isn't it comforting to know they can do the same for you?

# La Coupe

694 Madison Avenue                                    (212) 371-9230
New York, NY 10021                          Fax (212) 421-1358

La Coupe's Charles Booth was destined to make a career of hairdressing. His earliest recollections include pictures of his French grandfather cutting soldiers' hair during World War I and his mother's salon in London. Although he planned on an Oxford education, at his mother's suggestion he took time for an internship with Vidal Sassoon in London. Apparently, mother knew best because Sassoon, who was at the height of his fame, made Charles his personal assistant and introduced him to an exciting new celebrity-studded world. Oxford was nixed, and Charles opened his first salon in Montreal in 1967. It's been one success after another since then.

La Coupe — "the cut" — is the basis, according to Charles, of all modern hair design. It reigns supreme at his chic black-and-white New York salon, staffed by ten stylists (plus colorists, makeup artists, manicurists, and umpteen assistants), each the product of

Charles's intensive training program. No matter where else in the world they may have worked, they must serve a one- to two-year apprenticeship as assistants at La Coupe before Charles allows them on the floor as full-fledged stylists.

Star stylist Kim Lepine — La Coupe's International Design Director for both salons — practices her craft on Glenn Close, Mary Tyler Moore, Eileen Ford, and a host of other loyal fans who keep her booked weeks in advance. The only way you can get a last-minute date with Kim is if there's a blizzard and appointments have been cancelled. She starts work at 7:00 A.M. (for early birds), goes till 4:30 P.M., and charges $125 for a design/cut/shape/dry. For later risers, appointments are available on Wednesdays and Thursdays until 7:30 P.M. We also recommend Rosario Acquista, another hairstylist, who has, like Kim, been at La Coupe for many years and does beautiful work as well.

There are many different price ranges for hair-styling at La Coupe, starting at $40. And, there is even such a thing as a $10 cut here. Tuesdays after 5:45 P.M. are "model nights" when the assistants take over under the supervision of a stylist. Call that day (they prefer between 4:00 and 5:00 P.M.) to find out which technique (style or color) they're practicing. If it sounds like you, try it. If not, they'll keep your name and number on file for when they're perfecting something more to your liking. You can't beat the color prices: single process ($15), half-head highlights ($25), and full-head highlights ($35, instead of the usual $175 to $250!). And perms are $35.

Many of La Coupe's very visible clients depend on the extraordinary hair color genius of Daniel Galvin of London, who counts Princess Diana among his homebased clients (he does her highlights). He pops over to New York for a week every couple of months or so and is booked solid for the duration. Daniel's fee starts at $250 for custom-designed highlights, which he calls "Natural Movements." Stop by for a consultation to determine what he can do for you — no need for an appointment and no charge either (everyone at La Coupe offers a free consultation). Just check the desk for the dates he'll be in town so that you, too, can be treated like royalty.

Also specializing in color is Rita Starnella, Color and Perm Director, known fondly as "the queen of perms." Melanie Griffith and Rebecca de Mornay are taken care of by Rita when they're in town, as is Michael Bolton, just one of the many males (including businessmen) who are patrons of the salon. Another colorist, Emily Kim, does Natasha Richardson's hair.

If you're in the market for a manicure or pedicure, talk to Sophie, who has handled the hands of everyone from the Duke and Duchess of Windsor to Cindy Crawford. She subscribes to the old world Parisian school of nail care — lots of buffing and no cutting. A manicure takes about half an hour and costs $18. Plan on an hour and $36 for a pedicure. Her newest service is "Sophie's Choice" — she'll create a custom-mixed polish just for you to match a favorite outfit or color. No extra charge for the color, but you can take the bottle home for $25.

Not quite satisfied with his mastery of the cut and the two salons that execute it so well, Charles Booth's entrepreneurial nature has led him into the realm of hair-care products. His first line, La Coupe Collection Privee, encompasses twenty products and is available at the salon and in retail drug stores. Charles Booth Salon Collection is his newest baby; its two products — a deep conditioning cream treatment/detangler and a dandruff shampoo — are currently available only at the two salons.

Also available at the salon for between-color treatments at home is something called Veg (because of its all-natural ingredients) which is made up using your very own formula. You brush the $21 version (for two or three touch-ups) directly onto your highlighted areas, and you simply shampoo in the $10 version (six applications). Frankly, we prefer the latter; although it's not as strong as the other, it will get you by and it's easier to use.

Charles has also designed a collection of brushes (for pros and nonpros alike) including the La Coupe Salon clip brush, literally a brush with a clip that holds the ends of the hair in place while you blow it dry. For those of us who are klutzes with brushes, it's a dream come true. The phones rang off their hooks after an item about it ran in *Harper's Bazaar*. Available by mail order, it comes in four sizes ($10, $15, $20, $25) depending upon your hairstyle or hair length.

With all this and, we're told, more to come, La Coupe is grossing millions of dollars annually. We can't wait to find out what Charles will come up with next!

# GENTLEMEN'S
# SERVICES

## *Delta Men's Hair Stylists*

992 Lexington Avenue                    (212) 628-5723
between 71st & 72nd Streets
New York, NY 10021

At least there's one place left in New York where a fellow can still get a good old-fashioned, simple but first-rate haircut, and a manicure too, if he's so inclined. It doesn't have all the trappings of the fancy hotel tonsorial parlors. It doesn't have the fake, old interiors of some of those other chichi places on and off the avenues, especially on the Upper East Side. It does have, purely and simply, six great barbers who give you a no-nonsense cut for $17, which may be the best bargain you'll find in this book.

We found out about this little mirrored jewel on the corner of 72nd Street from George Elliott who ought to know something about hair — he's been coiffing the rich and famous for years in his salon in Florida's Jupiter Island Club during the winter and on Fisher's Island, playground of the quietly rich, in the summer. But when George comes to New York, he heads straight to Delta to get his locks shorn.

When he gets there, he heads straight for the chair of Peter, the amiable, soft-spoken Greek who's been cutting hair on this corner since 1962! Or he might (if Peter's on vacation) try Olga — an admittedly unlikely name for a perfectly marvelous men's coiffeuse. Mila is the new manicurist, and the full-service salon offers everything from a shoe shine ($2) or shave ($13) to a facial ($20).

Because of its location, because of Peter and his merry band, Delta has its share of New York notables who ring for the obligatory appointment (though if you're a regular, Peter will do his best to squeeze you in — provided it's not Saturday morning in the middle of the social season).

# EXERCISE

## *Lotte Berke*

23 East 67th Street            (212) 288-6613
2nd Floor
New York, NY 10021

If you wonder where all those beautiful bodies that grace New York come from, where those ladies go to stay so fit and trim despite the city's bountiful caloric temptations, chances are they are going to the Lotte Berke Studio.

A modest affair on the second floor of an old townhouse — no massage rooms, no sauna, no steam rooms — the studio owned by Lydia Bach is committed to hard work. It is work based on a method of rehabilitation exercise developed in London by Lotte Berke. Lydia adapted and further refined the method into what is now a combination of modern dance, yoga, and orthopedic stretching and strengthening exercises. Designed to be equally effective for men and women, the regimen yields truly remarkable results. Just look at manager Elizabeth and her husband, Fred.

Elizabeth grew up practicing the Lotte Berke method and credits it with her youthful, healthy, not to mention beautiful, looks. Fred, long and lean himself, is in amazing shape and has been teaching here for the last several years.

Betsy Aaron of CBS has been coming to Lotte Berke for years; we guess that her husband, CBS international correspondent Richard Threlkeld, couldn't stand to see her body get in such great shape — he now comes here, too. Other regulars include Pia Lindstrom, Ann Reinking, and Tom Wolfe (yes, that Tom Wolfe). Classes begin at 7:30 A.M., and the regulars who show up every day for the early class are all active, busy people. But don't worry, they have classes running all day. And there are evening and weekend classes as well, so that virtually anyone can fit them into their schedule. By appointment, and limited to twelve people, each session costs only $16, so there's no excuse for not keeping fit during a business trip or a New York weekend. You can sign up for a series to keep you occupied during longer stays at a slight discount.

However, you should bear in mind that this is serious exercise in a no-nonsense environment (yes, there are showers and some lockers, but this is not one of your high-tech fitness palaces). If you want a place to show off the latest in leotards or to socialize, look elsewhere.

# Radu's Physical Culture Studio

24 West 57th Street (212) 581-1995
New York, NY 10019

If Cindy Crawford hadn't hated exercising, she probably never would have met Radu Teodorescu. But Cindy needed to find a workable way to stay fit, so she sought Radu's services. Dubbed "the toughest trainer in town," he customized a fitness program to shape her body, which led to, in Crawford's words, a "fitness awakening." And thus, her now-famous "Shape Your Body" video was born, with workouts created by none other than our friend Radu.

Radu! RADU! you can almost hear muscular hordes chanting their leader's name. And believe us when we tell you there are any number of people in New York who swear Radu makes Attila look like a wimp. Radu runs a tight ship based on hard work — human body work.

In fact, his studio bears no resemblance to the gleaming temples of exercise loaded with tons of expensive equipment that seem so popular these days. His classes are held in an unair-conditioned facility with minimal accoutrements — some familiar- and used-looking exercise apparatus, a few mats thrown around for good measure. The only glamour is the clientele, including Candice Bergen, John Kennedy, Jr., Debbie Gibson, Regis Philbin, Calvin and Kelly Klein, and countless models besides La Crawford. But with regimens that typically produce sweat in the first seven to eight minutes, whatever starlike charisma they bring with them soon fades as they huff and puff along with everyone else.

Radu studied physical education at the University of Bucharest in his native Romania, before emigrating to the United States in 1972. Having attended one of the most prestigious physical fitness schools in the world, he was shocked by the sorry state of Americans' training efforts. Everyone was jogging like mad, but without benefit of proper training. Orthopedists were reaping vast rewards.

Radu discovered his true calling—making people safe for sports. He opened his gym in 1977 and developed a routine heavily reliant on gymnastics. His theory is that if you are in top physical form, as defined by his routines, you can avoid many common sports injuries. Word quickly spread that his students got the quickest results in the shortest period of time. It also got around that he was merciless. Potential students stayed away in droves. Still, he persevered, never altering his program to suit the lazy masses. Times were tough for a while, but now he's doing very well and reaping lots of publicity, particularly via the video. Success hasn't gone to his head, though, and he's still awfully severe when he thinks you're not working hard enough.

Of course, at his prices he's not running for Mr. Popularity, although he can be disarmingly charming. He's probably the best, and he certainly charges the most—$100 for an hour alone with the master. His staff trainers get $40 for half an hour, $65 for the full hour. Group classes run $16 each, but drop to $11 apiece if you buy a 120-class card for $1,320.

Not bad, especially if you might end up looking like Cindy Crawford.

## Vertical Club

| | |
|---|---|
| 330 East 61st Street<br>New York, NY 10021 | (212) 355-5100 |
| 139 West 32nd Street<br>New York, NY 10001 | (212) 465-1750 |
| 333 Madison Avenue<br>New York, NY 10017 | (212) 983-5320 |
| 350 West 50th Street<br>New York, NY 10019 | (212) 265-9400 |

Several years ago, there was just one Vertical Club; now there are four, and your membership entitles entrée into 350 clubs around the country. But don't count on getting into the Vertical Club if you're just a member of one of those 350 clubs—there's no reciprocity. The New York locations are that desirable. Also, it used to be that just anyone could buy a guest pass. You can't anymore, unless you happen to be staying at the Pierre, the Lowell, the St. Regis, or the Plaza Athénée, or if you're a non–New York member of the International Racquet Sports Association (IRSA). What's all the fuss about? Well, you could ask regulars like Arnold Schwarzenegger and Maria Shriver, Cher, Harrison Ford, Jimmy Connors, Tom Hanks, or Dustin Hoffman and they would probably wax poetic about the country club–like facilities, the training programs, or even the amenity-filled locker rooms.

Of course, all you have to do to become a member is plunk down $1,559 for the first year and $750 per year thereafter for everything except tennis privileges. Quite a bargain considering Vertical Club's superb services.

As the name suggests, each of the Vertical Clubs go up, up, and up. The three new locations are microcosms (except for tennis, racquetball, and squash courts) of the flagship facility on East 61st Street, which boasts seven floors and 175,000 square feet of fitness nirvana. There you'll find eight tennis courts (six indoors, two on the roof), five squash courts, three racquetball courts, a track, tanning rooms, a sundeck, and a lap pool. With upbeat music blaring throughout, the energy level here is phenomenal; if it could be tapped, the city would never suffer another blackout.

Not all that energy is totally committed to exercise. Sexual tension hangs in the air, almost tangibly. This is a coed club where many members are as intent on exercising their social skills as they are their muscles. Beautiful bodies abound, clad in show-off duds. While the staff is friendly, encouraging, and helpful, the clientele can be a bit intimidating, particularly if you have reason to be self-conscious about your love handles or thunder thighs.

Take heart — the club's one-on-one training program at $60 per hour can whip you into shape with maximum results in mininium time. It's just one of the many add-on options to the basic annual fees. Tennis memberships are available for $3,120 the first year, $1,040 annually thereafter. Full use of the club is incorporated in the fees, and there are no monthly dues.

If you're in town for the day and a guest of one of the aforementioned hotels, the $100-per-day guest pass for two includes two half-body suntans. IRSA members pay just $30 a day for use of the facilities.

The Vertical Club accommodates most schedules with long hours — 6:00 A.M. to 11:00 P.M. Monday through Friday, 9:00 A.M. to

9:00 P.M. weekends. Prime time for the tennis courts is defined by a $30 per hour court charge from 5:00 to 8:00 P.M. weekdays, 9:00 A.M. to 6:00 P.M. Saturday and Sunday. Off-peak hours can be had for $15 each. In either case, you can reserve up to forty-eight hours in advance — the same for squash and racquetball. Court charges for both are $10 an hour.

If you're not into racquet sports, you can save a lot of money at the Vertical Club. There's a never-ending series of classes, all day every day, for no additional charge. Use the helpful Definition of Classes to choose from such classes as "Funk & Step," "Hip Hop Express," "Challenge Aerobics," "Dynabands," and "Body Ultimate."

Most are held in the flagship's giant second-floor gym where you'll find every possible piece of state-of-the-art exercise equipment, including fifteen recently installed recumbent bicycles. A one-tenth-mile track circles the room overhead. It's three lanes wide, with a rubberized surface, and we understand the bird's-eye view of the action below is useful for more than breaking the monotony of running. It allows joggers to (literally) set their sights on the person to whom they would most like to introduce *their* body ultimate.

There's a juice bar on the lower level near the locker rooms, which, even as plush locker rooms go, are quite nice. Towels, hair-driers, and toiletries are available. On the same level you'll find the sauna and steam rooms, as well as the whirlpool. Rooms designated for massages are also located here. The staff masseurs charge $30 for a half-hour rubdown, $45 for an hour.

Whatever your approach to the club—whether you're looking for a meat market or a workout, as a regular member, tennis member, or regular guest—you're sure to enjoy its energy and be infused with a new sense of *joie de vivre.*

# CHAPTER EIGHT

# Miscellaneous Services

*"I can get it for you...."*

*A* bride with an off-the-wall sense of humor told me she had "registered" for wedding gifts at her neighborhood bank, in all denominations! Indeed, she had, and the couple began marital life with a lovely nest egg.

The point is that no matter what you think of, someone in New York is there to serve you. Anything, anytime, anyplace. It won't be a bargain, but you said you *wanted* it — and you didn't mention price.

There are people in New York who will save you time or save your ties, redecorate your home, cater to your whims, and paint your portrait, or your cat's portrait. We're not talking here about mundane services like dry cleaners and copy centers, though there are plenty of both. We're talking about the things that make life easier, more interesting, and downright spectacular — the daydreams, the sudden cravings, the item you could not get at the place you call home, but which you are sure exists in New York.

And it does, because New York is an Oriental bazaar and has everything from the fabulous to the fantastic. A visitor or longtime denizen has only to think of a want or desire not yet satisfied and there's a clairvoyant unlocking a shop or hanging out a shingle to do just that — to gratify their wish. Satisfaction guaranteed.

# *Alice S. Mason, Ltd.*

| 635 Madison Avenue | (212) 832-8870 |
| between 59th and 60th Streets | Fax (212) 832-7634 |
| New York, NY 10022 | |

The great smile is what you first notice about Alice Mason. Then there's her fabulous taste. Finally, you'd be mesmerized by the enormous double strand of white pearls. What you *should* realize immediately is that she is one smart cookie; therein lies the secret of her phenomenal success.

A native of Chestnut Hill, the tony Philadelphia suburb, Alice arrived in New York in 1952 at the tender but not unseasoned age of twenty, an aborted stab at college and one marriage behind her. She rented an apartment from a broker by the name of Gladys Miller, who also gave her a job. She worked for Miller's firm for five years before branching out on her own in 1958.

From the start, she broke barriers. At twenty-five, she was considered too young to be starting her own business, but that didn't stop her. Neither did the Social Registered co-op boards that spent their time denying applications of anyone they considered NOCD — Not of Our Class, Dear. Alice rightly recognized that there were a lot of NOCD types with a great deal of money to spend. She solicited their business, then set about becoming an expert on board psychology. Her success at getting the right clients into the right buildings became legendary.

Supposedly the model for the character of Maisie Verdurin in Dominick Dunne's novel *People Like Us*, Alice built an extraordinary network of contacts, which she carefully nurtures with her fabled dinner parties. They became a tradition early in her career, when she realized how fascinating it would be (and how good for business) for such diverse clients as Alfred Gwynne Vanderbilt and Marilyn Monroe to meet and mingle. Those dinner parties helped her build a business that keeps twenty-two brokers very busy selling the city's best residential real estate.

The parties keep her network so well oiled that she doesn't have to do much advertising, and she often seems to know when an exceptional property is going to come on the market even before the owner knows he's decided to sell! Somehow, folks just seem to trust Alice with their secrets or their suspicions. They know she's the soul of discretion. She's proved it over and over again by refusing to reveal who paid how much for what, even though her interests might have been better served if she had been a little less discreet.

The best of the best places to live, according to Alice in a recent *W* profile, are 960 Fifth Avenue ("just about the best building in Manhattan"), 834 Fifth Avenue ("most of the apartments have four master bedrooms and four maids rooms"), 740 Park Avenue, ("the smallest apartments are 12 rooms"), 720 Park Avenue ("extremely large dining rooms"), and One Sutton Place South ("wonderful libraries and living rooms").

Naturally, Alice is in her element at the top of the market, say $2 million or more. Indeed, she won't personally touch anything less, but she's got brokers on her staff who are as comfortable at the $200,000 level as she is in the millions. But if you want an invitation to one of her parties, you'd better be prepared to up the ante — considerably!

# *Herman Agar Co.*

(212) 695-1135

Herman Agar started his ticket agency in the Roaring Twenties, operating out of what is now the coat checkroom of what was then the city's most notorious speakeasy — the "21" Club. The establishment was as awash with Whitneys, Vanderbilts, and Astors as it was with illegal booze, and they all relied on Herman to secure their tickets for the era's most important events.

Herman is, alas, long gone, but the service he founded for the carriage trade remains intact under the experienced supervision of Paul Abramson and Phil Reisel. They've been in the business for decades and have thirty agents in their employ. For the right price, quoted on request and dictated by the degree of difficulty involved, we've never known them to fail to satisfy a client's request. And with clients like Bill Paley, the Bass and Hunt families, Estée Lauder, Douglas Fairbanks, Jr., and every serious investment house in the country, you can bet those requests have been pretty demanding and the right price pretty high.

Credit cards are accepted by the agency, but somewhat grudgingly. Paul and Phil prefer to deal with house accounts. It's so much more genteel, and no percentages are annoyingly subtracted from their profit. The only way to get an account, though, is to be recommended by an existing client. We suggest you roam through the Fortune 500 and see who you know.

Whether you're looking for tickets on or off the Great White Way, to the opera, the ballet (in Manhattan or any other city), or any sporting event in the world, you can count on Herman Agar. In fact, for megaevents like the World Series or the Super Bowl, they set up an office in the host city and somehow manage to snap up the very best seats.

Once you become a regular client, they'll extend their services to obtain impossible-to-get last-minute reservations at New York's most popular restaurants. Rumor has it that members of the Rothschild family call Herman Agar to arrange all their stateside activities, even before they book their Concorde flights. Maybe you should too. Remember, Paul and Phil are just a phone call away from making sure you're seen wherever you like.

## *Jerry Kravat Entertainment Services*

205 Lexington Avenue               (212) 686-2200
at 32nd Street                Fax (212) 689-9140
New York, NY 10016

Having a party for two, twenty, two hundred, or two thousand? Producing a corporate or institutional event? Is there a trade or industrial show, or perhaps the launch of a new product in your future? What about that benefit for your favorite charity? For anything that requires some form of entertainment, call the delightful Jerry Kravat. Founder of a completely unique service that matches talent to places and events, Jerry is relentless in making sure his clients' needs are satisfied.

And those needs are myriad. He regularly meets the entertainment demands of all the best places and people. Jerry's prestigious credits as entertainment director and regularly featured orchestra include the New York Palace, the Waldorf-Astoria, the Pierre, the Plaza, and the principality of Monaco (among others), all at the same time. Jerry always seems to have a unique understanding of and appreciation for what makes each event special and what kind of clientele it attracts. He says it's like solving a jigsaw puzzle, putting all the pieces together to make a perfect fit — to wed location, ambience, crowd, and entertainer(s). Jerry's marriages never fail. When Valentino tossed his thirtieth anniversary bash at the 7th Regiment Armory, he turned to Jerry's orchestra to entertain his glamorous guests. So did the organizers of New York Hospital's annual "Cabaret" ball, starring, naturally enough, Joel Grey. And Jerry's music and entertainment have been featured for many years on CBS-TV's "Happy New Year America."

No affair is too small or too special; from a small dinner party to a wedding (he was flown to St. Thomas for one) or a major event, anywhere in the world, Jerry Kravat has played a role. He's put together shows at the San Diego Zoo, Universal Studios in L.A., and Walt Disney World. In the process, he's hired the likes of Aretha Franklin, Bill Cosby, Cher, Ella Fitzgerald, Barbara Cook, Bob Hope, Lena Horne, Liza Minnelli, Luciano Pavarotti, Chita Rivera, Joan Rivers, Kenny Rogers, and Bobby Short. He's equally creative at finding the perfect strings to stroll through your next cocktail get-together or the pianist to create that appropriately romantic background for a little *dîner à deux*.

Whatever you have in mind for any occasion, give Jerry a call to be sure it is a very special event indeed.

# *Jill Gill*

90 Riverside Drive                    (212) 362-8440
New York, NY 10024

Jill Gill is into preservation — not wildlife, but our lives and yours. For nearly thirty years she's made a specialty of preserving important parts of people's lives by capturing them in wonderful watercolor and ink paintings — that glorious view from the office, a special garden in bloom, a room full of cherished memories, or a beautiful vista. Many of Jill's clients have her paint their townhouse to hang in their country house and vice versa. They also like to reproduce her paintings as postcards or Christmas cards; they make such a personal statement.

It all started with Jill's hobby of photographing, then painting, buildings and street scenes slated for demolition or radical change.

After seeing some of these watercolors, friends asked if Jill would paint a portrait of their house, and a new career was born.

In pursuit of that career, Jill visits with her clients in the surroundings they want immortalized. She chats with them about their feelings, about what makes the place so special to them. Then she takes pictures—lots of them. Armed with these, she retreats to her studio to immerse herself in painting and about six to eight weeks later emerges with the finished product.

Prices range from $2,500 to $25,000, depending upon size and scale; a facade is less costly than a garden or a room, which both require a three-dimensional approach. Clients like Zubin and Nancy Mehta and the late Pierre Matisse have engaged her services, and she has immortalized such legendary locations as the Russian Tea Room, the James Beard House, and the Actors Studio. She'll preserve for posterity your special piece of New York— or anywhere else for that matter. Jill's motto, she maintains, is "Have brush, will travel!"

# Michel Thomas Language Center

156 Fifth Avenue                                    (212) 688-8400
Suite 1011                                     Fax (212) 255-1728
New York, NY 10010

The French government called on Michel Thomas as a star witness in the trial of Gestapo leader Klaus Barbie. After all, it was Michel, as a young leader of the French Resistance during World War II, who faced an interrogation by Barbie and lived to tell the tale. He's now put the language skills that got him past that incident to work in a truly unique system for people anxious to learn a foreign tongue quickly and painlessly.

His way is really the only way to learn a new language, short of moving to its country of origin. In only ten days, Michel guarantees you'll be speaking, reading, and writing the language of your choice. He'll also find a teacher for any language in the world, though he specializes in the major tongues. And he's truly the master. Companies like Chase Manhattan, MCA, Lazard Freres, and Bertelsmann are terribly impressed with Michel and his system. He's taught any number of their top executives, not to mention Candice Bergen, Carl Reiner, and Walter Carley, our ambassador to France.

Michel's system has one ground rule — "never try to remember anything. The responsibility for the learning and remembering is with the teacher, not the learner." Having exhibited absolutely no facility for languages until we ran into Michel, we now buy his seemingly improbable line — since we can now *parle Français* with the best of them.

Four thousand eight hundred dollars buys you eighty hours of instruction and a schedule tailored to your own needs. The first phase of the center's course concentrates on the basics of vocabulary, grammar, tense, and syntax. Then Michel tailors the program to fit your needs, whether personal or professional. Whatever your pace or your schedule, Michel can add a new dimension to your life by giving you the ability to communicate effectively in a language other than English. *Comprendez-vous?*

# Spencer Realty

353 Lexington Avenue                    (212) 661-9440
New York, NY 10016

Fed up with hotels for long stays in New York and want a place you can really call home? For a pied-à-terre with character, charm, and at least a touch of class, call Brenda Spencer. Her business is rentals, furnished and unfurnished; her specialty is short-term leases. Whether you seek a turn-of-the-century brownstone, a prewar luxury apartment, or a loft in Soho, Brenda can find it for you. The whole of Manhattan is her inventory.

Monthly rates for a modest nest start at about $1,200, with the sky the limit. The minimum commitment is generally two months. A single month is possible, but difficult.

Corporate giants like First Boston, Philip Morris, Goldman Sachs, Bear Stearns, and Morgan Stanley count on Brenda to locate homes away from home for visiting execs. People from the entertainment industry regularly depend on her when they're in town to do a show or make a movie, as do any number of other world-class travelers who prefer private residences to hotels.

Brenda also provides free "settling in" services as a little bonus and to help make her clients comfortable as quickly as possible. They include arranging for maid service, cable TV, and garage space. She even maps out local restaurants, grocery stores, dry cleaners, and shoe repair shops.

Give her two or three weeks notice if you're looking for a place in New York, but one will do if you're really in a bind. Should you leave town for an extended period and wish to list your home with her, plan to do it one to two months before your departure.

# Tiecrafters

252 West 29th Street                          (212) 629-5800
New York, NY 10001

Andy Tarshis worries about neckties—not whether the red one goes with the gray suit, but whether the spot on the red tie will ever come out. For over forty years, Andy's been running one of New York's most unusual and most specialized businesses, one entirely dedicated to the proper care and feeding of ties. How many ties have you discarded because of stubborn stains or outdated widths? With Andy and Tiecrafters in your life, you may never throw a tie away again.

When it comes to cleaning, Andy's services may be the best in the world. He'll go to just about any length to remove that salad-dressing stain from your new Hermès. If necessary, Tiecrafters will open the back, release the stitching, clean the silk, and then resew the tie. All this, for $5 per tie, with a four-piece minimum.

As tie experts of long standing, Tiecrafters knows all the fabrics and all the styles. If you want to modernize your narrow ties by making them wider, bring them in to Andy's new street-level storefront location so he and his staff can work their magic. You'll have a new, fashionable cravat for only $7.50. And Andy will make your wide ties narrow when styles change again in a few years.

If you want to add to your wardrobe, as well as revamp it, remember Tiecrafters also makes ties—$40 each, including fabric. The charge is only $30, if you supply the goods.

And the best news is that you can take advantage of Tiecrafters services even when you're not in New York. Half their business comes from all over the United States and Canada via UPS, Federal Express, or any common carrier. Cleaning and alterations usually take about a week and a half if you drop off the ties or have Tiecrafters pick them up (from anywhere in Manhattan)— it's more like a two-week turnaround if you're working through the mail.

But if you have a real tie crisis and can get it to Andy by 11:00 A.M., you can have it back that same afternoon. Isn't it wonderful that Andy worries so much about ties, so you don't have to?

# Acknowledgments

*To Laura Segal Stegman*

*For all her time and talent in helping make this book a reality. It couldn't have been done without you!*

*To my friends and colleagues, whose kindness and professional cooperation made the research such fun. Thank you!*

Ferne

# Index

## A

Abrahams, Pema, 314
Abrahams, Simon, 314–315
Abrahams, Tenzing, 314
Abramson, Paul, 365, 366
Acquista, Rosario, 355
Adrienne Restaurant, 48
Agar, Herman, 365–366
Agnez, Marcel, 53
Ahlstedt, Johan, 76
Air travel, 6–9, 12–15
Akers, Karen, 20
Albin, Christian, 97
Alice S. Mason, Ltd. 364–365
Allen, Joe, 141–143
Allen, Julie, 114, 142
Alrae, Hotel, 51
Amato, Joe, 107
Amato, Tony, 241
Amtrak, 5–6
Aquavit, 74–76
Arizona Cafe, 78
Arizona 206, 76–78
Armani, Giorgio, 269–270
Arpels, Helene, 234–235
Arpels, Julien, 334
Art, 367–368
Arthur Gluck, Chemisiers,
    215–216
Asprey & Company, Ltd., 293–295
Asprey, William, 293
Astor, John Jacob, 63, 69
Astor, William Waldorf, 69
Aulenti, Gai, 327
Aureole, 79–80

## B

Baccarat, 295–297
Bach, Lydia, 358
Badescu, Afrodita, 269
Ballato, 81–82
Ballato, John, 81
Baloun, Philip, 208–210
Barbier, Christophe, 22
Barneys New York, 248–251
Baroni, Stephan, 205

Barye, Antoine Louis, 325
Battistini, Stefano, 97
Baum, Joe, 158
Beau Brummel, 216–217
Beauty and health, 336–337
    exercise, 358–362
    gentlemen's services, 357
    ladies' services, 343–349
    supplies, 337–342
    unisex services, 350–356
Bendel, Henri, 235–237
Bennis, Susan, 237, 285–286
Bergdorf Goodman, 251–254
Bergland, Robin, 211
Berliner, Harold, 194
Bernardaud, 297–299
Bernardaud, Michel, 298
Bernardaud, Pierre, 298
Berns, Charlie, 184–185
Berta, Andrea, 314
Biagiotti, Belia, 239
Biber, James, 140
Bickson, Raymond, 39
Bidder, Alex von, 96, 97, 98, 99
Bifulco, Gino, 288–290
Bifulco, Tom, 288–290
Billy Martin Western Classics,
    254–255
Bishop, Michael, 260–261
Blanc, Raymond, 13
Blom, David, 136
Bloomingdale, Joseph, 255
Bloomingdale, Lyman, 255
Bloomingdale's, 255–258
Blumert, Jerry, 303
Bocuse, Paul, 82
Bodey, Worthy, 322
Bonuso, Ed, 189
Booth, Charles, 354–355, 356
Borthwick, Jane, 303
Bottega Veneta, 258–259
Bouley, 82–86
Bouley, David, 82–85, 132
Bouley's, Grandmother, Rice
    Pudding. See Recipes
Boulot, Philippe, 38

Boulot, Susan, 38
Boyds of Madison Avenue, 337–339
Branson, Richard, 12–13
Bravo, Rose Marie, 284–285
Bridal wear, 244–247
British Airways, 6–7
Brooks, Henry Sands, 219
Brooks, John E., 219
Brooks Brothers, 218–220
Buccellati, 317–318
Buccellati, Mario, II, 317
Bulgari, 318–320
Bulgari, Constantine, 319, 327
Bulgari, Giorgio, 319
Bulgari, Marina, 327–328
Bulgari, Nicola, 319–320
Bulgari, Paolo, 319
Bulgari, Sotirio, 318
Bull and Bear, 72
Burberry, Thomas, 259–260
Burberry's, 259–261
Burdick, Lawrence, 194
Burke, David, 146–147

C
Cafe Botanica, 24–25
Café des Artistes, 86–89
Café Pierre, 50
Cafe Vienna, 253
Calvo, Helga, 300
Carey, Chris, 109
Car/limo services, 1, 15–16
Carlson, Charlotte, 341
Carlyle, The, 18–21, 27
Carnegie Delicatessen & Restaurant, 89–90
Carter, Dixie, 20
Cartier, 320–322
Cartier, Pierre, 320–321
Caruso, Enrico, 95
Cashmere Cashmere, 262–263
Cassidy, Una, 342
Caterers. See also Gourmet foods
Glorious Foods, 203–205
Great Performances, 205–206
Sylvia Weinstock Cakes, 206–208
Cellar, The, 278
Cenci, David, 220–221, 230–231

Cetta, Mike, 182–183, 184
Cetta, Pat, 182–183
Chanel, 228–230
Chanel, Coco, 228–229
Chaney, William R., 332
Chanterelle, 91–93
Charivari, 264–265
Cheung, Lilian, 351
Christofle, 300–301
Chrysler, Walter P., 48
Chu, Gloria, 99–100, 130
Ciner, Emanuel, 323
Ciner Fashion Jewelers, 323–324
Civetta, Nicola, 154–155, 156
Clarke, Charlie, 153
Clarke, Patrick Joseph "Paddy," 153
Cogan, Marshall, 184–185
Coles, Peter, 275
Contrapunta, 78
Corwin, Barry, 93, 94
Cosmetics, shopping for, 236–237
Coty, Roger, 306
Crispy Orange Beef from Fu's. See Recipes
Culter, Arthur, 93, 94

D
Dakota, The, 56
D'Amico, Andrew, 178–180
Dav-El, 15–16
Davi, Frances, 138
Davi, Frank, 138
Davi, Grace, 138
Davi, Margaret, 138
Davi, Natalino, 138
Davi, Vincent, 138
Davide Cenci, 220–222
D'Avino, Cathy, 107
D'Avino, Connie, 107
D'Avino, John, 106
D'Avino, Vincent, 107
Dawson International, P. L. C., 263
Dean & DeLuca, 191–193
Delouvrier, Christian, 24, 128–129
Delta Men's Hair Stylists, 357
Denning, Mary Kaye, 299
Destino, Ralph, 322
Dill, David, 205

Dillon, Kevin, 147
Dissin, Bruno, 168
Docks, 93–95
Doolan, Michele, 327
Doral Tuscany Hotel, The, 21–23
D. Porthault & Co., 301–303
Driscoll, Sean, 203, 204, 205
Dumas, Rena, 273–275
Dunn–Tompkins, Carol, 3
Duran, Rosa, 305–306

E
Edwardian Room, 56–57
Edwards, Warren, 237, 285–286
Eiji, 346
Elizabeth Arden, 343–344
Elliott, George, 357
Emporio Armani, 265–267
Entertainment services, 366–367
Epstein, Diane, 286–288
Essex House, 23–26, 27, 127–128
E. Vogel — Custom Boots to
    Measure, 267–268

F
Fader, Albert, 337
Fader, Carol, 337–338
Fagan, Charles, 281
Falk, Susan, 236
Felder, Bettina, 205
Feldman, William, 318
Fendi, 230–232
Fendi, Federica, 231
Fendi, Maria Teresa, 231
Fendi, Sylvia, 231
Feret, Philippe, 59
Ferrara, 95–96
Ferrara, Antonio, 95
Fifth Avenue Club, 284
Figueroa, Joe, 303
Finch, Christi, 199–200
Finocchario, Giorgio, 36
Fioravanti, Olga, 228
Fioravanti, Raquel, 227, 228
Fioravanti, William, 226–228
Fitness salons, 358–362
Flay, Bobby, 134–135
Floris, 339–341
Floris, Juan Famenias, 339
Florists
    Philip Baloun Designs, 208–210

Renny, 210–211
Robert Isabell, Inc., 212–213
Fornari, Tito, 42
Fortuna, Tony, 132
Fortunoff, 303–304
Four Seasons, The (restaurant),
    96–99
Four Seasons Hotel, The, 26–29
Frette, 304–306
Frizon, Maud, 240–241
Frobuccino, Marilyn, 77
Furs, shopping for, 230–232
Fu's, 99–102

G
Gallagher, Helen, 102
Gallagher's, 102–104
Gallery, 20
Galvin, Daniel, 355
Gandrille, Claude, 274
García, 344–345
Garth, Dave, 87
Georgette Klinger, 350–352
Gerard's, 67–68
Gianni Versace Uomo, 268–269
Gibilie, David, 287
Gill, Jill, 367–368
Gimbel, Adam, 282–283
Gimbel, Bernard, 282
Giorgio Armani, 269–270
Givenchy, 232–234
Givenchy, Hubert de, 232–234
Glorious Foods, 203–205
Gluck, Arthur, 215
Goitein, Adelaide, 309
Gold, Jehv, 193–194
Golden, Hope, 257
Goldman, Avram, 217
Goldsmith, Barry, 260
Goller, Ira, 194
Goodman, Edwin, 251
Gorevic, Cali, 325
Gorevic, Charles, 324–325
Gorevic, Ferdinand, 324
Gorevic, Roger, 324–325
Gorevic Collection, 324–325
Gossnel, Melissa, 85
Gotham Bar and Grill, 104–106,
    139
Gotham Lounge, 47
Gould, Michael, 257, 258

Gourmet foods, 191–203. *See also* Caterers
Dean & DeLuca, 191–193
Manhattan Fruitier, 193–194
Murray's Sturgeon 194–195
Orwasher's, 195–196
William Poll, 196–198
Word of Mouth, 198–200
Zabar's, 200–202
Zito's Bread, 202–203
Gourmet Gazelle, 278
Graham, Florence Nightingale, 343–344
Great Performances, 205–206
Green, Edward, 293
Greenstein, Jackie, 329
Gern, Armel, 121
Grimsbo, Lee, 193
Grodd, Clifford, 223
Grotta Azzurra, 106–108
Gucci, 271–272
Gucci, Aldo, 271
Gucci, Guccio, 271
Gucci, Maurizio, 271
Gustafsson, P. J., 180
Gutman, Steve, 217

H
Hale, Martin A., 35
Hallas, Marie, 57
Hampton, Mark, 19
Handler, Mark S., 279
Hardenbergh, Henry Janeway, 56
Harkavi, Ilana, 352–354
Hefferman, Kerry, 34, 105, 139
Heim, Alfred, 43, 44
Helene Arpels, 234–235
Helicopter service, 7–9
Heller, Nancy, 284
Helmsley, Harry, 43
Helmsley, Leona, 43
Hencken, Caren, 2, 3, 4
Henderson, Gordon, 284
Henri Bendel, 235–237
Herman Agar Co., 365–366
Hermès, 272–275
Hermès, Emile-Maurice, 273
Hermès Jean-Louis Dumas, 273
Hermès, Thierry, 272–273
Hill, David, 323
Hill, Douglas, 323

Hill, Jean, 323
Hill, Pat, 323
Hilton, Conrad, 69
Hoffman Travel Service, 2–4
Home, shopping for the, 293–315
Hotel Millenium, The, 29–31
Hotel Westbury, 32–34
Hotels, 17–18. (*See* individual listings following)
Carlyle, The, 18–21, 27
Doral Tuscany, The, 21–23
Essex House, 23–26, 27, 127–128
Four Seasons, The, 26–29
Hotel Millenium, The, 29–31
Hotel Westbury, 32–34
Lowell, The, 34–37
Mark, The, 27, 37–40
Mayfair Hotel Baglioni, 40–43
New York Palace, The, 43–45
Peninsula, The, 45–48
Pierre, The, 48–51
Plaza Athénée, 51–54
Plaza Hotel, The, 54–57
Regency, The, 57–60
Royalton, The, 60–62
St. Regis, The, 63–66
Stanhope, The, 66–68
Waldorf–Astoria, The, 69–72
Howard, Charles, 345
Howard, Josefina, 161–163
Hudson River Club, 108–111
Hunt Room and Bar, 44
Hutton, E. F., 48

I
Iacobiello, Franco, 156, 157
Il Makiage, 352–354
Inagiku, 72
Ingenito, Paul, 166
Isabell, Robert, 212–213

J
Jammet, Andre, 116, 117, 118
Jammet, Rita, 116
Jerry Kravat Entertainment Services, 366–367
Jet Aviation Business Jets, Inc., 14–15
Jewelry, shopping for, 316–335
J. G. Melon, 111–112

Jill Gill, 367–368
Jim McMullen, 112–114
Joe Allen, 114–116
John Sahag, 345–347
Johnson, Philip, 96
Jolly, Jay, 205
Jones, Daniel, 137
Journeys Bar, 24
J. S. Suárez, 237–238

**K**
Kalikow, Peter, 29
Kavanaugh, Mary, 253
Kaye, Sidney, 165
Kenneth Jay Lane, 326–327
Kiehl's 341
Kim, Emily, 356
King, Jill, 321–322
King Cole Bar, 63
King Cole Grill, 63
Klein, David, 15
Klein, Murray, 200, 201
Klinger, Georgette, 350–352
Klinger, Kathryn, 350
Kravat, Jerry, 366–367
Kretchmer, Jerry, 139
Kriendler, Jack, 184, 185
Kriendler, Pete, 185
Krupka, Otto, 180, 181
Kunz, Gray, 65, 129–130

**L**
La Caravelle, 116–118
Lackner, Bernard, 52–53
La Coupe, 354–356
La Côte Basque, 118–120
Lagerfeld, Karl, 228, 231
La Grenouille, 120–122
La Lingerie, 238
Lalique, 306–308
Lalique, Marc, 307
Lalique, Marie–Claude, 307
Lalique, René 306–307
Landsberg, Jeffrey, 328, 329
Landsberg, Jonathan, 328
Landsberg, Norman, 328–329
Lane, Kenneth Jay, 326–327
Lang, George, 87–88
Language services, 368–369
Laura Biagiotti, 239–240

Lauren, Ralph, 280–282
Lavezzo, Dan, III, 154
Lavezzo, Dan, Jr., 154
Lavezzo, Daniel, 153
Laxer, Sol, 216–217
Lazzarro, Larry, 78
Leather goods, shopping for, 230–232, 271–275
Le Bernardin, 122–125
Le Bistro Adrienne, 48
Le Café, 251
Le Cirque, 125–127
Le Coze, Gilbert, 122–124
Le Coze, Maguy, 122–124
Lee, Linda, 277–278
Leggiadro, 275–276
Leiderman, David, 201
Le Magueresse, Jacques, 124
Le Manoir aux Quatre Saisons, 13
Leonardo, 347–348
Lepine, Kim, 355
Le Regence, 53
Le Salon, 68
Les Celebrites, 24, 127–129
Lespinasse, 65, 129–131
Le Trianon, 44
Leuenberger, Niklaus, 47
Leung, Michael, 99–100
Levine, Bill, 170–171
Levine, Howie, 93, 94
Levine, Sarabeth, 170–172
Limousines, 15–16
Lingerie, shopping for, 236
Lamonaco, Michael, 185, 186, 187
Lorenzo, William, 335
Loring, John, 65, 333
Lotte Berke, 358–359
Lowell, The, 34–37
Lutèce, 82–83, 131–133
Lynch, Harold, 267
Lynch, Jack, 267

**M**
Macagnone, Anthony, 81
Macagnone, Anthony, Jr., 81
Macagnone, William, 81
Maccioni, Sirio, 125, 126
Macy, John, 194
Macy, Rowland H., 279

Macy's, 276–280
Mahon, John, 59
Malouf, Waldy, 108, 109, 110
Mancini, Claire, 240
Mancini, Rene, 241–242
Manhattan Fruitier, 193–194
Maniscalco, Louise, 250
Marcatilli, Valentino, 168
Marina B., 327–328
Mariotti, Dario, 40–43
Mariotti, Gabriella, 41
Mark, The, 27, 37–40
Martinez, Zarela, 188–189
Mason, Alice, 364–365
Masson, Charles, 120, 121, 122
Masson, Giselle, 120–121
Masson, Phillippe, 120–121, 122
Maud Frizon, 240–241
Maurizio, Tony, 222–223
Maurizio — Custom Tailors,
    222–223
May, Tony, 167–168, 169
Mayfair Hotel Baglioni, 40–43
McCormack, Maureen, 224
McCoy, Don, 205
McIntosh, Frank, 237
Mello, Dawn, 271
Men, shopping for, 215–228,
    248–293, 370–371
Men's Store, The, 251–254
Merritt, Eva, 310
Mesa Grill, 133–135
Metropolitan Museum, 68
Meyers, Marilyn, 294
Michel Thomas Language
    Center, 368–369
Miller, Bryan, 77
Miller, Gladys, 364
Miyake, Issey, 264
Mnuchin, Adriana, 263
Montmorency–Laval,
    Monseigneur de, 295–296
Montrachet, 82, 135–137
Moore, Gene, 333
Morgan, Colette Nerey, 254
Mori, Hanae, 374
Morse, Aaron, 341
Morse, Irving, 341
Morse, Jami, 341
Mourges, George, 111
Murray's Sturgeon, 194–195

N
Natalino, 137–139
Nathan, 348
Neary, John, 21
Nedelec, Jean Claude, 204
Neimark, Ira, 251
Neumark, Liz, 205–206
Newman, Kathy, 257
Newton, Doug, 254
New York Helicopter, 7–9
New York Palace, The, 43–45
Niccolini, Julian, 98
Nieporent, Drew, 135–136
Niven, Jamie, 339
Norman Landsberg, 328–329

O
Oak Bar, 57
Oak Room, 56
One Fifth Avenue, 139–141
O'Neil, Jack, 111
Ono, Tadashi, 117
Oroveanu, Ion, 150–151
Orso, 141–143
Orwasher, Abram, 195
Orwasher's, 195–196
Oscar's 72
Ostrove, Ralph, 223
Overholser, Genevieve, 259
Oyster Bar, 56

P
Palm Court, 56
Palmer, Charlie, 79, 80
Palmer, Clifford R., 313
Parioli Romanissimo, 143–145
Park Avenue Cafe, 36, 146–147
Parker, Milton, 89–90
Pascal, Guy, 237
Patsy's, 147–149
Paul Stuart, 223–225
Pei, I. M., 27
Pembroke Room, 36–37
Peninsula, The, 45–46
Peretti, Elsa, 332
Perrygore, Clive, 21, 22
Petricca, Bruce, 307
Petrossian, 150–152
Petrossian, Armen, 150–151
Petrossian, Christian, 150–151
Petrossian, Melkoum, 150

Petrossian, Moucheg, 150
Philip Baloun Designs, 208–210
Philippe, Louis, 292
Philipson, Robert, 318
Picasso, Paloma, 332
Pierre, Charles, 48
Pierre, The, 48–51
Pike, Anthony, 32
Pimienta, Michel, 34
Pines, Sylvia, 242–243
Pinto, Piero, 239
P. J. Clarke's, 152–154
Plant, Morton (Mrs.), 321
Plaza Athénée, 51–54
Plaza Hotel, The, 54–57
Pliessnig, Herbert, 49, 51
Poll, Stanley, 197, 198
Ponzek, Debra, 133, 134, 136
Pool Room, 97, 98
Portale, Alfred, 104, 105, 139–140
Portay, Sylvan, 126
Porthault, Madelaine, 301, 303
Porthault, Marc, 303
Post House, 36, 37
Powell, Yuta, 233
Pratesi, 308–309
Pressman, Barney, 248–249
Pressman, Fred, 249
Pressman, Phyllis, 249
Price, Kenyon, 172, 173
Primavera, 154–156
Primola, 156–158
Promenade, 160, 161
Pronsky, Paula, 271
Puckering, Andrew, 340
Puiforcat, 310–311
Puiforcat, Emile, 310
Puiforcat, Louis-Victor, 310

**Q**
*Queen Elizabeth 2*, 9–12

**R**
Rabalais, Nicholas, 48
Rachou, Jean-Jacques, 118–119, 120
Radu's Physical Culture Studio, 359–360
Rail transportation, 5–6
Rainbow Room, The, 158–161
Rainbow & Stars, 160–161

Ralph Lauren at 72nd Street, 280–282
Rathe, Richard, 139
Raymond, George, 322
Real estate, 364–365, 369–370
Recipes
 Crispy Orange Beef from Fu's, 101–102
 Grandmother Bouley's Rice Pudding, 85–86
 Rosa Mexicano's Chile Chocolate Truffles and Pumpkin Seed Praline, 164
 Tagliolini with White Truffles (Parioli Romanissimo), 145
 The "21" Club Crabcake Recipe, 186–187
Red Door Salon, 343
Reddy, Kantha, 226
Reddy, Uma, 225, 226
Regency Hotel, The, 57–60
Regency Lounge, 59
Reidy, Bryan, 103
Reisel, Phil, 365, 366
Remington Room, 185
Rene Mancini, 240–241
Rennard, Andre, 129
Renny 210–211
Restaurants, 73–74 (*See* individual listings following)
 Aquavit, 74–76
 Arizona 206, 76–78
 Aureole, 79–80
 Ballato, 81–82
 Bouley, 82–86
 Café des Artistes, 86–89
 Carnegie Delicatessen & Restaurant, 89–90
 Chanterelle, 91–93
 Docks, 93–95
 Ferrara, 95–96
 Four Seasons, The, 96–99
 Fu's, 99–102
 Gallagher's, 102–104
 Gotham Bar and Grill, 104–106, 139
 Grotta Azzurra, 106–108
 Hudson River Club, 108–111
 J. G. Melon, 111–112
 Jim McMullen, 112–114
 Joe Allen, 114–116

La Caravelle, 116–118
La Côte Basque, 118–120
La Grenouille, 120–122
Le Benardin, 122–125
Le Cirque, 125–127
Les Celebrites, 24, 127–129
Lespinasse, 65, 129–131
Lutèce, 82–83, 131–133
Mesa Grill, 133–135
Montrachet, 82, 135–137
Natalino, 137–139
One Fifth Avenue, 139–141
Orso, 141–143
Parioli Romanissimo, 143–145
Park Avenue Cafe, 36, 146–147
Patsy's, 147–149
Petrossian, 150–152
P. J. Clarke's, 152–154
Primavera, 154–156
Primola, 156–158
Rainbow Room, The, 158–161
Rosa Mexicano, 161–164
Russian Tea Room, The,
    165–167
San Domenico, 167–170
Sarabeth's Kitchen, 170–172
Sfuzzi, 172–174
Shun Lee, 174–176
Sidewalkers, 176–178
Sign of the Dove, 178–180
Snaps, 180–182
Sparks, 182–184
"21" Club, The, 184–187
Zarela, 188–189
Reynolds, Renny, 210–211
Richard, Laurent, 117
Ripert, Eric, 123
River Cafe, 79
Robbins, Karen, 286
Robert Isabell, Inc., 212–213
Rockwell, David, 59
Rogers, Jacqueline, 323, 324
Roney, John, 112
Rosa Custom Ties, 226
Rosa Mexicano, 161–164
Rosa Mexicano's Chile Chocolate
    Truffees and Pumpkin Seed
    Praline. See Recipes.
Ross, Ann, 275–276
Rossi, Rubrio, 143–145
Rostang, Michel, 53

Rotunda, The, 49–50
Round Bar, 61
Royalton, The, 60–62
Rubell, Steve, 60, 62
Ruiz, Nilda, 263
Runsdorf, Inc., 329–330
Runsdorf, Lee, 329–330
Runsdorf, Lucette, 329
Russian Tea Room, The, 165–167

S
Safro, Millicent, 287–288
Sahag, John, 345–346
St. Regis, The, 63–66
Saks, Horace, 282
Saks Fifth Avenue, 282–285
Sal Anthony's, 81
Saltzman, Ellin, 251
San Domenico, 167–170
Santo, Henny, 178
Santo, Joseph, 178
Santoro, Lori, 269
Santos, Berge, 77
Santos, Henny, 77
Santos, Joseph, 77
Sarabeth's Kitchen, 170–172
Sardi, Vincent, 114
Sartogo, Piero, 319
Schenck, John 105
Schoenegger, Theo, 169
Schrager, Ian, 60, 62
Schutz, Pierre, 132
Schwartz, Mark, 346
Schweithzer, Sandy, 311
Schweitzer Linens, 311–312
Scognamillo, Concetta, 148
Scognamillo, Joe, 148, 149
Scognamillo, Pasquale, 148
Scognamillo, Salvatore, 148
Scoppa, Enrico, 95
Scott, Keith, 270
Sea travel, 9–12
Segal, Rick, 64
Sfuzzi, 172–174
Sherwin, James, 21
Shoes, shopping for, 229–230,
    234–235, 240–242, 247–248,
    271, 285–286
Shopping, 214–215
    for bridal wear, 244–247
    for cosmetics, 229, 236–237

for flowers, 208–213
for foods, 191–208
for furs, 230–232
for the home, 293–315
for jewelry, 316–335
for leather goods, 229–230,
    237–238, 242, 271–274
for lingerie, 238
for men, 215–228, 248–293,
    370–371
for shoes, 229–230, 234–235,
    240–242, 247–248, 271,
    285–286
for women, 228–293
Short, Bobby, 20–21
Shulman, Mark, 236
Shun Lee, 174–176
Sidewalkers, 176–178
Siegfried, Darren, 75
Sign of the Dove, 178–180
Simkovics, Stefan, 32
Sirota, Jack, 90
Snaps, 180–182
Soane, Sir John, 38
Solombrino, Scott, 15–16
Solomon, Jack, 102
Soltner, Andre, 82, 131–133
Sommer, Walter, 286
Soule, Henry, 118
Sparks, 182–184
Spencer, Brenda, 369–370
Spencer Realty, 369–370
Spitalnick, Sylvia, 257
Spitzer, Michael, 215–216
Splan, Suzanne, 293
Stanhope, The, 66–68
Starck, Philippe, 60–61
Starnella, Rita, 355–356
Steiger, Walter, 247–248
Steinberg, Laura, 57
Sterling, Jack, 153
Steuben, 312–314
Stevens, Benny, 104
Stewart-Gordon, Faith, 165, 166
Stillman, Alan, 37
Stoj, Barbara, 287
Stout, Tom, 3
Strauss, Isidor, 279
Strauss, Nathan, 279
Suárez, José, 237–238
Suárez, Matthew, 238

Suárez, Ramona, 236
Susan Bennis/Warren Edwards,
    285–286
Sussman, Mark, 260
Sylvia Pines — Uniquities,
    242–243
Sylvia Weinstock Cakes, 206–208
Synder, Bruce, 185
Szule, Rosa, 305

T
Tailors, 215–228
Tamayo, Mark, 313
Tansky, Burton, 251
Tarshis, Andy, 370–371
Taylor, Victor, 131
Tender Buttons, 286–288
Tenzing & Pema, 314–315
Teodorescu, Radu, 359–360
Terme di Saturnia, 284
Thomas, Michel, 368–369
Ticket services, 365–366
Tiecrafters, 370–371
Tiffany, Charles, 331, 332
Tiffany & Co., 330–333
Time & Again, 22–23
Tisch, Jonathan, 57, 59
T. O. Dey, 288–290
To, Michael, 100–101
Tong, Michael, 174–176
Torres, Jacques, 127
Trader Vic's, 57
Transportation
    air, 6–7, 12–15
    car/limo, 1, 15–16
    helicopter, 7–9
    rail, 5–6
    sea, 9–12
Trapani, Francesco, 319
Travel services, 2–4
Travel writing, 374
Trimarchi, Antonia, 247
Trubowitch, Neil, 66, 68
Trump, Donald, 54, 56
Trump, Ivana, 54, 56
Tullis, Garner, 137
"21" Club, The, 184–187
    Crabcake Recipe. *See* Recipes

U
Ullman, Myron, E., III, 279
Uma-Reddy, Ltd., 225–226

Ungaro, 243–244
Ungaro, Emanuel, 243–244

V
Van Cleef, Alfred, 333–334
Van Cleef & Arpels, 333–335
Vargas, Carol, 244
Vera Wang Bridal House, Ltd.,
    244–247
Verge, Roger, 82
Versace, Gianni, 268–269
Vertical Club, 360–362
Virgin Atlantic, 12–13
Vogel, Dean, 267, 268

W
Waldorf-Astoria, The, 69–72
Walsh, Brendan , 77
Walter, Steiger, 247–248
Waltuck, David, 91, 92
Waltuck, Karen, 91
Walzog, David, 77
Wang, Vera, 244–247
Watts, Carroll, 254
Wayne Webb Technique, The,
    348–349
Webb, Wayne, 348–349
Weinstock, Sylvia, 206–208
Weiser, Barbara, 264, 265
Weiser, Jon, 264
Weiser, Selma, 264
Weiss, Rachel, 259
Werner, Elaine, 294

Westbury, Hotel, 32–34
William Fioravanti, Inc. —
    Custom Tailors for Men,
    226–228
William Poll, 196–198
Wilson, Leo, 153
Women, shopping for, 228–293
Word of Mouth, 198–200

Y
Yamamoto, Yoji, 264
Yellowfingers, 78
Young, John, 331
Yves Saint Laurent Femme,
    290–293

Z
Zabar, Eli, 201
Zabar, Louis, 201
Zabar, Saul, 200, 201
Zabar, Stanley, 200, 201
Zabar's 200–202, 278
Zarela, 188–189
Zito, Anthony, 202
Zito, Anthony, Jr., 202
Zito, Charles, 202
Zito, Charles, Jr., 202
Zito, Jimmy, 202
Zito, Josephine, 202
Zito, Julius, , 262
Zito, Vincent, 202
Zito's Bread, 202–203
Zuliana, Giuliano, 156, 157

# ABOUT THE AUTHORS
## *Ferne Kadish*

"A very elegant gypsy" is the most accurate description of Ferne Kadish, whose travels are endless in her quest for the best. Her discerning eye and impeccable taste have made her recommendations reliable, not just to the casual visitor but even to natives of the city she is examining.

Born in Chicago, she grew up in Beverly Hills, California, and continued her bicoastal life-style by attending Boston University and the University of Southern California.

She conceived and was coauthor of a series of seven upscale volumes on New York, London, Paris, and Los Angeles. The original idea was how to enjoy a city for $500 a day, but soon progressed to $1000 a day—before lunch! Somehow, she also found time to collaborate on a novel, *The Golden Circle*. She has lectured throughout the United States, and has been featured as the luxury travel expert on CNN and on "Lifestyles of the Rich and Famous." She has developed a pilot for a TV show presently under consideration at a major studio.

Ferne makes her home in Beverly Hills when she's not out researching the next book in her travel series or on a lecture tour. She is married to Emmy-award winning producer, Stan Margulies.

## *Shelley Clark*

Born in Lewes, Delaware, and raised in both Delaware and Maryland, writer/publicist Shelley Clark has had an eclectic career. After graduating with honors from Kenyon College, Shelley gained hands-on experience in a variety of fields, including tape editing, sales, marketing, and—finally—public relations. Her skills as a writer and publicist caught the attention of Hanae Mori, for whom she became director of communications based in New York City. Today, she works as director of marketing for a New York restaurant.